THE MICROECONOMICS
ANTI-TEXTBOOK

THE MICROECONOMICS
ANTI-TEXTBOOK

A Critical Thinker's Guide — Second Edition

Rod Hill and Tony Myatt

LONDON · NEW YORK · OXFORD · NEW DELHI · SYDNEY

Zed Books
Bloomsbury Publishing Plc
50 Bedford Square, London, WC1B 3DP, UK
1385 Broadway, New York, NY 10018, USA
29 Earlsfort Terrace, Dublin 2, Ireland

BLOOMSBURY and Zed Books are trademarks
of Bloomsbury Publishing Plc

First published in Great Britain 2022

ISBN: HB: 978-1-7836-0730-3
PB: 978-1-7836-0729-7
ePDF: 978-1-7836-0731-0
eBook: 978-1-7836-0732-7

Printed and bound in Great Britain

To find out more about our authors and books visit
www.bloomsbury.com and sign up for our newsletters.

CONTENTS

TABLES AND FIGURES

Tables

Figures

ACKNOWLEDGEMENTS

This book is the second edition of *The Economics Anti-Textbook*, first published in 2010. The new title, *The Microeconomics Anti-Textbook*, is a more accurate reflection of the subject matter as it does not deal with macroeconomics.

We have benefited from the feedback received from readers and users of the first edition. For their comments and suggestions, we thank Abdella Abdou, Graham Davis, Maggie Fitzgerald, Jesse Hajer, Tom Malleson, Andrew Secord, and Asad Zaman, as well as Michael Derrer and Jim Stanford, who published reviews of the first edition.

Thanks as well to our former editors at Zed Books, particularly Ken Barlow and Kim Walker, for their patience for the length of time this revision has taken.

As with the first edition, we dedicate this book to our respective children, Joan-Maki Motapanyane, and Rose and Thomas Myatt, as well as to all inquisitive economics students who want to think for themselves and not just believe what they're told.

ABOUT THE AUTHORS

Rod Hill grew up in Ontario, was educated at the University of Toronto, the University of Stockholm and the University of Western Ontario, where he obtained a PhD in economics. He has taught at the University of Windsor, the University of Regina and the University of New Brunswick, where he has been a professor of economics since 2003. His research interests have included international trade policy, taxation and the underground economy, and (as a result of growing dissatisfaction) the content of the introductory textbooks. He is a research associate with the Canadian Centre for Policy Alternatives and a member of the Progressive Economics Forum and the World Economics Association.

Tony Myatt received his PhD from McMaster University with distinction in theory. He has taught at McMaster University, the University of Western Ontario, the University of Toronto and the University of New Brunswick, where he has been professor of economics since 1992. His research interests have included the supply-side effects of interest rates, labour market discrimination, unemployment rate disparities, and the methods and content of economic education. He has developed several different introductory courses as vehicles for teaching principles of economics, including 'Economics of everyday life', 'Economics in the real world' and 'Economics through film'. Professor Myatt was the recipient of UNB's Arts Faculty Award for Excellence in Teaching in 2008.

INTRODUCTION: OUR GOALS, AUDIENCE AND PRINCIPAL THEMES

'If economics courses and textbooks matter, they do so because they willfully toy with our ideas about the world we live in.' Yanis Varoufakis[1]

'The enterprise of economics is better characterized by the content of elementary texts than by what goes on at the frontiers of economic theory.' Stephen Marglin[2]

In brief

The typical introductory economics textbook teaches that economics is a value-free science; that economists have an agreed-upon methodology; and they know which models are best to apply to any given problem. They give the impression that markets generally are sufficiently competitive that (for the most part) they lead to efficient outcomes; that minimum wages and unions are harmful to workers themselves; and that government regulation is either ineffective or harmful.

The *Microeconomics Anti-Textbook* points out that all this is a myth. Value judgements pervade economics and economic textbooks. These value judgements reflect a social and political philosophy and can be called an ideology or world-view. It is one that textbook writers are implicitly attempting to persuade the reader to accept. The *Anti-Textbook* makes this ideology, and the value-judgements behind it, explicit. The point is not so much to claim that this ideology is wrong, but simply to point out that it exists, and that there are always alternative views that one ought to consider.

Our aim is not to debunk mainstream (neoclassical) economics – just the textbook presentation of it. Partly, this is because the neoclassical paradigm is remarkably malleable. It is capable of transforming itself, of shedding many an unappealing feature.[3] Partly, it is because the boundaries of mainstream neoclassical economics are blurry. It is not clear, for example, whether work on behavioural economics lies within the neoclassical paradigm or is a direct assault upon it. In any event, the work since the 1970s on imperfect information by Joseph Stiglitz and others overthrows many of the neoclassical presumptions about efficiency and the harmfulness of government intervention, and whether this work remains within the neoclassical paradigm is debatable.[4] Though we are sympathetic to alternative paradigms and to heterodox views (one of us thinks of himself as a 'post-Keynesian' and the other doesn't identify with any single school of thought), the *Anti-Textbook* is not a presentation of alternative paradigms. Instead, we draw upon them in our critique of standard textbook microeconomics. They are particularly useful because of their emphasis on things that are systematically neglected by neoclassical economics.

This book is not 'anti' microeconomics, or even 'anti' mainstream microeconomics. It is 'anti' mainstream textbook microeconomics. An examination of their content reveals that the standard textbooks are remarkably similar and reflect a narrower range of world views than those held even by mainstream economists. Contrary to what the student might expect, the authors of these books are not free to present their own ideas about how to introduce the subject. Instead, as described by David Colander, himself the author of a widely used text, there is an unwritten 15 percent rule. A book's content cannot deviate from the 'standard' text by more than this, or it will endanger its chances of adoption by instructors, who would face costs of switching from whatever standard book they were currently using.[5]

Of course, there are a small but growing number of non-standard textbooks that have defied the 15 percent rule and still managed to get published. They comprise a very small share of the market in the English-speaking world. Unfortunately, the vast majority of first-year economics students are subjected to the standard mainstream textbook. It is for these undergraduate students, as well as the curious layperson, that we have written this book.

We hope that our book, by citing the views of many prominent economists from a variety of schools of thought, both mainstream and heterodox, will help students to understand that economics is much more diverse (and interesting!) than what they see in their standard introductory text.

The influence of the core content of the standard textbook extends well beyond the classroom. Dutch economist Peter-Wim Zuidhof writes that 'textbook accounts are also what journalists, commentators, policy advisors, economists, and noneconomists alike tend to draw on when having to explain economics in public'.[6] Citizens who pay attention to public policy discussions are in danger of falling victim to what James Kwak calls *economism*: 'Economism is what you are left with if you learn the first-year models, forget that there are assumptions involved, and never get your hands dirty with real-world data.'[7] Our book is intended to be an antidote to this ailment.

The structure

Our *Anti-Textbook* follows the structure of the typical introductory microeconomics textbook and can be read in conjunction with any standard text. Alternatively, it can be read on its own. Each chapter begins with a Standard Text section, a concise exposition of the conventional textbook material. (This is based on our surveys of the content of 10 North American texts, listed in the Addendum to this chapter.) This is followed by an Anti-Text section with our critique of the Standard Text. As such, we hope it will prove useful to students, to those professors who feel even slight discomfort with the hegemony of the conventional text, and to everyone else interested in understanding more about contemporary economics.

To help stoke the fires of revolution, each chapter contains 'questions for your professor'. These aim to sum up the weak points of the texts' exposition in the form of a question. If you are a student and you choose to ask one of these questions, remember that the goal is not to criticize your professor, who probably did not write your textbook and may not even have had the freedom to choose it. Nor is the goal to embarrass the professor, who might not know the answer. Instead, such questions could provoke a useful discussion of the limitations of the textbook models and their content. However, be warned – asking such questions may meet with a hostile reception if the professor is a true believer in textbook economics! Unfortunately, professors are not accustomed to being asked challenging questions in introductory courses.

Our thesis

Textbooks are necessarily selective. They must include and emphasize some things and exclude or downplay others. They ask certain questions and not others. They place some topics and questions in the forefront, and put others in the background or leave them out entirely. Those decisions usually reflect implicit, not explicit, value judgements about what is interesting and important. No 'objective' account is possible. For most people – including many economists – this is not a controversial claim.

Yet the textbooks cloak themselves in an aura of objectivity. They portray economics as a science dealing with facts and theories that make predictions. Economists are portrayed like scientists wearing white lab coats objectively developing theoretical models and coming up with policy prescriptions supported by a consensus of professional opinion.

The *Anti-Textbook* argues that this is a myth – one which is not only dangerously misleading but also bland and boring. Value judgements arise on the first page, where the textbook writers ask 'what is economics?' and attempt to define the subject and the main problems that it addresses. A variety of possible definitions exists, and each one would give rise to different lines of enquiry. One definition might stress the importance of using society's scarce resources to make total income and production as large as possible; another might stress the importance of eliminating poverty and deprivation so that everyone's basic needs are met. When an author gives one view and ignores alternative possibilities, a value judgement has been made.

Moreover, the hope that economics would one day become a positive science relying on the evidence to confirm or to refute theories has, up to this point, been in vain. There are long-standing disputes about the effects of relatively simple policy changes. For example, does an increase in the minimum wage increase unemployment? Many texts claim that economists have a consensus answer to this question supported by a clear body of empirical evidence. But nothing could be further from the truth. Contradictory evidence abounds; the dispute is sometimes heated and, as we show in Chapter 2, consensus among economists has broken down beginning in the 1990s. Some acknowledge that such disputes are a 'battleground for those who believe in free markets and those who do not'.[8]

Economics is inevitably a battleground between opposing ideologies. This isn't necessarily a bad thing. Recognizing this reality puts the controversy and excitement back into economics, and reveals a fascinating and vibrant field of study. John Maynard Keynes, perhaps the greatest economist of the 20th century, considered economics to be 'a moral science and not a natural science. That is to say, it employs introspection and judgements of value.'[9]

One of the major aims of our book is to point out where ideological issues arise, and where the textbooks make implicit value judgements that you may not share. One major area where such value judgements crop up are the decisions about what to leave out of the text. Alternative perspectives may not be discussed, inconvenient questions may not be asked and contrary empirical evidence may be omitted.

Indian economist Kaushik Basu commented: '[S]o much of what passes for interpretation and description of the world in the social sciences is a Panglossian justification for the current system, the distribution of power as it presently is, and the status quo of wealth. On some topics, where to justify the status quo would be too blatant, we have a conspiracy of silence; we say nothing in the hope that our attention will drift to less dangerous topics.'[10] There is no overt conspiracy, of course. Instead, in the case of the textbooks, there is a (perhaps subconscious) understanding that some things are not to be said lest that the book find itself far outside the 15 percent zone that guarantees respectability and a hope of adequate sales.

We offer examples of such omissions in the hope that students will get into the habit of thinking about what is *not* in the text as well as what is.

After all, the textbooks are not only trying to teach you how to think ('like an economist'), they are also trying to tell you what to think about.

We stress that our aim is not to trash the textbooks, nor are we portraying textbook writers (or economists generally) as propagandists or ideological hacks. All too often, the word 'ideological' is used as a term of abuse: one group that claims to be 'non-ideological' accuses others of being 'ideological'. 'Bias in favor of the orthodox is frequently mistaken for "objectivity". Departures from this ideological orthodoxy are themselves dismissed as ideological', as American political scientist Michael Parenti remarked.[11]

Our point is not so much to claim that the ideology of the textbooks is wrong, although admittedly we do not share it. Rather, we want to remind readers that it exists. Students should be consciously aware of it – and that there are alternatives on offer.

The world view of mainstream textbooks

So what is the worldview of the introductory texts? Harvard professor Dani Rodrik put it well in his book *Economics Rules*:

> much of what goes on in an introductory course in economics is a paean to markets. It gives little sense of the diversity of conclusions in economics, to which the student is unlikely to be exposed unless she goes on to take many more economics courses. ... Instead of presenting a taste of the full panoply of perspectives that their discipline offers, they focus on benchmark models that stress one set of conclusions.[12]

We agree that the typical text offers a 'paean to markets' – usually not in a crude way, but in a subtle way through its choice of themes, and through its emphasis on demand and supply (also called the model of perfect competition) as the central theoretical structure. Most of the standard textbook is spent developing and applying that structure. It describes a world of perfect markets in which given resources are allocated as if by an invisible hand in a way that maximizes the value of total production. The belief that this model approximates how markets operate in the real world is often referred to as 'market fundamentalism'.[13]

According to the late American economist Robert Prasch, 'market fundamentalism remains the perspective of virtually every introductory economics textbook'.[14] To further clarify the policy implications of emphasizing the perfectly competitive view of the world, Prasch says:

> Minimum wage laws, usury laws, truth-in-advertising laws, laws to regulate fraud, health-and-safety codes, anti-discrimination laws, building inspection codes, environmental laws, investor protection rules, and many other rules and regulations have each and severally been

breezily, even haughtily, dismissed by market fundamentalists and the many columnists and politicians who invoke their arguments.[15]

It's true that no mainstream textbook supports the elimination of such policies. They set out many qualifications to the market fundamentalist model. But these qualifications are made in such a way that they appear of secondary, rather than primary, importance. The theory of perfect markets is all too often applied reflexively to policy questions, without any discussion of whether it is relevant or appropriate. By offering a one-size-fits-all model, the texts fail to convey the idea that economics consists of many models and that selecting which model is most appropriate in a particular situation is critically important. If an inappropriate model is used, the conclusions will be equally inappropriate.

What's wrong with this worldview?

Market fundamentalism – the analysis that dominates the mainstream textbooks – assumes *perfect and costless information*. Much research in recent decades has explored the implications of relaxing this extreme assumption and considering what happens in a setting of imperfect information, where some people know more than others (termed 'asymmetric' information). The *Anti-Textbook* highlights the many places where this more realistic approach is relevant. With pervasive informational problems, the market economy systematically fails to produce the efficient allocation of resources that is the centrepiece of the textbook story.

Furthermore, the perfect markets of the texts are populated by large numbers of small firms, producing identical products, with no power to set their own product price. Does it matter that very few actual markets resemble this? Many economists think it does. In recent decades, a great deal of research has been devoted to markets in which there are a few large firms, or in which firms produce different products. Theories of international trade are now dominated by such approaches. The efficient allocation of resources that occurs in the perfect markets story does not happen in these more realistic approaches.

The focus on 'efficiency' that runs through the texts comes at the cost of neglecting issues of the distribution of income and wealth and of economic justice, which get short shrift in virtually all texts. In Chapter 9, we examine the textbook claim that income redistribution and greater social spending are a costly exercise that reduces economic growth; we argue that neither theory nor evidence support this view.

Another neglected topic is the problem of *externalities*. Even when people make their decisions with perfect information, they can still choose not to take into account the effects of their actions on others. Every kind of pollution, from the local to the global, is an example of this. We show in Chapter 7 that externalities are not the afterthought that the textbooks suggest, but are a pervasive problem that render the invisible hand story irrelevant as a description of the world we live in. The Postscript on the textbook treatment of climate change underscores this problem.

Questions of *power* are absent from the texts. Yet in reality sellers try to shape and to influence the preferences of consumers, while consumers may try to exert their power to get producers to produce products in more ethical or environmentally sustainable ways. Managers exert power over workers if business organizations are authoritarian and hierarchical, as is typically the case. Corporations, labour unions, citizens' groups and non-governmental organizations may struggle to influence the 'rules of the economic game' – tax law, regulation, government programmes and so on. A similar struggle takes place at the international level. Yet, as we argue, particularly in Chapters 4, 5 and 8–10, power of this kind, while important in the understanding of actual economic life, is virtually absent from textbook economics.

Economics textbooks often present hypotheses and policy prescriptions with surprisingly little or no supporting evidence, or (worse) they ignore inconvenient contrary evidence. Indeed, the textbooks contain very few references to the professional literature. Another goal of this book is, where relevant, to ask for the evidence and to show the student the way to the evidence that the texts omit. It is remarkable, for example, that the texts present no evidence at all about what determines individuals' well-being. They simply assert the materialist assumption that people are better off if they have more stuff. Yet the evidence we consider in Chapter 4 offers little or no support for this position.

Finally, the whole textbook structure is built on a view of human beings as rational calculators – a view that is rejected by psychologists and is increasingly being challenged within mainstream economics itself. It is being replaced with a view of human beings as having limited rationality, and capable of irrational exuberance and exaggerated herd-like reactions to economic events.

The shortcomings of the mainstream textbooks' world-view have not escaped all students. In 2000, a group of economics students in France circulated an open letter to their professors declaring 'We wish to escape from imaginary worlds!' and deploring the 'disregard for concrete realities' in their teaching. They asked for less dogmatism and more pluralism of approaches. Since then, student groups promoting change have proliferated around the world. In 2014 an International Student Initiative for Pluralism in Economics formed and issued an open letter calling for change.[16] This has since become Rethinking Economics, an umbrella organization of student groups around the world. Another student-run organization, Exploring Economics, has been established. (See the Resources and Suggestions for Further Reading at the end of this chapter.)

The textbooks and the Anti-Textbook

The Microeconomics Anti-Textbook presents a different picture of economics and a different vision of the economy – it's one that many economists see, but it has been filtered out of the mainstream introductory textbooks. It is not based on the ideas of an obscure fringe of the economics profession. We draw on the writings of many prominent economists – many winners of the Nobel Memorial Prize in economics, including even the authors of prominent introductory textbooks.[17]

We echo Akerlof and Shiller when they say: 'There is then a fundamental reason why we differ from those who think that the economy should just be a free-for-all, that the least government is the best government, and that the government should play only the most minimal role in setting the rules. We differ because we have a different vision of the economy.'[18]

Economics textbooks can and should be better. They need to incorporate the dimensions that are currently missing – power, history, institutions, a multiplicity of models. Textbooks need to convey the crucial art and difficulty of choosing the correct model. We need a vision of the economy that is far from the Panglossian portrayal currently in the textbooks. Real economies, even in the high income countries, feature persistent poverty, often growing inequality and economic insecurity, pervasive pollution, both local and global.

RESOURCES

Rethinking Economics (www.rethinkeconomics.org) is a network of dozens of student organizations around the world that promotes broadening of economics education beyond the narrow focus on neoclassical economics and solving mathematical problems that have nothing to do with real world issues.

Exploring Economics (exploring-economics.org) is a resource established by the Network for Pluralist Economics, founded in 2016. It has good introductions to 10 different schools of economic thought (in French, German, and Spanish as well as English), links to podcasts and to courses around the world, and much else.

SUGGESTIONS FOR FURTHER READING

The Econocracy: The Perils of Leaving Economics to the Experts, by Joe Earle, Cahal Moran and Zach Ward-Perkins, was written by some of the students who organized the economics student movement at the University of Manchester. In part, it's a critique of how economics is being taught and recommendations for how it can be improved.

The Rethinking Economics movement has produced *Rethinking economics: an introduction to pluralist economics*, edited by J. Christopher Proctor, Liliann Fischer, Joe Hasell, David Uwakwe, Zach Ward-Perkins, and Catriona Watson, is a collection of nine essays on approaches to economics that are neglected in the standard neoclassical textbooks.

What about alternatives to the standard texts? Several places maintain lists, although they are not necessarily complete or up to date. The US-based Union of Radical Political Economics has a list at urpe.org/resource/textbooks. The World Economics Association also has a list: worldeconomicsassociation.org/textbook-commentaries/alternative-texts.

We will keep a blog for this book, www.economics-antitextbook.com (the same one as for the previous edition) where, among other things, we will provide updated suggestions for further reading. Readers are invited to send us suggestions as well as comments about the book itself and questions to which we'll respond on our blog. Our email address is rodntony@gmail.com.

ADDENDUM: OUR SAMPLE OF STANDARD TEXTS

To ensure that the Standard Text section of each chapter is an accurate reflection of the textbooks, we have surveyed the contents of a sample of the 10 North American introductory microeconomics textbooks listed below. Nine are American editions and one is Canadian. They were chosen based on a combination of market share, longevity, and whether the book has been recently updated. Some of them also have international editions, indicated by an asterisk. The books are:

*William Baumol, Alan Blinder, and John Solow, *Microeconomics: Principles and Policy*, 14th edition, 2020.
*Karl E. Case, Ray Fair, and Sharon Oster, Principles of Microeconomics, 13th edition, 2020.
*David Colander, *Microeconomics*, 11th edition, 2020.
Robert H. Frank, Ben Bernanke, Kate Antonovics, and Ori Heffetz, *Principles of Microeconomics*, 7th edition, 2019.
*Paul Krugman and Robin Wells, *Microeconomics*, 6th edition, 2021.
*N. Gregory Mankiw, *Principles of Microeconomics*, 9th edition, 2021.
Campbell McConnell, Stanley Brue, and Sean Flynn, *Microeconomics: Principles, Problems, and Policies*, 22nd edition, 2021.
*William McEachern, *Microeconomics: A Contemporary Introduction*, 11th edition, 2017.
*Michael Parkin, *Microeconomics*, 13th edition, 2019.
Christopher Ragan, *Microeconomics*, 16th Canadian edition, 2020.

As we've claimed earlier, there are very substantial similarities across such books, but there are also differences. There are also inevitably grey areas around the border of what constitutes a standard or mainstream textbook.

Peter-Wim Zuidhof surveyed a selection of texts, including some of these, and distinguished four types. One he classified as 'liberal'. These texts portray markets as natural mechanisms in which forces act to move them to equilibrium. This leaves laissez-faire as an ideal and a limited role for government to correct 'market failures', should markets not allocate resources efficiently or fairly.[19]

A second category he classifies as the 'imperfect markets' approach, exemplified here by the Frank, Bernanke, and Solow text. They use the term 'market imperfections' instead of 'market failures', subtly suggesting that, instead of the failure of perfect markets, markets are commonly imperfect. Zuidhof writes: 'When imperfect rather than perfect markets are the norm, there is a natural place for government in the economy. In a world of imperfect markets, government intervention is no longer treated as a foreign or external intervention as was the case with market failure, but rather is seen as an integral part of the economy.'[20]

A third category is the 'free market' approach. The Baumol, Blinder and Solow text is an example. Here, 'the naturalism of the market in fact performs a double role in limiting government: first to show that one should not tamper with the market, and second that, in case markets fail, governments may fail for the same reasons.'[21] Baumol and co-authors set out a fundamental principle at the beginning of the text stating that 'attempts to repeal the law of supply and demand' by 'interference' with market prices 'usually backfire and sometimes produce results virtually the opposite of those intended'.[22]

Finally, Zuidhof identifies an 'institutionalist' approach, citing David Colander's text. He writes: 'Even though not overtly heterodox, Colander, unlike any of the other texts, introduces Austrian, institutionalist, radical, feminist, theological, and post-Keynesian approaches to economics that place a relative emphasis on institutions and history'.[23] The institutionalist approach emphasizes that markets are social constructs built on an institutional foundation. Here, government is not just legitimated by its role in dealing with market failures; it has a broader part to play in determining the ways in which economic forces should be channeled, markets being just one of them.

Where significant differences exist between the books in our sample, we try to give credit where credit is due. Not every point raised in the *Anti-Text* applies to each of these books.

Chapter 1

WHAT IS ECONOMICS? WHERE YOU START INFLUENCES WHERE YOU GO

'Introductory texts support an ethical system, one which authors fail to acknowledge. Clearly the selection of one ethical system over another is a normative choice, and it is… [a] choice which is consequential.' Emily Northrop[1]

1 THE STANDARD TEXT

1.1 Economics is the science of choice

It seems obvious that economics is about the economy; so a common sense definition of economics might be that it concerns itself with money, markets, business and how people make a living. But this definition is too narrow. Economics is not just the study of money and markets. It studies families, criminal behaviour and governments' policy choices. It includes the study of population growth, standards of living and voting patterns. It can also have a shot at explaining human behaviours in relation to dating and marriage.

The fact that economics can examine subjects traditionally studied by other social sciences suggests that *content* does not define the *discipline*. As long as a topic has a social dimension, we can look at it from the perspective of any social science.

Most textbooks define economics as the science of choice. It's about how individuals and society make choices, and how those choices are affected by incentives. This definition includes all aspects of life: a couple's choice to have a child, or a political party's choice of its platform. Its drawback is that it doesn't help to differentiate economics from the other social sciences, since they too look at how we make choices.

What distinguishes economics from other social sciences is its commitment to *rational choice theory*. This assumes that individuals are rational, self-interested, have stable and consistent preferences, and wish to maximize their own happiness (or 'utility'), given their constraints – such as the amount of time or money that they have. Social situations and collective behaviours are analysed as resulting from freely chosen individual actions. Just as science attempts to understand the properties of metals by understanding the atoms that comprise them, so economics attempts to understand society by analysing the behaviour of the individuals who comprise it.

1.2 Scarcity

Why is choice necessary? Economics assumes that people have unlimited wants. Therefore, no matter how abundant resources may be, they will always be scarce in the face of these unlimited wants.

A fundamental question in economics has always been how do we maximize happiness? Economists maintain that while we must allow people to decide for themselves what makes them happy, we know that people always want more. Therefore, society needs to use its resources as efficiently as possible to produce as much as possible; and society needs to expand what it can produce as quickly as possible. This explains why economists emphasize the goals of efficiency and growth.

But does the concept of unlimited wants mean that someone will want an unlimited number of new coats, or an unlimited number of pairs of shoes? No, it doesn't. Along with unlimited wants, economists normally assume that the more you have of something, the less you value one more unit of it. So, unlimited wants does not mean we want an unlimited amount of a specific thing. Rather, it means that there will always be something that we will desire. There will always be new desires. Our desires and wants are fundamentally unlimited.

1.3 Opportunity cost

Since resources are scarce, if we choose to use them in one way, we can't use them in another. Choosing more of one thing implies less of another thing. In other words, everything has a cost, and the real cost of something is what must be given up to get it. This is its opportunity cost – the value of the next best alternative forgone.

It's a cliché that *there's no such thing as a free lunch* – there is always an opportunity cost. Even if someone else buys you lunch, there is still a cost. There is a cost to society for all the resources used to grow the food, ship it to the restaurant and have it prepared. Your free lunch even costs you something: it uses up some of your scarce time that you could have used to do something else.

1.4 Marginal thinking: costs and benefits

You are familiar with the margin on a page – it lies at the edge. And when someone describes a soccer player as being *marginal* they mean he is a fringe player, on the edge of inclusion. Economists use the word marginal in a similar way. Marginal cost is the cost at the margin – or to be more precise, the cost of an additional unit of output or consumption. Thus, the marginal cost of wheat is the additional cost of producing one more unit of wheat. Similarly, marginal benefit is just the benefit someone gets from having one more unit of something. We might measure benefit in hypothetical *utils of satisfaction*; or in dollar terms – the maximum willingness to pay for one more unit. As the science of choice, the core economic framework is remarkably simple: *all activities are undertaken to the point where marginal cost equals marginal benefit.* Why? Because at this point total net benefit is maximized. An example will help.

Imagine we are old-style Soviet planners, trying to determine the quantity of Russian-style fur hats to produce. Let's assume that the marginal cost of producing a fur hat increases the more we produce – so we draw it as the upward-sloping line in the upper diagram of Figure 1.1. Further assume that the more hats are produced, the less one more hat is valued – so the marginal benefit line slopes down. How many hats should we produce? If we produce only Q_1 units, the marginal benefit of one more hat is $6, but the marginal cost is only $3. This means that the extra benefit of one more unit is greater than the extra cost of producing it. Therefore, we can improve society's well-being by producing one more. This remains true as we increase production to Q*. But we should not produce more than Q*. Beyond that point marginal cost exceeds marginal benefit, reducing total net benefit from hat production. Total net benefit is shown in the lower diagram of Figure 1.1. Clearly, this is maximized at an output of Q*.

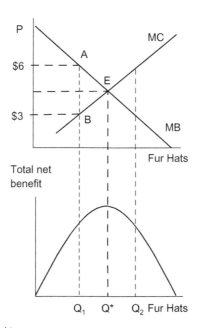

Figure 1.1 Marginal thinking

This marginal-cost/marginal-benefit framework can be applied to everything we do, buy, hire or produce. If I want to maximize my satisfaction from studying economics, I should study until the marginal cost of one more hour of study just equals the marginal benefit. If I want to maximize my satisfaction from buying oranges, I equate marginal cost to the marginal benefit of one more orange.

When textbooks claim '*rational people think at the margin*' it is this framework they have in mind. But are people rational?

1.5 Rational and self-interested individuals

Critics claim the foundations of economics are shaky – people are not rational, they say, nor solely self-interested. But rationality in economics means something quite different from its colloquial meaning. All it means in an economic context is that individuals are goal oriented and have consistent preferences (or tastes). So if John prefers apples to oranges, and oranges to grapefruit, he must prefer apples to grapefruit.

Economists assume everyone has the same fundamental goal: to be as happy as possible, or (to use economic jargon) to maximize their utility (or satisfaction). But different things bring happiness to different people. One person prefers to give their money to charity and live a simple ascetic life. Another prefers to spend their money on the fast life – the American comedian W. C. Fields famously quipped, 'I spent half my money on gambling, alcohol, and wild women. The other half I wasted.' Economists do not judge the things that bring utility to people. To be 'rational' in economics simply means that given your preferences, you choose to allocate your time and money to maximize your utility.

Further, individuals are not assumed to think only of themselves. Someone's utility may depend on the well-being of others. The altruist is viewed as no better or worse than the miser, since they are both trying to be as happy as possible. Selfish and selfless, virtue and vice, have no meaning in economics – they're just different preferences.

If individuals are rational, they respond to incentives in predictable ways. Thus, if we wish to encourage people to give blood we could pay them for their time. Or, if we wish to encourage people to recycle bottles, we could make them pay a bottle deposit that is refunded upon return.

1.6 Markets are usually a good way to organize economic activity

We don't need economic planners; as long as we have competitive markets they organize the economy in a way that maximizes the value of total production and thus the incomes that are earned by producing it. This is better than the perfect planner for two reasons: first, it doesn't require an expensive planning bureaucracy; second, it doesn't require that anyone be altruistically motivated.

We will develop the argument over several chapters, but let's have a quick synopsis right now. Here it is in three sentences:

In competitive markets, prices and quantities are determined by demand and supply. But demand is just marginal benefit, and supply turns out to be just marginal cost. So, competitive markets guarantee that the right quantities are produced and society's net benefit is maximized.

This is the technical argument for laissez-faire, the view that governments should leave the economy alone. Let's consider the argument developed by Adam Smith in *The Wealth of Nations*, published in 1776. In an analogy that has become iconic, Smith compares competitive market forces to an *invisible hand* that guides self-interest into socially useful activities. He wrote: '*It is not through the benevolence of the butcher, the brewer or the baker, that we expect our dinner, but from their regard to their own interest.*' In a later passage he added: '*Every individual... by directing that industry in such a manner as its produce may be of the greatest value, he intends only his own gain, and he is in this, as in many other cases, led by an invisible hand to promote an end* [the public interest] *which was no part of his intention.*'[2] The novel twist in Smith's argument is that he turns selfishness into a virtue. Government intervention is not needed because a competitive market system naturally leads to a *harmony of interests*. In Smith's example, it leads to the optimal quantities and lowest possible prices for meat, beer and bread. In other words, it leads to an efficient outcome.

1.7 Governments can sometimes improve market outcomes

The central message is this: if *all* markets were competitive and there were markets for everything, laissez-faire would produce an efficient outcome in three key aspects: it would produce the optimal quantity of each good; it would produce these quantities at the lowest possible cost; and it would distribute the output to those who 'value' it most. This situation is called Pareto optimal, and it has the property that it is not possible to make anyone better off without making at least one person worse off – in other words, there would be no waste anywhere in the economy.

The condition that *all* markets must be competitive can be violated in two ways, however. First, some markets may be *non-competitive*, as in the case of monopoly (a single seller). Second, some markets *may not exist*, such as the market for unpolluted air. Both cases lead to 'market failure'. In such situations, government intervention can (in theory) improve upon the inefficiency produced under laissez-faire. Thus, the role of the government is critically dependent on two factors: first, how competitive existing markets are; and second, upon how many markets don't exist.

1.8 Another government role: providing equity

In the special situation of complete and competitive markets, laissez-faire leads to a Pareto-optimal situation – an ideal situation in an efficiency sense. But that doesn't mean that the outcome would be fair or humane. It might be a situation where widows and orphans are starving while everyone else has three homes and a luxury yacht. So the government has another role in the economy: to redistribute income to make market outcomes more equitable. But redistributing income necessarily creates inefficiencies, and this creates a trade-off between efficiency and equity.

1.9 The efficiency–equity trade-off

Trade-offs follow from scarcity and opportunity cost: we are always trading off more of one thing for less of another. While this kind of trade-off is familiar from everyday life, economics also emphasizes a more abstract trade-off: that more equity always comes at a cost of less efficiency. This view is encapsulated in American economist Arthur Okun's leaky bucket metaphor: redistributing income is like carrying water from the rich to the poor using a leaky bucket – the result may be more equitable, but comes at a cost of water wasted on the ground.[3]

The argument hinges on two kinds of adverse incentive effects – direct and indirect. The direct effect is this: the more the government helps people, the less incentive they have to help themselves. For example, the so-called 'social safety net' comprises things like unemployment insurance benefits and old-age pensions. The first of these state-provided benefits reduces the incentive to work and the second reduces the incentive to save (and hence to work). Therefore, they reduce efficiency by distorting people's incentives.

The indirect effect operates via the necessity to pay for the social safety net: this requires various forms of taxation, which also cause inefficiencies. For example, income taxes affect incentives to work. Sales taxes increase prices so buyers demand less of the taxed goods, leading to a decrease in production. If an optimal amount was previously being produced, sales taxes lead to a sub-optimal or inefficient situation.

How much efficiency should be traded off for an increase in equity is a political issue about which economics can say nothing. That is because it is a *normative* question – it depends on people's values and priorities, something about which economists as citizens have opinions, but no professional expertise to offer. The job of the economist is to explain why there is a trade-off, and to suggest ways of improving the nature of the trade-off so additional equity can be had at a lower cost.

2 THE ANTI-TEXT

2.1 The inherent tension with macroeconomics

As we mentioned one seminal book in economics, Adam Smith's *The Wealth of Nations,* let's mention another: John Maynard Keynes's *The General Theory of Employment, Interest and Money.* Published in 1936 during the Great Depression, it attempted to explain how unemployment could persist, and what governments could do about it. In doing this, Keynes became the founding father of macroeconomics. This is the study of large aggregates, and explains such things as unemployment, inflation, exchange rates and interest rates; whereas microeconomics deals with smaller units, such as individual markets.

Keynes's message is the opposite of Smith's. Whereas Smith emphasized that a capitalist market economy can be self-regulating and efficient, Keynes emphasized that it was inherently prone to cycles of boom and bust – and those periods of bust are terribly inefficient. Whereas Smith emphasized that rational decision-making leads to an efficient outcome, Keynes emphasized that people's behaviour, particularly regarding business investment, is driven by waves of spontaneous optimism and pessimism and (implicitly) fuelled by greed, fear and the herd instinct.

When it comes to macroeconomics, Keynes's thinking still dominates. It is generally accepted that the government must intervene in the economy to prevent both recessions and overblown expansions, and that it must regulate some sectors. Yet, when it comes to textbook microeconomics, the thinking of Adam Smith dominates. It's an uneasy coexistence.

> Question for your professor: Microeconomics emphasizes
> the efficiency of the individual competitive market. Yet
> when all markets are studied together in macroeconomics,
> the result can be the inefficiency of mass unemployment.
> Can you explain this apparent inconsistency?

2.2 Scarcity and unlimited wants? Reconsidering the economic problem

According to the texts, the 'economic problem' is making choices that allocate our scarce resources in the best way given our unlimited wants. Difficult trade-offs are inevitable. But this view of the economic problem can be challenged in several ways.

Economists in the 'post-Keynesian' school reject scarcity as a fundamental truth. In their view, economies typically have unemployed resources. If those resources could be put to work, more of everything could be produced. We could have our cake and eat it too; there would be no opportunity cost if all the resources being put to work had been involuntarily unemployed. As Canadian economist Marc Lavoie writes, '... since full employment of resources is not assumed, the discussion of their efficient allocation is not a major issue. Rather, what is emphasized among post-Keynesian economists is the degree to which these resources are utilized.'[4]

> Question for your professor: Would there be an
> opportunity cost to putting people back to work(and
> producing more goods) even in a deep recession? If
> not, then does scarcity depend on full employment?

Post-Keynesians aren't the only ones who reject scarcity as a basic economic condition. For example, Emily Northrop questions whether the texts' assertion that people's wants are insatiable is true. She notes that some people manage to resist consumerism and choose different lifestyles embodying simplicity, balance or connection (to the earth and to others). The fact that some are able to do this suggests unlimited wants aren't innate. As she points out, the texts ignore the 'cultural and economic institutions that nurture human wants', such as advertising. Their assertion of insatiability effectively legitimates and promotes consumerism.[5]

Northrop also points out that the notion of unlimited wants puts all wants on an equal footing: one person's want for a subsistence diet is no more important than a millionaire's want for precious jewellery. This equality of wants reflects the market value system that no goods are intrinsically more worthy than others – just as no preferences are more worthy than others. This is clearly a value judgement and one that many people reject. Yet economics, which unquestioningly adopts this approach, claims to be an objective social science that avoids making value judgements!

If we accept this view of unlimited wants, the economic problem can never be solved once and for all. But if we reject the view that all wants have equal merit, the economic problem can be redefined in a way that has a solution. Northrop cites John Maynard Keynes's view that the economic problem is the 'struggle for subsistence' and that it could be solved if everyone's basic needs were met. Keynes distinguished between two kinds of needs: those which are 'absolute in the sense that we feel them whatever the situation of our fellow human beings may be, and those which are relative', which depend only on what others have and may indeed be unlimited. However, for Keynes, absolute needs took priority and he foresaw the possibility of the economic problem being solved (in the then developed countries at least) within a century of the time that he was writing.[6]

This definition of the economic problem clearly requires a value judgement about which needs get moral weight, just as the one in the text does. But Keynes's definition puts equity and the distribution of income front and centre. It contrasts with the textbook approach of treating equity as a political issue outside the scope of economic analysis.

In general, we could think of economics as being about 'how societies organize themselves to support human life and its flourishing' – or about how they fail to do so. Such a 'provisioning' definition of economics encompasses both markets and families, both money and care', as Julie Nelson puts it.[7]

Kate Raworth goes a step beyond this in stating that the economic problem is achieving 'human prosperity within a flourishing web of life'. This requires meeting everyone's basic needs while keeping the socio-economic system within sustainable limits imposed by the Earth's finite resources.[8]

Another economist who rejects the idea of 'innate unlimited wants' is Stephen Marglin.[9] He sees the source of consumerist materialism in the destruction of community ties, which creates an existential vacuum: all that's left is the pursuit of more material goods. Having more stuff substitutes for meaningful relationships with family, friends and community. His conclusion: as long as goods are a primary means of solving existential problems, we will always want more. But what or who is responsible for undermining community ties and bonds? Marglin argues that the assumptions of textbook economics, and the resulting policy recommendations of economists, undermine community. Let's consider how this works.

2.3 The individual versus the community

According to Marglin, the textbook focus on individuals makes the community invisible to economists' eyes. But it is our friendships and deep connections with others which give our lives meaning. So community ties, built on mutual trust and common purpose, have a value – a value that economists ignore when recommending policy.

Furthermore, Marglin argues that rational choice theory – emphasized in the mainstream textbooks – reduces ethical judgements and values to mere preferences. Are you working for the benefit of your community? That's your preference. Are you cooking the books to get rich quick? That's your preference. Being selfish is no worse than being altruistic, they are just different preferences.

Indeed, according to mainstream textbook economics it is smart to be selfish. It not only maximizes your own material well-being, but through the invisible hand of the market it also promotes the public interest. This view influences the cultural norms of society and indirectly erodes community. This influence of economics on attitudes isn't mere speculation. As we will describe shortly, there is evidence that studying economics can change students' behaviour, and not for the better.

Marglin's key point concerns the uneasy relationship between markets and communities. Textbook economics praises the efficiency of markets, and economists generally favour expanding the reach of the market. For example, economists favour free trade agreements because they expand markets. But free trade creates winners and losers and sometimes the losers are concentrated in geographical areas. Sometimes whole communities are wiped out. Still, as we will explain in Chapter 10, economists argue that free trade is beneficial because the gains outweigh the losses. But this accounting ignores the cost of community destruction. Marglin notes '[I]n practice compensation [for those made worse off] is not forthcoming. And how do you compensate somebody for the destruction of the community in which she grew up, is raising a family, and hopes one day to retire and look after her grandchildren?'[10]

Marglin argues that economists fail to do an appropriate cost–benefit analysis on whether extending the influence of markets is a good idea. They see the benefits, such as higher material living standards, but since the community is invisible, they don't see the costs. As a result, they fail to address the question: What limits should be placed on markets for the sake of community?

> Question for your professor: Since it is our friendships and deep connections with others which give our lives meaning, why does cost–benefit analysis always give a *zero* value to community ties?

2.4 The individual versus the corporation

Marglin argues that the textbook focus on individuals is problematic. John Kenneth Galbraith went further. He thought the textbook focus on individuals was a source of grave error and bias because in the real world the individual is not the agent that matters most. The corporation is.

By having the wrong focus, economics is able to deny the importance of power and political interests.

Textbooks assume that rational individuals with stable preferences, uninfluenced by advertising, allocate their spending to maximize their own happiness. This suggests that individuals, through their spending, exercise ultimate control over both what is produced and how it is produced. Of course, entrepreneurs and corporate managers actually make those decisions. But (so the conventional argument goes) they are governed by their anticipations of market response – they cannot survive if customers don't buy. Thus, even large corporations are subordinate to the market.

Further, textbooks assume that the state is subordinate to individuals through the ballot box. At the very least, government is assumed to be neutral, intervening to correct market failure as best it can, and to redistribute income to make market outcomes more equitable.

But this idealized world is so far removed from the real world that it is little more than a myth, or 'perhaps even a fraud'.[11] The power of the largest corporations rivals that of the state; indeed, they often hijack the state's power for their own purposes. In reality, we see the management of the consumer by corporations; and we see the subordination of the state to corporate interests.

Galbraith saw economic life as a bipolar phenomenon. In one part of the economy there are vast numbers of small-scale businesses, where the market is paramount and the state is remote. This is the part featured in economic instruction and in political speeches, even as it fast disappears. 'For the small retailer, Wal-Mart awaits. For the family farm, there are the massive grain and fruit enterprises and the modern large-scale meat producers'.[12]

The other part of the American economy consists of a few hundred enormously powerful corporations. What they need in research and development, or environmental policy, or public works, or emergency financial support, becomes public policy. Government policy is influenced in widely accepted ways. 'Between public and private bureaucracies – between GM and the Department of Transportation, General Dynamics and the Pentagon – there is a deeply symbiotic relationship. Each of these organizations can do much for the other. There is even, between them, a large and continuous interchange of executive personnel'.[13]

In the United States, a prime example of how corporate interest has taken over public interest is provided by the 'military-industrial complex'. President Dwight Eisenhower coined this term in 1961 in his last address to the nation as he warned about the dangers to democracy of its growing power. Military industries provide employment across the country and funds for politicians. In recent decades, a 'prison-industrial complex' has arisen in the United States, with corporations profiting from mass incarceration.[14] The 'surveillance-industrial complex' is a combination of private and public security organizations and corporations routinely gathering and sharing massive amounts of information to monitor, track and surveil the population.[15] The newest addition to this family of American complexes is the 'political-industrial complex' that supports its two political parties; it includes wealthy donors, lobbyists, partisan think tanks, consultants, and the media.[16]

In Galbraith's view, the biggest corporations have power over markets, power in the community, power over the state, and power over belief. As such, the corporation is a political instrument, different in form and degree but not in kind from the state itself. Textbook economics, in ignoring and thus concealing that power, is part of the problem. As such it becomes an 'ally of those whose exercise of power depends on an acquiescent public'.[17]

> Questions for your professor: What the biggest corporations need in environmental policy, public works, or emergency financial support, they usually get. Does our textbook discuss the political power of large corporations? If it doesn't, doesn't this stop us from seeing how we are really governed?

2.5 The trade-off between efficiency and equity reconsidered

The textbook argument for an efficiency–equity trade-off revolves around the disincentive effects from having a social safety net, and the inefficiencies created from the taxation necessary to pay for it. We will examine this in Chapter 9, but for now let's just note a couple of things. First, taxes do not necessarily influence behaviour in undesirable ways. And second, there are beneficial incentive effects from living in a more equitable society.

Taxes need not cause inefficiencies When it comes to pollution we actually want to create disincentives. As we see in Chapter 7, a tax on emissions of pollutants can improve economic efficiency and give society a double dividend: not only does the tax reduce a harmful activity, but society also gains the additional government spending financed by the tax. In general, we should first be taxing things that society doesn't want, such as pollution, before taxing things that society wants, such useful commodities.

Inequality might be bad for efficiency Inequality might be bad for efficiency for many reasons. Let's begin by considering two obvious ones. First, a high degree of inequality leads to high crime rates, which increases the social costs associated with law enforcement, the judicial process and individuals' efforts to protect themselves and their property. This reduces the resources available for other things. Second, inequality and poverty are associated with the lack of educational opportunities for the poor and worse health outcomes for everyone. A better-educated and healthier workforce is more productive than a less-educated one.

Inequality has numerous, more subtle, effects. It influences 'social cohesion' and the economic pay-off from trust and cooperation. These are part of a society's 'social capital' and play an important role in facilitating economic life. Low levels of inequality promote social cohesion and trust, whereas high levels of inequality weaken people's sense of reciprocity and increase the sense of 'us' versus 'them'. For example, greater inequality significantly reduces expressed levels of trust.[18] Lower levels of trust are, in turn, associated with lower levels of average individual satisfaction with life.[19]

Trust and cooperation matter for many reasons. Whereas trust between workers and management facilitates the adoption of new and more productive techniques, polarized groups engage in wasteful conflict that brings production to a standstill. Where there is trust, parties can reach handshake agreements; without trust, elaborate contracts are required. In general, the importance of trust and mutual cooperation is demonstrated by the fact that when workers 'work to rule' (and do nothing except what they are contractually obliged to do) output falls and delays increase. Clearly, workers normally do much more than they are contractually obliged to do.

Greater social cohesion also has political advantages. In *Making Democracy Work*, American political scientist Robert Putnam shows that engaged citizens have better government. Social cohesion leads to more political participation and better monitoring of government, which increases governmental efficiency and reduces corruption. The economic benefits take the form of better roads and sewerage systems, better regulation of business, more effective enforcement of contracts, and overall a better quality of life.

> Questions for your professor: Aren't there good reasons to think that equity might enhance efficiency, for example, improved trust, less crime and violence, less waste of human potential, better health, better governance? Why does the text mention only how efficiency might be reduced?

2.6 The *Homo Economicus* Assumption and Its Pernicious Effects

The core textbook assumptions about human behaviour are deliberately unrealistic. The economic decision makers in the texts (and in much of economic theory) are rational thinkers, who make plans, carry them out, never experience regret, and are purely self-interested. Because they are plainly not human, their species has been given the name *Homo economicus*. The idea must be that even though the assumptions are unrealistic, they have the advantage of simplicity and provide a good enough approximation to be useful.

In *Doughnut Economics*, Kate Raworth traces the origins of Homo economicus back to John Stuart Mill, who thought that political economy should assume that individuals seek to maximize their own wealth, while disliking work, and desiring luxuries. She writes that Mill 'justified his caricature, confident that no "political economist was ever so absurd as to suppose that mankind are really thus constituted", while adding that "this is the mode in which science must necessarily proceed" '.[20] In other words, simplifying assumptions are needed to deduce conclusions from the theory.

We'll discuss the role of simplifying assumptions in the next two chapters, but for now let's note that further assumptions were later added to Mill's wealth maximizer. The English economist William Stanley Jevons, who in the 1870s pioneered the kind of marginal thinking described earlier in this chapter, had Homo economicus maximizing his well-being. The creature was given insatiable wants by Alfred Marshall in his famous text *Principles of Economics*, which first appeared in 1890. By the 1920s, American economist Frank Knight had added perfect knowledge and perfect foresight.

If the self-interested behaviour of Homo economicus leads to a socially desirable outcome, it is easy to think that the mainstream textbook message is that this is how people *should* behave, just like Adam Smith's butcher, brewer, and baker. It not only maximizes their own material well-being, but through the invisible hand of the market it also promotes the social good. As Joan Robinson put it: 'By this means the moral problem is abolished. The moral problem is concerned with the conflict between individual interest and the interest of society. And this doctrine tells us that there is no conflict, we can all pursue our self-interest with a good conscience'.[21]

What effect does this have on economics students? In a pioneering study in 1981, Gerald Marwell and Ruth Ames found that exposure to economics generates less cooperative, less other-regarding, behaviour. Later, Robert Frank and co-authors showed that uncooperative behaviour increases the more individuals are exposed to economics.[22] Others find similar results, but as we will see in the next chapter, empirical results in economics are rarely conclusive. An alternative possibility is that economics students are different from other students from the start; their different characteristics could be the result of self-selection, rather than indoctrination.[23] Perhaps some students may find the reputation of the subject off-putting in the first place, leaving the more self-interested ones in the classroom. Perhaps it is a mix of both as some studies have also found.[24]

The lesson should be clear: economics students should be careful not to take the textbook model of Homo economicus as a guide about how to behave. In any case, as we will see, purely self-interested behaviour does not lead to socially desirable outcomes. Let's now consider the other attributes of Homo economicus, particularly its rationality.

2.7 Reconsidering the assumption of rationality

No one maintains that people are rational in the sense that Homo economicus is assumed to be. Indeed, the term "hyper-rational" may well be more appropriate than the commonly used "rational", because it emphasizes that this is something that no human could achieve.[25] As psychologist Gerg Gigerenzer remarks in his book, *Rationality for Mortals*, 'all relevant information is assumed to be available to Homo economicus at no cost. This classical version of Homo economicus has a distinctive Christian flavor: He is created in the image of an omniscient God.'[26]

The relevant question is whether people, on average, behave in a way that is close enough to the way Homo economicus would behave to allow the theory to be useful. At first glance, it's not easy to say because, while it's assumed that people are acting rationally to attain their goals, we don't know what people's preferences and goals are.

For example, can rational choice theory explain addictive behaviour? Addiction to soft drugs like tobacco seems to conform to the theory's predictions. Both the amount smoked and the decision to quit respond in systematic ways to the abolition of advertising, to health warnings, to rules governing smoking in public places, and to the price of cigarettes.

But can it explain getting addicted in the first place? And what about addiction to hard drugs that destroy people's lives relatively quickly? A resolute defender of the rationality assumption could assert that if people are doing these things that is because that is their preference. If they later express regret, then it can only be the case that their preferences must have changed.[27] The theory, expressed in such a way, is hardly satisfactory because it cannot be refuted.

In fact, research suggests that the key element is inadequate understanding and inadequate information – people systematically underestimate the power of the addictive craving. Not only is this underestimated by those who have never experienced such craving. The power of future craving is underestimated by addicts as soon as they have a fix.[28]

But once we allow for *systematic* deviations from rational choice, where do we stop? If this were extended beyond the realm of addictive behaviour to behaviour in general, what would be left of rational choice theory? So, the question of such systematic mistakes or 'biases' is an important issue, one that has been explored by Daniel Kahneman – who, despite being a psychologist by training, received the 2002 Nobel Memorial Prize in economics.

Systematic mistakes As Kahneman describes in his book *Thinking, Fast and Slow*, the mind works in two quite distinct ways. *System 1* is best described as a system of short cuts, rules of thumb (or *heuristics*) that allow the mind to jump to intuitive conclusions relatively easily. Its advantage is its speed; it is also associative, uncontrolled and essentially automatic, and these constitute its areas of vulnerability. On the other hand, *System 2* is systematic, logical and rule bound; it is controlled and deliberate. It is *System 2* which is rational in a calculating sense. But most of the time we operate using *System 1* – usually with remarkable success. Unfortunately, it is prone to making systematic errors, even with very simple mathematical questions.

For example, suppose a bat and a ball cost $1.10 in total. The bat costs $1 more than the ball. *How much does the ball cost?* What do you say?

According to Kahneman most people answer 10 cents, including half of the students at Princeton, an elite university![29] Even actuaries and researchers make similar errors. (The right answer: the ball costs 5 cents since $0.05 + $1.05 = $1.10.) We are poor at calculating some things, especially probabilities, and our intuitive answers are systematically biased: we underestimate the likelihood of mundane things happening, even as we overestimate the likelihood of frightening or exciting things happening. We are overly influenced by the decisions of others – to the point of sitting quietly in a room filling up with smoke, as long as there are others in the room doing likewise.[30] We give undue weight to the most recent past, and when making life decisions we systematically underestimate the importance of the distant future. Nevertheless, we are confident – overconfident in fact – of our ability to make judgements.

One of Kahneman's most interesting findings is that our preferences depend on inconsequential differences in the way choices are *framed*. Take two mathematically identical options and dress one up as a loss, and the other as a gain, and we choose the one dressed up as a gain. For example, if the risk associated with a medical procedure is expressed as a 10 per cent risk of dying, fewer people will accept the procedure than when the risk is expressed as a 90 per cent chance of living.[31]

2.8 Behavioural economics

Research in psychology such as Kahneman's has inspired some economists to integrate these ideas into economics. The most prominent of these, the American economist Richard Thaler, was awarded the Nobel Memorial Prize in 2017 for his work over the previous 40 years in behavioural economics. This is the field of economics that uses more realistic psychological assumptions about behaviour than the Homo economicus approach.[32] Behavioural economics focuses on individual choices such as consumer behaviour and the choices people make in financial markets. It allows human nature to be bounded in three ways: bounded (or limited) rationality, bounded willpower and bounded self-interest. (All of these are unbounded for Homo economicus.)

With regard to bounded rationality, it is surprising that economists are just now catching on to the importance of framing – advertisers have understood this concept for years. They understand that choice depends on how the decision-maker describes the object to himself and what associations can be given to it. Advertising attempts to frame the choice in a way that skews the buyer's decision in favour of the seller. If the seller is successful, the buyer may no longer be acting entirely in his own best interest. Instead of the presumption that markets will make everyone as well off as they can be, now all bets are off.

With regard to bounded willpower, behavioural economics recognizes that once we make a choice, we often fail to follow through. We want to lose weight and exercise more. But it's tempting to do all that tomorrow, not today. An important example of this procrastination is saving behaviour. It is generally accepted that Americans should save more, and apparently they want to. But they don't. It has proved an intractable problem. But through a better understanding of our psychology, Richard Thaler came up with a solution: the Save More Tomorrow programme.[33] The idea is that people commit a portion of their *future* salary *increases* into a retirement savings account. Brilliant! There is no sacrifice today; we do our savings tomorrow as we would prefer. When this plan was offered in several firms in the United States, a high proportion (78 per cent) joined. Those enrolled increased their saving rates from an average of 3.5 per cent to 13.6 per cent.

As to our bounded selfishness, most of us want to 'do the right thing'. This means that financial incentives can actually reduce altruistic behaviour, leading to perverse effects. For example, Richard Titmuss showed that paying blood donors in the USA not only reduced the quantity of donated blood, but it also reduced its quality.[34] As a result of his work, the World Health Organization in 1975 urged its member states to 'promote the development of national blood services based on voluntary non-remunerated donation of blood'.[35]

Another classic example of how actions are motivated by 'doing the right thing' is that the introduction of small fines for parents who arrive late to collect their children from a nursery school causes parents to arrive late more often than before. The payment reduces the guilt about arriving late, and parents treat the situation as if they are paying for a service.[36]

Given these results, should we pay households for recycling waste? Should we give tax relief to those who buy greener cars? The issues aren't trivial. Financial incentives can backfire.

Another interesting aspect of our bounded selfishness is that besides having a social conscience and altruistic motivations, we exhibit consideration for total strangers – and expect it in return. Giving tips in restaurants we will never again visit is one example. But systematic evidence has been provided by the *ultimatum game*: player A is given a sum of money to split with player B; if B accepts A's offer, they divide the money accordingly; but if B rejects A's offer, both players get nothing. Textbook economics says that player B should accept any offer greater than zero. Yet in thousands of trials around the world, with different stakes, people generally reject offers of 30 per cent (or less) of the total sum. The results hold even when the players are anonymous and when the sum involved is up to three months' income.[37]

This has applications to all areas in economics. An individual's willingness to pay for an object is influenced by knowing what the workers who made it were paid. A union may be prepared to jeopardize the future of the whole enterprise if it decides that the offered wages are too unfair. And empirically we find that unskilled workers in more profitable sectors or companies are paid more than identical unskilled workers elsewhere. When textbook economics ignores our instinct for fair shares, it misses a critical element of many economic interactions.

The impact of behavioural economics Behavioural economics has entered the mainstream, at least in a limited way. Many economists work in the field and publish in major journals. Despite this, Homo economicus lives on. One possible reason for this is that many behavioural economists, such as Richard Thaler, are not challenging one of the fundamental pillars of neoclassical economics: they still see a value in using the Homo economicus assumption as a kind of benchmark, a point of comparison with actual behaviour.[38] As we've seen, the lessons of behavioural economics can be used to 'nudge' people in (hopefully) the right direction. Real people also 'need protection from others who deliberately exploit their weaknesses—and especially the quirks of System 1 and the laziness of System 2', as Daniel Kahneman puts it, giving as an example the recommendation that all contracts be written in plain language that everyone can understand.[39]

It's worth noting that whether to retain the rationality benchmark is controversial. 'A true theory of bounded rationality does not cling to optimization theories, neither as descriptions nor as norms of behaviour', according to psychologist Gerd Gigerenzer, who asks: 'A systematic deviation from an "insane" standard should not automatically be called a judgmental error, should it?'[40] The results of behavioural economics only show that the rational actor assumption often makes poor predictions about actual behaviour.

What about behavioural economics in the textbooks? Almost all texts mention behavioural economics, but with rare exceptions it usually gets just a few pages of discussion.[41] Examples of a few behavioural 'anomalies' are given, but the impression is left that the Homo economicus assumption works well enough. Obviously, behavioural economists disagree.

> Question for your professor: Behavioural economists
> have shown that financial incentives may reduce
> altruistic behaviour, and produce perverse results
> (examples: blood donors, late fines at day care
> centres). How do we know when to use financial
> incentives, and when not to?

In Marglin's view, 'if the research agenda of behavioural economics were to be carried through unflinchingly, the results might well be devastating for the self-interested, utility-maximizing individual who has had the leading role in economics since its emergence as a separate discipline'.[42] Whether this new psychological realism will eventually revolutionize the subject remains to be seen. Either way, it leads nicely into our next chapter on methodology.

2.9 Concluding comment

Textbook economics starts out on the wrong foot by asserting, without discussion, that the subject matter of economics is the choices rational individuals make when faced with scarcity created by their unlimited wants. The value judgements involved in this and the alternatives to it go unmentioned. The 'economic problem' then becomes how to use those scarce resources in the most efficient way, subject to some equity goals that are costly to attain.

As Julie Nelson puts it, 'when we say that economics is about "rational choice in the face of scarcity", we stack the deck in favor of individualism and selfishness. Contrast this to saying that economics is about "who gets to eat and who does not". The latter packs a visceral punch and directs us towards investigating social relations'.[43] The issue of who gets to eat is not hypothetical. Even in the wealthy countries of North America and Europe, 15 million people – about 1.4 percent of the population – go some days in the year without eating. For the world, it's 10.2 percent, some 769 million people.[44]

She has also been rightly critical of the narrow focus of the typical introductory course, writing 'We haven't just *forgotten* to teach Econ 101 students that caring, power differences, ethical concerns, the ability to work together, and the health of our physical world are important, too. We teach them that, for the purpose of understanding economic life–this huge part of our social world! –paying attention to those things is *unnecessary.*'[45]

The texts' portrayal of a world of atomistic individuals each caring only about themselves misses the tension between the individual and society that is expressed by the words of the first century Jewish sage Hillel, quoted by Marglin: 'If I am not for myself, who will be? And if I am only for myself, what am I?'.[46] As we've seen, it seems all too easy for economics students to think that economic theory is saying that they should be only for themselves.[47]

Behavioural economics reminds us that we are not Homo economicus but the far more interesting Homo sapiens. Theories that incorporate bounded rationality, bounded willpower and bounded self-interest are better at explaining people's actual behaviour than the Homo economicus assumption used in the textbooks.

SUGGESTIONS FOR FURTHER READING

In her 1993 essay 'The Study of Choice or the Study of Provisioning? Gender and the Definition of Economics', Julie Nelson critiques the standard textbook definition of economics and offers a broader alternative approach.

Emily Northrop's essay 'Normative foundations of introductory economics' is highly recommended. Unfortunately, it remains as relevant today as it was when it was written in 2000.

Kate Raworth's *Doughnut Economics*, Chapter 3 'Nurture Human Nature: from rational economic man to social adaptable humans', traces the history of *Homo economicus* and the evidence about people's actual behaviour.

Daniel Kahneman's *Thinking: Fast and Slow* describes the psychology behind behavioural economics and his role in developing it with his long-time collaborator, the late Amos Tversky.

Richard Thaler's 2015 book *Misbehaving: The Making of Behavioral Economics* is an engaging account of his research.

Chapter 2

INTRODUCING ECONOMIC MODELS

'Whether you can observe a thing or not depends on the theory which you use. It is the theory which decides what can be observed.' Albert Einstein[1]

'Economics is the science of thinking in terms of models joined to the art of choosing models which are relevant to the contemporary world.' John Maynard Keynes[2]

I THE STANDARD TEXT

1.1 Model building and model testing

Science is a method – a process of forming hypotheses, making predictions and testing the predictions against the facts. Sometimes a hypothesis will emerge from inference: looking at the world and making a generalization about it. Sometimes it will emerge from a process of deduction: thinking about the world in a systematic way. Usually deduction involves trying to separate what is essential about a problem from its irrelevant details. When we do this, we have created a simplified version of reality, or a *model* of reality. Thus, building models necessarily entails making assumptions that are *unrealistic* – otherwise they wouldn't be *simplifying*.

A map does something similar; only those details relevant to the map's purpose are included. The details that are left out don't matter if the map is useful. Similarly, if a model makes good predictions, then those aspects of reality that are ignored don't matter. Therefore, it's inappropriate to judge the usefulness of a model by the realism of its assumptions; the only relevant test is the accuracy of the model's predictions.

1.2 Examples of economic models

The production possibility frontier (PPF) Let's begin with a simple two-person economy where things are produced. We can imagine the situation faced by the fictional 18th-century shipwrecked sailor, Robinson Crusoe. Crusoe on his island has to divide his time between two activities, fishing and gathering coconuts. Devoting more time to fishing implies less time for coconuts; the opportunity cost of one more fish is the number of coconuts forgone.

Next, Crusoe meets Friday, who also fishes and gathers coconuts. Friday is less productive at both tasks, but especially at gathering coconuts; when it comes to fishing he is only slightly worse than Crusoe. Having met, should they continue to work in isolation? Since Crusoe is more productive in everything, could it be in his best interests to continue to go it alone?

It turns out that specialization and exchange (trade) can benefit them both. It doesn't matter that Crusoe is more productive (or has an 'absolute advantage') in producing both fish and coconuts. Crusoe should spend more time gathering coconuts (at which he is much better), and Friday should spend more time fishing (at which he is only a little worse). Such an arrangement will increase their total production of fish and coconuts.

To demonstrate this in a more interesting context, let's replace individuals with countries. This allows us to see the gains from international trade. The model has two purposes: to illustrate some important concepts as simply as possible, while making predictions, in this case about the pattern of production and trade between two countries.

Our story will feature two countries (England and Canada), two industries (wheat and cloth) and one scarce resource, or 'factor of production', labour. This parallels the demonstration of comparative advantage by David Ricardo in 1817, and for that reason is often called the Ricardian model of trade.

Comparative advantage and the gains from trade Suppose that one unit of labour can produce 5 bushels of wheat or 10 yards of cloth in England; whereas one unit of labour can produce 100 bushels of wheat or 50 yards of cloth in Canada. These data are shown in Table 2.1 below.

Clearly, Canadian labour is more productive in both industries; so Canada has an absolute advantage in both. But the opportunity cost of producing cloth is lower in England than in Canada.

In particular, it takes one tenth of a unit of labour to produce 1 yard of cloth in England. But one tenth of a unit of labour could have produced half a bushel of wheat in England. Thus, the opportunity cost of a yard of cloth is half a bushel of wheat in England. Following the same logic, the opportunity cost of 1 yard of cloth in Canada is 2 bushels of wheat.

Table 2.1 Labour's productivity in England and Canada

| | One unit of labour can produce: | | Opportunity cost of 1 yard of cloth |
	Wheat (bushels)	Cloth (yards)	
England	5	10	½ a bushel of wheat
Canada	100	50	2 bushels of wheat

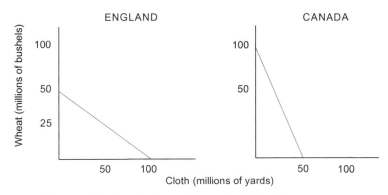

Figure 2.1 Wheat and cloth production in England and Canada

England's lower opportunity cost of cloth means that it has a *comparative advantage* in cloth. Both countries will benefit by specializing according to their comparative advantage. This can be demonstrated using production possibility frontiers.

Suppose that England has 10 million units of labour. Devoting all its labour to wheat production, it could produce 50 million bushels. Alternatively, if it devoted all its labour to cloth production it could produce 100 million yards of cloth. We plot these two extremes in the left-hand panel of Figure 2.1 and connect the two points with a solid straight line to show England's current production possibility frontier (PPF). As we assume constant output per unit of labour input, the PPF is linear. England could choose to produce anywhere along it.

Assume that Canada has 1 million units of labour available for production per month. Referring back to Table 2.1, Canada could produce 100 million bushels of wheat and no cloth, or 50 million yards of cloth and no wheat. Joining these points yields Canada's production possibility frontier, shown in the right-hand panel of Figure 2.1. If each country specializes a little more in the commodity in which it has a comparative advantage, then total world output of both goods will be increased. Let's see how.

Suppose that in England international trade causes 100 units of labour to move out of wheat and into cloth production. From Table 2.1, English wheat output falls by 500 bushels and English cloth output increases by

Table 2.2 Changes in world output

Wheat (bushels)		Cloth (yards)	
England	- 500	+ 1,000	
Canada	+ 1,000	- 500	
world	+ 500	+ 500	

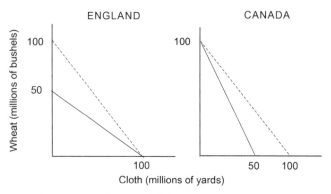

Figure 2.2 Expanded consumption possibilities

1,000 yards per month. In Canada, let's suppose that international trade causes ten units of labour to move out of cloth and into wheat production. As a result, Canadian cloth output decreases by 500 yards, and Canadian wheat output increases by 1,000 bushels. Table 2.2 summarizes the result.

World output increases as a result of each country specializing a little more in that commodity in which it has a comparative advantage. Since world output increases, it is clear that mutually beneficial trade is possible.

Could one country seize most of the benefits for itself? It is possible, depending on the terms at which they trade. Since England is exporting cloth, the higher the price of cloth (in terms of wheat) the more England benefits (and the less Canada benefits). But as long as trade is voluntary, both countries must gain something to induce them to trade at all.

Before trade, the price of each good is determined by its opportunity cost. So, in England the price of a yard of cloth is half a bushel of wheat. It will export cloth providing it can get a better price than that. In Canada the price of a yard of cloth is 2 bushels of wheat. It will import English cloth if it can pay less than 2 bushels of wheat per yard of cloth. For illustrative purposes, suppose they settle on a price halfway between the two extremes, a price where they both benefit equally: a price of 1 yard of cloth for 1 bushel of wheat.

Without trade, consumption possibilities are limited to what each nation can produce for itself. Trade expands the consumption possibilities, however, out to the dotted lines in Figure 2.2. Since both nations have expanded their consumption possibilities, people in each country can potentially consume more of each good. Both countries can be better off than before trade.

I.3 Positive and normative economics

Economic models can be used only to shed light on questions of fact. This is the subject matter of *positive economics*, which focuses on the way the world actually works; it can help us to determine whether positive statements, or statements about fact, are true or false. For example, 'an increase in the minimum wage will increase unemployment for young and unskilled workers' is a positive statement. It may not be true, but it is still a positive statement in so far as it can be refuted or confirmed by appealing to the empirical evidence.

On the other hand, economic models can't be used to shed light on how the world *ought* to be. This involves making value judgements, often involving questions of fairness or equity, and is the subject matter of *normative economics*. For example, the statement 'there should be no homeless people in rich developed countries' is a normative statement based on values – it cannot be tested by appealing to empirical evidence.

This distinction helps to explain why there is a public perception of widespread disagreement among economists. Economists, like other citizens, have different values; therefore they often disagree over normative issues. But on positive issues decided by economic analysis and empirical evidence, there is widespread consensus. For example, a 2011 survey of American economists found that 74 percent agreed with the statement 'A minimum wage increases unemployment among young and unskilled workers.' 95 percent agreed that 'Tariffs and import quotas usually reduce general economic welfare'.[3] (We set out a model of the minimum wage in the next chapter and look at tariffs in Chapter 10.)

Positive economics occupies most of economists' time and effort. On normative issues, economists have no more expertise than anyone else and so they can offer no scientific answers to those questions. For example, what constitutes a fair or equitable distribution of income or wealth is a matter of individual judgement. What economic policy should do to improve equity is ultimately something that society's political institutions will have to decide.

2 THE ANTI-TEXT

Economics is a social science, dealing with aspects of human behaviour and social organization, not a natural science like physics or chemistry. Yet students of economics will notice concepts from the natural sciences, particularly physics, being put to work in economic models. There will be "laws" proposed, "forces" at work moving markets towards "equilibrium".

But compared with the natural sciences, a social science like economics faces added difficulties. Unlike inanimate material, people are sentient and their motivations and behaviours are complex. For example, their choices are influenced by evolving social norms, which could even be influenced (for better or worse) by ideas in economics itself![4] A theory that could work in one social setting, might be inadequate in another. As social animals whose nature has been shaped by evolution, people are concerned with relative position, status and power. Being cooperative animals, as well as competitive ones, they form alliances to further their objectives (e.g. industry associations, political parties, labour unions and citizens' movements).

As we will see, in this complex environment, firm knowledge in positive economics is hard to attain. For example, the effects of policy changes can be unpredictable and even hard to sort out after the fact. Testing models is easier said than done, and definitively rejecting a model may be almost impossible. Finally, it is impossible to cleanly separate positive and normative economics because value judgements and ideological outlooks permeate pretty well everything that we do.

2.1 Textbooks ignore their own methodology

Textbooks emphasize that models cannot be judged by the realism of their assumptions, but only by the accuracy of their predictions. Yet in this chapter of the typical mainstream textbook several models are presented and their predictions are *not* tested against the facts. Instead, predictions about the benefits of specialization and trade (for example) are stated as if they have been *demonstrated* by the model. This lack of testing can perhaps be forgiven in such an early chapter of a textbook. But this same omission continues throughout subsequent chapters. Rarely is any evidence presented to back up a model's predictions, let alone a systematic consideration of evidence.

Further, the textbooks often fail to clarify the comparative nature of model testing. The real issue is always how well a model performs relative to an alternative model; how well one set of assumptions performs relative to an alternative set of assumptions. In practice, a poorly performing model will not be abandoned unless we have an alternative that can do better. Textbooks don't mention difficulties associated with model selection.

Why don't the textbooks consistently apply the test of predictive power to the models they present? One possible answer is that predictive power isn't all it's claimed to be. Predictive power may be fine in the natural sciences, such as physics or chemistry, but in a social science like economics, where there are so many variables that are impossible to control, it simply doesn't give us conclusive answers. Consequently, if we restrict ourselves to talking about things that have been conclusively settled by empirical evidence, then we'd have little to say. Let's consider this problem in more detail.

> Question for your professor: In this course, are we going to decide which models to use by the relative accuracy of their predictions?

2.2 Testing economic theories in practice

If the official methodology of positive economics worked reliably, there should be widespread consensus among economists about positive questions. Indeed, many texts claim that is the case. For example, Gregory Mankiw claims that 79 percent of economists agree that 'minimum wage increases unemployment among young and unskilled workers'.[5] Clearly, the figure comes from a 1990 survey cited in Table 2.3. Let's consider this purported consensus. There have been four surveys published, the results of which are shown in Table 2.3.

From Table 2.3 we see that to get 79 per cent agreeing with the minimum wage proposition on the 1990 survey, one must add the 'generally agree' category to the 'agree with provisos' category. This is taking a bit of a liberty, isn't it? What if the proviso is related to the size of the minimum wage increase? For example, suppose a doubling of the minimum wage would increase youth unemployment, but a 20 per cent increase would not. If that were the proviso then the economists who 'agreed with provisos' would hold 'heretical' beliefs. As we will see in the next chapter, the textbook prediction is that *any* increase in minimum wages would increase unemployment. Since we really don't know what the provisos are, we simply shouldn't group the two categories.

Comparing the results of the four surveys, we see a clear trend: a decline in the percentage of those who generally agreed and a rise in the percentage of those who disagreed. If these surveys show anything at all, they show the gradual breakdown of consensus with regard to the minimum wage proposition.

This breakdown of consensus almost certainly reflects the work of David Card, Lawrence Katz, Allan Krueger and others, much of it published in the early 1990s, which concluded that minimum wage increases often have a zero or even a positive impact on employment. These results were the subject of a lively debate, discussed in Card and Krueger's 1995 book *Myth and Measurement*.[6]

The tone of the debate has often been rather heated. Card and Krueger have been accused of practicing 'politically correct' economics and of

Table 2.3 Percent in agreement with the proposition: 'minimum wages increase unemployment among young and unskilled workers'

Year of Survey	Mid-1970s*	1990†	2000‡	2011‡‡
Generally Agreed	68%	56.5%	45.6%	39.4%
Agreed with provisos	22%	22.4%	27.9%	34.0%
Disagreed	10%	20.5%	26.5%	25.2%

Sources: * Kearl et al. 1979; † Alston et al. 1992; ‡ Fuller and Geide-Stevenson 2003; ‡‡ Fuller and Geide-Stevenson 2014

deliberately using suspect data in one of their studies.[7] For their part, Card and Krueger have presented evidence of 'publication bias' that makes results that are contrary to textbook conventional wisdom harder to publish.[8]

Hristos Doucouliagos and T. D. Stanley found support for this claim of publication bias. They examined 1,474 (!) estimates of the effects of minimum wages on employment in the United States. They found publication bias favouring the conclusion that increases in the minimum wage reduce employment. When the effects of this bias were removed by sophisticated statistical techniques, they concluded that the evidence supported Card and Krueger's conclusion that the observed changes in the minimum wage have had essentially no effect on employment.[9] This means that the conventional model of the labour market is inadequate and that other theories (which we discuss later) would be more appropriate.

Incidentally, the problem of publication bias is not confined to the American debate about the minimum wage. It is pervasive in economics, while similar issues have been discovered in other disciplines.[10]

The key point for our discussion of methodology is that one team of authors would consistently find results different from another team. David Levine, editor of the journal *Industrial Relations*, attributed this phenomenon to 'author biases', which he diplomatically defined as 'conscious or unconscious biases in searching for a robust equation.'[11]

What does searching for a 'robust' equation mean? The point is that testing hypotheses is not an easy matter. For the minimum wage proposition, other things besides minimum wages affect the unemployment of young and unskilled workers, and these other influences need to be 'controlled' for, or taken into account. For example, we need to control for the number of school leavers entering the labour market searching for jobs, and for the overall state of the economy, whether we are in a recession or boom. And so on, and so on. A full set of such controls needs choosing, defining and measuring, and the choices we make may influence the result.

On top of this, there are well-known statistical pitfalls to avoid. If the data don't have certain statistical properties, it is possible to erroneously find significant evidence where there is none in reality. To add to the difficulty, there may be more than one way to avoid such pitfalls, and the choice of method may influence the result.

Finally, a statistical result may be dependent on a very particular time period. It may be that addition or deletion of observations changes the result.

These are examples of non-robustness. Indeed, in the case of the minimum wage proposition, all these small decisions evidently did affect results to such an extent that different teams consistently found different results, leading to apparently serious economists being reduced to name-calling.[12]

It's not just differences in research design which can lead to different results. In a famous 1986 study, William Dewald and his co-authors showed that many published results could not be *replicated*. Using exactly the same data, definitions and statistical procedures, they could not arrive at the same results as those published. Replication is an essential component of scientific methodology, and is the only way to create a defensible, coherent body of knowledge. Yet seldom are results replicated. They note: 'It is widely recognised that errors occur in empirical economic research and appear in published empirical articles. Our results ... suggest that such errors may be quite common.'[13] Later studies suggest that things have not improved even now.[14]

Question for your professor: How can we have confidence in empirical claims in economics when economists can't even replicate many of each other's results?

In practice, hypothesis testing is problematic. It relies on econometrics – statistics applied to economic theory – and 'econometrics ... has not been able to deliver as a tool for falsification of theories', as Cambridge economist Frank Hahn observed.[15] We have illustrated this point using the minimum wage controversy, but there are many, many more.

The minimum wage debate became surprisingly heated given how little is at stake – a prediction of the standard textbook competitive model of the labour market, which, as we'll see in the next chapter, requires many highly unrealistic assumptions. It is astonishing that so many economists are so committed to believing in the empirical relevance of this model that they feel extreme discomfort when its predictions are challenged. Indeed, some textbook writers (or the economics professors who adopt certain textbooks) apparently feel so much discomfort that they continue to assert that a *consensus* exists about the effect of minimum wages!

Clearly, many cling dogmatically to their favourite views and can do so because of the difficulties with empirical testing that we have described. But it's not entirely hopeless. As we've seen with the minimum wage example, opinions do slowly change, perhaps with generational turnover, as evidence accumulates. Some textbooks are following, albeit with a lag.

What about natural experiments? Unlike natural scientists, social scientists like economists can rarely carry out controlled experiments on whole societies. However, they can take advantage of 'natural experiments' in which some event, like a policy change, takes place in one location but not in another similar location.

For example, in the early 1990s the state of New Jersey raised its minimum wage relative to neighbouring Pennsylvania. This is a potentially attractive natural experiment since both states had similar economic and social structures – especially on either side of the state boundaries. This natural experiment is precisely what Card and Krueger's 1994 article was about. However, their critics contended that were important differences in the operating environment of firms on different sides of state boundaries: in taxes, for example, and in the way in which wages were reported and therefore measured. Unfortunately, natural experiments do not eliminate the need to choose and measure relevant control variables, nor do they eliminate the dangers of statistical pitfalls. So, it is not at all clear that natural experiments have a significant advantage over everyday econometric hypothesis testing.

2.3 Core propositions are incapable of refutation

According to the philosopher Imre Lakatos the central propositions of any theoretical framework are surrounded by what he termed a 'protective belt' of 'auxiliary assumptions' that prevent them from being refuted.[16] For example, in the minimum wage case the central proposition that is being tested is that the standard textbook competitive model has empirical validity – that it is an empirically accurate portrayal of how actual markets function. This proposition gives rise to testable predictions; one is the minimum wage prediction. The auxiliary assumptions involved in testing this prediction include: that the correct control variables are selected; that they are measured in the correct way; that statistical pitfalls are properly corrected; and that there are no errors in the computations.

The auxiliary assumptions provide a protective belt because negative evidence can be discounted by the true believer on the grounds that the auxiliary assumptions didn't hold: the authors of some particularly damning piece of empirical research must have made poor decisions or errors that led them to fail to identify the true minimum wage effects that are surely latent, waiting to be discovered. A true believer taking that view would be consoled by the occasional appearance of a paper that seems to uncover such evidence.

> Question for your professor: Since any negative result could always be blamed on the specific way the hypothesis was tested, can a hypothesis ever be categorically rejected?

So the official methodology, that models whose hypotheses are rejected by econometric methods will be discarded and replaced by better models sounds like a fine ideal, but is very difficult to carry out in practice. This is certainly the case for core assumptions such as utility maximization, as we saw in Chapter 1. As Yanis Varoufakis remarks: 'Actually it is no accident that the foundations of neoclassical economics cannot be tested. Shielding one's theory from empirical testing is one way of defending it, of making it immune from criticism. ... In general, the most important aspects of different schools of thought are assumptions which are deliberately put beyond empirical testing.'[17]

In practice, as Dani Rodrik explains: 'Knowledge accumulates in economics not vertically, with better models replacing worse ones, but horizontally, with newer models explaining aspects of social outcomes that were unaddressed earlier. Fresh models don't really replace earlier ones. They bring in a new dimension that may be more relevant in some settings.'[18] As a social science, economics does not lend itself to a search for some grand unified theory to explain big questions such as what determines the pattern of trade between countries. Instead, as we'll see, a variety of models need to be developed that take critical details of the context into account. It's then a matter of judgement as to which model is most appropriate in any given situation.

2.4 When is a particular model useful?

All too often, models are presented as if they were true and can be applied directly to real-world situations without further discussion. In his book *The Craft of Economics*, Edward Leamer disagrees:

> We would make progress if we could agree that our models are neither true nor false; *our models are sometimes useful and sometimes misleading.* The craft of economics depends on the subtle skill of judging when a model is useful and when it is not. We don't teach this in graduate schools, but we should. What we do is very much the opposite. We often teach and speak as if our models were true.[19]

As we will see, Edward Leamer's comment applies equally well to the undergraduate teaching and textbooks.

If only economists could start their theorizing process from axioms – from assumptions that are self-evidently true – then they would not need to test the predictions of theory. If they made no errors of deduction, the conclusions would be as sound as the axioms they were based on. But unfortunately, such axioms don't exist. Instead, as we've seen, economists have no choice but to begin with assumptions which are unrealistic; at best, they are simplified descriptions of a complex situation. Indeed, the official methodology is proud of its unrealistic assumptions, claiming only that successful explanation and prediction are what counts.

Let's look again at the Ricardian model of the production possibility frontiers and trade between England and Canada in the Standard Text part of this chapter. If you examine it carefully you will realize that among the assumptions made in that story were: wheat and cloth are exchanged directly for each other, so currencies and exchange rates are ignored; the value of each country's exports equals the value of its imports – so there are no trade deficits or surpluses; wheat produced in Canada is exactly the same as English wheat, and the same is true of cloth; products in both countries are produced at constant opportunity costs; opportunity costs differ between the two countries, perhaps due to different technologies, natural resources or climates; technologies and quantities of productive resources don't change; and neither workers nor productive capital, such as machinery, can move between countries but they can move freely between wheat and cloth production within each country.

That's quite a list and clearly not all those assumptions are going to be literally true. But if this model is going to offer a general explanation of *all* international trade, it must be the case that the violation of any of these assumptions must have a negligible effect on the model's predictions about trade. This is called the *negligibility assumption.*[20] Having made that assumption, we can make a *domain assumption*: namely that this model explains the patterns of international trade that we see in the world.

But suppose that some of these negligibility assumptions are false. That is, there are non-negligible consequences for the model's explanations or predictions if some of these assumptions were not true. That would mean that this model would not apply in those circumstances. The domain assumption stated earlier would now be false and a more modest claim about the *domain of applicability* of the Ricardian model would have to be made, restricting it to those cases where the negligibility assumptions are true. Let's consider a specific example where Ricardo's model does not apply.

Every undergraduate textbook on international trade sets out the Ricardian model of comparative advantage that we have described. As we've seen, it explains trade based on differences between countries. But these textbooks then go on to explain that the predictions of this model – trade in dissimilar products between countries that have large opportunity cost differences – does not fit the facts for much of the trade that we see in the world. A large part of international trade takes place between high income countries where technology and productivity are relatively similar. So, we would expect no great differences in opportunity costs between these countries. Moreover, much of that trade consists of trade in similar products – German cars for Japanese cars, or Swiss chocolate for Belgian chocolate, and so on.

Instead, trade between industrialized countries is better explained by a different model that incorporates two alternative assumptions. First, goods from different countries are not perfect substitutes for each other, unlike in Ricardo's model. Second, on the production side, opportunity costs are not constant; instead, average costs typically decrease at higher rates of production of specific manufactured goods (a situation called increasing returns, examined in Chapter 5). This means that we are likely to see large firms in each country specialized to make a limited range of products at lower average cost than if they produced a larger variety of goods at home. International trade then allows buyers in all countries to have a greater variety of goods at lower prices than would otherwise be the case. Comparative advantage plays no role in these models. The situations they examine lie outside its domain of applicability.[21]

We will look in more detail at international trade in Chapter 10. But the point here is that, as we'll see throughout this book, there are a variety of models or theoretical frameworks that can be used to try to understand economic phenomena. For example, we will see several models of individual markets for a good or service. It is essential that models come with some guidelines about when it's appropriate to use them, or in the terminology here, their domain of applicability. But typically, they don't.

Edward Leamer remarks that 'we rarely discuss their domains of usefulness. On the contrary, we usually make the domain of usefulness seem large with a sleight of words — using affectless language for expressing our assumptions.' As an example, he gives the assumption that productive resources can move freely between industries, as we saw in the Ricardian model. But this assumption really amounts to saying 'workers operating sewing machines in Los Angeles could equally well solder welds in automobile assembly plants in Detroit, and that sewing machines could equally well serve as office buildings in New York.' Putting it that way makes it immediately clear that for this negligibility assumption to be true, the model can only apply to some long period of time as the economy is slowly restructured. But then, he asks, what are we to make of the other assumptions of fixed technologies and fixed quantities of productive resources? Those negligibility assumptions are false, because we know that both change significantly over long periods of time.[22]

The result? Because of the contradictory nature of its assumptions, perhaps this simple framework has no domain of applicability at all!

In general, he says 'the domain of usefulness of our models is mostly an unsolved mystery.' For that reason, he prefers to describe theories as fictional stories, where it is up to the reader's judgement to determine its applicability. Beginning students, however, make the mistake of taking the models literally.[23] As we will see, the introductory textbooks are of little help, all too often offering their central model of a competitive market as a good enough description of reality that it is applicable to almost all settings.

> Questions for your professor: How could we test the theory of comparative advantage to see if it predicts patterns of trade? If we can do that, does it pass the test?
>
> The textbook says that simplifying assumptions are needed in economic models. If the assumptions that lie behind a model in our textbook are not strictly true, how do we know where and when we can apply the model and when we would need a different model?

2.5 The Rhetoric of Economics

Deirdre McCloskey began writing about the 'rhetoric of economics' in the 1980s, urging economists to recognize the literary and rhetorical nature of their work. Her purpose was 'to study the rhetoric of economic science.... the conversation economists have among themselves for purposes of persuading each other'.[24] Here rhetoric means 'the art of probing what men believe they ought to believe, rather than proving what is true according to abstract methods'.[25] By science, McCloskey means a systematic and disciplined inquiry, something broader than just an inquiry involving measurement and statistics. Thus McCloskey writes: 'My own science of economics was literary, like physics, or mathematics, or biology, a persuasive realm where the work was done by human arguments, not godlike Proof.'[26]

The official methodology (as seen in the Standard Text) is that positive economics is theory, measurement, and statistical hypothesis testing. The unofficial, but actual, methodology is broader, and rightly so. Economics, and indeed all sciences, are inescapably literary. It is a conversation among economists as they try to decide what conclusions are reasonable. It involves debate, storytelling, and attempts at persuasion. McCloskey hopes that awareness of this will help to prevent people from being persuaded by things that they shouldn't be.

As we've seen, for Edward Leamer, 'a model is only a metaphor', a rhetorical device, a fictional story which may or may not be useful.[27] Others prefer to call them fables or parables. In any case, the point is that they should not be taken literally. It's a matter of judgement as to whether they are useful and insightful or not. Nobel Memorial prize winner Wassily Leontief once lamented: 'Page after page of professional economic journals are filled with mathematical formulas leading the reader from sets of more or less plausible but entirely arbitrary assumptions to precisely stated but irrelevant theoretical conclusions.'[28]

Let's go back again to our Ricardian model. We began by looking at trade between two people (Robinson Crusoe and Friday) and then metaphorically said trade between two countries is like trade between two people. How good a metaphor is this? Countries consist of many people and, in this case, that makes an important difference. When Crusoe and Friday trade voluntarily, we can say that both must be better off than before. But the same cannot be said of two countries. It's easy to see that some people in each country may well be worse off than they were before. For example, as Canada specializes in wheat production for export, people whose resources were employed in cloth production will be worse off if we make the more realistic assumption that they cannot move costlessly into wheat production. As we will discuss further in Chapter 10, a value judgement needs to be made as to whether the country as a whole is better off or not.

Let's consider the central model, introduced in Chapter 1, of rational choice where actions are taken up to the point where marginal benefit just equals marginal cost. Economists don't test this model by asking people whether this is what they are trying to do. Instead, the model relies on an analogy, another rhetorical device. It's claimed that when maximizing utility or maximizing profits people act *as if* they were equating marginal benefits with marginal costs.

The usefulness of this analogy was explained by Milton Friedman in a famous 1953 essay on methodology.[29] He wrote that to explain or to predict the actions of a skilled billiards player, you could make the unrealistic assumption that the player understands and uses the laws of physics in making his shots. The player may never have studied physics at all, but a model that assumed that he had would do a good job. The player acts *as if* the assumption were true. Friedman's persuasive analogy has exerted a powerful influence over economists and helps to explain their extreme scepticism that anything can be learned about economic behaviour by asking people directly.

2.6 The inseparability of positive and normative economics – and a word on the Art of Economics

The typical textbook maintains, wrongly, that the scientific part of economics, positive economics, can be separated from normative economics, the part that involves value judgements and ideas about the goals of economic policy. To see why this is incorrect, one can look at any non-mainstream textbook for a simple explanation.

While doing positive economics, David Colander writes that 'some value judgments inevitably sneak in. We are products of our environment, and the questions we ask, the framework we use, and the way we interpret the evidence all involve value judgments and reflect our backgrounds.'[30]

In their text *Understanding Capitalism*, Samuel Bowles and his co-authors point out: 'Nobody can be equally interested in all aspects of the economy, and your values will help you decide which economic questions you would most like your economic investigations to illuminate.'[31] An economist who is ideologically hostile to government regulation of economic life may be inclined to try to investigate whether and how much a larger government reduces economic growth. An economist with an egalitarian outlook might do research on how much existing economic inequality comes from inherited wealth and what the consequences of an inheritance tax would be.

Suppose instead that our egalitarian economist was concerned about poverty. 'How many people are living in poverty?' is a positive question, but it cannot be addressed without defining poverty. That requires some normative or ethical judgements about what constitutes poverty in a particular society.[32] The positive and normative cannot be separated.

The art of economics Even if the standard textbook story were correct, it is still missing an essential idea. Normative economics can help to determine an economic policy, but to implement that policy requires the ability to apply what knowledge we have from positive economics. This is the *art of economics.*

Why is this an art? Because it's not at all obvious how best to go about achieving the desired goal. For example, suppose we want to reduce poverty to a certain level by a certain time. How would we best go about doing that? As David Colander emphasizes, policy conclusions do not follow from positive economics alone.[33] This is because the art of economics 'requires a knowledge of institutions, of social, political, and historical phenomena, and the ability to use available data in a reasonable way in discussing real-world economic issues.'[34]

Dani Rodrik nicely sums up the challenge of putting it all together:

> Economics provides many of the stepping stones and analytic tools to address the big public issues of our times. What it doesn't provide is definitive, universal answers. Results taken from economics proper must be combined with values, judgments, and evaluations of an ethical, political, or practical nature. These last have very little to do with the discipline of economics, but everything to do with reality.[35]

The textbooks' discussion of policy ignores this and, as David Colander remarks, focuses 'on economic efficiency ... giving the impression that discussions of efficiency belong in positive economics. However, achieving economic efficiency is not an end in itself, but is a debatable, normative goal which often will conflict with other normative goals society might have.'[36] Instead, economists and the textbooks should explicitly acknowledge the value judgements they make in their policy recommendations.

Questions for your professor Are positive and normative economics really two separate things? For example, haven't the authors of our textbook made normative judgements in deciding where to place particular topics in the textbook and how much coverage to give them? [You might look at the treatment of income and wealth inequality, poverty, or climate change in the book.]

2.7 Paradigms and ideology

While the word *paradigm* doesn't appear in most economics textbooks, it is a simple and important concept: it is the *world-view* shared by members of a scientific community. It defines what is to be investigated and the methods and abstractions that are regarded as legitimate. In short, a paradigm refers to a coherent 'school of thought'.

One reason mainstream textbooks don't mention the word 'paradigm' is that they typically don't mention alternative schools of thought. They teach exclusively within the dominant paradigm called neoclassical economics. But it's not the only one. Perhaps you could ask your professor about alternative economic paradigms and how their view of the world differs from the textbook view.

In the figure on the left, do you see the young woman looking over her right shoulder? Or do you see the older woman looking down towards the left? In the figure on the right, viewed one way, one sees the old hag; viewed upside down, one sees the beautiful princess. In a way, paradigms operate just like this. Confronted with the same reality, some perceive the benefits of a free-market capitalist economy; while others see the opposite and predominantly perceive the costs.

Figure 2.3 Different perceptions of reality

Thomas Kuhn, who gave the word 'paradigm' its contemporary meaning, argues that paradigms are a kind of necessary indoctrination – necessary because research needs rules.[37] It is difficult enough to push forward the frontiers of science without always questioning the fundamental assumptions upon which it is based. While this provides an advantage, there is an obvious drawback: scientists trained to think in a specific paradigm have difficulty thinking 'outside the box'. This is what Keynes had to say about the difficulties he encountered writing *The General Theory* – his macroeconomic explanation for the Great Depression of the 1930s:

> The composition of this book has been ... a long struggle of escape ... from habitual modes of thought and expression. The ideas which are here expressed so laboriously are extremely simple and should be obvious. The difficulty lies, not in the new ideas, but in escaping the old ones, which ramify ... into every corner of our minds.[38]

What we are trained to see influences what we actually do see. And reality can be perceived in many different ways, as Figure 2.3 illustrates. Furthermore, no paradigm – especially in the social sciences – can be value free.

This certainly applies to one's choice of a paradigm. Steve Cohn puts it very nicely: 'Because the reasons for choosing one paradigm over another are subjective (somewhat analogous to the reasons for choosing one academic major over another), the allegedly objective status of "positive" analysis within a paradigm is already heavily infused with the subjectivity of paradigm choices.' He advises thinking 'about the values, goals, and subtexts that animate different paradigms as these can easily color "positive" appearing claims.'[39]

As well, he advises looking at any economic question from the point of view of several paradigms, including in particular those that challenge the status quo.[40] Why? Economic knowledge is produced within a particular social context and he remarks that there 'is strong precedent for expecting social systems to produce cultural and ideological justifications for their social hierarchy.' And indeed, as we will see in this book, he is right to contend that '[m]uch of textbook economics tends to justify the status quo'.[41]

A paradigm is not much different from an ideology. An ideology is a view of the way the world works, especially as applied to politics. It embodies a view of human nature and the possibilities for change. It embodies value judgements about what's good and bad. Different political ideologies give rise to different schools of thought in the social sciences. So, one might argue that an ideology is more fundamental than the paradigm it gives rise to. But the point is that any paradigm is necessarily infused with an ideological perspective.

What is the ideological perspective with which neoclassical economics is infused? Well, that's what this book is about. We argue that it is possible to infer the values of neoclassical economics from the textbook presentation of the subject: from the emphasis given to certain topics and the lack of emphasis given to others, from the unsupported claims, from the questions that are never asked, and from the propositions that are believed as articles of faith and can never be refuted.

It's not the only possible approach. We could have taken an approach that traces the intellectual history of ideas and pointed out that the roots of neoclassical economics go back through Adam Smith to the classical liberals – to John Locke and then later to John Stuart Mill – and their fundamental values of individual responsibility, freedom of choice, the sanctity of private property, and minimal government presence in the market economy. In other words, neoclassical economics is aligned with a political philosophy that in the eighteenth and nineteenth centuries was called classical liberalism and today would be called conservative.

Yet another approach is taken by David George. He analyses carefully the language used in textbooks. He says: 'it is the rhetorical practices of introductory texts more than it is the "received theory" that convey a conservative (or "classical liberal") world-view'.[42] For example, he shows that some textbooks emphasize the opportunity cost associated with public spending, but private expenditures would never be characterized as a diversion of real resources from the public sector. Some talk about the resources 'used up' by the government, as if the citizens get no benefit from them, and about the government 'imposing' taxes, which suggests an authoritarian government going against the popular will.

Question for your professor: It is generally accepted that all paradigms reflect a particular world-view or ideological perspective. What is the ideological perspective of neoclassical economics?

2.8 Concluding Remarks

As we've explained, models are much trickier things than the texts let on. We have to think carefully about where and when any particular model is useful and insightful. This is as much an art as a science. It's all too easy to forget this and to treat the model as an actual description of reality. This is what the texts invite us to do when they fail to discuss where a model is applicable and where it isn't.

We also shouldn't forget that the models are developed within a broader framework that reflects the paradigms and ideologies accepted by their creators and users. The scientific method, with its impartial observers creating models, testing their predictions against the data, and rejecting those that fail the test, and keeping only those that have not yet been rejected is a useful ideal. But we must be aware, especially in the social sciences, that reality is messier and ends up far from that ideal. This doesn't mean that we should give up; as a first step, we need to be aware of what we're doing. That can help us understand that, as with individual models, different paradigms or theoretical frameworks may be more useful in some contexts than in others.

SUGGESTIONS FOR FURTHER READING

On methodology and the minimum wage controversy, a very good source is still Card and Krueger's 1995 book, *Myth and Measurement: The new economics of the minimum wage.* Focus on Chapter 1 ('Introduction and overview', pp. 1–20) and on Chapter 12 ('Conclusions and implications', pp. 387–401).

Dani Rodrik's book *Economics Rules: The Rights and Wrongs of the Dismal Science* shows that economics consists of a large variety of frameworks, each offering a different interpretation of how the world works, with different implications for public policy. The book then offers ideas about how to navigate among these.

Ha-Joon Chang's *Economics: A User's Guide* devotes Chapter 4 ('Let a Hundred Flowers Bloom') is a concise guide to nine schools of economic thought, of which neoclassical economics is just one.

A good Internet source that describes different schools of thought in economics is the History of Economic Thought website developed by Gonçalo Fonseca with the support of the Institute for New Economic Thinking. See www.hetwebsite.net/het/. See the link 'Schools of Thought'.

Chapter 3

HOW MARKETS WORK (IN AN IMAGINARY WORLD)

I THE STANDARD TEXT

1.1 What is a competitive market?

There is no 'competing' behaviour in a competitive market – no advertising, no price-setting strategies, no rivalry. This is because all buyers and sellers are *price-takers*. This requires large numbers of buyers and sellers, with no one buyer or seller having a significant market share, and all firms producing an identical (or homogeneous) good or service.

1.2 The demand curve

An individual's demand curve describes the relationship between the quantity demanded and the good's own price *ceteris paribus* (holding all other influences constant). These other influences include the individual's preferences, income and the prices of related consumption goods. These may be either complements (such as DVDs and DVD players) or substitutes (such as chicken or beef). Expected future prices may also be important in determining how much is bought currently.

An individual's demand curve is a frontier – it tells us the maximum price he or she is willing to pay to obtain any given quantity. If any of the other influences change, the demand curve *shifts*. To obtain the market demand, we sum the amounts every individual wishes to buy at any given price. Thus the size of the population influences demand.

The shape of the market demand curve shows the responsiveness of quantity demanded to price changes. Normally, as the price increases, quantity demanded decreases, as seen in Figure 3.1.

The responsiveness of quantity demanded to a change in price is measured by the *price elasticity of demand*. It is defined as:

$$e_d = \frac{\% \text{ change in quantity demanded}}{\% \text{ change in price}}$$

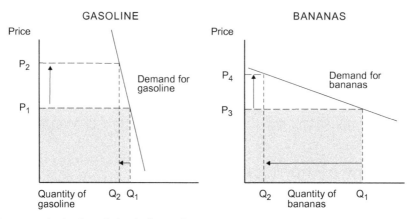

Figure 3.1 Inelastic and elastic demand

Suppose a 50 per cent increase in the price of gasoline leads to a 10 per cent decrease in the quantity demanded. The price elasticity of demand for gasoline is 0.2 (10 per cent divided by 50 per cent). In contrast, the demand for bananas is more sensitive to price changes: suppose a 40 per cent increase in the price of bananas leads to an 80 per cent decrease in the quantity demanded. The price elasticity for bananas is 2. Elasticities depend on the availability of substitutes among other things. There are many substitutes for bananas (other fruit), but few substitutes for gasoline (or petrol), at least over a short time period.

Total revenue is price multiplied by quantity. Elasticity of demand determines how total revenue changes when price changes. For example, when the price of gasoline is P_1, total revenue equals the shaded box in the left-hand diagram of Figure 3.1. When the price goes up to P_2 the height of the total revenue box increases by 50 per cent, and its width decreases by 10 per cent. It is clear that the new total revenue box is bigger than before.

Similarly, when the price of bananas is P_3, total revenue equals the shaded box in the right-hand diagram in Figure 3.1. When the price goes up to P_4 the height of the total revenue box increases by 40 per cent while its width decreases by 80 per cent. Clearly, the new total revenue box is smaller than before.

As an application, suppose the London tube system is losing money. If the objective is solely to increase total revenue, should the tube authority increase or decrease fares? If the demand for tube rides is inelastic, they should increase fares; if it is elastic they should decrease fares. If the elasticity is equal to one (a so-called 'unit-elastic' demand curve) then a fare change would have no effect on total revenue.

1.3 The supply curve

The supply curve describes the relationship between the quantity of a good supplied and its own price, *ceteris paribus*. It too is a frontier, showing the *minimum* price that sellers are willing to accept for any given quantity. Generally speaking, as the price of a product increases, the quantity supplied goes up. The responsiveness of quantity supplied to a change in price is measured by the *price elasticity of supply*.

$$e_s = \frac{\% \text{ change in quantity supplied}}{\% \text{ change in price}}$$

The six key things that affect the position of the supply curve are: the weather (especially important for agricultural products); changes in the prices of goods that makers of this product could produce instead; changes in input prices (or prices of 'factors of production'); changes in technology; changes in the number (and size) of firms in the industry; and changes in expectations about future prices. Comparing the factors that shift demand with those that shift supply, we see only one identical item: expectations of future prices.

1.4 Market equilibrium

When prices are free to fluctuate, market forces move the actual price (and quantity) towards the equilibrium price (and quantity). The left-hand diagram of Figure 3.2 shows that at a price P_1, which is above the equilibrium price, P^*, there is an excess supply (or surplus) equal to 400 units per period. This creates downward pressure on the price, causing it to fall until equilibrium is restored at P^*. The right-hand diagram shows that when the price is below equilibrium there is an excess demand (or shortage). This creates upward pressure on the price, causing the price to increase until equilibrium is restored at P^*.

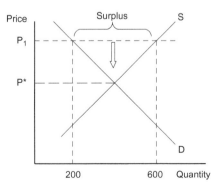

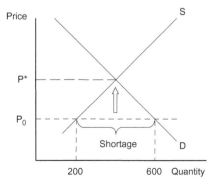

Figure 3.2 Movement towards equilibrium

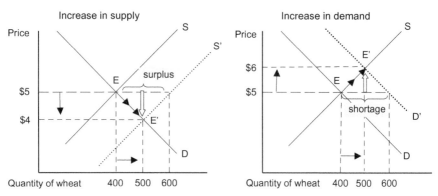

Figure 3.3 Comparative static analysis

1.5 Comparative static analysis

How does a change in one of the factors underlying demand or supply affect the market equilibrium? 'Comparative statics' compares one static equilibrium position with another. The analysis is timeless (we don't know how long anything takes) and ahistorical (it doesn't matter in what order things happen).

In the left-hand diagram of Figure 3.3 we show the effect of an increase in the supply of wheat from S to S' – perhaps caused by a fall in the price of fertilizer. At the original price of $5 there is now a surplus of wheat. This causes the price to fall to $4, eliminating the surplus. In the right-hand diagram of Figure 3.3 we show the effect of an increase in the demand for wheat – perhaps caused by an increase in incomes. The original demand line shifts rightwards to D', causing a shortage at the original equilibrium price of $5. This causes the price to increase to $6, at which point the shortage is eliminated.

Note that an expectation of a future price increase causes supply in the market today to shift leftwards as suppliers store some current production to sell at a higher price in the future.

1.6 A government-regulated price ceiling: rent controls

Governments often try to control market prices using price ceilings and price floors, i.e. maximum and minimum prices set by regulation. Rent control (an example of a price ceiling) is an attempt to help low-income families afford the cost of accommodation. Unfortunately, attempts to overrule market forces often lead to unintended effects that usually hurt the very group the government is intending to help.

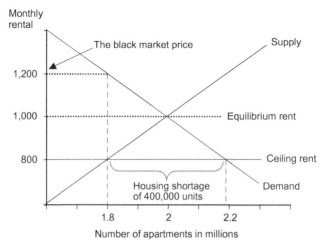

Figure 3.4 The effect of rent control

Figure 3.4 shows the market for apartments in Montreal assuming all apartments are identical. The going rent is $1,000 a month and 2 million units are rented. When the government imposes a rent ceiling of $800, fewer apartments are offered for rent and more demanded, causing a shortage of 400,000 rental units. The shortage is likely to get worse the longer the rent control is in effect, as apartment buildings are knocked down or converted to condominiums.

Shortages induced by price controls in competitive markets lead to *inefficiency*: missed opportunities to make some people better off at no cost to anyone else.

The first inefficiency is an inappropriate distribution of apartments among renters. For example, 'empty-nesters' want to downsize, while households with new children want something bigger. These moves benefit both parties, but are hampered by the shortage created by the rent control.

A second inefficiency is the wasted time, energy and money spent searching for an apartment.

A third inefficiency is that the quality of apartments will become undesirably low. Some tenants would be happy to pay for better conditions, and landlords would be happy to provide them for increased rent. This is a missed opportunity.

Finally, price ceilings encourage *illegal activities*, specifically the emergence of black markets – side payments (or bribes) to obtain an apartment. Given the shortage of apartments under rent controls, Figure 3.4 indicates that buyers are willing to pay up to $1,200 a month – $400 more than the legal ceiling. So, we can expect side payments as high as $400 a month.

Our analysis contains predictions that we will state generically (not tailored to the market for apartments). First, price ceilings in competitive markets lead to shortages that get worse the longer they are in effect. Next, the fundamental reason shortages are bad is that they are inefficient, and this inefficiency manifests itself in three distinct ways: an inefficient distribution of the good among buyers; wasted resources trying to buy the good; and an inefficiently low quality of the good. Finally, whenever there are unsatisfied wants because of legal restrictions, crime will arise to profit from them.

1.7 A government-regulated price floor: minimum wages

Figure 3.5 depicts a competitive market for unskilled workers. The equilibrium wage is $9 an hour, and total employment is 15 million workers. Suppose the government decides that $9 an hour is not a living wage, and imposes a minimum wage of $15 an hour. The impact is 3 million fewer jobs, 3 million more people willing to work and unemployment (or a surplus of labour) of 6 million workers.

Any minimum wage above the equilibrium has the same qualitative effect; but the higher the minimum wage, the worse it is.

The surplus caused by a price floor creates inefficiencies – missed opportunities – that resemble those created by price ceilings. First, there is an *inefficient allocation* of sales among sellers. With a minimum wage there may be some job seekers who really want to work but cannot find a job, and others who have a job but are almost indifferent as to whether they work or not. Second, sellers (job seekers) waste time and effort searching for a buyer (an employer). Third, suppliers offer an inefficiently high quality to try to attract buyers, who might have preferred the original quality at a lower price. Finally, price ceilings provide an incentive for *illegal activity* – only in this case it is

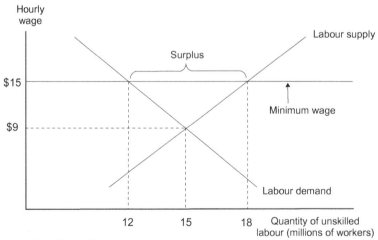

Figure 3.5 The effect of a minimum wage

sellers (job seekers) bribing buyers (employers), or employment arrangements out of sight of the law.

1.8 Who bears the cost of sales taxes?

Contrary to popular belief, the person who ends up 'paying' a sales (or excise) tax is not necessarily the same person on whom the tax is levied. Rather, the incidence of the tax depends on the relative size of the price elasticities of demand and supply. This can be shown using demand and supply diagrams.

The left-hand diagram of Figure 3.6 shows supply and demand for parking spaces. We assume the government collects the sales tax from producers of parking spaces. This adds to producers' costs, so a $4 per unit sales tax shifts the supply curve upwards by $4 per unit for each level of output. According to the diagram, the effect is to raise the equilibrium price from $6 to $7. Effectively $1 of the tax has been passed on to consumers in higher prices. The remainder, $3 per unit, is paid by producers. Finally, the tax raises $1,600 in revenue for the government ($4 x 400 units).

In the right-hand diagram, we have supply and demand for milk. A sales tax of $1 per litre of milk shifts the supply curve up by $1 per litre. According to the diagram, the tax raises $40 million in government revenue ($1 x 40 million litres), and raises the equilibrium price by 90 cents. In contrast to the previous example, where producers paid most of the tax, here most of the tax is passed on to consumers, and only 10 cents per litre is paid by producers. What causes this difference in who bears the burden of the tax?

It turns out that the incidence of the tax depends on the relative size of the price elasticities of demand and supply at the equilibrium prices and quantities. The actual formula (found in more advanced textbooks) is:

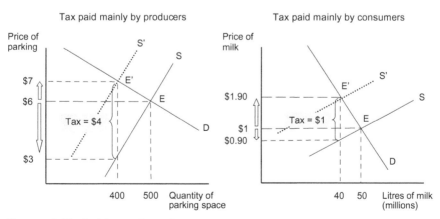

Figure 3.6 The incidence of taxation

$$\text{Formula 1}: \text{proportion of sales tax borne by consumers} = \frac{e_s}{e_s + e_d}$$

$$\text{Formula 2}: \text{proportion of sales tax borne by producers} = \frac{e_d}{e_s + e_d}$$

where e_s and e_d are the elasticities of supply and demand in equilibrium. Note that the proportions sum to one – the total tax is split between buyers and sellers.

The formulas show that the greater the price elasticity of supply, and the smaller the price elasticity of demand, the more the tax is paid by consumers. If we understand elasticity to mean 'responsiveness', this amounts to a claim that if producers are responsive (or flexible, or elastic) to price changes, while consumers are unresponsive (or inflexible or inelastic), the more the tax burden falls on consumers. In general, the less elastic side of the market pays the larger share of the tax.

1.9 The costs of taxation

In Figure 3.6 the tax on milk reduced consumption by 10 million litres. This is milk that would have been consumed in the absence of the tax, to the mutual benefit of both producers and consumers. Nobody would have been worse off. So, an excise tax creates inefficiency. This represents a cost of the tax over and above the money paid to the government in taxes. This extra cost is referred to as the excess burden or deadweight loss of the tax. Economists say that the real cost of a tax is not the tax payments themselves, which are used for public purposes, but it is the mutually beneficial trades that no longer occur because of a tax.

2 THE ANTI-TEXT

2.1 The demand and supply model is sold as a generic tool

The material summarized in the previous section is sometimes called 'How markets work'.[1] It follows a discussion of models and methodology that emphasizes the importance of predictive power, and it contains applications to a broad range of labour and product markets. The range of these applications, the position of these chapters near the front of the text, and the immediately preceding methodological discussion that plays down realism of assumptions, *all suggest that the supply and demand framework is a generic tool that can be applied to all markets.* As David Colander puts it, 'supply and demand are the lens through which economists look at reality'.[2]

But the supply and demand framework is actually a simplified representation of a perfectly competitive market, one of four types of market classifications described in the texts. Many textbooks are quite explicit about this, but usually much later, when they discuss perfect competition. For example, Krugman and Wells state in their Chapter 12: 'The supply and demand model, which we introduced in Chapter 3 and have used repeatedly since then, is a model of a perfectly competitive market'.[3]

We set out the model of perfect competition in the Standard Text part of Chapter 6, but for now we just need to understand that a supply curve only exists in perfectly competitive markets. These are markets in which a very large number of firms, all small relative to the size of the market, sell a standardized product (such as a type and quality of rice) at the going market price. No producer is large enough to affect the market price, so each simply chooses the quantity to produce. As a result, there is a unique relationship between market prices and supply by each individual firm and the total supplied by all firms. This is the market supply curve.

In all other market types, described in the next section, there is no "market price". Instead, firms can choose the price-quantity combination that maximizes their profits. The best price depends on the position of the demand curve. As we show in more detail in Chapter 6, there is no unique relationship between price and the quantity produced, and therefore no supply curve.

Since supply curves exist only in perfectly competitive markets, we need to know: first, how many markets are perfectly competitive in the real world? And second, even though the competitive model is not (strictly speaking) applicable to non-competitive markets, can it be usefully applied as an approximation? We address those questions next.

> Question for your professor: If an industry is not perfectly competitive, can we still draw the industry supply curve?

2.2 How many markets are perfectly competitive?

To this point we've talked vaguely about 'non-competitive' markets. Let's be more precise. Textbooks categorize markets according to the number of producers and the type of product, as shown in Table 3.1.

Non-competitive markets fall into three types: monopolistic competition, oligopoly and monopoly. Firms in all three non-competitive markets have 'market power', which means they face a downward-sloping demand curve, and so can choose the price of their product rather than simply accept a 'market price' like the perfectly competitive firm. Market power derives from the firm being large relative to the industry, or from

Table 3.1 Types of market structure

How many producers are there?	Are products differentiated?	
	no	yes
Many	Perfect competition	Monopolistic competition
Few	Oligopoly	Oligopoly
One	Monopoly	Monopoly

having a product that is unique (or differentiated) in some way, or for both reasons. The question is: how prevalent is perfect competition relative to the other market structures?

The key requirement for perfect competition is price-taking behaviour on the part of both buyers and sellers. In other words, no buyer or seller has any power over the market price.

This can happen only if there are many buyers and sellers, all of whom are small relative to the size of the market. The sellers must be selling identical products, as otherwise they would have some power to set their own prices. Both buyers and sellers must have perfect or complete information about all relevant aspects of the market. Only in that way can a single price emerge in the market: all sellers must charge the same price, because buyers have perfect information about selling prices and always buy at the lowest price. Information plays other vital roles in the model, as we will see shortly.

However, in our sample of 10 texts, only three mention the necessity of perfect information.[4] Three others failed to mention the subject at all.[5] The remaining four offered somewhat weaker versions; market participants are "well-informed" or "fully informed" about prices and perhaps product characteristics or production technologies. By deemphasizing or failing to mention the requirement of perfect information, the texts widen the apparent applicability of the supply and demand/perfectly competitive model to real world markets.

This apparent difference in opinion among the textbooks is particularly strange given the research on the implications of imperfect information in recent decades. This has revealed the crucial importance of the perfect information assumption. Joseph Stiglitz, who received the Nobel Memorial Prize for his work on information economics in 2001, explains:

> For more than 100 years, formal modeling in economics has focused on models in which information was assumed to be perfect. Of course, everyone recognized that information was in fact imperfect, but the hope ... was that economies in which information was not too imperfect would look very much like economies in which information was perfect. One of the main results of our research was to show that this was not

true; that even a small amount of information imperfection could have a profound effect on the nature of the equilibrium.[6]

Why could even a small amount of imperfect information have a profound effect? Stiglitz gives the following example:

> Assume for example, as in the standard theory, that all firms were charging the competitive price, but there were an epsilon cost of searching, of going to another store. Then any firm which charged half an epsilon more would lose no customers and thus would choose to increase its price. Similarly, it would pay all other firms to increase their prices. But at the higher price, it would again pay each to increase price, and so on until the price charged at every firm is the monopoly price, even though search costs are small.[7]

In the above quote, 'epsilon' stands for an arbitrarily small quantity. Just an epsilon of costs of acquiring information could lead otherwise competitive firms to charge the monopoly price. The point is that even slight departures from free, and hence perfect, information have large consequences.[8]

If imperfect information undermines the competitive model, is there a better alternative? Stiglitz explains: 'a central consequence of imperfect information is that … product markets are more aptly described by models of imperfect competition, where … [firms] perceive themselves facing downward sloping demand schedules'.[9]

Apparently, the prevalence of perfectly competitive markets depends on the likelihood of having perfect information. To appreciate how implausible the assumption of perfect information is, it helps to realize that many information asymmetries (some people knowing more than others) are inevitable. Job applicants know more about their ability than prospective employers; workers know more about their work effort than management; management knows more about their firms than potential investors; borrowers know more about their likelihood of default than lenders; people buying insurance know more about their efforts to avoid risk than insurers. According to Stiglitz, information imperfections are so pervasive 'it is hard to imagine what a world with perfect information would be like'.[10]

Opinions differ as to whether perfect competition actually describes many real-world markets. Those textbooks that include *perfect* information as a requirement state that perfect competition has very limited applicability. For example, Baumol and co-authors say that the requirements for perfect competition are 'rarely, if ever, found in practice'.[11] Those that don't insist on perfect information make stronger claims for the existence of perfectly competitive markets. For instance, Krugman and Wells state: 'important parts of the economy are fairly well described by perfect competition'.[12]

Many texts claim that the markets for agricultural products are perfectly competitive. For example, Mankiw writes 'There are some markets in which the assumption of perfect competition applies perfectly. In the wheat market, for example, there are thousands of farmers who sell wheat and millions of consumers who use wheat and wheat products. Because no single buyer or seller can influence the price of wheat, each takes the market price as given.'[13] But this description of the wheat market is completely inaccurate. When was the last time you bought a sack of grain from a farmer?

In reality, most wheat is sold to firms that mill the grain. In turn, the flour is sold to firms that will make bread, pasta, and other wheat products. Those may be sold to grocery retailers and then on to the final consumer. Each of the transactions in this chain involves a different market. A serious discussion of the US market for wheat would examine how farmers sell their wheat to the wheat flour milling industry. One American study does just that and concludes that three large companies have a dominating presence in the US industry. Instead of being price takers, the milling firms set prices on a take it or leave it basis for farmers. They conclude that the buyers have market power and 'that the analysis suggests that the general assumption that competitive models may be a good approximation for imperfectly competitive agricultural markets does not necessarily hold'.[14]

Buyer power is even greater in agricultural markets where distance is important. For example, cattle, hogs, and chickens cannot be transported long distances for slaughter and processing, giving slaughterhouses and processing plants considerable power. Yet the assumption of perfectly competitive markets implicitly assumes that all transactions occur in a single location, reducing transportation costs to zero.

At least in North America, many farmers and fishers are increasingly squeezed by the market power of the few firms that supply their inputs and the few buyers of their outputs – including supermarket chains and the fast food industry.[15] But even assuming that the whole of agriculture, forestry, fishing and hunting were perfectly competitive, their combined output is only a very small fraction of total production in the industrialized economies.

Evidence that price-taking behaviour is rare is provided by a team led by Alan Blinder. They surveyed 200 representative firms in the United States, excluding agriculture. They say: 'First of all, we took it for granted that almost all firms in our economy are price-makers rather than price-takers – an assumption amply justified by the survey responses'.[16] They find that prices are 'sticky' – set by firms and periodically reviewed; they are not determined instantaneously by supply and demand. They say:

> First, the evidence gathered in this study emphatically supports the mainstream [macroeconomic] view that sticky prices are the rule, not the exception, in American industry. According to our respondents, the median number of price changes for a typical product in a typical year is

just 1.4, and almost half of all prices change no more often than annually. Among firms reporting regular price reviews, annual reviews are by far the most common. At the other end of the spectrum, only about 10 percent of all prices change as often as once a week, and about 7 percent of all firms schedule price reviews at least weekly.[17]

In contrast, perfectly competitive firms are price-takers. They never need to review their price schedules. Their prices change continually with shifts in demand and supply. *None* of the firms surveyed by Blinder and his co-authors fell into that category.

```
Question for your professor: Most firms in the real
world set their own prices. Does the supply and
demand model apply to them?
```

2.3 Is the competitive model a useful approximation?

No two hairstylists are equally skilled. They sell a differentiated product. Each stylist faces a downward-sloping demand curve, implying that the supply curve for haircuts does not exist, as stated earlier. Furthermore, there is no unique price for haircuts, but instead a range of prices – each price *set* by the hairstylist – depending on the stylist's quality, reputation, location and clientele. This is a non-competitive market.

Nevertheless, can the competitive model be applied to this market as an *approximation*? Assume away all the complications. Assume all hairstylists are identical. Assume perfect information. Won't the competitive model give us insights into the determinants of the average price of haircuts? Won't the things that cause supply curves to shift left – an increase in the costs of production (shampoo prices go up), or a decrease in the number of firms (hairstylists) – increase the average price of a haircut? If so, the competitive model provides a *useful approximation* even to this non-competitive market.

If this were generally true, the textbook emphasis on competitive markets as a generic tool would be justified. Maybe it's like the law of gravity: strictly speaking it holds only in a vacuum; but it can be usefully applied in everyday life.

This is the position taken by Krugman and Wells, who, after noting that oligopoly is by far the most common market structure, ask, 'Given the prevalence of oligopoly, then, is the analysis ... based on perfect competition still useful?' They argue that it is because '[i]t is also true that predictions from supply and demand analysis are often valid for oligopolies'. Given the complexity of oligopoly models, 'in situations where they do not expect the complications associated with oligopoly to be crucial, economists prefer to adopt the working assumption of perfectly competitive markets'.[18] In other words, the competitive model is simpler and can be applied even to non-competitive markets, because it gives us accurate predictions.

Let us, then, consider the predictive power of the competitive model, focusing on the core applications emphasized in introductory textbooks.

Predictions concerning minimum wages Does the evidence support the predictions of the supply and demand framework concerning the effects of minimum wages? We addressed this question in detail in Chapter 2. In brief, the empirical studies conflict to such an extent that we used it as a case study to illustrate the limitations of hypothesis testing and predictive power as criteria for model selection. The consensus concerning the effects of minimum wages has broken down – though this is not generally reported in the textbooks.

What we have yet to explain is why moderate increases in the minimum wage might *not* reduce employment of low-wage, low-skilled workers. The explanation depends on 'frictions' in the labour market: imperfect information and the costs workers face in getting a new job.

Such labour market frictions mean that employers are not simply wage-takers: they have some short-run (or temporary) power to set wages lower than other firms without losing all their workers. This power may derive from the time and resources necessary for a worker to find a new job, or because taking another job might entail moving home or increased costs of commuting. Either way, moderate minimum wage increases may offset the market power of employers without causing job losses – indeed, they may even cause job gains (as we explain more fully in Chapter 8).

The minimum wage application is precisely about whether frictions in the labour market are significant. The easiest way to account for the array of mixed evidence is to concede that frictions are important in certain cases. So, when discussing the effects of minimum wages the predictions of the perfectly competitive model should be compared with those from a simple noncompetitive model. In this case, that would be a monopsony, the term that describes a market with a single buyer.

Even after more than 20 years of controversy about the effects of the minimum wage, a survey of 25 American textbooks found that only nine also connected their analysis of the minimum wage with the monopsony model.[19] In our sample of 10 texts, only three made a direct comparison.[20] But the average textbook continues to apply the competitive model as if it were the only model relevant to the minimum wage question. Some of these briefly mention the empirical controversy. For example, Mankiw still writes: 'Although there is some debate about how much the minimum wage affects employment, the typical study finds that a 10 percent increase in the minimum wage depresses teenage employment by 1 to 3 percent.'[21] Krueger tracked down this "typical" study to an influential survey paper published in 1982![22]

> Question for your professor: Does the empirical
> evidence support the predictions of the supply and
> demand framework concerning the effects of minimum
> wages? (Best answer: It's mixed, but the consensus
> seems to be shifting; see Chapter 2.)

Predictions concerning rent controls The main prediction of the competitive model – shortages that get worse the longer the rent control is in effect – depends on the rent ceiling remaining below the equilibrium level: it must be *binding*. If the extent to which it is binding lessens – if the ceiling rent moves towards the equilibrium rent – then we would not expect shortages to worsen. On the contrary, we'd expect them to moderate. But knowing the extent to which the ceiling rent is binding over time is complicated by the fact that we cannot observe the equilibrium rent.

A second complication is that the type of rent control prevalent nowadays is very different from the type assumed in textbooks – a rigid rent freeze. Controls of this sort were introduced in major US cities during the Second World War, but every city (apart from New York) had abandoned this 'first-generation' rent control by the early 1950s. 'Second-generation' rent control, first introduced in the 1970s, is significantly more flexible. For example, it commonly allows automatic rent increases geared to increasing costs, excludes luxury high-rent buildings and new buildings, restricts conversions, decontrols between tenants, and provides incentives for landlords to maintain or improve quality.

A third complication is that housing units are assets, the desirability of which is impacted by many other factors besides rent control: interest rates, inflation, profit opportunities elsewhere, the local real estate cycle, government housing and tax policies, and expectations about the future.

In reviewing the empirical evidence on rent control, urban economist Richard Arnott says: 'The impact of these other factors is likely to be significantly greater than any effect due to controls. Trying to discern the effects of rent control in such a situation is akin to trying to hear a whispered conversation across a street of roaring traffic'.[23] He suggests that with the exception of New York City (which retained its first-generation controls) and perhaps Toronto (which had poorly designed second-generation controls) the effects of rent control in North America have been almost imperceptible. This is a dramatic contrast to the treatment in the textbooks. By assuming that the rental housing market is perfectly competitive, and by considering a crude form of price ceiling, most texts suggest that rent controls necessarily have destructive effects.

Why are most textbooks (and most North American economists for that matter) so negative on rent controls? Arnott suggests two reasons: 'The first is ideological. The debate over rent control has been a battleground between those who believe in the free market and those who do not. The echoes of the debate carry over to other policy arenas where its resolution has far more quantitative import. The second is methodological'.[24]

The methodological battle is about whether the competitive model is good enough as a generic approximation to most markets and in particular, whether it can be used to analyze the effects of price controls in the rental housing market. The housing market has many non-competitive elements: apartments vary in size, quality, and location; search costs are substantial (as evidenced by agents' fees), as are moving costs; and there is a lack of information about who's a good landlord and who's a good tenant. Are these merely details that can be ignored as irrelevant? Most housing economists believe that these are too important to be ignored in practice. Since the mid-1980s most of them have turned their attention to non-competitive models – models that emphasize search costs and the importance of contracts.

Because of this different methodological perspective, they are much less critical of rent control. Arnott conjectures: 'Perhaps a majority, at least among the younger generation, would agree with the statement that a well-designed rent control program can be beneficial'.[25] Yet this research seems to have had no impact on the principles textbooks.

Question for your professor: Would rent controls necessarily cause shortages if the rental housing market were imperfectly competitive? (Right answer: No.)

Predictions concerning the incidence of taxation If the evidence presented for the effects of minimum wages and for rent controls is weak, things are even worse when it comes to the incidence of sales taxes: the textbooks present almost no evidence at all.

This is strange because the competitive model makes clear predictions: the proportionate burden of a sales tax is determined by the relative elasticities of supply and demand. The texts illustrate this idea using relative slopes of supply and demand in a wide variety of markets. The problem is that the markets are not perfectly competitive, so they have no supply curves whose elasticity could be measured. For example, Michael Parkin draws supply and demand curves for the cigarette market.[26] Yet cigarette production in the United States is highly oligopolistic. David Colander uses the example of luxury boats, where products are clearly differentiated.[27] There is no "market price" for yachts. William Baumol and co-authors draw a supply curve for Cadillacs, for which there is obviously only one manufacturer![28]

The text models do illustrate the idea that one or both parties in a transaction may ultimately pay the tax. This can be the case in imperfectly competitive markets as well. But why do we need the supply and demand model to show us this? The same result can be shown in models of imperfect competition. Again, the supply and demand model is being sold as a generic model of a market, without any discussion of whether this is appropriate.

Question for your professor: Can the demand and supply model predict the incidence of taxation in imperfectly competitive markets?

2.4 But don't price floors cause surpluses and price ceilings shortages?

Price ceilings Price ceilings have been imposed on different commodities, in different countries, in different times. During the Second World War, there were price ceilings on many commodities in Britain, Canada and the USA – commodities such as meat, milk, eggs, sugar and gasoline. In every case, shortages developed. Doesn't this confirm the usefulness of the competitive model?

Not really. In Chapter 6 we show that the textbook model of monopoly contains the same prediction: if price ceilings are sufficiently low there will be shortages. Similarly, shortages are also a likely outcome in textbook models of oligopoly and monopolistic competition. The fact that shortages develop in response to price ceilings doesn't demonstrate the superiority of the competitive model.

We quote Krugman and Wells as preferring the competitive model because models of oligopoly (where strategic interaction is the key) are so complex. But as we will see in Chapter 6 the monopoly model is simple – just as simple as the competitive model. Why not use that? Why not champion the usefulness of the monopoly model as a generic tool?

The reason is that such an analysis would tell the 'wrong story'. For all the qualifications that are later tacked on to it, the central textbook story is how the market economy works like an invisible hand, efficiently allocating resources among alternative uses. As we'll see, an economy populated with firms that have market power has no invisible hand allocating resources efficiently – hence the necessity to study an imaginary economy rather than something resembling the real one.

So, we're not arguing that price ceilings do not cause shortages. The issue is whether the assumption of perfect competition can be applied to every market as a decent enough approximation. If we accept the official methodology, of hypothesis testing and predictive power, then in each case we need to ask which works better: the competitive model or a non-competitive model.

> Questions for your professor: If price ceilings
> were low enough, would they cause shortages in non-
> competitive markets too?(Answer: Yes.)So, if price
> ceilings caused shortages in the Second World War,
> that can't be taken as empirical support for the
> demand and supply model, can it?

Price floors Similarly, we are not arguing that price floors don't cause surpluses. All economists would agree that if the minimum wage were raised high enough, employment could fall significantly. Where the minimum wage controversy begins is when we ask whether moderate increases have the same effect. As we've explained, the issue revolves around whether labour markets are *perfectly* competitive, or whether there are significant imperfections.

Perhaps one reason for the popularity of the one-sided minimum wage application is its ideological usefulness in undermining a labour market regulation that students will be inclined to take for granted as a good thing. After all, most of them will have worked at minimum wage jobs at this point in their lives. But if we are to be more charitable, there aren't a lot of examples of price floors where governments do not act as 'buyers of last resort' and make up the difference between quantity demanded and quantity supplied. This complicates the analysis considerably. A well-known example of such a policy is the Common Agricultural Policy of the European Union, a complex system which includes price floors for some products and purchases of surplus production from the EU budget. This arrangement has certainly produced surpluses, mockingly labelled butter and grain 'mountains' and milk 'lakes'.

In the case of the minimum wage, governments do not stand by to offer jobs to anyone who loses theirs as a result of a minimum wage increase. But in most countries, they do stand by to offer unemployment insurance, other forms of income assistance, and subsidized education to those who need it. This is typically ignored by those who oppose any minimum wage increase on the grounds that it will hurt those whom it is most trying to help.

> Question for your professor: The demand and supply
> model seems to suggest that suppliers will increase
> supply when binding price floors are imposed, despite
> observable surpluses. That seems irrational, so what
> do they actually do? (Answer: there is no answer!
> The model can say nothing about this situation. See
> the next section.)

2.5 What the texts don't tell you about the competitive model

The competitive model only works in equilibrium The perfectly competitive demand and supply model seems to make sense in equilibrium. Everyone takes prices as given, which is fine since everyone trades the amount they want, and no one has any incentive to change. But when something happens to disturb equilibrium the story starts to unravel.

Let's go back to the comparative static analysis, explained earlier using Figure 3.3. In the left-hand diagram we assumed a fall in the price of fertilizer shifted the supply curve of wheat to the right. This caused a surplus of wheat at the original equilibrium price. As a result, we are told prices fall. But how do they fall?

Kenneth Arrow pointed out the 'logical gap' in the theory: 'there is no place for a rational decision with respect to prices as there is with respect to quantities'.[29] As a result 'each individual participant in the economy is supposed to take prices as given and determine his choices as to purchases and sales accordingly; there is no one left over whose job is to make a decision on price.' The model says nothing about how people might behave in disequilibrium, by changing prices and quantities for example. He concludes that 'perfect competition can prevail only at equilibrium'.[30]

One "solution" to this is to come up with a theory of an economy that is always in equilibrium. The job of doing this is given to an auctioneer, who is 'the visible, if imaginary, embodiment of the invisible hand. He has no economic involvement in the market: no mention is made of his objectives or constraints', as British economist Huw Dixon puts it.[31] This fictitious character, who originated with the 19 century Swiss economist Leon Walras, fills the glaring gap in the demand and supply model to adjust prices in response to excess supply and demand in order to restore equilibrium.

If having to invent an auctioneer is bad enough, what's worse is that the auctioneer can't allow any trades to occur until he finds the equilibrium solution. This is because the auctioneer needs eventually to end up at the intersection of the demand and supply curves. If we allow trades before equilibrium is reached, people will have spent some of their budget. As a result, they would not be able to buy what they otherwise would have bought at what would have been the new equilibrium price.

The demand and supply curves are derived assuming market participants can buy or sell all that they wish at the going market price. But they can't do that when there are shortages or surpluses. Out of equilibrium these curves are only 'notional'. They don't tell us how much buyers would try to buy, or sellers would try to sell, if there were a surplus or shortage.

Rather than resorting to the abstract and unrealistic Walrasian auctioneer, the texts prefer to deal with disequilibrium situations by telling a superficially plausible story of price adjustment that is not actually part of the theory, as Arrow pointed out long ago. The assumption of buyers and sellers being passive price takers is cast aside. Texts often tell stories about how sellers notice surpluses or shortages, acquire the ability to set their own prices and start to adjust them accordingly.

For example, if a surplus appears as the result of a decrease in demand (the reverse of what is illustrated in the right-hand panel of Figure 3.3), sellers apparently do not realize that immediately, despite the assumption of perfect information. Instead, for some time they keep bringing to the market a quantity consistent with the original price, as shown by the supply curve. They then observe an unexpected amount of unsold goods and react by reducing prices.[32]

Here is a typical text account of how a perfectly competitive market reaches equilibrium: 'For example, if automobile dealers find themselves with unsold cars in the fall when the new models are coming in, you can expect to see price cuts. Sometimes dealers offer discounts to encourage buyers; sometimes buyers themselves simply offer less than the price initially asked'.[33] This market does not remotely resemble a perfectly competitive one; it describes a story of price adjustment in an oligopolistic market with imperfect information where buyers also have some bargaining power.

The textbook story of a shortage parallels this. 'When excess demand occurs in an unregulated market, there is a tendency for price to rise as demanders compete against each other for the limited supply. The adjustment mechanisms may differ, but the outcome is always the same', namely a rise in the market price.[34] As in the case of a surplus, textbook authors are understandably vague about what the price adjustment mechanisms are. The theory of perfect competition has nothing to say about how prices are set and what happens out of equilibrium.

Nevertheless, the textbooks maintain that market participants will start to raise prices if shortages appear and will lower prices if there is a surplus. But, as we explain in the Addendum to this chapter, when markets are out of equilibrium there is no guarantee that such price adjustments in each market will lead all markets back to equilibrium.

> Question for your professor: If everyone is a price taker in the competitive demand and supply model, who makes prices fall when there is a surplus?

The requirements for perfect competition are mutually incompatible In 1926, Piero Sraffa, a young Italian economist at Cambridge, made some very inconvenient observations about the supply and demand theory of perfect competition. In particular he argued that the conditions necessary for independence between the supply and demand curves are unlikely to exist in reality.

As we have seen, the supply and demand model examines a single market in isolation. It is implicitly assumed that events in this market do not have impacts on other markets that, in turn, feed back into this market. As a result, what happens in other markets can be neglected. This is called partial equilibrium analysis in contrast to general equilibrium analysis which considers the simultaneous equilibrium of all markets in the economy. (See the Addendum to this chapter for a more detailed discussion.) It is also assumed that demand and supply are independent of each other; shifts in demand do not also cause shifts in supply and vice versa. However, Sraffa pointed out that this is rarely the case in practice. A simple example illustrates the point.

Let's suppose that strawberries are produced in a perfectly competitive market and that the demand for strawberries increases for some reason. In the standard analysis, the quantity supplied increases as the price rises in the market. (In a diagram, the equilibrium point moves up to the right along a stationary supply curve, as seen in the right-hand panel of Figure 3.3). But that may well not be the end of the story! As more strawberries are produced, the demand for things needed to produce strawberries, such as farm labour, increases. If that increases the price of farm labour, then the supply curve of strawberries must also change because the price at which strawberry producers are willing to supply depends on their cost of production. The supply curve then shifts to the left, further increasing the price of strawberries.

This is only the beginning of the complications. The increase in the price of farm labour would change the costs, and thus the supply curves, in other fruit industries, such as cherries. If people consider strawberries and cherries to be substitutes for each other, the rising price of cherries increases the demand for strawberries.... In short, we have a mess on our hands: the interdependence of supply and demand conditions renders the partial equilibrium framework incapable of providing a clear and determinate result. Another assumption is required to rescue the supply and demand model, but it brings more trouble in its wake.

The assumption that is needed is that each perfectly competitive industry does not influence the prices of any of the inputs that they use. In other words, each industry contributes only a negligibly small share of the total demand for inputs. In that case, the expansion of strawberry production in the previous example would have no effect on the price of farm labour or on any other input price. The supply and demand curves are once again independent of each other.

However, this solution leaves unresolved another question raised by Sraffa, which we will examine in more detail in Chapter 5: could an individual farm expand its production indefinitely without raising the costs of producing an additional basket of strawberries? Imagine a farmer replicating her strawberry field over and over, expanding the size of the farm. What limits its size? If individual firms can expand like this, nothing guarantees that this market will remain perfectly competitive with a very large number of firms, each negligibly small relative to the size of the market.

Sraffa's critique led to the development of the model of imperfect competition: many firms, each selling a differentiated product. As we will see in Chapter 5, what limits the size of the firm in this context is that the size of its market is limited by a downward-sloping demand curve.

> Question for your professor: Our text assumes that
> the supply and demand curves are independent of
> each other, so one can move without the other also
> moving. What do you think of Piero Sraffa's critique
> of that assumption? Do you think the "solution" to
> his criticism is very realistic?

Multiple equilibria Nothing guarantees that the demand and supply curves are linear. They might have backward-bending regions, giving rise to multiple intersection points. For example, Robert Prasch explains that when needs are an important consideration, the labour supply curve could look like that shown in the left-hand diagram of Figure 3.7.[35]

The standard story (often found in textbooks) describes the section of the curve above W_s. As wages rise, the opportunity cost of leisure increases, causing people to substitute leisure for more work. This is the effect that initially dominates between W_s and W_L. On the other hand, people want to 'buy' more leisure as their incomes rise. When wages get high enough, this effect dominates, leading to a backward-bending section above W_L.

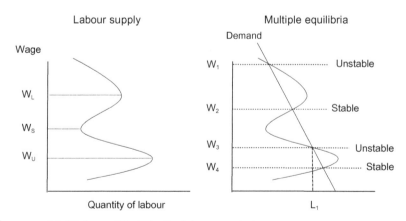

Figure 3.7 Multiple equilibria in the labour market

Prasch supplements this standard story by considering what happens when wages fall towards (and even go below) subsistence levels. He argues that when wages go below the level necessary to maintain minimum living standards with normal working hours, households increase their labour supply to abnormal levels. They might hold two jobs or work fourteen-hour shifts. So, below the subsistence wage, which we assume to be W_S, labour supply increases, accounting for another bend in the labour supply curve at W_S.

As wages continue to fall, they will eventually reach the point where the total hours of work required to maintain a socially acceptable standard of living are too long to be sustainable. Below the unsustainable wage, W_U, working hours fall precipitously. Prasch says: 'the primary worker and his or her family will be forced by exhaustion, disease, despair, and disrepair to abandon their effort to maintain a standard of living consistent with effective membership in the labour force and, consequently, civil society. They become homeless, petty thieves, or beggars, with strong prospects for a relatively short and miserable life.'[36] This explains the third bend occurring at W_U.

When we confront this labour supply curve with a standard downward-sloping labour demand curve, we get four possible equilibrium points, as shown in the right-hand diagram of Figure 3.7. Of these, both W_1 and W_3 are unstable. (At a wage slightly below either of these levels, supply exceeds demand, causing wages to continue to fall; similarly, at a wage slightly above either of these wage levels, demand exceeds supply, causing wages to continue to increase.) This leaves two stable equilibria – one of which offers wages quite a bit higher than the subsistence level, W_2; while the other is a poverty trap where wages are substantially below subsistence, W_4.

Prasch uses this construction to show the potential usefulness of minimum wage laws and maximum hours provisions. Either a minimum wage set above W_3, or maximum hours restriction set below L_1, would preclude the poverty trap equilibrium. Interestingly, in this model the legislation pushes the economy to a desirable equilibrium, but once at this equilibrium neither restriction appears 'binding'. That is to say, the equilibrium wage would be above the legal minimum wage and the offered hours would be less than the legal maximum. Prasch notes that this is 'a nice illustration of how market forces can interact with legislation to bring about results that are not immediately evident or expected'.[37]

Multiple equilibria might also arise out of imperfect information. Joseph Stiglitz explains that if there is a lack of information about quality differences between workers (or goods), then all those workers (or goods) will be lumped into a general category and sell for a wage (or price) that reflects the average quality. Clearly, those selling the better quality have an incentive to try to demonstrate this so they can command a premium price.

Conversely, those selling the inferior quality have an incentive to impede the flow of information, to sow confusion and doubt. This leads to the possibility of multiple equilibria, one in which information was fully revealed (the market identified the high and low ability people) and another in which it was not.[38]

Questions for your professor: If markets have multiple equilibria, are some more desirable than others? Is there a role for government in attaining the more desirable ones?

Self-fulfilling prophecies Yet another source of non-uniqueness arises from self-fulfilling prophecies as illustrated in Figure 3.8. According to the texts, expected future prices influence both the demand and supply curves. Suppose both consumers and producers expect future prices to increase by 10 per cent. Consumers will try to buy more now before prices increase, thus shifting up the demand curve from D_1 to D_2. Producers will withhold sales now in the expectation of getting higher prices in the future, thus shifting the supply curve left from S_1 to S_2. It is even possible that these shifts will increase the price from P_1 to P_2 by 10 per cent. In any case, there has been a self-fulfilling prophecy: the price has risen because people expected it to rise.[39]

Question for your professor: Changes in expectations about future prices shift both the demand and supply curves. But then what's efficient about the resulting prices?

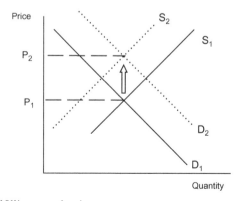

Figure 3.8 Self-fulfilling prophecies

© Andy Singer

Destabilizing speculation and bubbles We've had the Japanese property and stock market bubble (which burst in 1990), the technology stock bubble (which burst in 2001), the Chinese stock market bubble (which burst in 2008) and housing price bubbles in numerous countries which precipitated the financial collapses that began in 2008. Imperfect information is an understatement when it comes to thinking about the future. Yet the textbooks scarcely mention issues of time and uncertainty, the role of speculators or the possibility of price bubbles (i.e. unsustainable price increases driven by expectations that end in a price collapse).

Perhaps some of these issues are beyond the scope of first-year textbooks, but the role of speculators is important enough to warrant consideration. Suppose there are ongoing price fluctuations – for instance, a cycle of boom and bust in commodity prices; what role do the speculators play? Do they make things better or worse? The traditional textbook answer is that if speculators make money, they must buy low and sell high. This extra buying when prices are low, and extra selling when prices are high, implies their activity must act to smooth price fluctuations. Hence, speculators add to the efficiency of markets.

But economists now realize that there are important limits to this argument. First, in the face of irrational traders, the speculator may privately benefit more from trading that helps push prices in the wrong direction than from trading that pushes prices in the right direction. Put another way, it may often pay 'smart money' to follow 'dumb money' rather than to bet against it.[40] For example, if speculators buy when prices are rising, and sell when prices are falling, they could still make money but would add to the amplitude of the price fluctuation.

> Question for your professor: The world price of oil hit an all-time high of US$147/barrel in July 2008. Many believed that this was in part driven by speculators.[41] How does speculation fit into the demand and supply model?

Scandals Examples of corporate misbehaviour are numerous and (after the fact) well-known. To take one example at random, consider the cheating on emissions tests in the United States and Europe orchestrated by companies producing diesel powered cars.

These problems arise where there is imperfect and asymmetric information. Using the competitive model as a generic tool for all markets obscures the importance of information imperfections and the legal and regulatory framework that's necessary to oversee markets and make sure they work as we want them to. More on this in Chapters 6 and 8.

The legal framework: the case of eviction protection legislation The standard textbook world is implicitly one of perfect information and contracts that are costless to negotiate and enforce. The legal framework within which markets operate gets scarcely a passing mention. These assumptions certainly simplify the discussion, but they also impart a subtle laissez-faire message hiding between the lines of the text itself. It implicitly says that the legal and regulatory framework is (at most) of secondary importance.

The nature of the legal and regulatory framework is crucially important for the efficient functioning of markets, as we'll see repeatedly throughout this *Anti-Textbook*. An example relevant to the rental housing market is the nature of eviction protection legislation. Should tenants be liable for eviction after failing to pay one month's rent? If not, after how many? Should the rule be modified in the depths of winter? Does it matter how high the general level of unemployment is? The wrong balance in eviction protection legislation can create an imbalance in the rental housing market as severe as the first-generation rent freeze did in New York City. The case study here is Paris.

During the severe recession of the early 1980s, many people lost their jobs and became unable to pay their rent. People were being thrown out on to the streets. To prevent that, legislation was passed that gave tenants increased eviction protection that shifted the balance of power between landlord and tenant so much in favour of the tenant that it resulted in only about 70 per cent of all rents being paid.[42] Landlords had to embark upon months and sometimes years of legal wrangling to evict tenants who defaulted on their rent.

The consequences were in many ways similar to a binding rent freeze: an increase in the quantity of units demanded, a decrease in the quantity supplied, and an excess demand for units. The one difference was that since better-quality tenants were less liable to default on their rent, landlords did have an incentive to upgrade their units. Clearly, Paris had the balance wrong in its eviction protection legislation. But what is the right balance?

As Ha-Joon Chang puts it: 'The free market doesn't exist. Every market has some rules and boundaries that restrict freedom of choice. A market looks free only because we so unconditionally accept its underlying restrictions that we fail to see them.'[43] By failing to emphasize this fundamental point, the texts leave the way open for people to fall victim to arguments that removing certain regulations will restore the "free market" or that introducing certain regulations will be an unwarranted departure from the "free market". Chang writes: 'Recognizing that the boundaries of the market are ambiguous and cannot be determined in an objective way lets us realize that economics is not a science like physics or chemistry, but a political exercise'.[44]

```
Questions for your professor: Is the legal framework
within which markets operate important in determining
the efficiency of markets and the equity of market
outcomes? Is this ever going to be discussed?
```

2.6 Summing up

Using the competitive model as a generic tool applicable to a broad range of markets irrespective of the number of producers, heterogeneity of the product or information imperfections creates an inbuilt bias against government market intervention. It loads the dice against measures such as rent controls and minimum wages.

The textbooks justify the generic application of the competitive model because it supposedly gives accurate predictions and because it is simpler than non-competitive alternatives. But the claim about predictive power is backed up by only cursory empirical evidence (minimum wages and rent control), and sometimes by no evidence at all (the proportionate burden of the sales tax). Further, the predictive power of the perfectly competitive model is not compared against that of alternative models. The key issue should be: which model better applies to any given situation? Answering this would require comparing the full array of predictions and a serious look at the evidence.

With regard to the claim that the competitive model is simpler than noncompetitive alternatives, no criteria are proposed to evaluate it. It is a matter of subjective judgement. Alone it is not enough to justify the generic use of the competitive model. This is obvious once one considers coming to an alternative judgement – that the monopoly model is the simplest market structure. Would that then justify applying the monopoly model generically throughout the whole economy? It certainly would not give the required impression of a well-functioning self-regulated market system. Stiglitz concludes that the competitive paradigm has survived so long 'partly because the belief in that paradigm, and the policy prescriptions that were derived from it, has served certain interests'.[45] In other words, it is an 'enabling myth'. Certainly, the overemphasis given to it in the textbooks is hard to explain in any other way.

The consequences of placing the supply and demand model at the heart of the textbook and applying it to a wide variety of policy questions are not innocuous. Norbert Häring and Niall Douglas sum up the problem nicely: '[I]t is with this textbook-presented caricature that most students of economics, and even more of those who take only the basic economics courses, leave university. They become policymakers, journalists or managers, thinking that the idea of perfect competition, while being a little exaggerated, contains the essence of capitalist economics and delivers robust and sensible recommendations.'[46]

SUGGESTIONS FOR FURTHER READING

Robert Prasch's book, *How Markets Work: Supply, demand and the 'real world'* is insightful reading. Particular emphasis could be put on Lectures II to VI.

Economism: Bad Economics and the Rise of Inequality by James Kwak is a superb examination of the pernicious influence of the simplistic supply and demand framework which pervades not only "Econ 101" but has also successfully penetrated the broader social discourse. Its purpose: to justify the existing social order.

ADDENDUM: THE INDETERMINATE AND UNSTABLE ECONOMY

This brief addendum considers two questions: Is there likely to be a unique equilibrium for the economy as a whole? And if the economy is not in equilibrium, is there some price adjustment process that will bring it to equilibrium? While these are questions that are normally considered in upper-level courses, the concepts should be understandable even to introductory students.

General equilibrium and partial equilibrium 'General equilibrium' is when all the markets in an economy are in equilibrium. For example, the 'production possibilities frontier' presented in Chapter 2 is a general equilibrium model of a very simple two-good economy. In this construct, impacts on wheat explicitly have implications for cloth. Both markets are simultaneously in equilibrium. 'Partial equilibrium' looks at just one market at a time, as in the supply and demand model in this chapter. For the most part, introductory microeconomics courses use a partial equilibrium approach despite the serious shortcomings pointed out by Sraffa.

Multiple equilibria and why they matter In Figure 3.7 we illustrated a situation in which an individual market had several possible equilibria, two of which were stable. That meant it was not possible to predict where the market price and quantity might end up. It might, perhaps, require knowing where the market price was originally. In such a situation, it might be possible to take action to achieve the most desirable equilibrium.

The same result can hold for the economy as a whole. That is, there could be many possible equilibria in a general equilibrium model, some of which might be stable and others unstable. Indeed, if the whole economy were to consist of only perfectly competitive markets, like the ones considered in this chapter, a theoretical result called, the Sonnenschein-Mantel-Debreu (or SMD) Theorem implies that the resulting general equilibrium may not be unique. As a result, it's impossible to say which of the possible equilibria is the one at which the economy would settle.[47] The economy is fundamentally indeterminate. Occasionally the SMD Theorem is referred to as the 'Anything Goes Theorem'.

This may sound like an abstract, technical point of no real relevance, but that's not the case. Economists, when trying to assess the effects of policy changes, sometimes make computer simulation models of the entire economy. Naturally, like any economic model, these general equilibrium computer simulation models are highly simplified descriptions of the real economy. Do these models miss the possibility of multiple equilibria? If so, a researcher could simulate the effect of a policy change (implementing free trade, for example) and reach one conclusion, while perhaps the economy would actually end up in quite a different position. Yet, as Hildenbrand and Kirman observe: 'Almost all of the economic literature, theoretical and applied, turns around models in which the nature of "the equilibrium" is discussed and analysed,' as if that equilibrium were unique.[48]

Does the economy find its way to equilibrium? The question is whether, when the economy is not in equilibrium, some price adjustment process returns the economy to equilibrium. In introductory economics, in the partial equilibrium context, students are told (as in Part One of this chapter) that a market can be brought back into equilibrium by lowering the price when there is excess supply (and raising it if there is excess demand). But Hildenbrand and Kirman note that 'as soon as we leave the two-good case this is no longer true'. To explain, they say: 'Think for a moment of two goods, cars and gasoline. Suppose prices were such that cars were in excess demand and gasoline in excess supply. Normal behaviour ... would be to raise the price of cars and lower that of gasoline'.[49] But raising the price of cars also lowers demand for gasoline, increasing the excess supply of gasoline, while lowering gas prices raises the demand for cars, increasing excess demand there. Price adjustments may lead around in circles, with differences between demands and supplies not approaching zero.[50] In the final analysis, the competitive economy has neither a unique equilibrium nor is there a way to reach an equilibrium without the intervention of the fictitious Walrasian auctioneer.

Chapter 4

PEOPLE AS CONSUMERS

'In standard neoclassical economics, with what does the textbook begin? It begins with a highly philosophical assumption that is presented as fact. It is the assumption that society comprises of atoms, of individuals who are characterised fully and exclusively by their preferences. All that they each do in life is to try to satisfy their own bundle of preferences. This is the utility maximisation principle.' Yanis Varoufakis[1]

I THE STANDARD TEXT

This chapter focuses on consumers, buyers in markets for final goods and services. 'Goods' are tangible things, such as economics textbooks or automobiles, while services are intangible, such as economics lectures or automobile repair work. For simplicity, we'll just talk about 'goods'. Final goods are consumed by the buyer rather than used as inputs in making something else. An apple bought by a bakery to put into an apple pie is an 'intermediate good', not a final good. We're concerned here only with final goods.

1.1 Utility maximization and individual demand

Demand for individual goods results from consumers' attempts to make themselves as well off as possible, or to maximize 'utility', a word that comes from the nineteenth-century English philosopher Jeremy Bentham, the originator of 'utilitarianism'. Utility is the benefit you get from having or doing something. We use the word interchangeably with 'benefit' or 'welfare' or 'well-being'.

The more of a good that a person consumes in a period of time, the greater the total benefit (s)he gets from it, but as total consumption increases, the extra benefit (or 'marginal utility') from having more of it eventually gets less and less. Consider the utility you get from drinking glasses of water during a day. The first one feels much needed; the tenth one could be a chore. This illustrates the 'law

Table 4.1 Mary's benefit from eating pizzas

Pizzas (per week)	Total benefit	Marginal benefit	Net benefit of consuming an additional pizza (if price is $12/pizza)	Total consumer surplus
1	$25	$25	$13	$13
2	$45	$20	$8	$21
3	$60	$15	$3	$24
4	$70	$10	-$2	$22

of diminishing marginal utility'. (It is termed a 'law' because of the confidence we have in its validity.)

To get the highest benefit from a given income, a person must spend appropriately on the goods and services available. Consider a simple example where there are only two goods: pizza and Pepsi. To get the appropriate balance in your total spending, you must avoid spending 'too much' on any one thing. If the last dollar you spend on pizza gives you less extra benefit than the last dollar you spend on Pepsi, you're spending too much on pizza. Spend less on pizza and more on Pepsi and you'll make better use of your income. The appropriate balance is reached when the last dollar you spend on pizza gives you the same extra benefit as the last dollar you spend on Pepsi.

A consumer's demand for a good summarizes the quantities that would be purchased at various possible prices. In principle, we can ask the consumer (whom we'll call Mary) the maximum amount she would be willing to pay for various amounts of the good (given her income and the characteristics and prices of all other goods) and construct the demand curve from that. Table 4.1 shows her benefit, measured in dollars, from eating pizzas.

The second column shows that she would be willing to pay at most $25 to get one pizza/week, reflecting her $25 marginal benefit from it. The second pizza gives her only $20 of marginal benefit, reflecting the law of diminishing marginal utility. That's why she'd be willing to pay only a maximum of $45 ($25 + $20) for two pizzas/week.

The table also illustrates the 'net benefit' she gets from her purchases. This is the difference between how much she values the good, as reflected by the maximum amount she's willing to pay for it, and the amount that she actually has to pay. If pizzas happen to cost $12 each, buying the first pizza gives a net benefit valued at $25 − $12, or $13. The second pizza gives a net benefit of $8 ($20 − $12), and so on. A running total of these net benefits (seen in the final column) shows the total net benefit that results from buying different numbers of pizzas.

This total net benefit is called the 'consumer's surplus'. If a consumer is spending just the right amount on each good, as described earlier, she is getting the maximum net benefit from her purchases and is maximizing her utility or well-being. If the price happened to be $12/pizza, Mary should buy three pizzas per week to maximize her surplus. Buying the fourth pizza would be an inefficient use of her budget because its marginal benefit is less than the price; the negative net benefit from that would reduce consumer surplus. In general, the consumer should buy more of the good as long as its marginal benefit is greater than or equal to its price.

The left-hand diagram in Figure 4.1 summarizes this. The rectangles show the marginal benefit of each additional pizza; the part of them above the $12 price shows positive additions to consumer surplus from buying that additional pizza. If the price falls to $9/pizza, we can see that it would now be worthwhile to buy the fourth pizza. In general, the marginal benefits tell us the consumer's demand at various possible prices. This example has supposed that pizzas have to be bought in whole units and can't be divided. If we allowed for that, so that people could buy fractions of a pizza (or slices of any size), we could draw marginal benefit as the smooth line in the diagram.

This line is the consumer's demand curve. The consumer's surplus is the area between the demand curve and the price. It's the same as the area of the three shaded rectangles showing the consumer surplus from each individual pizza (with the exception of any surplus from buying a small amount of the fourth pizza, now that pizzas can be bought by the slice).

Other things also influence the amount a consumer wants to buy at each price, such as the income available, and the prices of other goods. They lie in the background here. Changes in any of those other things change demand: an increase in income, for instance, could increase the amount of pizza a person buys at any given price, moving demand as shown in the right-hand diagram of Figure 4.1. Or, if income increases a lot, it could reduce demand, as caviar is consumed instead of pizza. In general, more income allows someone to have a different, more preferred, mix of goods giving greater total benefit or utility.

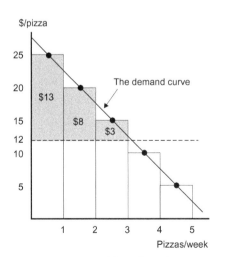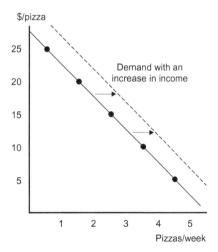

Figure 4.1 Marginal benefit and price

1.2 Market demand

Demand by all consumers is just their total demand at various possible prices. If the price of a pizza is $12, Mary in Figure 4.1 buys three pizzas per week, while weekly demand by all the persons in the market – perhaps a particular geographic region – is 30,000 pizzas, as shown in Figure 4.2. Reflecting individual demands, market demand shows the benefit (measured in dollars) consumers as a whole get from buying various quantities of pizzas. At $12 per pizza, consumers' surplus of all consumers added together is the difference between the maximum prices consumers would be willing to pay (shown by the demand curve) and the market price, the shaded triangle shown in Figure 4.2.[2] If the price falls, consumers buy more and their surplus expands.

The example shows three things: first, the marginal benefit curve is the same as the demand curve; second, the area under the demand curve represents the total benefit from consuming the good; third, the shaded area below the demand curve and above the going price is the net benefit (or consumer's surplus) from buying that good.

If the distribution of wealth and income were different then, in general, individual and total demands for goods would change; prices and the amounts produced and sold would also be different. The analysis assumes a particular distribution of income and wealth among people.

For every good, each consumer makes the choices that maximize his or her consumer's surplus, and in aggregate (given everyone's limited budgets) the total surplus of all consumers is maximized too. If something forces consumers to alter their choices compared with this 'free market' outcome, they will be worse off.

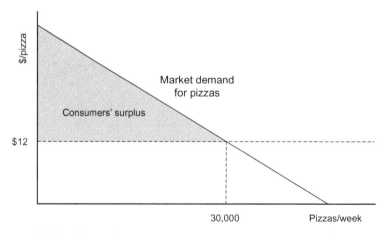

Figure 4.2 Market demand

2 THE ANTI-TEXT

The previous account of consumer choice offers a superficially plausible way of thinking about the demand for pizza and how that might change if income changes, the sort of uninteresting question that the textbooks consider at length. But the approach has serious shortcomings that should be a source of concern if we use it as the central or 'default' model to assess the outcomes of consumer decisions in particular markets and in the economy as a whole. In Chapter 1, we described the work of behavioural economists who have examined people's bounded rationality and bounded willpower, concepts that can be applied to understanding consumer behaviour. Here, we will examine further issues that our textbook story quietly swept under the rug.

First, this account says nothing about where our consumer's preferences for pizza, Pepsi or anything else have come from. *Preferences are simply 'given'.* As Milton Friedman put it in his graduate text: 'The economist has little to say about the formation of wants; this is the province of the psychologist. The economist's task is to trace the consequences of any given set of wants'.[3]

This narrow view unduly limits the questions that economics can address. Do some producers and retailers have real influence through advertising and marketing over people's preferences? Why does it matter?

Second, it is assumed that buyers have *perfect information* about what they're buying. When people buy pizzas, if the green peppers on them contain carcinogenic pesticide residues, no worries! The buyers take this into account in their rational calculations when they ask for them on their pizza. In reality, however, *imperfect information* is the rule, not the exception. As well, information is *asymmetric* – in this case the producers of goods have more and better information than their potential customers. Does imperfect and asymmetric information result in important systematic errors when buyers make spending decisions?

Third, the benefit a person gets from consumption in the textbook story has *no social context.* It is entirely unrelated to what other people in the surrounding society have. What happens if social context matters?

We'll consider each of these points in turn. The ideas and their implications are not difficult to understand, so their absence from the textbooks can't be blamed on that. However, they spoil the rosy picture of the operation of the unregulated market economy that an innocent reader can easily take away from the textbook account.

2.1 What if preferences are not 'given'?

The textbook account implicitly assumes that people's wants originate within themselves. For example, a buyer's preferences about pizza and willingness to pay for it reflect how good it tastes compared with other things. If that's true, we don't really have to consider where our taste for pizza comes from; it's just a part of our nature, shaped by evolution to induce us to satisfy our needs for nutrients. This way of thinking clearly does not apply to all goods and services. But the economists who developed the theory of demand were not trying to develop a real theory of people's 'wants'. They sought only a simple account to explain the demand curve, a building block in the supply and demand model that in turn produces a theory of prices, their real goal.[4]

Why shouldn't we acknowledge that wants are, in part, determined by people's previous consumption experiences, the social environment in which they live, and attempts by firms to influence individuals' wants?[5] Textbook economics has long been criticized for ignoring this; if preferences are influenced in important ways within the economic system itself, it's hardly convincing for Friedman to claim that it's not economists' business.

Advertising

> 'Advertising may be described as the science of arresting the human intelligence long enough to get money from it.' Stephen Leacock.[6]

Advertising is the most obvious attempt to influence people's preferences. In textbook economics, people are perfectly informed, so advertising must just provide consumers with accurate information about product characteristics, sellers' locations and prices. This assumes away persuasive advertising that tries to change people's wants and stimulate new wants; and it assumes that advertising never provides biased or misleading information.

The supply and demand model at the heart of textbooks doesn't permit such questions about advertising to arise. Each firm has a very small share of the market and all make identical products, such as a particular variety of apples, for example. We can imagine apple farmers having roadside stands with signs reading 'apples, $4/kg', but no farmer will be so foolish as to try to boost sales by paying for billboards with pictures of celebrities eating apples. (Advertising is acknowledged only later in the textbook when discussing industries dominated by one or a small number of firms, but this has no impact on the theory of consumer behaviour.)

The advertising industry is large. In the United States, probably the world's most advertising-saturated country, it has constituted about 2 percent of US gross domestic product since the second half of the 20th century.[7] In his 1958 book *The Affluent Society*, John Kenneth Galbraith wrote that advertising expenditures 'must be integrated with the theory of consumer demand. They are too big to be ignored'.[8] Yet textbook economics still relegates them to the sidelines.

Some people accuse advertising of contributing to consumerism and an excessively materialistic culture. Clearly, this can't be the goal of any particular advertiser, who, like the apple farmer, is only trying to sell a product, but it may be a side effect of the activity of the advertising industry as a whole.

© Andy Singer

For example, in her study of the commercialization of childhood, *Born to Buy*, Juliet Schor summarizes the results of studies of children's exposure to Channel One. Channel One is a daily news and advertising broadcast shown in a quarter of US middle and secondary schools in exchange for video equipment. They find that the programme affects children's attitudes, making them more likely to agree with statements expressing materialistic views ('designer labels make a difference').[9]

The problem of changing preferences Some economists have given the formation and change of preferences serious thought and reached conclusions that undermine the textbook account. A straightforward example illustrates the central idea.

Suppose that you are the editor of a top fashion magazine. You use a simple flip phone and have no use for the features that a smart phone offers. Photographers spot you at a public event with your unfashionable phone and you are mocked in the tabloid newspapers. The next time you appear in public you are carrying the latest model smart phone. Evidently your preferences changed.[10]

How would we evaluate this situation? If we use your initial preferences, when you placed no value on the smartphone's extra features, we must conclude that you are worse off: you've paid good money for something you thought was not worth it. If we use your new preferences, we must conclude that you got some consumer surplus from the deal and are better off after the purchase.

The fundamental problem is that it's not always obvious whether the preferences before or after the change are the ones to use in judging your situation. You have the freedom to change your preferences, after all. On what grounds can we say which preferences are the most valid? Does it depend on why you changed your preferences? The problem is even more complex if people's preferences continually change because of their experience and their changing social environment.

The textbooks implicitly claim that the origin of wants is unimportant by simply ignoring the question. The only thing that apparently counts is the wants of the moment and the extent to which they are being satisfied. But this claim involves a value judgement that reasonable people may – and do – disagree with. How people's preferences are formed is important. While the great economists of the past were often willing to make explicit value judgements about people's wants, now most economists remain silent.[11]

Even on the rare occasion when a text acknowledges the existence of persuasive advertising that gets consumers to pay high prices for inferior products, it adopts what American economist Steve Cohn calls the 'note but ignore' rhetorical strategy – not letting the inconvenient observation have any fundamental impact on the analysis.[12]

To open wants up for scrutiny and debate, textbook economics would have to admit that its method of using consumer surplus in judging individual and social outcomes doesn't always work. Rather than deal with the thorny issues that advertising and marketing raise, the textbooks direct students' attention to socially innocuous questions such as how the demand for pizza might be affected by changes in the price of beer or anchovies.

Controlling advertising in the public interest

> 'Every time you're exposed to advertising, you realize once again that America's leading industry, America's most profitable business is still the manufacture, packaging, distribution and marketing of bullshit.' George Carlin.[13]

In the real world, these issues are too important to ignore and citizens' concern about the harmful effects of advertising and marketing on wants sometimes forces governments to regulate and restrict it in the public interest. Children are particularly vulnerable to the army of psychological experts deployed against them. 'Marketing snoops, with cameras, notebooks, and videotapes, can be found in toy stores, clothing shops, and supermarkets, hanging out in the aisles and watching what kids do,' writes Juliet Schor.[14]

Young children can't tell the difference between entertainment programmes and advertising on television, one reason why some western European countries ban the use of children in TV advertising.[15] Sweden, Norway, Brazil and the Canadian province of Québec all ban domestic TV advertising directed at children under the age of twelve. Other countries have a variety of regulations; for example, the United Kingdom there is a ban on the advertising of unhealthy foods high in fat, sugar and sodium that is directed towards children. Such junk food is the focus of most advertising directed towards children in the United States, who reportedly see an average of 20,000 commercials a year just on television.[16]

Children have a large direct and indirect influence on household spending, which is why they are targeted by advertisers. To reach them, companies' marketing campaigns are combining traditional media with 'campaigns in schools, internet, digital marketing, packaging, and cross-promoting through popular movies or television characters.'[17]

Example: marketing tobacco to children Much of tobacco companies' advertising and marketing efforts have been directed at children and youth, who will be the adult smokers of the future. The World Health Organization's Framework Convention on Tobacco Control calls for a ban on all forms of tobacco advertising, promotion, and sponsorship including the retail display of tobacco products. Restrictions have been put in place in many countries, but investigations have shown that serious problems remain.

With smoking on the decline in many high-income countries, tobacco companies' efforts are increasingly directed towards developing countries with growing incomes and lax enforcement for what rules there are. Based on a 22 country, four continent study, *The Guardian* reported that 'Marlboro cigarettes made by Philip Morris and British American Tobacco brands such as Pall Mall, Kent, Dunhill and Lucky Strike were being sold and promoted within 300 metres (1,000ft) or closer to schools in nearly all the countries researchers examined in a series of studies'. In New Delhi, for example, researchers 'saw single cigarettes and tiny sachets of chewing tobacco for sale alongside sweets directly opposite school gates', in violation of the law.[18]

Example: marketing infant formula One of the most notable examples of an attempt to limit marketing and advertising is the World Health Organization's International Code of Marketing Breast-Milk Substitutes, established in 1981. The Code bans advertising and promotion of infant formula, sets strict labelling requirements, and requires producers to inform potential buyers that breast milk is best for babies. It also requires that formula be used only after consultation with medical professionals. The Code came about after campaigns in the 1970s by nongovernmental organizations against producers, particularly the Nestlé boycott.

The World Health Organization and UNICEF agree that for the first six months of life, all babies should be fed only breast milk rather than infant formula. If this happened worldwide, every year it could prevent more than 800,000 deaths of children under the age of five as well as 20,000 deaths of mothers due to breast cancer.[19]

In developing countries, bottle-fed babies are much more likely to die than breast-fed babies, largely because of the use of contaminated water. Even in the developed countries, bottle-fed babies have significantly poorer health outcomes than breastfed babies. Yet despite all this, only about 40 percent of infants worldwide are breastfed at some point during their first six months.[20] Why?

According to UNICEF and the WHO, 'aggressive marketing of breastmilk substitutes creates a major barrier to breastfeeding'.[21] As one study reports, 'Formula advertisements portray formula milk to be as good as or better than breastmilk, or present it as a lifestyle choice rather than a decision with health and economic consequences.... Marketing messages can also convey that breastfeeding is difficult and that breastmilk substitutes help to settle fussy babies.'[22]

For example, an investigation in the Philippines found that representatives of infant formula companies were a ' "constant presence in hospitals", handing out "infant nutrition" pamphlets to mothers, which appear to be medical advice but in fact recommend specific formula brands and sometimes have money-off coupons.' In further violation of Philippine law, formula producers 'Nestlé, Abbott, Wyeth and Mead Johnson were found to be offering doctors, midwives and other health workers meals, cinema and theatre tickets and gambling chips, as well as all-expenses-paid sponsorship for attendance at lavish medical conferences'. As a result, 'many women were found to be spending up to three-quarters of their income on formula for their babies, sometimes denying themselves food to afford it. Some were living without running water and electricity, causing problems when trying to sterilise bottles.'[23] The effects of this on infant mortality are all too predictable.

Individual governments must implement the Code in their own laws and monitor compliance, but many drag their feet. In the United States, the Code's restrictions are not even legally binding.[24] The editors of the *International Breastfeeding Journal* write that 'the lack of a breastfeeding culture in most industrialized nations is the legacy of decades of commercial marketing of infant formula, often endorsed by medical practices', which leaves parents woefully ignorant.[25]

The bottle-feeding culture has slowly been reversed in some places. This requires a halt to commercial marketing, government support for adequate paid maternity leave, and the implementation of UNICEF's Baby Friendly Hospital Initiative, which helps mothers begin breastfeeding right after birth.

> Questions for your professor: How do we measure consumer surplus if advertising and marketing change people's preferences? Does it matter if they buy things they would not want with perfect information?

2.2 Incomplete and asymmetric information

The textbook economics story of consumer choice with its implicit assumptions of informative advertising and perfect information leading to optimal choices is particularly misleading in situations where incomplete and asymmetric information is a central feature. This provides an opportunity for manipulative marketing by producers. Let's consider a couple of examples.

Example: marketing prescription drugs No one should have been surprised when a study finally revealed that Prozac, the popular antidepressant taken by 40 million people, and three other drugs in its class are no more effective for most people than a placebo (a sugar pill that the patient believes is a drug). The study 'examined all data available on the drugs, including results from clinical trials that the manufacturers chose not to publish at the time'.[26]

While the drug companies raked in tens of billions over the decades these ineffective drugs have been on the market, patients were unknowingly exposed to risks of lethal side effects, such as suicide – a problem the drug companies were aware of, but concealed.[27]

Unfortunately, the Prozac story is no aberration. Pharmaceutical drugs are complex products that their ultimate users are in no position to understand or assess. Consumers rely on drug companies and supposedly independent researchers, medical journals, healthcare providers and government regulators to make safe products available and to prescribe them properly. This system has been deeply compromised according to exposés.[28]

Between 1999 and 2019, almost 247,000 Americans died from overdoses related to prescription opioids.[29] The origin of the drugs behind the opioid epidemic ravaging the United States has been traced back to the mid-1990s with the development and aggressive marketing of OxyContin, a painkiller produced by Purdue Pharma, an American company. It became the 'gateway drug to the most devastating public-health disaster of the twenty-first century' in the United States, as Barry Meier describes it in his book *Pain Killer*.[30]

Drug companies have discovered that they can expand their markets by having drugs prescribed to healthy people. Recent decades witnessed highly profitable increases in the number of 'depressed' people, children with 'attention deficit hyperactivity disorder', people with 'high' cholesterol, and on and on. Even shyness has become a major epidemic labelled 'social anxiety disorder' – and a powerful antidepressant (with 'horrendous withdrawal symptoms') found a huge new market.[31] The earlier and the longer people can be put on drugs, the more money can be made.

Advertising directed at consumers is effective in inducing prescriptions from doctors, particularly for new drugs that are very expensive and no better than older, less expensive ones or perhaps no better than nothing at all. Citizen groups, such as Commercial Alert, want such ads banned in the United States, but corporate power has blocked it, although such advertising is banned in every other developed country except New Zealand.[32]

Researchers studying drugs and sitting on panels writing guidelines for doctors very often receive money as 'consultants' from the companies whose products they study or recommend. According to a former editor of the *New England Journal of Medicine*, the influence of the industry is such that much published research may be 'seriously flawed', misleading doctors who rely on it to judge the efficacy and safety of new drugs.[33] A significant number of articles published in medical journals have been 'drafted by drug company-sponsored ghostwriters and then passed off as the work of independent academic authors'.[34]

The main targets of drug company marketing are the doctors who write the prescriptions. Sales representatives, who regularly visit doctors' offices to ply their wares, shower them with "gifts". Companies spend millions flying doctors on all-expenses-paid trips to conferences where they are presented with one-sided marketing dressed up as "medical education".[35]

Little wonder, then, that combined with the political power of the companies (which we look at in the next chapter), the drug makers are regularly among the most profitable corporations in the world.

Example: food The food industry is crucial in satisfying one of our most fundamental needs. We can see, smell and taste what we eat and drink, but to find out what it contains at the molecular level is no easy matter.

Books such as Eric Schlosser's *Fast Food Nation* helped to reveal what really goes into the products of the fast food industry – everything from shit from slaughtered animals in hamburger meat to the 'natural and artificial flavours' conjured up by the chemists of the flavour industry. Such exposure, however, has had only a minor effect on an industry that maintains an enormous advertising budget to bolster its image, much of it directed at children, whose food preferences form early in life.[36]

Lack of information is a problem even for those who try to eat in a more healthy way. Fresh fruit and vegetables are increasingly designed to look good to the buyers, but their nutritional content is plummeting. The same is true of industrially produced meat.[37]

People are also increasingly interested in how their food is produced. Public awareness of the treatment of animals, particularly in factory farming, is rising. For example, in Britain 'free-range' eggs produced by cage-free hens able to walk outside exceed the value of eggs from caged hens. In most cases, however, shoppers are not given the information they would need to make ethical choices about the food they are buying.[38]

If demand for a product (such as adulterated factory-produced chicken meat) in the presence of imperfect information is greater than it would be in the presence of perfect information, then consumers really do not use their budgets efficiently to maximize their well-being. The misallocation of resources parallels what we saw in the earlier example, where preferences were altered by advertising and other social influences.

The real default case: incomplete and asymmetric information Despite the pervasiveness of informational problems and the inefficiencies they give rise to, textbook economics focuses on the improbable assumptions of given tastes and perfect information that helps make Adam Smith's good-news story of the invisible hand work for consumers. But incomplete and asymmetric information – that is, buyers and sellers knowing different things – is a better description of reality for almost all goods. As the examples we give suggest, ignorance about what we buy and use is commonplace and in many situations buyers' ignorance has important consequences.

How flammable is your children's clothing? How will your automobile respond to crashes of various kinds? Did you get cheated by the mechanic when you had the car repaired? What hidden defects are there in the house you are considering buying? What are your chances of being a victim of medical malpractice? What chemicals are leaching out of plastics into your food and drink and what are the consequences? And so on. You can be sure that the producers of these goods or services know much more about the answers than their customers. Even if the customers suspect there is a potential problem, they are unlikely to undertake the time-consuming and perhaps technically demanding research on their own.

What about the news media? Don't investigative reporters uncover problems and inform the public? Don't governments monitor the market and act on the public's behalf, regulating or providing information? We explain the economic basis for corporate power in the next chapter, but for now let's just note that the media corporations that provide most people with their news are primarily interested in profits; systematically upsetting other corporations (which may be major advertisers) is not profitable.

How governments behave depends on the strength of the country's civic life and the social norms supporting it. Where civil society, and thus democracy, is weak and the power of big business is strong, governments can be expected often to act against the interests of the vast majority of the population. (We return to this issue in Chapter 9.)

Everywhere, people and economic institutions try to cope with informational problems. It's not all bad news. Think, for example, of the investments some companies make in a reputation for quality, or those that offer real guarantees and warranties to distinguish their higher-quality products from those of competitors. None of these commonplace features of the business world has a place in the textbook world of perfect information.

In the United States, Ralph Nader has spent a lifetime improving the odds for consumers through organizing citizen and consumer groups and pressing government to level the playing field through law and regulation. He, and others around the world, have won important victories for consumers, but the cards remain stacked in favour of producers. Business lobbies are always trying to roll back consumer gains.[39]

```
Questions  for  your  professor:  Isn't  incomplete
and  asymmetric  information  an  important  problem
for  consumers?  Does  the  default  assumption  in  the
textbook of complete and perfect information divert
attention away from these problems? If so, in whose
interest?
```

2.3 Preferences and relative position

Advertising and other actions by producers are not the only way in which people's tastes are shaped within the economic system itself. We are, after all, social animals: we see what others have and that influences our own wants and the utility we get from the things we have.

According to evolutionary psychology, the way we think about our place in society has been shaped, like all the other processes of our minds, by evolutionary forces. A concern for status and security is central to the individual's ability to survive, to find mates and to reproduce. We have an innate concern about our relative position in our 'reference group', those people with whom we compare ourselves. As Juliet Schor reminds us, 'While most critics of consumer society focus on ads and the media, it's important to remember that the more powerful stimulator of desire is what friends and family have.'[40]

The implicit assumption in textbook economics is that the utility people get from things is entirely independent of what others have.[41] But what is the evidence about how other people's consumption affects our utility? The textbook account presents none. How does considering utility in a more realistic way change our judgements about how well the economy is functioning?

John Kenneth Galbraith expressed a central aspect of the problem in his 1958 classic *The Affluent Society*:

> If the individual's wants are to be urgent they must originate with himself. They cannot be urgent if they must be contrived for him. And above all

they must not be contrived by the process of production by which they are satisfied. For this means that the whole case for the urgency of production, based on the urgency of wants, falls to the ground. One cannot defend production as satisfying wants if that production creates the wants.[42]

Production creates wants through people's desire to emulate others. 'One man's consumption becomes his neighbour's wish ... The more wants are satisfied the more new ones are born,' as Galbraith wrote.[43] If this is true, we keep working to produce more and more, yet we remain in the same place in terms of the utility we get from those things. Is there evidence to support this view?

```
Question for your professor: According to our
text, people get utility from the things that they
themselves consume. But what others have apparently
doesn't affect their utility. Do you think that is
true in reality?
```

2.4 Beyond textbook utility: measuring what matters

When British economist Richard Layard decided to study economics he rightly believed that the discipline "was originally founded in order to discover which institutions would produce the greatest happiness for the people". Disappointment soon followed. "I was quickly shocked by the narrow view economists had about what actually causes happiness. Essentially they thought it was about purchasing power, plus a few other bits and pieces.'[44]

The narrow view Layard describes still dominates the textbooks, but a growing number of economists are thinking much more broadly about well-being or happiness. We'll first describe what has been learned by studying direct measures of well-being, based on people's subjective judgements. Then will have a brief look at objective measures that are being used as well to assess genuine progress.

The evidence: surveys of subjective well-being In 1974, the American economist Richard Easterlin wrote a path-breaking essay in which he drew economists' attention to work in sociology and psychology that tries to measure individuals' feelings of satisfaction and happiness. These are called measures of 'subjective well-being' (SWB) because they rely on people's own, subjective, assessments rather than objective measures, such as how much income they have.

Measures of SWB fall into two broad categories. One asks about happiness or emotional well-being in people's everyday experience. For example, 'Taken all together, how would you say things are these

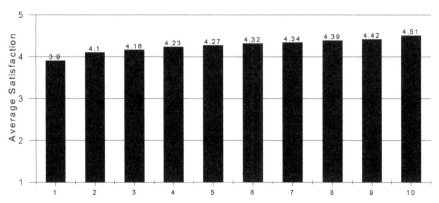

Figure 4.3 Satisfaction with life, Canada, 2007–2008, by income decile
Source: Sharpe et al. (2010), Table 9

days – would you say that you are very happy, pretty happy, or not too happy?' The second asks people to reflect on their satisfaction with their lives as a whole. For example, people can be asked directly about their satisfaction, as in the happiness question. A variant asks them to rate their current lives on a 'ladder scale' where 0 is 'the worst possible life for you' and 10 is 'the best possible life for you'. These questions measure things of importance to people and are potentially useful for economic and social policy. While these questions are measuring somewhat different things, this area of research is often just called the study of 'happiness' and its determinants.

Happiness within countries across income groups: Within countries, people with more income have higher average happiness and life satisfaction, as the textbook model would predict. Figure 4.3 shows an example for Canada where the respondents in a national survey are divided into ten equal-sized income groups or deciles. It shows average responses to the question 'How satisfied are you with your life in general? 1) very satisfied 2) satisfied 3) neither satisfied nor dissatisfied 4) dissatisfied 5) very dissatisfied.'[45] While no one claims that any one person's reported level of subjective well-being can be directly compared with any other person's, the average differences across the groups are meaningful and reflect real differences.

However, the size of the effect is surprisingly small. Richard Layard summarizes the results of thousands of surveys done around the world: 'holding all else constant, a person with double your income will be 0.2 points happier than you are [on a scale of 0–10]. Similarly, a person whose income is one half of yours will be 0.2 points less happy. These are not huge differences and in most countries income inequality explains under 2 percent of the variance of happiness.'[46]

There is some evidence that the well-being benefits of higher incomes may even eventually end in some countries. Kahneman and Deaton report that average happiness in the United States rises with household income up to about the 6th decile, when it flattens out. They write:

> More money does not necessarily buy more happiness, but less money is associated with emotional pain. Perhaps $75,000 is a threshold beyond which further increases in income no longer improve individuals' ability to do what matters most to their emotional well-being, such as spending time with people they like, avoiding pain and disease, and enjoying leisure.[47]

Others have since found a similar result for happiness and for life satisfaction using data for countries from around the world.[48]

Average happiness within countries over time: Easterlin also examined how average happiness changed over time within a country. Figure 4.4 is an example illustrating his central finding. It shows measures of satisfaction with life in Japan between 1958 and 2013. Per capita GDP was more than five times higher in 2013 than in 1958, yet life satisfaction seems virtually unchanged. Easterlin has given a similar example for the United States, where surveys of happiness go back to 1946 – again, no upward trend despite much greater material affluence.[49]

More recently, Easterlin and co-authors examined results of surveys of subjective well-being in China conducted between 1990 and 2012. GDP per capita was more than seven times higher in 2012 than it was in 1990.[50] Yet as the economy grew rapidly, life satisfaction fell until the early 2000's when it rose back close to its 1990 level by 2012. They attribute the decline in life satisfaction and its recovery to movements in unemployment and changes in the social safety net.[51]

Some have challenged Easterlin's contention. For example, Betsy Stevenson and Justin Wolfers carefully re-examined the data for Japan shown in Figure 4.4, showing that for the separate survey questions asked

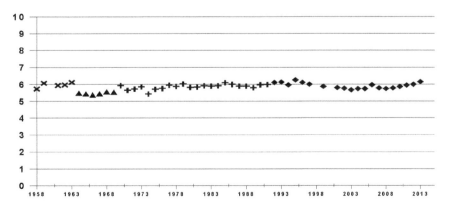

Figure 4.4 Satisfaction with life, Japan, 1958-2013
Source: Veenhoven (2020).

(indicated by different markers in the Figure) life satisfaction was positively related to GDP per capita if changes in unemployment were also taken into account.[52] Not everyone was convinced that they had refuted Easterlin's general claim.[53] Easterlin himself contended that their results showed what was already known – well-being fluctuates in the short term with the state of the economy – whereas his claim was about the long-term relationship.

For now, let's heed the words of Richard Layard: 'the most we can say is that economic growth is no guarantee of increased happiness. We should surely welcome it, but only as one of a whole range of ways to make the world happier. We should certainly not sacrifice too much else in the pursuit of higher income. And this is what seems to be happening.'[54]

The 'Easterlin Paradox' The evidence we have reviewed has paradoxical features. At any time within a country, higher-income persons have a higher level of subjective well-being on average (perhaps up to a point.) So shouldn't higher average incomes be associated with a similar increase in average subjective well-being? Yet it is possible that there is no significant positive relationship between average income and average subjective well-being for a country as a whole over long periods of time, even when incomes have grown substantially. This puzzle has been dubbed the 'Easterlin Paradox'.

Easterlin's own explanation is straightforward: people evaluate their well-being using a standard or norm based on the social conditions they experience. If material conditions improve, the social norm changes with it. As a result, on average people feel no improvement in their well-being. Norms and aspirations rise to cancel out the effects of higher real incomes and consumption. People don't seem to realize that a gradual rise in norms will take place. Instead, they believe that they'll be happier in the future with higher incomes than they really turn out to be.[55] This is perfectly consistent with higher-income individuals reporting themselves happier or more satisfied than lower-income individuals at any particular time.

Easterlin suggests a simple thought experiment: 'Imagine that your income increases substantially while everyone else's stays the same. Would you feel better off?' Of course you would. 'Now, suppose that your income stays the same while everyone else's increases substantially. How would you feel?' He asserts that most people would feel less well off than they did before.[56]

The Easterlin Paradox is also consistent with the idea that people adapt to changes in income. More income may initially give a feeling of greater wellbeing, but it wears off because we judge our circumstances relative to our own recent experience. This is a familiar concept in psychology because our senses exhibit this feature. What feels like a warm day in winter would seem like a chilly one in the summer, even if the temperature is the same on both days.[57]

Another factor that might contribute to the Easterlin Paradox is that consuming commodities takes time – a scarce commodity. Yet in the textbooks, as the Swedish economist Staffan Linder pointed out long ago, 'consumption is regarded as some sort of instantaneous act'.[58] Growing material affluence means greater access to goods, but with no greater time in which to consume them the scarcity of time increases. Linder predicted 'an increasingly hectic tempo of life', less 'time devoted to the cultivation of mind and spirit' and an increase in ultimately unsatisfying materialism.[59] While textbook economics remains blind to this issue, some people, such as those experimenting with 'simple living' and 'voluntary simplicity', are seeking ways out of the dilemmas that Linder identified.

> Question for your professor: What does the evidence
> say about whether economic growth and higher average
> incomes in a country increases feelings of well-
> being, on average?

What really matters? While happiness, however measured, doesn't vary much with incomes, it does vary a lot across the population. There is a lot of inequality in happiness levels. For example, in the British population the happiest 10 percent have an average of 9.4 on a scale of 0–10, while the least happy 10 percent average only 3.8.[60] What explains such differences in subjective well-being?

Health, both mental and physical, is very important, as are the quality of family and work life. Being unemployed has a large negative effect separate from its effect on income alone.[61] Also important are social connections, doing things for other people, having the freedom to choose what to do with your life, and whether or not you perceive widespread corruption in business and government, which indicates something of the level of trust in society and its institutions.[62]

The average values of people's responses to survey questions about these factors – social supports, generosity, freedom, absence of corruption– are important indicators of a country's social environment. Along with GDP per capita and estimates of healthy life expectancy, these explain (statistically speaking) three quarters of the variation in average happiness between countries.[63]

Figure 4.5 shows data on average national happiness from Gallup World Polls. Participants assess their lives by answering a question like: "Imagine a ladder with steps numbered from 0 to 10, where the top represents the best possible life for you and the bottom of the ladder represents the worst possible life. Where on the ladder do you feel you personally stand at the present time?" The figure shows average responses for each of 152 countries compared with their GDP per capita.[64]

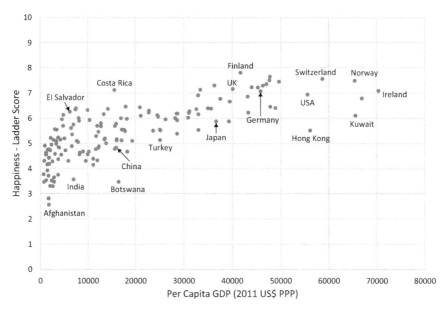

Figure 4.5 World happiness, 2017–2019

Source: Helliwell et al. (2020), Figure 2.1, data available at worldhappiness.report/ed/2020.

It's apparent from Figure 4.5 that increasing GDP per capita increases average happiness, but the relationship is relatively small. A doubling of GDP per capita increases average happiness by just over 0.2 on the scale of 0 to 10. The effect is the same if it rises from $5,000 to $10,000 or from $20,000 to $40,000. So, as average incomes increase, and extra $1000 increases happiness by decreasing amounts.

At any given level of per-person GDP, happiness varies considerably – compare Costa Rica with Botswana, or Norway with Kuwait, so other things besides income must be responsible. The presence of social supports are very important; average happiness would rise by about 2.3 points if everyone in a country had a friend or relative that they could rely on in a time of need, compared with no one having such support. Freedom to make life choices (as opposed to its absence) raises average happiness by about 1.2 points. Generosity, measured by making charitable donations, would raise happiness by 0.7 (compared with no one doing so). If everyone perceives widespread corruption, in part reflecting levels of trust in the society, happiness falls by 0.6 compared with the absence of corruption.

Such studies of happiness, both in individual countries and between countries, illuminate what really matters to people. The standard textbook story overstates the importance of greater material consumption, particularly in already affluent countries. At the same time, it completely ignores the importance of health, social connections and supports, the quality and security of work, and important characteristics of social and civic life. Many of these can be influenced by economic policy.

Measures such as happiness and life satisfaction are surely components of what is meant by 'utility', but they are not the whole story. As Angus Deaton put it, '[p]eople may adapt to misery and hardship, and cease to see it for what it is. People do not necessarily perceive the constraints caused by their lack of freedom; the child who is potentially a great musician but never had a chance to find out will not express a lack of life satisfaction'.[65]

Objective measures, such as the actual freedoms and capabilities that people have, address such concerns. This is an approach that has long been advocated by the Indian economist Amartya Sen. Rather than focusing on high or growing incomes, which are not ends in themselves, it proposes goals such as a long and healthy life, political freedoms, freedom to exchange goods and labour with others, and the ability to participate in social life.[66] These things are also important in determining happiness so, to some extent, these approaches complement each other.

2.5 Summing up

The decisions about what and how much to buy are central to the textbook account of how markets work. The textbooks describe consumers who save and spend optimally to maximize their well-being. Yet a careful look reveals just how limited its range of applicability really is. It would work nicely for Robinson Crusoe, living in isolation on an island and trying to decide whether to have a banana or a coconut for breakfast. But when applied to the world in which we live, its assumptions about preferences and information and its omission of social context raise serious problems.

It's obvious that the perfect-information model of rational consumer choice is not realistic. The important question is whether the model describes and explains consumer behaviour in a useful way.

Given the systematic ways in which consumers' tastes and information are shaped by producer power and by the social environment around them, the textbook model is a poor guide. It suggests that any voluntary purchase must leave buyers better off. Yet people do not benefit from consuming things they would not want if they had accurate information about their characteristics. Businesses can often make it hard for consumers to obtain relevant information. This is only one aspect of the disproportionate power of business organizations in society.

The texts ignore the fact that the utility people get from buying more stuff depends on how quickly they get used to having it and also on what other people have. Blinding students to these psychological and social realities makes critiques of consumerism almost impossible to understand. It also gives students the impression that economic growth is more important for the well-being of the population than actually seems to be the case. If economics is about finding the institutions that promote 'the greatest happiness for the people', as Richard Layard wrote, then this narrow approach to utility/happiness needs to be abandoned.

SUGGESTIONS FOR FURTHER READING

The cycle of working and spending and how we might escape it is the subject of Robert and Edward Skidelsky's thoughtful book *How Much is Enough? The Love of Money, and the Case for the Good Life*. The same theme has animated the research of American economist Juliet Schor, whose classic *Born to Buy: The Commercialized Child and the New Consumer Culture* is highly recommended. Her 2011 book *True Wealth: How and Why Millions of Americans Are Creating a Time-Rich, Ecologically Light, Small-Scale, High-Satisfaction Economy* reports on grassroots movements in the United States attempting to escape consumerism while living in a more sustainable way.

There are now many books and documentaries on the sad state of the modern industrial food system. British investigative reporter Felicity Lawrence's book *Not On the Label: What Really Goes into the Food on Your Plate* remains a standout.

The study of subjective well-being has assumed a prominent place in economics research, even if it is ignored in the textbooks. The annual *World Happiness Report* contains the latest research and is available at worldhappiness.report/. Richard Layard, one of its editors, has co-authored *Can We Be Happier? Evidence and Ethics*, summarizing the current state of knowledge and how it might be applied to improve people's well-being.

Advanced undergraduates will be able to appreciate the critique of consumer theory in Part 1 of Yanis Varoufakis's *Foundations of Economics* as well as Chapter 2 of Ben Fine's *Microeconomics: A Critical Companion*.

Chapter 5

THE FIRM

'[with] the great concentrations of power in the multinational corporations ... the text books are still illustrated with U shaped curves showing the limitation on the size of the firms in a perfectly competitive market.' Joan Robinson[1]

I THE STANDARD TEXT

The business firm is an organization within which factors of production – workers, capital (buildings, machinery, equipment and so on) and land – are used with inputs purchased from other firms (raw materials, parts, security services, for example) to produce goods and services for sale. The organization can have different legal forms: a sole proprietorship, a partnership, a cooperative or a corporation.

Although non-profit firms (such as universities) are not uncommon, the firm's goal is assumed to be profit maximization. More precisely, this is the maximization of the present discounted value of the profits it will earn now and into the future.

1.1 Production

The firm's managers (who may or may not be its owners) make decisions about such things as how much to produce, how they will produce it and what prices to charge. To do this, they have to know the 'technology' of production available to them. 'Technology' just describes how inputs produce outputs. So a peasant weeding a field with a hoe is a possible technology for producing a crop.

Let's consider the example of a firm that produces loaves of bread using 'labour' (workers, all identical in skills and effort) and 'capital' (all the things such as ovens, buildings and so on that workers use to make loaves of bread). Table 5.1 summarizes the 'production function', which relates input use to different rates of bread production.

Table 5.1 Inputs and output in the short run (with 10 units of capital)

Units of labour	Output or total product	Marginal product
	(dozens of loaves per day)	(dozens of additional loaves per day)
0	0	-
1	3	3
2	8	5
3	16	8
4	20	4
5	22	2
6	22	0

Some inputs can be more quickly and easily changed than others. For example, managers can more easily hire or lay off a worker than build a new building. In our simple two-factor setting, this amounts to saying that capital is effectively fixed for a time, so managers have only choices about varying labour if they want to change production. The period of time during which they face such decisions is 'the short run'. In Table 5.1, the firm is using ten units of capital to produce bread. The first two columns show how bread output (or total product) varies with labour input. The third column, labelled 'Marginal product', shows how output changes as one more worker is hired. (Units of labour are workers per day. Units of output are dozens of loaves of bread.)

The third column illustrates the law of diminishing marginal returns. This shows that increasing the use of any one input, holding all other inputs fixed, eventually reduces the marginal product. This is just a claim about an empirical regularity that economists believe so strongly they label it a 'law'.

The law of diminishing returns does not rule out an initial period of increasing marginal returns. Thus, in column three, the marginal product of the second worker is five dozen loaves of bread, greater than the three dozen of the first worker. Increasing marginal returns occur because, as more workers are used, complicated tasks involved in bread making can be broken up into a series of simple tasks in which workers specialize. This is the idea of the 'division of labour', a concept emphasized by Adam Smith. But once the benefits from the division of labour are exhausted, diminishing marginal returns set in. If they did not, it would be possible to bake all of the world's bread in this one bakery by adding more and more labour inputs. Marginal productivity of labour must eventually diminish because of the fixed amounts of other inputs it has to work with. While workers can use more flour and yeast (intermediate inputs purchased from other firms) to make more bread, there are only so many dough mixing machines and ovens to use. Figure 5.1 sketches out these general ideas.

The law of diminishing returns determines the shape of all the product curves: marginal, total and average. The marginal product must be an inverted

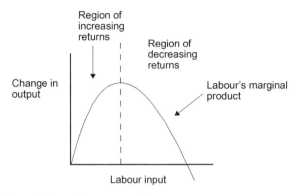

Figure 5.1 The law of diminishing marginal returns

'U' shape as diminishing returns set in. The total product can be derived from the marginal by summing the contribution of each unit of labour. The average product could be derived from the total product by dividing it by the labour input.

1.2 Costs of production in the short run

We can derive the costs of bread production by using the data in Table 5.1 along with information about the costs of labour and capital. Let's suppose that fixed costs (i.e. costs unrelated to the rate of production) are $250/day, and labour costs $150/day. Table 5.2 shows the results (for which a cup of strong coffee would be a useful accompaniment).

Column (1) contains the output data from Table 5.1. Column (2) assumes a fixed cost of $250. Column (3) shows total variable cost, which is $150 times the number of workers hired. Column (4) is total cost, which is the sum of fixed and variable costs.

Table 5.2 Costs in the short run ($)

(1) Total output	(2) Total fixed cost	(3) Total variable cost	(4) Total cost	(5) Average fixed cost	(6) Average variable cost	(7) Average total cost	(8) Marginal cost
0	250	0	250	∞	∞	∞	
3	250	150	400	83.3	50.0	133.3	50
8	250	300	550	31.3	37.5	68.8	30
16	250	450	700	15.6	28.13	43.8	18.8
20	250	600	850	12.5	30	42.5	37.5
22	250	750	1,000	11.4	34.1	45.4	75
22	250	900	1,150	11.4	40.9	56.8	∞

Note: Calculated using Table 5.1, assuming capital costs $250/day and labour costs $150/day.

The next three columns show average costs (average fixed costs, average variable costs and average total costs), obtained by dividing the appropriate 'total' column by output. Note that average fixed cost declines continually as more is produced. Average variable cost falls at first, but later increases as diminishing marginal returns set in. Average total cost falls quite rapidly at first, owing to the rapidly falling average fixed costs and the falling average variable costs. But as the fall in average fixed costs moderates and average variable costs begin to increase, eventually average total costs increase. Like average variable costs, average total costs are U-shaped.

The final column shows the cost of producing additional output, or marginal cost. When the first worker is hired, variable costs rise by $150 and three dozen loaves of bread are made, so their marginal cost is $150/3, or $50 per dozen loaves. We really want the extra cost of producing one more unit of output, but output jumps from zero to three as the firm hires one unit of labour. So, dividing by three units of output gives us an approximation: the average of the marginal costs as we increase output from zero to three.

When the second worker is hired, costs go up by $150 again, and the bakery makes five dozen more loaves. Their marginal cost is $150/5 or $30 per dozen loaves. The marginal cost of bread falls initially, reflecting increasing marginal returns, but increases later as diminishing marginal returns set in.

Figure 5.2 sketches out these short-run average and marginal costs. (The marginal cost in the numerical example rose in steps as an additional worker was hired for a day; if the firm can hire labour for any length of time it wants, the marginal cost line becomes smooth.)

Note the central importance of the law of diminishing returns; it determines the shape of all the cost curves: marginal, average and total. If marginal productivity rises as additional workers are added, the marginal cost of bread falls. When diminishing returns begin and marginal productivity falls, marginal cost begins to rise. (Compare Tables 5.1 and 5.2 when the fourth worker is hired.)

To maximize profits, the firm's managers apply the rational-choice logic of marginal benefit equals marginal cost that we saw in Chapter 1. In this case, consider a perfectly competitive bakery that faces a 'market price' for bread.

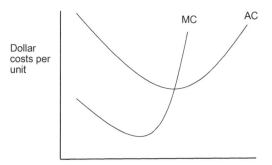

Figure 5.2 Marginal and average costs

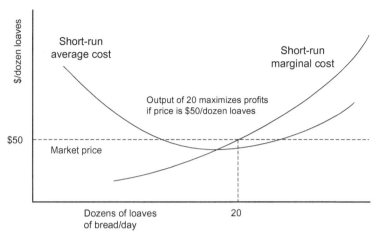

Figure 5.3 Marginal benefit and market price

The marginal benefit of selling a dozen loaves of bread is the market price of (let's say) $50. This is shown in Figure 5.3 as a horizontal line. The firm maximizes profits when the extra revenue from making and selling a dozen loaves of bread just equals the extra costs incurred.

Using the data from Table 5.2, let's suppose that the twentieth unit of output has a marginal cost of just $50 per dozen loaves. (Recall that $37.50 is the average of the rising marginal costs between units sixteen and twenty.) To produce more than that involves a marginal cost greater than $50, which would reduce total profits. The difference between price and average cost, $7.50 (i.e. $50 – $42.50), is profit per dozen loaves of bread; total profits are a princely $150. Using Table 5.1, we can see that in the short run the bakery will hire four workers.

1.3 Production and costs in the long run

In the short run, the firm could not vary all its inputs. But in the 'long run' it can. This varies the 'scale' of the firm's activities. If, for example, the firm doubled the inputs it used, production must rise, but in what proportion?

Economists classify the possible outcomes into three categories. The first is 'constant returns to scale': output changes in the same proportion as inputs. It's easy to imagine a simple example: the firm could have two identical bakeries producing twice as much bread as the bakery in the earlier example.

The second category is 'increasing returns to scale'. As the name suggests, output rises in greater proportion than the change in inputs. Doubling capital and labour inputs more than doubles bread production. There are many reasons for economies of scale. One of the most obvious is that greater scale permits greater division of labour and more specialized capital equipment.

The third category is 'decreasing returns to scale', or 'diseconomies of scale', in which output rises by a smaller proportion than the increase in inputs.

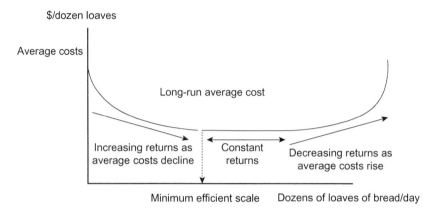

Figure 5.4 Long-run average cost

This could be due to problems experienced by management in coordinating production activities as the firm gets large.

The nature of a particular firm's returns to scale is important in describing its long-run costs, and this, in turn, ends up determining how many businesses can survive and coexist in a particular market.

At least initially, firms typically experience increasing returns to scale; doubling inputs doubles costs, but more than doubles output. Average costs must be declining as production increases. (We assume that the firm hires inputs at constant market prices, so that hiring more labour doesn't raise wages, for example.) This is seen in the left-hand part of Figure 5.4.

When increasing returns to scale end, the firm has attained the lowest average cost that is possible with current technology and input prices. This output rate is called the 'minimum efficient scale'. At that point, the firm could replicate its activities and expand at constant average cost. However, these constant costs eventually come to an end when the firm begins to experience decreasing returns to scale. Long-run average costs begin to increase, giving the long run average cost curve its U-shape.

1.4 Profit maximization for perfectly and imperfectly competitive firms

Figure 5.5 shows the profit-maximizing output in the long run in the case of the perfectly competitive firm, which takes the market price as given. Using the usual profit-maximizing logic, the firm produces output up to the point where its long-run marginal cost equals its marginal revenue, in this case the market price. In the situation illustrated, the firm is just covering all of its costs. (Chapter 6 explains how the assumption of easy entry of firms into the industry ensures this outcome occurs in perfectly competitive industries.)

The alternative case is that of the price-setting firm, rather than the price-taking firm. These are the firms that appear in all other markets other than

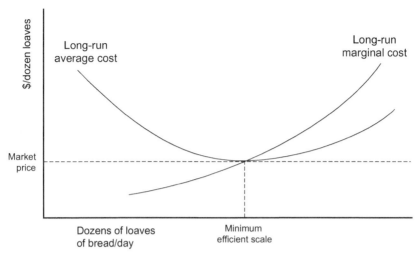

Figure 5.5 The long-run equilibrium for the competitive firm

Table 5.3 Downward-sloping demand and marginal revenue

| The demand curve | | Total revenue | Marginal revenue per |
Price ($)	Quantity	($)	additional loaf ($)
10	100	1000	–
9	200	1800	8
8	300	2400	6
7	400	2800	4

the perfectly competitive one. (These markets are examined in the next chapter.) Such a non-competitive firm has a choice of prices, as described by the demand curve for its product. In this case, marginal revenue is not the market price. Table 5.3 gives an example.

The first two columns show four points on a downward-sloping demand curve facing the firm. The third column is total revenue (price times quantity sold). The fourth column shows marginal revenue: how the firm's revenue changes as it lowers its price to sell more. (As in Table 5.2, marginal revenue is expressed as the additional revenue per loaf. If the price is lowered by $1 to sell 100 more loaves and total revenues rise by $800, the marginal revenue per loaf is $8.) Comparing Columns 1 and 4, we see that marginal revenue is consistently less than price. To sell one more unit the firm decreases its price *not just on the last unit, but on all the output that it previously sold at the higher price.*

Figure 5.6 shows the general relationship between demand and marginal revenue. Just like the competitive firm, the non-competitive firm maximizes profits by producing output where marginal revenue equals marginal cost. Once the quantity is determined in this way, the demand curve determines the price, at $7 per loaf in this case.

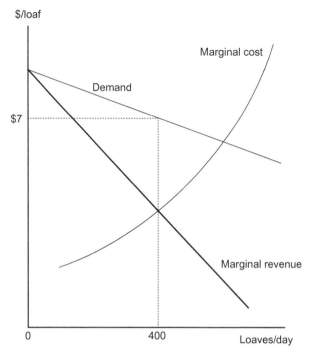

Figure 5.6 Relationship between demand and marginal revenue

Implications for market structure Given consumer demand for the good, the number of firms in the industry (the 'market structure') depends on the typical firm's minimum efficient scale (MES) compared with demand. If demand is large relative to MES, there is room for many firms. If economies of scale persist over a wide range of output, there may be room for only a few firms, or perhaps just one.[2]

2 THE ANTI-TEXT

The textbook firm is a strange thing, sketched out with thought experiments and invented data of the sort we used in the previous Standard Text section. The supposed objective of the firm itself – profit maximization – is not based on evidence of firms' actual behaviour but is chosen for analytical convenience. We consider alternative perspectives.

   While the textbooks keep students focused on technical details and elaborate diagrams, some important features of the firm are ignored entirely or are so taken for granted that they're invisible. In standard theory, firms maximize profits by comparing the extra revenues they get by producing more goods or services with the costs of the inputs needed to produce them. But many firms also find it profitable to incur costs to influence their external environment. These activities are a visible aspect of the political power of business and are the subject of the second section.

Power within the firm is unmentioned too. The firm remains a 'black box', its internal structure ignored. We'll peek inside the black box in the third section.

Although the texts focus most of their attention on the relationships between inputs and outputs and between outputs and costs, they offer no empirical evidence. The fourth section shows how the evidence contradicts the textbook story. We conclude with a look at alternative ideas and evidence about how firms actually set prices.

2.1 Profit maximization re-considered

> 'The directors of such companies, however, being the managers rather of other people's money than that of their own, it cannot well be expected, that they should watch over it with the same anxious vigilance with which the partners in a private copartnery frequently watch over their own. ... Negligence and profusion, therefore, must always prevail, more or less, in the management of the affairs of such a company.' Adam Smith[3]

The textbooks assume or assert that firms are managed to maximize profit. Some obvious exceptions, such as nonprofit firms, are sometimes noted and then ignored. At the other end of the ideological spectrum, Marxian economics also assumes that capitalist firms seek to maximize profits. So, both the neoclassical and Marxian models claim to be universally applicable across time and space. The two schools reinforce each other on this assumption and help to normalize it.

Just in terms of numbers, most businesses are proprietorships with a single owner or partnerships. While making an economic profit (as opposed to simply covering all opportunity costs) may be a goal, why shouldn't we expect owners to try to maximize their utility? Utility could depend on profits, but also on other things such as leisure and lifestyle. As Emily Northrop also points out, 'profit might be willingly sacrificed to provide more generous wages and benefits for employees, to allow production processes that are more environmentally sustainable, or to provide monetary or in-kind support for community charities'.[4] The same could be said for family-owned private corporations. Let's then focus on publicly traded corporations.

Inside the black box of the firm The textbooks treat the firm as if it is a single unit that operates with a clearly defined purpose. But a large corporation consists of many different kinds of actors: the owners or stockholders, boards of directors who are supposed to oversee the management on behalf of the stockholders, different layers of management and a complex workforce, possibly spread over many locations and many countries. Even if the stockholders were solely concerned about maximizing profits, they may well have difficulty getting managers to do what they want. Managers, in turn, may have difficulty getting workers to work as hard as they can.

The imbalance of power between owner-shareholders and their board of directors on the one hand, and the managers the board appoints on the other, has been recognized for a long time, as shown by the earlier quotation from Adam Smith. Texts treat profit maximization as the firm's only goal, but there is room for managers to have their own objectives. This is an example of the agency or principal-agent problem, studied by economists in recent decades. The principals (usually shareholders) elect their agents (the board of directors) who appoint managers (the agents of both shareholders and the board) whose assignment is (assumed to be) profit maximization.

However, managers have better information than do shareholders and their board about the firm's true performance and the nature of their own efforts. Although outside observers such as auditors, bond-rating agencies and analysts for brokerage firms are supposed to help oversee management, they suffer from imperfect and asymmetric information too. As well, scandals in recent decades have revealed the potential for conflicts of interest and corruption.[5]

The second difficulty is shareholder-voters' lack of incentive to inform themselves, particularly if none have a significant block of shares. Top management may gain effective control of the firm, aided by the considerable influence managers exert over boards of directors.

The plundering of shareholder assets by managers has become hard to overlook. In their study *Pay without Performance*, Harvard Law School professors Lucian Bebchuk and Jesse Fried argue that '[t]he pervasive role of managerial power can explain much of the contemporary landscape of executive compensation'.[6] (We examine the bloated pay of senior corporate executives in Chapter 8.) When these informational problems are considered, the claim that the firm's managers simply maximize the firm's value (i.e. the present value of expected profits) is not very convincing.[7]

Alternatives to profit maximization A more plausible description of management's goals was sketched out by John Kenneth Galbraith in the 1970s:

> there must be a relatively high threshold level of profits to keep the stockholders and creditors quiet, ... to avoid takeovers, to minimize recourse to banks, to secure the autonomy of management and the technostructure [his term for the corporate bureaucracy]. In addition, an increase in the profit level from year to year remains an important test of the efficacy of the management and the technostructure ... an important justification for their continued autonomy, power and independence.[8]

In his landmark book *The Visible Hand*, business historian Alfred Chandler agrees, proposing that growth and stability are the main goals of the managers who run firms.[9]

Post-Keynesian economic theory also rejects the assumption of profit maximization. Unlike the textbook neoclassical approach, post-Keynesians see firms operating in an environment of *fundamental uncertainty*. For example, if a firm makes an investment in plant and equipment, the resulting profits or losses cannot be described as a set of possible outcomes with known values, with each outcome having a probability. (For example, a profit of 100 with a probability of 0.9 and a profit of 10 with a probability of 0.1, gives an 'expected profit' of 91). Instead, the values of the possible outcomes are unknown, and no probabilities can be attached to them.[10]

In such an environment, a firm's ultimate goal is to reduce the uncertainty that it faces by acquiring power over its economic, political and social environment. This will improve its chances of survival in the long-term. Pursuing growth helps to attain that objective. In turn, profits contribute to growth by providing funds for investment and facilitating access to credit. However, the firm consciously sacrifices some profit to achieve greater growth.[11]

There is also some empirical evidence that firms do not maximize profits. Figure 5.6 shows that where profits are maximized, marginal revenue equals marginal cost. Except for the rare instances where marginal cost is zero, this implies that marginal revenue must be positive. But Marc Lavoie notes that estimates of the demand facing individual firms suggest that marginal revenue is often zero or negative![12] He also cites the survey by a team led by Princeton economist Alan Blinder of 200 large American firms.[13] They found this same result for marginal revenue for more than 80 percent of the firms in their survey. This implies that prices are lower and sales are higher than would be compatible with profit maximization.

What do firms' managers themselves have to say about their goals? Survey results, reviewed by Blinder's team, provide mixed evidence: profit maximization, target rate of return, and maintaining market share, among other things.[14] But on the rare occasion that such evidence of goals other than profit maximization are acknowledged in a textbook, it is brushed aside with the assertion that these are simply a means to the ultimate goal of maximizing profits.

What is the origin of the dogma of profit maximization? Northrop points out that the concept originated with the 19 century French economist Augustin Cournot, who pioneered the application of calculus to the problem. His assumption of profit maximization was required for the mathematics and was not based on any observation of how firms actually behaved. That approach has been maintained to the present day, with the account in the introductory texts using words and diagrams in place of calculus.[15]

Citing Adam Smith, Northrop explains that prior to Cournot businesses were viewed as seeking profit, but not necessarily to the exclusion of other goals. Indeed, she remarks that Smith wrote disapprovingly of the 'mean rapacity' of those 'merchants and manufacturers' who went so far as to try to keep imports out of the domestic market. She contrasts such ruthless profit-maximizing behaviour with the benign profit-seeking motives of Smith's example of the butcher, brewer, and baker that we mentioned in Chapter 1.

What about 'corporate social responsibility'? Real firms can have a variety of possible goals, including *profit-making* but not necessarily *profit maximizing*. The firm's managers could voluntarily refrain from actions that might be legal but could be viewed as socially irresponsible. Such socially responsible behaviour could come from the owner/managers own beliefs or it could be a response to ethical views shared with workers, customers, or communities.

For example, the emission of harmful pollutants into the air or water could be reduced below what is required by regulation, although it raises the firm's costs. If this reduces profits, any additional benefits (enhanced reputation, for example) would not offset the increased costs but would still be rational if we assume choices which involve considerations beyond just profit.

In a famous essay, Milton Friedman condemned the idea for ethical reasons. If shareholders desired maximum profits, which he presumed was the case, managers would be spending shareholders' money without their consent. Managers should see that the firm obeys the law and does not violate ethical custom, but no more.[16] This is a more restrained version of profit maximization than the 'mean rapacity' of corporate criminals (of which there is, unfortunately, no shortage), who view fines as just a cost of doing business.

However, Friedman would have no objection if the corporation were explicitly established to pursue more than one goal. For example, some corporations have adopted a 'Triple Bottom Line', pursuing a balance between financial, social, and environmental goals. Colander's text is exceptional in mentioning the existence of these 'for-benefit' firms, giving the Danish pharmaceutical company Novo Nordisk as an example.[17] As of 2020, more than 3,200 such firms have received independent certification of such behaviour.[18]

Nor should Friedman object if 'socially responsible' actions were done openly; shareholders would be free to choose whether to invest in such firms or not. In fact, many large firms voluntarily undertake independent certification of social and environmental standards.[19]

Most texts ignore the issue of corporate social responsibility completely, but those that mention it dismiss it for one of two reasons. Some assert that it is ineffective or impossible to carry out because of competitive pressures.[20] Alternatively, it is unnecessary *if* consumer-citizens are keeping a close eye on corporate behaviour and *if* governments are setting laws and regulations in the public interest.[21] (Those are big ifs.)

The texts also ignore Friedman's qualification that firms conform to the society's 'ethical custom'. It may be perfectly legal for a firm to use an intricate network of shell companies located in tax havens to avoid corporation income taxes, but does it violate ethical custom? Public anger at the exposure of such behaviour suggests that it does. By sweeping ethical considerations under the rug, the texts promote the acceptance of any behaviour that is not explicitly constrained by law, law that is itself influenced by corporate power, as we discuss below.

What can we conclude so far? There are good reasons to think that different firms can and likely do pursue different goals. The one-size-fits-all assumption of profit maximization is not convincing either theoretically or empirically. But the single-minded insistence on profit maximization raises the following question.

What effects might the emphasis on profit maximization have? In Chapter 1, we mentioned the evidence that studying economics, with its emphasis on Homo economicus, may influence students' outlooks by encouraging selfishness and discouraging cooperative behaviour. Israeli economist Ariel Rubinstein conducted surveys of economics students and people with other backgrounds. His survey explored attitudes about the trade-off between profit maximization and other possible objectives, like the interests of other stakeholders such as workers. Respondents were to imagine that they were a senior manager who had to 'decide whether to maximise the company's profits by laying off half its workforce or to make do with lower profits by firing less than that number'.[22] In this scenario, fired workers would have difficulty finding a job and a new job would likely have a lower wage.

The results? Economics students, whether undergraduate or graduate, were much more inclined to sacrifice workers' interests to maximize profits than were other students – even MBA students – and the general public. Rubinstein thinks that the mathematical way in which profit maximization is taught to economics students conceals the ethical complexity of the situation, neglecting the need to balance the interests of owners and workers.[23]

Indeed, firms whose managers fail to take the interests of their employees into account could pay a significant price. The resulting lack of trust in the workplace has a large impact on the subjective well-being of employees.[24] To the extent that competition in the labour market forces firms to compensate workers for the unpleasantness of their work, a reduction in trust could be expensive indeed.

Questions for your professor: The text assumes that *all* firms maximize profits, but why wouldn't the owners of private firms maximize their utility instead? For publicly owned corporations, doesn't the separation of shareholder ownership and managerial control give managers room to pursue their own objectives? Should firms pursue profit maximization to the exclusion of any other considerations?

2.2 Shaping the external environment: using power for profit

Austrian economist Kurt Rothschild made the following insightful observation about economic theory long ago:

> More or less homogeneous units – firms and households – move in more or less given technological and market conditions and try to improve their economic lot *within the constraints of those conditions* ... [But] people will use power to alter the mechanism itself; that uneven power may greatly influence the outcome of market operations; that people may strive for economic power as much as for economic wealth; these facts have been largely neglected.[25]

And indeed, textbook economics almost entirely ignores the power that some firms, particularly large ones, have to shape their external environment to their advantage. We've already seen examples in the previous chapter in thinking about the use of advertising and marketing to influence potential buyers of the firm's goods and services. But the power of business is most evident in its efforts to shape public policy. This touches on virtually every aspect of public affairs, including foreign and military policy, international trade policy, tax policy, environmental regulation, laws about intellectual property (such as patents and copyrights), transportation policy, subsidies to business, unemployment insurance, pensions and other social income supports, and product safety regulation.

More than a century ago, Thorstein Veblen wrote: 'Representative government means, chiefly, representation of business interests. The government commonly works in the interest of the business men with a fairly consistent singleness of purpose.'[26] Despite important advances in democracy in many countries since Veblen's time, his remark retains some relevance today.

'Think tanks' funded by corporations and foundations established by the very wealthy churn out policy papers guaranteed to reach the desired conclusions; they provide talking heads for television and opinion pieces for the newspapers. Capital cities swarm with business lobbyists. In Washington, a city consumer advocate Ralph Nader refers to as 'corporate occupied territory', registered lobbyists outnumber members of Congress by twenty-two to one and spend about $290 million a month to advance their clients' interests.[27]

Corporations can also influence policy in other ways. For example, the International Life Sciences Institute (ILSI), an organization established by a Coca-Cola executive in 1978 and funded, in part, by Coke, Nestlé, McDonalds, and PepsiCo has spent 20 years establishing itself as a major influence over public health policy in China. It did this by developing institutional, financial, and personal linkages that have resulted in ILSI establishing its office inside the Chinese Centre for Disease Control and Prevention, a branch of the health ministry. The worsening obesity epidemic – nearly one in five urban Chinese children are obese – has been met with industry-friendly policies emphasizing exercise.[28]

Why do the mainstream textbooks ignore this behaviour? After all, investments in influencing public policy are economic decisions just as much as the building of a new production facility or spending on research and development. Non-mainstream texts recognize this simple fact of life. As noted earlier, in his text on post-Keynesian economics, Marc Lavoie identifies power as the ultimate objective of the firm. That includes attempts to influence its legal and regulatory environment.[29]

Perhaps part of the blame for ignoring power can be put on the disciplinary division between economics and politics. But this division has been crumbling since the 1950s, ever since economists and political theorists began applying the framework of individual rational choice to politics. Despite its drawbacks (which we will examine in Chapter 9), that approach, called 'public choice', can help explain an apparent puzzle: how can the few dominate the many? How can a few hundred large corporations and business organizations wield such disproportionate influence in society? If the policies that business owners want are not in the interests of the majority of the population, why don't the citizens simply block them and institute the policies that they prefer? After all, they have democratic institutions at their disposal and corporations have no votes.

Explaining corporate power Before the development of public choice theory, it was often assumed that groups of people with common economic interests would act to further those interests just as a single person would act to further his or her interests, as the late American economist Mancur Olson remarked in introducing his path-breaking book *The Logic of Collective Action*.[30] As the title of the book suggests, he was trying to explain when groups of people would take collective action to promote their interests. By applying the logic of rational choice, the comparison of marginal benefit and marginal cost, Olson showed that some groups would find it much easier to act in their collective interest than others would.

Let's consider a simple example in which apple farmers have an interest in restricting competition from foreign apple growers. Would it pay an apple farmer to retain a lobbyist to persuade the government to limit imports of foreign apples? The answer is clearly 'no' for the same reason we saw in Chapter 4 that it didn't pay the farmer to pay for 'Eat Apples!' billboards. The cost to him would likely exceed the benefits even if he were successful.

© Andy Singer

If an association of apple farmers existed that could hire the lobbyist, the cost to the association might be less than the total benefits all apple farmers would get. But for such collective action to come about, the apple farmers would have to make a contribution to the association. Again, each would have an incentive not to pay and to 'free-ride' on the benefits it might produce (such as government measures to restrict imported apples). Olson predicted that because of this 'free rider problem', such organizations would either not exist or would be small and weak unless they could provide individual farmers with some private benefits they could not otherwise get (cheap crop insurance, for example).

Crucially, the free-rider problem is less severe for small groups. If a few firms account for most of the total production in an industry, they can more easily engage in collective action. The firms will act either together or individually to produce a collective good that benefits them all to some extent. As a result, '*there is a systematic tendency for "exploitation" of the great by the small*', wrote Olson.[31]

Olson explained that 'The high degree of organization of business interests, and the power of these business interests, must be due in large part to the fact that the business community is divided into a series of (generally oligopolistic) "industries", each of which contains only a fairly small number of firms'.[32]

The tobacco industry provides a good example. Cigarette production is dominated by just a few firms in many countries; worldwide five companies, led by British American Tobacco and Philip Morris, dominate the global market.[33]

The industry, whose products kill 6–7 million people annually, carries out extensive lobbying worldwide, with considerable success. It tightened its grip on Washington under Trump, with recipients of tobacco money having prominent positions in his administration.[34] With cigarette smoking on the decline in high income countries, the industry is trying to expand sales in developing countries, particularly Africa. A number of African countries have been pressured by companies to 'axe or dilute the kind of protections that have saved millions of lives in the west'.[35] Phillip Morris, one of the world's largest publicly traded tobacco companies, has been busy worldwide attempting to block or undermine provisions of the Framework Convention on Tobacco Control (FCTC), the first treaty negotiated under the World Health Organization. In effect from 2005, its goal is to reduce the demand for tobacco. (The United States and a handful of other countries, including Switzerland, have not yet ratified it. By coincidence, Phillip Morris International's operational headquarters is in Switzerland.) Phillip Morris lobbies delegates to biannual FCTC conferences where antismoking guidelines are developed, while trying to influence the composition of national delegations. Along with other tobacco companies, it is had significant success in delaying action and watering down the results of FCTC conferences.[36]

A favourite tactic of corporations and their lobbyists is to create front organizations and phoney 'grassroots' groups that appear to be representing hard-to-organize large groups.[37] The tobacco industry has spent millions supporting such organizations, alongside 'insurance, oil and gas, chemical and pharmaceutical companies, medical associations, and auto manufacturers'. The message of these organizations is 'a sly deception', equating 'the efforts of injured consumers to recover damages' with 'lawsuit abuse', according to the Centre for Justice & Democracy at the New York Law School.[38] Efforts to limit people's ability to sue (marketed in the United States as 'tort reform') can be a profitable investment for insurance companies and for businesses that produce products that harm or kill people.[39]

The tobacco companies and corporate propaganda (or 'public relations') firms have also been at the forefront in sponsoring front organizations that hang the label 'junk science' on scientific research detrimental to corporate interests. Fossil-fuel interests have taken up the 'junk science' crusade in fighting action on climate change. (Chapter 7 gives many other examples of effective collective action by business.)

The flip side of corporate power: public inaction and ignorance Public choice theory also explains why business interests are often able to organize to shape legislation to protect their profits at the expense of the vast majority of the population. For example, the millions of American buyers of overpriced health insurance and pharmaceutical drugs find it difficult to respond to defend their interests with anything like the resources deployed by industry. Despite the supposed power of numbers and of the ballot box, they tend to fall victim to the free-rider problem in two ways. Becoming informed and acting on that information may not seem worth the trouble.

As in the earlier example with the apple farmers, if each person compares the costs of political action with the likely benefits, they may not act. Writing to their elected representatives or contributing to a public interest group may seem like a waste of time and money. The individual bears all the costs of his or her contribution (which may seem too small to make a difference), while the benefits (if any) largely go to others. It's tempting to free-ride and leave the organizing up to someone else.

There are many large groups in society that might have a similar problem organizing to further their collective interests, even where the total benefits to the group would exceed the costs of acting. For example, taxpayers, the unemployed and poor people face difficulties in forming groups to work together effectively. Of course, some such organizations, such as consumer groups, do exist. The theory simply predicts that they will likely be much smaller and less powerful than they would be if people could somehow overcome the free-rider problem.

It often does not pay the individual member of a large group to know the facts about the issues. In public choice theory, this is called 'rational ignorance'. Information about public policy is not free, and what are the benefits? As a citizen, you can know your interests and thus decide what causes to support. But if you're not going to act (as we've just discussed), becoming informed would be a waste of time. As a voter, you can cast a more informed vote, but your vote will likely have no effect on the outcome. A more informed vote provides benefits (if any) largely to others, just like any contribution to further the interests of a large group. It pays to 'free-ride', in this case on others' informed votes.

Nor can one expect the mass media to act as 'watchdogs' and hold politicians accountable on the public's behalf. The large corporations that control the media (outside of public broadcasting) have their own goals and taking on corporate power and companies that may be big advertisers is not among them. As Edward Herman and Noam Chomsky contend, one of the functions of the mass media is to 'inculcate and defend the economic, social and political agenda of privileged groups that dominate the domestic society and the state', and 'to fulfil this role requires systematic propaganda'.[40]

Claims about the rational ignorance and inaction of the public should not be taken too far or viewed as a cause for despair. If many people are already organized for other reasons – for example, into labour unions for collective bargaining – then those organizations can be used for collective action to counteract the power of big business. Social media, whatever its faults, has also lowered the costs of organizing groups of people with common interests.

We will examine the shortcomings of public choice theory in Chapter 9, but for now let's note that its individualistic assumption of narrow self-interest and the predictions of ignorance and inaction that follow from it are overly pessimistic. After all, many people inform themselves about public affairs instead of about the private life of Justin Bieber. They participate in community and national life in many ways, perhaps out of a sense of solidarity with others, or because they find pleasure in the activities themselves, or because they feel it is the right thing to do, perhaps influenced by social norms. We also have our emotions to make us act, something that cold-blooded rational choice theory ignores.[41] Injustice, whether to ourselves or to others, leads to indignation that, in turn, can lead to action.

Rational ignorance does not apply to businesses if there are substantial profits at stake. In capital cities, small armies of corporate lawyers and lobbyists work full time watching laws, regulations and public policy that might affect their clients' interests. Politicians will be under great pressure to look good to the voters, but to be good to big business.

American philosopher John Dewey once described politics as 'the shadow cast on society by big business'.[42] But the power of big business doesn't cast any shadows in economics textbooks.

```
Questions for your professor: If firms can make
investments to change public policy to increase
their profits, why does the text not discuss this?
Where does the text discuss the connection between
economic power and political power? If it doesn't,
is it sweeping the reality of corporate power under
the rug, and in whose interest?
```

2.3 Power and hierarchy within the firm

In the textbooks, not only does the firm exert no power in the outside world, there is also no power visibly exerted within the firm itself. Factors of production show up for work and output somehow gets produced, as described by the production function. The nature of the firm's ownership and its internal organization is implicitly assumed to be of no importance.

While everyone understands that 'political freedom' requires democratic political institutions, 'economic freedom' apparently doesn't require democratic economic institutions. It means only the freedom to buy and to sell with whomever you want, or 'the freedom to shop', in James Galbraith's sardonic phrase.[43]

The capitalist firm of the textbook is not democratic; it's authoritarian and hierarchical as a matter of principle. Self-employment aside, most workers have only the freedom of choosing 'which hierarchy to work in or which boss to work under', as Samuel Bowles and co-authors put it in their nonstandard text.[44]

Yet the presence or absence of democracy matters for firm behaviour. Managers would pursue different goals if they were elected by the workforce rather than appointed by a board of directors representing only shareholders. For example, managers in some industries knowingly expose their workers to hazards that lead to injury, illness or death rather than accept reduced profits. The workforce itself would choose differently if given the chance. Similarly, if demand for the firm's product falls, some workers may get laid off in the capitalist firm, but democratic firms seem to prefer to share the work and to avoid layoffs. Capitalist firms also invest in developing and refining techniques for maintaining hierarchy and control of the workforce; workers in democratic firms would invest in 'technologies, work methods, and forms of organization that promote the effective use of the firm's resources, including their own time and energy'.[45]

The idea of economic democracy is just an extension of the movement for greater democracy that's gone on for centuries. Nevertheless, as Samuel Bowles and co-authors explain:

> Texts that ignore the power that is exercised in corporations will find nothing in them to democratize. Moreover, the right of people to participate in a decision-making process, the outcome of which affects their entire community, is not considered to be a problem that falls within the purview of economics.[46]

Although standard textbooks mention no alternative to the status quo, the idea of workplace democracy has a long history in economic thought. In the mid-nineteenth century, John Stuart Mill wrote of the experiments with worker-managed firms in his *Principles of Political Economy*, the definitive textbook of that time, describing economic democracy as the way of the future.

> The form of association, however, which if mankind continue to improve, must be expected in the end to predominate, is not that which can exist with capitalist as chief, and workpeople without a voice in the management, but the association of the labourers themselves on terms of equality, collectively owning the capital with which they carry on their operations, and working under managers elected and removable by themselves.[47]

Democratic firms are not fictional constructs, like the perfectly competitive firm. Both consumer-owned and worker-owned cooperative firms exist in many countries and are important in some sectors of the economy. Yet they have virtually vanished from the textbooks.[48]

For worker cooperatives, there is evidence that worker productivity is higher than in comparable capitalist firms, in part because of better incentives. There is no principle-agent problem, because the workers are the owners.[49] The most famous worker cooperative is the Mondragón Corporation, centred in the Basque region of Spain. It developed from a single small co-op founded in 1956.[50] As of 2019, it consisted of about 100 cooperatives employing about 81,000 people. It is a prototype of a cooperative economy in which the primary, manufacturing, financial and service sectors form an interlinked network.[51]

But there are real barriers to the growth of democratic firms that leave them greatly outnumbered by capitalist firms. They have trouble raising financial capital from banks and worker-owners face significant risks by having to invest much of their wealth in the same business in which they also have their jobs. Being less willing to take risks, innovation in product design and production processes would suffer. This could result in higher costs that are not offset by benefits such as greater productivity. In contrast, capitalist firms are typically owned by wealthier individuals who can diversify their risks.[52]

It is curious, and revealing, that while the textbooks claim their subject is about choices between alternatives, no alternatives are discussed when it comes to the central institutions of economic life. The capitalist firm is the only game in town.

> Questions for your professor: Why does the textbook suppose that democracy must end at the workplace door? In whose interest is it that economic democracy remain off the agenda?

2.4 What do firms' costs actually look like?

The theory of production and cost is oriented towards the perfectly competitive firm, as Joan Robinson says in the epigraph at the beginning of this chapter. Unfortunately, both the stories about diminishing marginal returns in the short run and decreasing returns in the long run are contradicted by the evidence about production and costs. As we will see, acknowledging the evidence would leave no place for the perfectly competitive firm,

Costs in the short run: is the 'law' of diminishing marginal returns relevant?[53] The standard textbook story about production is remarkably sloppy about the distinction between the *stock* of factors employed (the number of workers, the number of machines, for example) and the *flow* of services that those factors provide (labour services per hour, machine hours). A proper description of production has flows of input services producing a flow of output.[54]

Mankiw's text offers a typical example of short run production that has a fixed stock of capital – a plant and equipment to make cookies – while the number of workers can be varied.[55] Output is described as a flow of 'cookies per hour'. A student could easily think that at each rate of production the capital input is the entire stock of capital, not the hourly services of those parts of the capital equipment that are being employed. Mankiw gives the standard story of diminishing returns: eventually additional hours of work in conjunction with the fixed capital stock produce less and less additional output.

This account implicitly assumes that in exchange for the wage each worker provides an hour of labour services of some constant quality. In their nonstandard text, Samuel Bowles and co-authors explain that 'every capitalist labor process necessarily combines both a social organization and a technology of production; these two elements shape, and are shaped by, the conflict between employers and employees over wages and the intensity and conditions of work.'[56] The standard text takes the social organization for granted and assumes that the conflict between employers and employees has somehow been settled. In doing so, it sweeps under the rug the power relations that are a central feature of real workplaces.

If production were described correctly, as flows of services producing flows of output, it is easy to imagine how diminishing returns could be postponed until production reached the maximum possible level, the plant's 'capacity'. Consider the bakery we described in the Standard Text. Suppose the bakery has some unused capital services held in reserve, in this case dough mixers and ovens that were unused or could be used for more hours per day. If the bakery uses more labour services alongside these additional capital services, it can produce more output. For example, the bakery might hire an extra shift of workers who would work the mixers and ovens for more hours.

An important feature of many manufacturing processes is that labour and capital services are used in fixed proportions.[57] A fixed number of worker-hours are required to operate a dough mixer for an hour, for example. Adding one more worker-hour would add nothing to output; removing one worker-hour reduces the time that the mixer can work. As output expands, there is no reason to expect diminishing returns. Additional bundles of labour hours and machine hours produce constant additional loaves of bread per hour.

As we saw in Chapter 3, all firms in the industry are assumed to be price takers in input markets, so hiring more labour hours does not raise the wage. Without diminishing marginal returns, marginal costs will be constant as output expands, at least until the capital stock is being used to maximum capacity. Beyond that point, it becomes, in effect, infinitely costly for the firm to produce any more output. The firm's marginal cost curve has the shape of a laterally inverted L, as shown in panel A of Figure 5.7. As American economist Richard Miller points out, this description of costs was first set out by Richard Kahn, a student of Keynes, in a dissertation at Cambridge in 1929![58] It is standard fare in the post-Keynesian approach to the firm and can be found in non-standard texts.[59]

What would be the implications of such marginal costs in the short run? The situation is illustrated in panel A of Figure 5.7, where marginal cost is $1 per loaf of bread at all levels of output up to the firm's capacity. At capacity, marginal cost becomes effectively infinite because the firm is unable to produce any more no matter how much it spends on additional variable inputs. If the market price is greater than the marginal cost, the firm will produce at capacity. If the price is less than marginal cost, the firm produces nothing. If the price just equals to marginal cost, output is indeterminate: the marginal revenue from producing an extra loaf of bread is $1 and the marginal cost is also $1 at any level of output. Whether it produces something or not, the firm has a loss equal to its fixed costs.

As Miller remarks in his analysis of the situation, 'most firms most of the time produce outputs between zero output and capacity output. A determinate solution in this range would require a negatively sloped demand curve', as in a modified version of Figure 5.6 where marginal cost is constant.[60] He recommends discarding the model of the perfectly competitive firm.[61]

Instead, the response has been to insist upon the assumption of diminishing marginal returns. This ensures that the firm's marginal costs rise in the short run, as we have seen.

But does the claim of rising short run marginal costs conform to the facts? A widely used intermediate-level text by the late Edwin Mansfield was unusual in offering a review of the evidence. He wrote that

> ... [an] interesting conclusion of the empirical studies is that marginal cost in the short run tends to be constant in the relevant output range. This result seems to be at variance with the theory presented earlier ..., which says that marginal cost curves should be U-shaped ... Although marginal costs may well be relatively constant over a wide range, it is inconceivable that they do not eventually increase with increases in output.[62]

And so the theory of upward-sloping marginal costs remained, despite the evidence.

More recently, the survey by Alan Blinder's team of 200 large American businesses, mentioned earlier, asked about marginal costs in the short run and reported 'overwhelmingly bad news here (for economic theory)': 48 per cent of firms reported constant marginal costs, 41 per cent claimed that marginal costs were decreasing, and only 11 per cent said they had increasing marginal costs.[63]

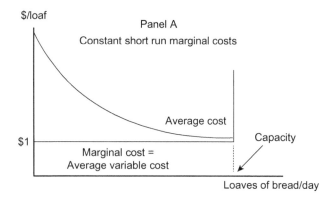

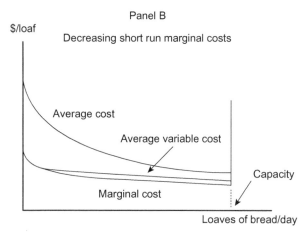

Figure 5.7 Short-run marginal costs

The arithmetic shows that if short-run marginal costs are constant, so are short-run average variable costs; average total costs decline because average fixed costs are falling, as we see in panel A of Figure 5.7. If short-run marginal costs are also declining, then average total costs decline even more rapidly, as shown in panel B of Figure 5.7. They conclude, 'While there are reasons to wonder whether respondents interpreted these questions about costs correctly, their answers paint an image of the cost structure of the typical firm that is very different from the one immortalized in the textbooks'.[64] After quoting this same sentence, Marc Lavoie remarks: 'Ironically, despite all this, when Baumol and Blinder present U-shaped cost curves based on the law of diminishing returns in their first-year textbook, they assert that "this so-called law rests simply on observed facts; economists did not deduce the relationships analytically" '![65]

But is the 'law' of diminishing marginal returns really wrong? After all, it only claims that the additional output produced by variable factors *eventually* diminishes. This can never be proven false. It can be defended, as Mansfield did, by saying that in particular cases we simply haven't reached the point where diminishing returns begin.

The point of the evidence we've cited is that the 'law' is apparently *not relevant* in most circumstances. In practice, the firm's production is constrained by the demand for its product. In such imperfectly competitive markets, examined in the next chapter, constant or decreasing marginal costs pose no theoretical problems.

Costs in the long run: are decreasing returns relevant? When we look at the evidence we find that the standard textbook theory about long-run costs fares no better than the short-run theory. Recall that a perfectly competitive market can exist only when each firm experiences decreasing returns at an output level that is small relative to the size of market demand. Then the firm's response to any rise in price would be constrained by rising long-run marginal costs (as shown in Figure 5.5). Increasing managerial costs in coordinating a larger scale of production or obtaining accurate information are the reasons typically given for this. As a result, any increase in demand in the market will, in the long run, be met by the entry of new firms and price remains the minimum of long-run average cost. (Chapter 6 explains the details.)

Piero Sraffa claimed that these convenient U-shaped cost curves didn't resemble the costs of actual businesses. He contended that business people 'would consider absurd' the textbook model's claim that it is rising costs which limit the expansion of a firm's production.[66] Instead, he claimed that average costs would typically be falling as output rose. What ultimately limits firms' production is limited demand for their product: a downward-sloping demand curve, in other words. The assumption in perfect competition that firms face a given market price 'differs radically from the actual state of things'. Sraffa's 1926 essay and the debate it sparked led, by the early 1930s, to work on theories of imperfect competition that we consider in the next chapter.

In his text, Edwin Mansfield also reviewed the evidence about long-run average costs and wrote that 'the long-run average cost function in most industries seems to be L-shaped ... not U-shaped. That is, there is *no evidence* that it turns upward, rather than remaining horizontal, at high output levels (in the range of observed data)'.[67] Figure 5.8 shows this; we see initially increasing returns and then constant returns. The key point here is that if firms don't experience decreasing returns, there's nothing to stop them growing large enough to be able to influence the market price, which is incompatible with a perfectly competitive market. Most introductory textbooks include one diagram like Figure 5.4, with a brief flat part conceding the possibility of constant returns but insisting upon eventual diseconomies of scale.[68] After this one brief cameo appearance, it is never seen again.

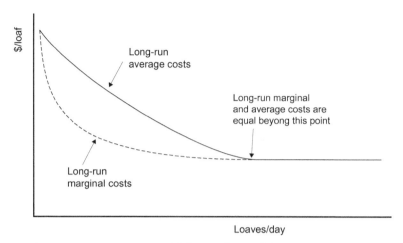

Figure 5.8 Long-run average cost with increasing and then constant returns

Incidentally, standard texts discuss long-run average costs in the context of a single production location or plant. Stories about economies of scale and the identification of the minimum efficient scale (see Figures 5.4 and 5.5) are about the optimum size of a *plant*, not the optimum size of the *firm*. But many firms produce the same product in different plants. It's easy to see how, by building more plants, firms could expand production at constant average costs in the long run.

The texts' justification for diseconomies of scale for the firm as a whole is typically a single line, with no evidence offered. 'The challenge of managing a large enterprise is the main source of diseconomies of scale', writes Michael Parkin.[69]

The textbook account seems to treat the attention of the entrepreneur or management as a kind of "fixed factor", bringing back the idea of diminishing marginal returns even in the long run, a period of time when all factors are supposed to be variable. As Avi Cohen points out, this 'does not stand up to even casual logical scrutiny, let alone to the empirical evidence on non-increasing costs'.[70] He adds: 'Just as there is a range of available techniques of production in the long run, we should expect a range of available techniques of management, including techniques better adapted to large scale enterprise', citing writers going back to the 1950s who show that 'there is no necessary reason why management cannot efficiently change or adapt to larger scale output'.

In his nonstandard text, Peter Dorman explains how this can be done. Corporations that produce a variety of products and services can construct managerial hierarchies for each product, or for each subsidiary, where managers in those areas operate with considerable autonomy. The very top management, which oversees the entire operation, act as planners, making strategic decisions, allocating resources in a general way between one area and another. This 'permits corporations to grow as large as they wish without overtaxing their operational management'.[71]

Theories with no empirical support live on The short-run and the long-run U-shaped average costs curves that inhabit the pages of the textbooks and which pose as typical cost curves are bogus constructions that owe their place to the desire to construct and justify a theory of perfect competition. They are not based on empirical evidence about actual costs. This sad state of affairs led Herbert Simon, a Nobel Memorial Prize recipient, to exclaim:

> I think the textbooks are a scandal.... The most widely used textbooks use the old long-run and short-run cost curves to illustrate the theory of the firm. I find that inexcusable. I don't really expect economists to purge their texts of these invalid theoretical elements, certainly not soon. But I don't know of any other science that purports to be talking about real world phenomena, where statements are regularly made that are blatantly contrary to fact.'[72]

As this is a chapter about firms, we could leave it at that, but this is a good spot to consider why this has happened, and why, as Simon says, it is likely to persist. It sheds some light on why the mainstream texts, which claim to respect empirical tests of theories, discard the evidence to protect the theory of perfect competition. Avi Cohen explains that the answer lies in what is seen as the even more unattractive nature of the alternative. If nothing limits the growth of the firm, 'the chaotic indeterminateness of oligopoly' (which we examine in the next chapter) replaces 'the elegant determinateness of perfect competition. An indeterminate theory serves little useful purpose'.[73]

As we sketched out in Chapter 2, a paradigm is not abandoned unless there is a more attractive one waiting to replace it. Since the 1930s, initially in response to Sraffa's critique of the competitive model, many economists have been working on potential alternative paradigms. Some of these have centred on models of imperfect competition. Since the 1970s, much work has been done exploring the implications of imperfect and asymmetric information. Joseph Stiglitz argues that 'information economics represents a fundamental change in the prevailing paradigm within economics'.[74] That may well be the case in terms of the cutting edge of economic theory, but it has not yet trickled down to the core of the undergraduate textbooks.

A paradigm's core theoretical framework is surrounded by what Imre Lakatos termed a 'protective belt' of 'auxiliary assumptions' to prevent it from refutation, as we described in Chapter 2. This is the role of the assumptions of diminishing marginal returns in the short run and decreasing returns to scale in the long run. Avi Cohen explains that 'These auxiliary assumptions provide a basis for questioning and discounting empirical evidence of non-increasing costs and thereby retaining the theory.' Without that, 'normal science – problem-solving activity within the context of an accepted theoretical framework or paradigm' – would not be possible.[75] He asks,

> What happens when you combine the necessary emphasis on unrealistic assumptions in model-building, the clarity of outcomes of simple, unrealistic models, a desire to convince students of the empirical relevance of the *outcomes* of the models, and the tremendous time pressure to cover too much material? It is no wonder that introductory instructors often take the shortcut of claiming that real-world outcomes are just like the outcomes of simple, perfectly competitive models.[76]

As we are stressing throughout this book, real-world outcomes are typically very different. At best, the model of the imaginary perfectly competitive market or of the perfectly competitive economy provides a benchmark of very limited usefulness against which the actual world can be assessed, a theme pursued further in the next chapter.

Questions for your professor: Why does the text not refer to evidence about the costs of actual firms? Is there evidence that such firms experience diminishing marginal returns? Is there evidence that most actual firms experience decreasing returns?

2.5 How do firms really set prices?

The story about how the profit maximizing firm sets prices is contradicted by empirical evidence. This applies both to how prices are set and how they change. Let's consider price changes first.

In the case of the competitive firm, as shown in Figure 5.3, the firm's price is the market price, which changes continually as demand and supply change. For the noncompetitive firm, seen in Figure 5.6, price depends on both demand (and thus marginal revenue) and marginal cost, and will change if either of them changes.

However, economists have long recognized that while prices change almost continuously in some markets, prices in other markets remained fixed for long periods of time. These are often called flexprice markets and fixprice markets, the terminology of the English economist John Hicks. Stock markets and commodity markets are flexprice markets. But most of the goods we buy in our everyday lives are purchased in fixprice markets. The sellers set prices and keep them fixed for a significant length of time. Demand may fluctuate, but prices don't change. Instead, firms respond by selling from or adding to inventories and, if needed, changing the rate of production. Firms typically keep excess capacity to be able to do this. This avoids price wars among firms when demand falls; when demand rises, firms keep prices unchanged to maintain their relationship with customers, who might look for other suppliers if prices increase.[77]

There is an additional problem with raising prices when demand increases. Daniel Kahneman and co-authors carried out a survey of the general public to test the fairness constraints that firms face in setting prices. The Canadian respondents were told: 'A hardware store has been selling snow shovels for $15. The morning after a large snowstorm, the store raises the price to $20. Please rate this action as: Completely Fair, Acceptable, Unfair, Very Unfair.' Take a moment to think about what your answer would be.[78]

You probably won't be surprised that 82 percent considered the action to be either unfair or very unfair. Using the original $15 price as a reference point, people see the firm gaining $5 per shovel at the expense of buyers. Such a price increase would run afoul of community standards of fairness, which people expect firms to adhere to.

Yet Richard Thaler reports that, when given the same question, 76 percent of his MBA students found the price increase either completely fair or acceptable. He calls this *'theory-induced blindness':* they now thought like what Thaler calls Econs, the Homo economicus decision-makers in economic models.[79] Fortunately for their long-term profitability, most firms seem to recognize these fairness constraints on profit-seeking and don't raise their prices in such circumstances, even if shortages occur.[80] However, there are some notable exceptions, such as airline fares and hotel prices, where such price changes have come to be regarded as acceptable.

What about price changes in response to cost changes? Firms are willing to change prices when costs rise significantly, a reason that customers can accept as fair. If all firms in the market experience similar cost changes, each can raise prices without the risk of losing market share.

However textbook theory predicts that the only costs that matter are variable costs and the marginal costs derived from them. Changes in fixed costs are irrelevant in setting the profit maximizing price.

How do firms actually determine what prices they will charge? Considerable evidence exists that many firms use 'markup pricing' – setting prices based on average costs.[81] Some firms may do this because they don't have enough information to estimate the profit maximizing price and use a markup over costs as a rule of thumb. Alternatively, some firms' managers may be setting prices to reach a target rate of return that will satisfy shareholders.

Because average costs reflect both fixed costs and variable costs, this contradicts the standard model's predictions that only variable costs matter. Cost-based pricing is also consistent with the relative unresponsiveness of prices to fluctuations in demand. While average costs vary with the rate of output, as seen in Figure 5.7, the price is set using the average cost at the average output rate expected by the firm's managers. As the rate of production rises or falls with changes in demand, prices remain constant.[82]

All in all, at least for fixprice markets, the textbook model does a poor job of explaining how prices are set and how and why they will change. This conclusion is further reinforced by the earlier discussion of the assumption of profit maximization. To the extent that other objectives prevail, prices will differ systematically from the levels predicted by standard theory.

```
Questions for your professor: (1) The model of
pricing in the text predicts that prices will change
whenever demand or costs change, but most goods have
fixed prices that don't change very often. How does
the model explain that? (2) In 1999, the CEO of Coke
got the idea of raising the price of Coke in vending
machines on hot days when demand would be higher,
and selling it more cheaply on cold days. Would that
be a good idea? (Answer: no. Coke had to beat a
humiliating retreat in the face of consumer anger.)[83]
```

2.6 Summing up: the firm in the textbook and the firm in reality

The textbooks' assumption that all firms only seek to maximize profits is too unrealistic to produce good predictions of behaviour. The owners of private businesses can trade off profits for other objectives if they choose. Managerial control of many public corporations allows for systematic departures from profit maximization.

All questions of power are ignored. Apparently, firms sit on the political sidelines, failing to try to shape their environment to their advantage. Power within the firm is assumed not to exist. So the question of whether or not there are alternatives to the traditional autocratic capitalist firm does not arise.

Students get a fictitious account of production and costs that ignores the evidence about what real firms experience. Acknowledging the facts would underline the irrelevance of the perfectly competitive firm as a description of reality.

The stories of how prices change are at variance with the everyday experience of fixed prices in many markets. Ignored are fairness constraints on firm behaviour. Finally, there is good evidence that firms set prices based on markups over some measures of average costs, prices that are systematically different from what would be predicted by the textbook theory.

All of this combines to give a bloodless and boring account of production that evades questions of real interest. There is no excuse for this dismal state of affairs.

SUGGESTIONS FOR FURTHER READING

John Kay's book *Obliquity: why our goals are best achieved indirectly* picks up on the fundamental uncertainty stressed in the post-Keynesian view described earlier. See in particular Chapter 3, 'The profit-seeking paradox – How the most profitable companies are not the most profit oriented'.

In chapter 4 of his book *What Prices the Moral High Ground?*, Robert Frank asks 'Can socially responsible firms survive in a competitive environment?' While theory can't provide a definitive answer, Frank makes the case that socially responsible behaviour gives a firm a number of advantages that might allow it to compete successfully.

Canadian law professor Joel Bakan's book *The Corporation: The pathological pursuit of profit and power* also inspired a thought-provoking documentary film, *The Corporation*, directed by Mark Achbar and Jennifer Abbott. It is freely available on YouTube. Bakan's sequel, *The New Corporation: How "Good" Corporations Are Bad for Democracy*, is also highly recommended.

Firms' exercise of growing economic and political power and the threat it can pose to democracy in the American context is described in Luigi Zingales' 2017 article 'Towards a political theory of the firm' in the *Journal of Economic Perspectives*.

In *Governing the Firm: Workers' Control in Theory and Practice*, Gregory Dow explores the normative case for worker control, the evidence of how worker-controlled firms work, and why such firms are so rare.

Tom Malleson's *After Occupy: Economic Democracy for the 21ˢᵗ Century* examines the costs and benefits of extending democracy to economic life, considers how various parts of the market economy might be democratized, and lastly sketches out what a democratic market economy might look like.

Richard Miller's 2000 article 'Ten Cheaper Spades: Production Theory and Cost Curves in the Short Run' in the *Journal of Economic Education* is highly recommended for students beyond the introductory level.

Chapter 6

MARKET STRUCTURE AND EFFICIENCY – OR WHY PERFECT COMPETITION ISN'T SO PERFECT AFTER ALL

'Perfect competition never did exist and never could exist because, even when firms are small, they do not just take the price as given but strive to make the price. All the current textbooks say as much but then they immediately go on to say that the cloud-cuckoo-land of perfect competition is the benchmark against which economists may say something significant about real-world competition ...' Mark Blaug[1]

The point of this section of the standard textbook is to show how firm behaviour and overall efficiency depend on market structure. The exercise supposedly demonstrates that perfect competition represents an ideal market structure, while all other scenarios involve a loss of efficiency. If this were true, it could provide a compelling reason for the emphasis on the competitive market in the standard textbook. But if this isn't the case, the emphasis on perfect competition is misplaced.

I THE STANDARD TEXT

1.1 Types of market structure

As introduced briefly in Table 3.1, markets are classified according to the number of buyers and sellers and the nature of the goods and services being exchanged. Also important is how easy it is for firms to enter or to leave the market. In this chapter, we will describe and analyze each of these 'market structures'. In all cases, there are many buyers in the market, enough that no individual buyer has any bargaining power over the price. As well, buyers and sellers are assumed to have perfect, costless information about things such as prices and product quality.

1.2 Perfect competition

We have already seen a perfectly competitive market in Chapter 3, which introduced the supply and demand model. All firms produce identical products and there are 'many' firms in the market, meaning that each firm is too small for its production to influence the market price in a significant way. Each firm is said to be a 'price taker', meaning that it has no ability to set a price for its product that is different from the market price.

Firms don't need to advertise or worry about their competitors, since they can sell all they wish at the market price. The price – being unaffected by an individual firm's output – is both the firm's average *and* marginal revenue. We analysed the behaviour of such a firm in the previous chapter. As seen in Figures 5.3 and 5.5, the price-taking firm produces up to the point where marginal cost equals marginal revenue, which equals the market price.

Derivation of the competitive firm's supply curve Figure 6.1 shows the process in action. The left-hand diagram shows supply and demand in the market as a whole. The right-hand diagram shows a typical firm producing a few thousand litres of milk, which in a market of millions of litres will have no discernible impact on price. The firm equates marginal revenue (or price) to marginal cost. If the market price is $5 per litre, the firm produces 8 thousand litres. If market price increases to $7 a litre (because market demand increases to D_2), the firm produces 9 thousand litres. The key point is that the firm's marginal cost line is the firm's supply curve.

There is only one wrinkle: in the short run the price must be above the firm's average variable cost. The difference between variable and total cost is fixed cost. But in the short run, fixed cost is unavoidable. So, as long as the price exceeds average variable costs, the firm's losses are less than its fixed costs, and the firm will stay in production – in the short run at least.

So, more accurately, the firm's supply curve is the section of the firm's marginal cost line that lies above its average variable cost. Summing what each firm would supply at any given price determines market supply. This means the market supply curve will shift for two reasons: first, the position of the typical firm's marginal cost curve could shift; second, the number of firms in the industry could change. Chapter 5 explained the factors that could

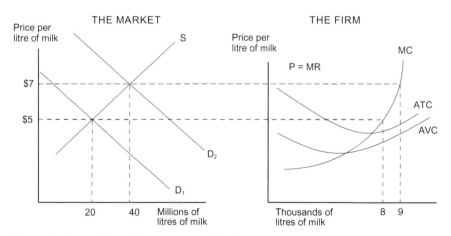

Figure 6.1 Derivation of the competitive firm's supply curve

shift the typical firm's marginal cost curve: changes in prices of factors of production, changes in technology, or changes in the size of the firm. What's new is the dependence of the industry supply curve on the number of firms in the industry.

Equilibrium in the long and short runs In economics, cost is always defined as opportunity cost, which includes the cost of the next-best opportunity forgone. When a firm is just breaking even, it is said to be earning *normal* profit – the same as it could have earned in its next-best opportunity elsewhere. When a firm is earning *economic* profit, it is doing better than it could have done elsewhere. If firms are earning an economic profit, there is an incentive for firms in other industries to enter this industry to share in those higher profits. As new entry occurs, the market supply curve shifts right, which reduces the price. This continues until the economic profit disappears, leaving firms earning only normal profit in long-run equilibrium.

To keep things simple, firms' inputs are often assumed to be homogeneous – every unit of labour, capital, and land have the same productivity. But this need not be the case. Suppose that some of the farms producing milk have a particularly productive breed of cow. Because of the assumption of perfect information, the price farmers are willing to pay for such cows will reflect their productivity. That will raise the cost of such cows, offsetting the benefits of their higher productivity. The cost per litre of milk produced will therefore be the same for all farmers, leaving profits the same as well.

This same mechanism works for all other factors that could lead to differences in costs. Any differences in efficiency between factors will be completely offset by differences in costs. Thus, all existing firms, and potential new entrants, have the same profits.

Let's compare the short run and long-run equilibria using diagrams. In Figure 6.2 the milk industry is initially in long-run equilibrium at a price of $3 a litre. Each firm produces 5,000 litres and just covers its long-run average

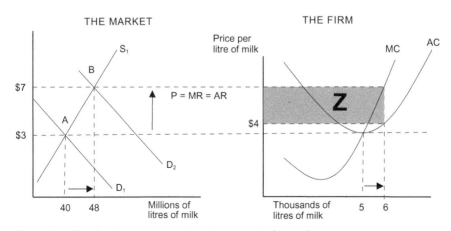

Figure 6.2 The short-run response to an increase in demand

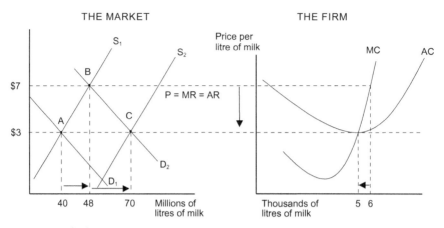

Figure 6.3 The long-run response to an increase in demand

costs. There is no tendency for firms to enter or to leave. Now suppose demand increases to D_2. In the short run, this drives up the price to $7. The firm maximizes profits by equating price (equal to marginal revenue) to its marginal cost. It produces 6,000 litres at an average cost of $4 per litre. Economic profit per litre is $3 (= $7 − $4). Total economic profit is $3 x 6,000 = $18,000, shown as the shaded rectangle, Z. This encourages new firms to enter the industry.

As new firms enter, so the market supply curve shifts to the right and the price is driven back down. How far to the right does the supply curve shift? As shown in Figure 6.3, the supply curve will have to move to S_2, so that the price is bid down to the minimum point on the typical firm's long-run average cost curve. At this point, no firm earns economic profit, and the incentive to enter the industry disappears. The decrease in price from $7 back to $3 causes the original firms to reduce their output from 6,000 litres back to 5,000 litres. But the increase in the number of firms more than offsets this decrease, and ensures that industry output increases from 48 million litres to 70 million litres.

The efficiency of perfect competition We showed in Chapter 4 that the demand curve for a commodity is the sum of all individuals' marginal benefit curves. We have just shown that the supply curve is the sum of all firms' marginal cost curves. Hence, the intersection of demand and supply can be reinterpreted as the intersection of the aggregate marginal benefit and marginal cost schedules. Provided there are no benefits or costs unaccounted for, i.e. no 'externalities' (no pollution, for example), this intersection gives us the efficient quantity, Q^*, as shown in Figure 6.4. (Externalities are discussed in Chapter 7.)

At Q_1 (which is less than Q^*) the extra benefit of one more unit exceeds the extra cost. Producing this unit increases net benefit. On the other hand, at Q_2 (which exceeds Q^*) marginal cost exceeds marginal benefit, and the production of that unit lowers net benefit. In conclusion, the intersection of demand and

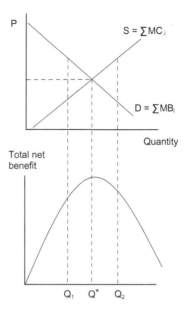

Figure 6.4 The optimal quantity

supply yields the optimal output, which maximizes total net benefit from the production of that good.

The above argument applies to any competitive equilibrium – even the short-run equilibrium at point B in Figure 6.3 where the price exceeds its long-run value. But free entry and exit ensures that the market moves to long-run equilibrium, shown in Figure 6.4, where there is the optimal number of firms, and where each firm produces at the lowest possible cost per unit. Furthermore, this optimal quantity is distributed to those who value it most.

To see this, suppose we have a fixed quantity of goods – say 1,000 loaves of bread. Now imagine the Ideal Planner, whose job it is to distribute those goods to maximize total benefit. Who should get the bread? The Planner should equate the marginal benefit of a loaf of bread across individuals.

For example, suppose that Muriel's marginal benefit is $4 per loaf, while Virginia's marginal benefit is $9 per loaf. The Planner should take a loaf away from Muriel and give it to Virginia. Muriel's benefit has fallen by $4 but Virginia's has increased by $9. On balance, total benefit increases by $5. As you take bread away from Muriel her marginal benefit of one more loaf increases. As you give bread to Virginia her marginal benefit falls. The Planner can continue to increase total benefit by reallocating bread from Muriel to Virginia until they both have the same marginal benefit. Total benefit is not maximized until everyone has the same marginal benefit of a loaf of bread.

But this is what competitive markets do automatically! We already know that each individual maximizes her own net benefit by buying up to the point where her marginal benefit equals the price. In a competitive market, all consumers face the same price and so all will have the same marginal benefit. So competitive markets work just as an Ideal Planner would only without all the expense we'd need for the Planner's staff, not to mention the immense informational problems the Planner would face.

1.3 Non-competitive markets: there is no supply curve

In non-competitive markets, firms have no supply curve. The reason is that competitive firms take the market price as given, whereas non-competitive firms do not. They are price makers, not price takers. Competitive firms equate the given price to marginal cost, giving rise to a unique quantity supplied for any given price; whereas non-competitive firms set their prices, and realize that the quantity they can sell depends on the price they set. Since the best price will depend on the shape and position of the demand curve, there is no unique price necessary to induce the supply of a given quantity – it depends on the nature of demand.

Just like the competitive firm, the non-competitive firm maximizes profits by producing up to the point where marginal revenue equals marginal cost. In the left-hand diagram of Figure 6.5, this occurs at an output of 400 units. Once the quantity is determined in this way, the demand curve determines the price, at $7 per unit.

As shown in the right-hand diagram, if demand shifted to D_2 (with associated marginal revenue of MR_2) the new marginal revenue curve would cut the marginal cost curve at the same point as before. Therefore, the firm would produce the same amount, but it would now sell the output at a price of $5. This shows that there is no unique price necessary to induce a given supply, and therefore no supply curve. This is the case for any non-competitive firm.

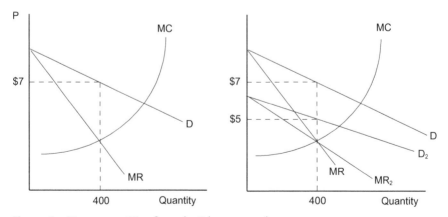

Figure 6.5 Non-competitive firms don't have a supply curve

1.4 Monopoly

Monopoly is the simplest non-competitive market structure since, by definition, there is only one seller. Maintenance of a monopoly position requires barriers to entry associated with: (1) control over at least one crucial input; (2) economies of scale; (3) technological superiority; or (4) a government-created barrier such as patent protection. If the barriers to entry are low, the threat of competitors entering the market would affect the monopolist's pricing decision. (Such a market is referred to as "contestable".) To keep things simple, we'll focus on the case where barriers to entry are high.

Comparing monopoly to perfect competition Suppose all the firms in a perfectly competitive industry were taken over and merged into a single monopolistic supplier. What would be the effect on efficiency and the distribution of income?

The key element in the comparison of the two industry structures is the dual role played by the competitive firms' marginal cost curves. As shown in Figure 6.6, their (horizontal) summation is the supply curve under perfect competition; but under monopoly that same summation is simply the monopolist's marginal costs.

Under perfect competition, demand and supply intersect at point A. After all the firms are merged, however, the monopoly maximizes its profit by equating marginal cost to marginal revenue at point B. Given output of Q_M, the demand curve determines the price, P_M, at point C.

As shown, monopoly restricts output below the socially optimal level. The monopolist realizes that if it sells less, the price can be raised, whereas each competitive firm cannot raise the price by reducing output, since they are too small to influence it.

We can measure the net loss associated with this output restriction. The value to consumers of the lost output is the area under the demand curve between Q_C

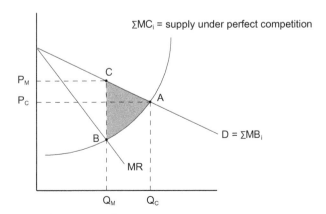

Figure 6.6 Monopoly versus perfect competition

and Q_M. The cost of producing this output is the area under the marginal cost curve between Q_C and Q_M. Therefore, the *net* loss (or *'deadweight loss'*) due to monopoly is the difference: the shaded area ABC.

Two other adverse effects of monopoly stem from the fact that monopolies tend to earn above-normal profits. First, these excess profits probably involve a regressive redistribution of income towards those who are already rich. We can call this the *'equity cost'* of privately created monopolies. Second, individuals will devote time, effort and expertise to secure monopoly profits, perhaps through seeking legal or regulatory protection from potential competitors. This *rent-seeking* behaviour is a further inefficiency – a waste of society's scarce resources over and above that of the deadweight loss.

Deadweight loss and price discrimination There is one interesting exception to the above conclusion: when a monopolist is able to perfectly discriminate among consumers on the basis of their willingness to pay, it produces the efficient amount, and deadweight loss is zero. Perfect price discrimination means that the monopolist is able to sell each unit at a different price, the maximum price given by the demand curve. In effect, the demand curve becomes the marginal revenue schedule, and the monopolist maximizes its profits by producing the competitive quantity at point A. Because the monopolist converts the entire consumer surplus into extra profits, however, perfect price discrimination worsens the equity cost of monopoly.

Perfect price discrimination is extremely rare because the monopolist doesn't know the maximum amount each consumer would be willing to pay. Instead, the monopolist seeks ways to segregate the market into different groups – those willing to pay more versus those who will only pay less. For example, those with less income are willing to cut out coupons in newspaper flyers, or are willing to stay over an extra night to get a cheaper airline ticket. Similarly, we may think student (or senior) discounts are justified on equity grounds, though they too are attempts at price discrimination.

Less than perfect price discrimination means that the monopolist will produce more than Q_M and less than Q_C in Figure 6.6. It lessens the deadweight loss but increases the equity cost of monopoly.

Regulating monopoly If monopoly is socially inefficient, government intervention can improve the market outcome. It can put in place anti-trust laws (or competition laws) that prevent monopoly from arising in the first place. If monopoly already exists, it could break up the monopoly into separate firms or it could regulate it.

For example, in certain circumstances price ceilings can eliminate the deadweight loss. The left-hand diagram of Figure 6.7 shows that a price ceiling of P_C causes the demand curve to have a kink. It does not stop the price from falling *below* P_C, so when output is greater than Q_C, the price is given by the original demand schedule. Since the price is constant between P_C and A, however, price equals marginal revenue in this range. Now when the monopolist equates

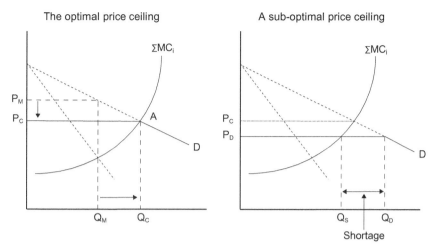

Figure 6.7 Price ceilings and monopoly

marginal revenue to marginal cost, he finds that they are equal at point A, and produces an output of Q_C. This price ceiling succeeds in getting the monopolist to produce the socially efficient output level. Therefore, we may call this an 'optimal price ceiling'.

This result stands in stark contrast to the effects of price ceilings in competitive markets (analysed in Chapter 3). In the competitive context, price ceilings necessarily cause shortages and black markets. In the monopoly context, those results appear only if the price ceiling is too low – as shown in the right-hand diagram in Figure 6.7. Any price ceiling less than P_C (but still high enough to allow the monopolist to cover costs) results in a shortage since it is *below* the point of intersection of demand and marginal cost.

The government's policy options are more limited in the case of 'natural monopoly'. This occurs when there are large fixed costs of doing business. For example, electricity (and gas) companies incur huge set-up costs to get the grid of cables (or pipes) in place; and they have low and roughly constant marginal costs of adding new users to the network.

Figure 6.8 shows this cost structure. Average costs fall as output increases, because fixed cost is spread over more and more units. Average cost never starts to rise because marginal costs are constant. If several firms were initially in this industry, the biggest firm would have lower costs than its rivals, allowing it to underprice them and capture even more market share – leading to an even greater cost advantage. The logical conclusion is only one firm in the industry.

Trying to establish a competitive industry in the context of a natural monopoly would (a) be doomed to failure, and (b) would result in higher average costs in the unlikely event it succeeded. Anti-trust laws should not be applied to natural monopolies. Nor can price ceilings induce a natural monopolist to produce the socially efficient output level. A price ceiling cannot be set where marginal cost cuts the demand curve since this would involve setting a price below average cost and the monopolist would be put out of business. Thus, in Figure 6.8 a price ceiling of P_C is not feasible.

Nevertheless, price ceilings can still be beneficial; they lower profits and prices, while increasing output. Without regulation, the monopolist in Figure 6.8 maximizes profits by producing Q_M where MR = MC. The resulting price is P_M and the shaded box shows economic profits. A price ceiling of P_R (where the average cost curve cuts the demand curve) increases output to Q_R and eliminates economic profit. Since output moves towards the competitive level (at Q_C) efficiency is increased.

This all looks terrific: consumers are better off, profits are eliminated, overall welfare increases. Unfortunately, things are rarely that easy in practice. The main problem is that regulators don't have the information required to know where the demand curve crosses the average total cost curve. If they set the price too low, they create shortages; if they succeed in setting price exactly equal to average costs on an ongoing basis, the monopolist loses all incentive to keep costs down.

Even worse, regulators may lose track of the public interest – they may become 'captured' by those they attempt to regulate. This could happen through corruption or, more innocently, through cross-hiring. Regulators tend to hire ex-industry personnel because of their expertise. Industry tends to hire ex-regulators for their insider connections.

Creating temporary monopoly through intellectual property Governments may actually facilitate the creation of monopoly by enforcing rights to intellectual property: patents, copyrights and trademarks. For example, if a pharmaceutical company has a 20-year patent on a particular drug, it has the exclusive right to produce it or to licence its production for as long as the patent is in effect.

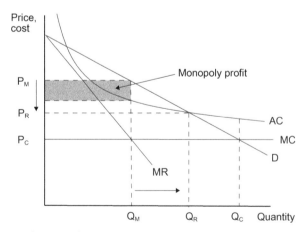

Figure 6.8 Natural monopoly

This gives it the incentive to bear the risk and expense of the research and development to develop the drug.

From a social point of view, in setting the length of patent protection the cost of a temporary monopoly must be weighed against the long-run benefits of having more new products and processes developed than would otherwise exist. The same is true for the copyright of artistic and literary works, such as this book. Trademarks protect firms' brand names and logos, which give buyers a guarantee of the authenticity of the goods on offer.

1.5 Other market structures

Perfect competition and monopoly represent two extreme forms of market structure. Both models are relatively simple, and both yield relatively clear-cut predictions. But most markets in modern industrial economies fall between the extremes. There's usually more than one firm in an industry, but rarely are there so many that they are all price-takers. These intermediate market forms – monopolistic competition and oligopoly – rarely lend themselves to definite predictions. But the consensus view is that prices and quantities in those markets fall within the bounds set by the two extremes. The more firms there are, and the more substitutable their products, the more results tend to the perfectly competitive outcome; the fewer the firms, and the less substitutable their products, the more they tend to the monopoly outcome.

Monopolistic competition This market structure occurs when there are many firms making slightly different products, with relatively easy entry into (and exit from) the industry. Differentiated products mean that each firm faces a downward-sloping demand curve for its product, giving it some 'market power' or choice over the price it sets.

Edward Chamberlin and Joan Robinson independently developed the theory in 1933.[2] They recognized that goods and services could be differentiated not just by their physical characteristics but by the creation of brands as well as by the location of sellers. Think, for example, of the barbershops or hair salons scattered across a large city.

One of the few predictions we can make in such markets concerns long-run equilibrium. Easy entry (and exit) ensures that in the long run no firm makes more than normal profit. Therefore, in long-run equilibrium the firm's price equals its average cost. As shown in Figure 6.9 this implies that monopolistically competitive firms produce an inefficiently small output (at Q_{MC}), where marginal benefit (or demand) exceeds marginal cost. Nor do these firms minimize their unit costs of production. In effect, they have 'excess capacity'. This means that the firms could produce more at a lower average cost, but it's not profitable to do so. On the other hand, buyers benefit from the variety offered by product differentiation. Just how much variety is optimal remains unclear.

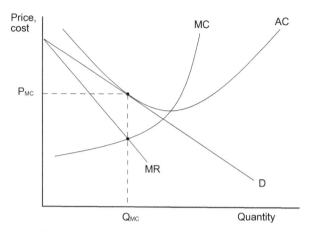

Figure 6.9 Monopolistic competition

Oligopoly There is no strategic interaction between firms in monopolistic competition because they are all too small to pay attention to each other. In contrast, strategic interaction is the core problem in the last industry structure – oligopoly. It occurs when there are relatively few firms in an industry, whether they differentiate their products or not. Strategic interaction makes it the least predictable market structure of all, since no firm knows precisely how its rivals will react to any move it makes.

Basic concepts from game theory help to explain the conditions under which firms may try to collude to achieve the (shared) monopoly outcome. With only two firms the simple 'prisoner's dilemma' is shown in Table 6.1. The strategies available to Enron are shown in the top row, and those to Esso in the left-hand column. Each combination of strategies results in a particular outcome for each company. In this case, neither firm trusts the other and any collusive agreement (or implicit cartel) invariably breaks down. For example, suppose that if Esso and Enron collude by agreeing to charge the monopoly price, each sees profits rise by $2 billion. But if only one of them honours the agreement while the other cheats (by offering price discounts), the cheater gains $6 billion and the other

Table 6.1 A pay-off matrix illustrating the prisoner's dilemma

	Enron honours the collusive agreement	**Enron offers price discounts**
Esso honours the collusive agreement	Enron = +$2 Esso = +$2	Enron = +$6 Esso = – $4
Esso offers price discounts	Enron = –$4 Esso = +$6	Enron = 0 Esso = 0

loses $4 billion. Finally, if both firms cheat (by offering price discounts) they make zero excess profits; each earns only normal profits.

Now suppose each firm rationally decides on its best strategy. Esso reasons as follows. So, if Enron honours the collusive agreement (the first column in the table), Esso would be better off by offering price discounts. And if Enron offers price discounts (the second column in the table), Esso would still be better off by offering price discounts. So no matter what Enron does, Esso's best strategy will be to cheat (and offer price discounts).

Since the situation is exactly analogous for Enron, neither honours the price-fixing agreement and the firms do not collude. This happens despite the fact that both of them would be better off if they did collude.

This appears to be good news for the consumer – collusion is difficult even when there are only two firms. Repeated plays of the same game, however, allow participants to build reputations. Developing the reputation of always playing 'tit-for-tat' (I'll do to you next period what you do to me this period) brings about a situation where it is in both firms' best interests to abide by the collusive agreement. Table 6.2 illustrates the first five periods of an open ended interaction between these two firms. Assume Esso plays 'tit-for-tat' and compare three strategies for Enron – honouring the collusive agreement throughout; honouring it only in the first period and cheating thereafter; and honouring it in every period except one (period 2 in this case). The reader can verify the table entries using the profit data from Table 6.1. Clearly, given Esso's 'tit-for-tat' strategy, the best strategy for Enron is to honour the collusive agreement and cooperate (illegally) with Esso.

It is interesting that game theory uses logic and incentives to explain how 'cooperative' (or collusive) behaviour can arise even though neither player is trustworthy. In the repeated game, each trusts that the other will not violate the agreement, because they know that the other is a rational calculator who operates only in their own best interests.

Table 6.2 Repeated plays when Esso plays 'tit-for-tat'

Period	Enron colludes throughout	Enron colludes in period 1 only	Enron cheats in period 2 only
1	+ 2	+ 2	+ 2
2	+ 2	+ 6	+ 6
3	+ 2	0	- 4
4	+ 2	0	+ 2
5	+ 2	0	+ 2
total	+ 10	+8	+ 8

2 THE ANTI-TEXT

Our version of the Standard Text has shown that supply curves exist only in perfectly competitive markets. Therefore demand and supply is just another name for the perfectly competitive model.

Under perfect competition, price ceilings necessarily lead to shortages and black markets. This chapter shows that those predictions do not apply to non-competitive markets. Whenever a firm's demand curve is downward sloping, a price ceiling (as in the cases illustrated in Figures 6.7 and 6.8) leads to an increase in quantity supplied without causing a shortage.

It is strange, therefore, that textbooks seem to regard the predictions of the supply and demand/competitive model as a generic model with wide applicability to all market structures. One would suppose the reverse to be true: since most markets are non-competitive, wouldn't the predictions of non-competitive models be most applicable? At the very least, textbooks should be highlighting the importance of model selection.

Why is the competitive model given such prominence in the typical textbook? In Chapter 3, we evaluated whether this could be justified by the prevalence of competitive markets in the real world, or by the model's predictive power even in markets that were not strictly competitive. We found neither of these explanations compelling.

This chapter evaluates another possible reason for the emphasis given to perfect competition. Even if no markets were perfectly competitive, and even if the model had no predictive power, perfect competition might still be important as a standard of static economic efficiency against which to compare other market structures, and for evaluating policies. (By static efficiency, we mean the efficiency with which these markets allocate society's scarce resources at a point in time.) If government policy brings a market closer to the competitive ideal, it is a good policy, at least in terms of the static efficiency criterion.

Unfortunately, the idea that perfect competition is an ideal market structure is seriously flawed. First, perfect competition could lead to an ethically unjust outcome. Can something really be ideal if it is not equitable? Second, perfect competition is an ideal only when we focus exclusively on static efficiency, but this ignores the issue of dynamic efficiency, with its development of new technologies and new products. Third, even in terms of static efficiency, there are many reasons to doubt that perfect competition is an ideal. We'll begin by expanding these arguments before looking at other limitations of the textbook treatment.

2.1 Can something be ideal if it is not equitable?

Perfectly competitive industries produce the efficient quantity, in the most efficient way, and ensure that it is distributed to those who value it most. What could be more ideal than that? Your answer probably depends on your income.

In explaining the efficiency of perfect competition, we compared it to how an Ideal Planner would operate. In order to maximize total benefit the Ideal Planner takes bread away from those with the lowest marginal benefit, and gives it to those with the highest. The final distribution of bread leaves everyone having the same marginal benefit per loaf. That sounds fair, doesn't it?

Actually, it is not necessarily fair at all. Remember, we are measuring benefit in terms of willingness to pay money for one more unit of the good. If people have the same preferences but different incomes, the rich will be more willing to pay more money for one more unit of a normal good than are poor people.[3] We also know that an increase in income shifts the demand curve for a normal good to the right. Since the demand curve *is* the marginal benefit curve, this means that it shifts the marginal benefit curve to the right. The greater is our income, the higher is our marginal benefit curve for most things.

Going back to our earlier example, suppose we know that Muriel's marginal benefit of a loaf of bread is $4, while Virginia's is $9. Efficiency in distribution requires taking bread away from Muriel and giving it to Virginia. But we don't know why Virginia has a high marginal benefit. It could be because she has five children to feed (compared to Muriel's one); or it could be because Virginia is rich, and therefore has a higher willingness to pay. Efficiency in the distribution of goods is not necessarily equitable.

Furthermore, any redistribution of income would change the relative demand for goods. For example, taking money from the very rich and giving it to the very poor would mean fewer luxury yachts and less champagne demanded, and more basic housing. So if all markets exist and they are all perfectly competitive, the economy would produce an efficient quantity of goods *given* the existing distribution of income. But this does not ensure that we produce *the* optimal quantity of goods (or the 'right' goods) in an ethical sense. Only when the actual distribution of income is 'just' will the efficient outcome represent a social optimum.

This is an important point to remember: it's okay to say that perfect competition produces an efficient outcome, but that should not be confused with an 'optimal' outcome. We want to avoid implicitly downgrading the equity objective to the point where it is always subservient to the efficiency objective. To rephrase the point using more technical language, perfectly competitive market prices reflect *marginal social valuations* only when the distribution of income is considered socially desirable. Then the marginal social value of a dollar would be equal for all individuals.

Incidentally, more advanced economics courses ignore this problem in a more sophisticated way. Preferences are assumed to be such that changes in the distribution of income leave the total demand for each good unaffected. In this special case, prices must equal marginal social valuations. This means, however, that a transfer of $1 from a rich person to a poor person does not affect the demand for anything, which is clearly untrue.

David Colander points out that 'most authors of principles books ...do not discuss the implications of an existing undesirable income distribution for measures of efficiency'.[4] An efficiently functioning market economy could produce a combination of goods and services that could appear woefully inadequate to meet the needs of society's members, although not their demands. In such situations, singing the praises of the invisible hand seems beside the point.

> Question for your professor: If part of the
> population of a country were starving because they
> had too little income to buy food(perhaps bad weather
> destroyed their harvest), would it be inefficient to
> subsidize their purchases of rice? (The right answer
> is 'yes': allocative efficiency means rice goes to
> those who are willing to pay the most for it.)

2.2 Static efficiency is less important than dynamic efficiency

The texts' examination of perfect competition and monopoly emphasizes efficiency, specifically *static* efficiency. Monopoly power is criticized for its inefficiency, although the argument given is hardly persuasive (as we explain in the next section). Even if this criticism were correct, it overlooks the issue of *dynamic* efficiency: the efficiency with which resources are used over time. The development of new technologies and new products must be a central part of the story of dynamic efficiency, yet this typically gets little mention in the textbooks.

Its relative neglect is strange because innovation is a central feature of capitalism and is widely agreed to be responsible for most long-term economic growth. Marx and Engels expressed it vividly in 1848 in *The Communist Manifesto*:

> The bourgeoisie, during its rule of scarce one hundred years, has created more massive and more colossal productive forces than have all preceding generations together. Subjection of Nature's forces to man, machinery, application of chemistry to industry and agriculture, steam-navigation, railways, electric telegraphs, clearing of whole continents for cultivation, canalisation of rivers, whole populations conjured out of the ground— what earlier century had even a presentiment that such productive forces slumbered in the lap of social labour?[5]

Writing a century later, a century that had seen the appearance of such things as electric light, radio, automobiles, and aircraft, the Austrian economist Joseph Schumpeter described the 'perennial gale of creative destruction' that produces such change. He wrote that 'in capitalist reality as distinguished from its textbook picture' the kind of competition between firms that is important is not price competition in an environment with given technology and market structures. Instead, it's 'the competition from the new commodity, the new technology, the new source of supply, the new type of organization ... – competition which commands a decisive cost or quality advantage and which strikes not at the margins of the profits and the outputs of the existing firms but at their foundations and their very lives.'[6]

In this view, monopoly profits are the reward for those who are successful in this struggle. They only continue if the firm keeps innovating at least as quickly as its competitors. Even so, it may fall by the wayside as completely new products are developed that substitute for what it produces.

It is easy to think of examples. For a few decades IBM had a near-monopoly in the production of computers. This was swept aside by the development of the personal computer which then saw intensive competition to develop smaller, lighter and faster devices. Similarly, Intel maintained a large advantage in microchip manufacture from the 1970s until the 1990s, but now it shares the market with many other firms such as Samsung and Advanced Micro Devices. A long-term struggle among many companies is underway to develop the electric automobiles of the future. Competition is ongoing to develop ever better battery technology to store the electricity from solar and wind power. And so on.

In this Schumpeterian story, if monopoly power is relatively short-term, or if the companies themselves undertake steady innovation to try to maintain it, any static inefficiencies of monopolies may be more than offset by their dynamic efficiencies. As Schumpeter himself put it: 'Capitalist reality is first and last a process of change. In appraising the performance of competitive enterprise, the question whether it would or would not tend to maximize production in a perfectly equilibrated stationary condition of the economic process is hence almost, although not quite, irrelevant.'[7]

Nevertheless, the textbooks continue to emphasize the static inefficiency of non-competitive markets, putting in the background the issue of dynamic efficiency. In our sample of 10 North American texts, four had nothing to say about these Schumpeterian ideas.[8] Most of the rest offered little more than a few paragraphs.[9]

Their focus on static efficiency is likely a by-product of their emphasis on perfect competition. Schumpeter thought that monopoly profits (or more generally, profits from market power) were critical in financing research and development. But perfectly competitive firms would have little or no profits to invest. As well, any knowledge they produce could quickly be acquired by other firms, so it would not pay any one firm to invest in producing that knowledge. It is not surprising that, at least before the appearance of multinational agribusiness, most research and development in agriculture was carried out by governments.

> Questions for your professor: Are firms that have
> significant market power more likely to invest
> in innovation and new products than perfectly
> competitive firms? If so, where are the benefits of
> that shown in a diagram like Figure 6.6?

Schumpeter was right about rising standards of living being largely due to innovation and about the relative lack of it in industries with large numbers of small firms. But whether the actual monopoly profits we observe are a temporary reward for innovation is an empirical question. There can be markets where innovation isn't particularly important and where monopoly profits can persist. Joseph Stiglitz points to the example of locally delivered services such as 'one firm servicing each brand of car or tractor, one or two Internet providers, one or two cable TV companies, a few providers of finance to small businesses.'[10]

Even in markets where innovation is important, there is no reason to think that the amount of innovation that firms carry out is the right one from a social point of view. When a firm produces knowledge through research and development, it will consider only the expected benefits to itself, ignoring beneficial spillovers to other firms or other sectors in the economy. From a social point of view, it underinvests in knowledge production.[11]

Missing from Schumpeter's original story was the critical role of the state in funding the basic research that occurs in research universities and government laboratories. These lie at the base of an economy's 'innovation system', to use the terminology of Joseph Stiglitz and Bruce Greenwald, who set out a broader vision of a 'learning society'.[12]

Schumpeter may also have been too optimistic about competition quickly eroding monopoly power. It's easy to imagine a situation in which a dominant firm has such a technological lead that potential competitors invest little in trying to challenge it. The dominant firm itself could rest on its laurels and invest little.

Such a firm could also invest in keeping out the competition. In many countries, competition policy tries to prevent dominant firms from abusing their power. But powerful firms can also lobby governments for changes in the rules. For example, they can persuade governments to strengthen patent and copyright protection, excluding competitors for a longer period.

To sum up: there is no reason to think that the outcome of this system of innovation and growth has been dynamically efficient any more than it has been statically efficient. Both concepts of efficiency are just theoretical benchmarks, but the textbooks give disproportionate attention to static efficiency.

It is true that as capitalism has spread around the world, it's brought about a spectacular growth in material living standards. As we saw in the previous chapter, its impact on subjective well-being is debatable, but it has certainly expanded people's capabilities in important ways. But, as the next chapter describes, it has also been accompanied by excessive pollution and environmental degradation, culminating in the risk of catastrophic climate change examined in the Postscript.

> Questions for your professor: Why does the text emphasize the static inefficiency of imperfectly competitive markets? What about the dynamic efficiencies that could come from competition and innovation in such markets? Isn't that more important than the static efficiency offered by (nonexistent) perfectly competitive markets?

2.3 Perfect competition is flawed even as a standard of static efficiency

Even if we ignore the issue of dynamic efficiency, there are many reasons why perfect competition is flawed as a standard of static efficiency. Some of these reasons are hardly mentioned in the textbooks despite being well known and routinely taught in upper-level courses.

Let's begin with *the theory of the second-best,* first set out by Richard Lipsey and Kelvin Lancaster in the 1950s.[13] Remember that in a world of competitive markets, the demand for every product reflects its marginal social benefits, while the supply reflects its marginal social costs. The equilibrium that results in each market maximizes net social benefits. But suppose that this is not the case in one of these markets and that, for whatever reason, that cannot be corrected by policy. Lipsey and Lancaster showed that it might be possible to reach a more socially desirable outcome by acting in other markets in ways that would at least partially counteract the problems created by the first market. Such actions would superficially appear to be creating more inefficiencies but would really be steps towards a 'second-best' outcome, given the constraints policymakers face.

Consider a concrete example. Suppose that the price of oil and the products made from it, such as gasoline, do not reflect their true social costs because of problems like air pollution and climate change. As we explain in the next chapter and in the Postscript, if the prices of such products are 'too low' from a social point of view, an appropriate response is a tax that raises their prices. But suppose that such taxes are not politically feasible. Because cheap fossil fuel has influenced decisions about the kind of vehicles people buy, the amount of public transit they take, and how much they fly, those markets have socially undesirable equilibria. Policymakers might respond by imposing fuel efficiency standards on automakers, subsidizing public transit, and refusing to allow new airport runways.[14]

The theory of the second best is not a criticism of perfect competition itself. Rather it is a criticism of the erroneous idea that incremental changes that remove 'distortions' facing decision-makers in individual markets will necessarily improve the allocation of resources in the economy. Yet this is precisely the impression that students could take away from typical textbook discussions of such things as price controls and subsidies.

This illustrates the weakness of the textbook claim that 'the operation of a purely competitive economy provides a standard, or norm, for evaluating the efficiency of the real-world economy' and serves as 'a benchmark for judging policies'.[15] As Mark Blaug asks: 'But how can an idealized state of perfection be a benchmark when we are never told how to measure the gap between it and real-world competition? It is implied that all real-world competition is "approximately" like perfect competition but the degree of the approximation is never specified, even vaguely.'[16] He goes on to add that the focus on perfect competition allows economists to give precise answers to relatively unimportant questions. Better would be to try to say something, however imprecisely, about the messy reality of actual competition as a dynamic process, as Schumpeter attempted to do.

> Question for your professor: I read that the theory of second best suggests that perfect competition is of little use as an ideal benchmark to guide government regulation. Do you agree?

© Andy Singer

Next, in showing the deadweight loss associated with monopoly, textbooks assume the monopoly has an *identical costs* to the perfectly competitive industry with which it is compared. But there is really no sound basis for such an assumption. The monopolist's costs might be lower, or higher, than the sum of the costs of the competitive firms it replaces.

Lower costs are possible if there are synergies or economies of scale or if the monopoly is the result of technological superiority. On the other hand, if barriers to entry are high, the lack of competitive pressure can leave monopolists with less incentive to keep costs down. The result could be what American economist Harvey Leibenstein called X-inefficiencies.[17]

Economists have long recognized that the assumption that costs are independent of the market structure is not true. Writing in the 1850s, French economist Augustin Cournot was aware that a monopoly's cost structure would differ from that of a perfectly competitive industry. Alfred Marshall's elaboration of this in his *Principles* in the 1920s 'actually amounts to denying the existence of a presumption that the price usually set by an industrial monopoly is higher and the quantity produced by it is lower than would be the case if the same commodity were produced under free competition', as Schumpeter pointed out.[18]

Finally, the textbook demonstration of deadweight loss assumes that the perfectly competitive industry has an *identical market demand* to the industry with which it is compared. But whereas monopolists have an incentive to advertise, perfectly competitive firms do not, as we noted in Chapter 4. (Consumers have perfect information and all firms sell the same product, so advertising by any one firm to increase demand for the product in general would not pay.) If the monopolist's advertising increases demand for the product, we cannot assume that both industry structures face identical demand.

Given all of these problems, the texts have shown nothing about the efficiency of perfect competition when compared with monopoly. Their claim that they have shown something is just a bluff.

Furthermore, if perfect competition is ideal, it has to be better than all other non-competitive alternatives. But as soon as we consider market structures where products are differentiated – oligopoly and monopolistic competition – the notion of identical market demand breaks down. As soon as products become differentiated instead of homogeneous, consumers have more choice, a benefit that potentially offsets other costs to society, as most texts recognize.

Question for your professor: With regard to the deadweight loss supposedly associated with monopoly, is there either evidence or theory to suggest the monopolist would have the same demand and the same costs as the perfectly competitive industry with which it is compared?

2.4 The textbooks concede the point

The texts implicitly concede that perfect competition is of little use as an ideal benchmark. At the very point they begin to discuss government attempts to move markets closer to the competitive 'ideal', they admit that the cure might be worse than the disease. They talk about the benefits of economies of scale; about the problems associated with regulating prices at average costs; about how regulators might become 'captured' by those they attempt to regulate. They raise the possibility that the costs of 'market failure' may be smaller than the costs of 'government failure' found in real political systems.

All the above points are genuine concerns. The real world is complicated and these complications mean that perfect competition is of very little use as an ideal market type. This brings us back full circle to the question: why is the competitive model given such prominence in the typical textbook?

2.5 Evidence, please!

For those who think that perfect competition gives us the 'ideal' output level, the natural question to ask is: how close do we come to it? In a famous 1954 paper, Arnold Harberger made the first stab at estimating the deadweight loss associated with monopoly power. He concluded that the efficiency cost was less than 0.1 per cent of GDP – so small that economists were wasting their time studying it! Naturally, this stimulated a flurry of methodological criticism and alternative estimates. As a 'make-work project' for economists, this was one of the better ones. Economists worked on refining and critiquing each other's estimates for the better part of thirty years before it finally went out of fashion in the mid-1980s.

Figure 6.10 gives a flavour of the issues involved. Harberger simplified the problem by assuming constant long-run average costs (LRC in the

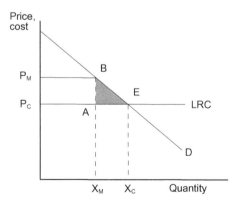

Figure 6.10 Estimating the deadweight loss of monopoly

diagram), which determine the competitive price. The monopoly price is somewhat higher, depending on whether the monopolist needs to discourage a potential rival from entering the market. We don't need to say how much higher, since that can be determined empirically. The difference between the two prices is the height of the deadweight loss triangle. It can be measured by dividing total profits by total output to get profit per unit, which is the same as price minus average costs, or P_M minus P_C in Figure 6.10. Given the height of the triangle, knowing the elasticity of demand would allow us to calculate its length.[19] Harberger simplified by assuming the elasticity to be 1.

The subsequent debate involved a host of questions. One tricky issue is that data on profit will include all profit – even what economists think of as 'normal' profit. But since economists treat 'normal' profit as an opportunity cost, it needs to be subtracted from total profit. Harberger estimated 'normal' profit as the average profit in his data. But depending on the data used, this could end up throwing out the baby with the bathwater. If all firms had equal monopoly power, he would conclude there was no monopoly power at all! A second tricky issue is that reported profits will include profits from price discrimination (which increases supply and reduces welfare losses). Such profits also need to be subtracted out but are very difficult to estimate. A third issue is how to measure the actual elasticities of all the demand curves.

If these issues seem complicated enough – and they are – by far the most awkward measurement issues are the very ones that undermine the notion that perfect competition is an ideal. For example, Stephen Littlechild critiqued the whole approach for ignoring dynamic efficiencies. He argued that profits are a short-term phenomenon arising from successful innovation, without which the product *wouldn't be available* to society. If so, both the monopoly *profit* and the consumer surplus at the monopoly output represent a social *gain*.[20]

> Question for your professor: For thirty years (from the mid-1950s to the mid-1980s) economists attempted to estimate the dead weight loss associated with monopoly power. What did they conclude?

Many also questioned whether costs would be unaffected by market structure. If Leibenstein's X-inefficiencies of monopoly are already embedded in the cost curves of Figure 6.10, Harberger's method will underestimate the deadweight loss. One study concluded: 'Sadly, all these arguments must remain at the level of speculation since we have no better evidence on the matter than was available at the time Leibenstein originally wrote.'[21]

In the third edition of their widely used text on industrial organization Frederic Scherer and David Ross comment: 'In the strictest sense, we operate with a measuring rod (or triangle) of distressingly elastic rubber. In principle, we cannot even tell the direction of the measurement error imparted by neglecting second-best and other general equilibrium repercussions.' They continue: 'Faced with this reality we have two options. We can give up trying to measure the allocative burden of monopoly, or we can cross our fingers and hope the errors from proceeding in a partial equilibrium framework are not too serious.' They admit that they lean towards the second alternative 'more on faith' than logic.[22]

The first edition of this text guesstimated the deadweight loss of monopoly power at 6 per cent of US gross national product (GNP), with a range of uncertainty running from 3 to 12 per cent of GNP. By the third edition, they avoided offering numbers because 'truth was not well served' – the numbers were picked up by journalists or politicians who didn't understand the caveats.[23] Instead, they say: 'The most that can be said with reasonable confidence is that the social costs directly ascribable to monopoly power are modest.'[24] Given all the caveats, however, the faith rather than logic, and given the huge range of uncertainty (from 3 to 12 per cent of GNP!), it seems that Scherer and Ross could just as easily have concluded that we really don't know the deadweight loss associated with monopoly. Indeed, we don't really know for many of the same reasons that perfect competition isn't really an ideal benchmark in the first place.

Nevertheless, the conclusion that the deadweight loss is 'modest' somehow became the consensus (or at least the majority) view. It could be taken to mean that the economy is reasonably close to the perfectly competitive ideal (an ideal which also assumes perfect information). This interpretation could be used to argue that government 'interference' is not worth the trouble. It could justify blanket deregulation – despite the fact that Scherer and Ross themselves cite the role of anti-trust policy in keeping the costs of monopoly power 'modest'.

As Robert Prasch writes: 'Since the late 1970s American economic policy has been almost exclusively informed by ... market fundamentalism. For a remarkable range of issues ... the "conventional wisdom" has been to aggressively promote deregulation and privatization.'[25] This trend began around the time that economists concluded that the social costs of monopoly power were 'modest'. It was surely a contributing factor to the swing towards market fundamentalism. And this is surely ironic. Instead of concluding that perfect competition isn't really of much use in assessing the performance of actual markets, this result was sold as indicating that the actual economy was pretty close to being efficient! Instead of concluding that existing regulation was working quite well, it justified widespread dismantling of regulation!

2.6 The omitted legal framework

Unfortunately, the textbooks have a very limited interpretation of the word 'regulation'. Their focus is almost entirely on regulations that control prices or quantities (quotas). But in the broadest sense, market regulations are the legal framework within which markets operate. They are a key factor in determining what markets are allowed to exist and whether those markets function well. We illustrated their importance in Chapter 3 by showing the effects on the rental housing market of poorly designed eviction protection legislation. Yet the legal and regulatory framework is generally neglected in textbooks.

Moral and ethical judgements are reflected in many aspects of public policy, and in the law and regulations which implement it. Where the textbooks champion the efficiency of mutually beneficial exchanges, they avoid discussing exchanges that raise sensitive moral questions, as David Colander points out. He asks: 'Where is the market failure in selling babies? You have a willing buyer, a willing seller, and a clear case of comparative advantage'.[26] Despite such trades being 'efficient', they are typically prohibited.

Just as selling babies is considered immoral, so too are other markets prohibited or heavily regulated in most countries. Think of the markets for fresh human kidneys, sexual services or many 'recreational' drugs. Apparently, such regulations and prohibitions reflect a collective decision that the efficient market outcome would be socially and ethically undesirable. Its efficiency means that there is no 'market failure', but there are what Colander terms a 'failure of markets' – a failure to reach an ethically acceptable outcome. The same thing happens, as we discussed earlier, if an efficient market economy leaves many people without the necessities of life.

More broadly, the texts shy away from policy questions that 'must be decided within a broader moral framework', presenting them as side issues, not core issues. As a result, Colander worries that thoughtful students who are interested in moral questions may drift away from economics to study other subjects, while the 'less thoughtful students ... come out of the course thinking that policy is an easy task if only people listened to economists and understood economic theory'.[27]

The moral and legal framework for economic life was not always neglected, as Prasch points out. 'A hundred years ago the teaching of economics, especially in the United States and Germany, began with a discussion of property and contract law ... [which] provides readers with a sense of how the economy is embedded in a set of institutions and norms, rules that may even come to be codified in the laws.' He attributes the modern textbook neglect of the legal framework partly to an oversimplified view of what is exchanged. Textbooks focus on 'an abstract good, by tradition termed a "widget" ... to illustrate the "essence" of the market process'.[28]

The widget is an example of what Prasch calls an 'inspection good' – a good whose qualities can be determined by inspection, and is purchased in a 'spot' market. (In a spot market, the transaction is negotiated and settled 'on the spot' during a single meeting or interaction – as in a suburban yard sale.)

The opposite of an 'inspection good' is an 'experience good' – the quality of which can be determined only through long-term experience of it. The opposite of a spot transaction is a 'relational contract', where people (at least implicitly) commit themselves to ongoing business relationships. Such contracts are pervasive in the modern economy. They are involved whenever companies subcontract the production of parts, whenever individuals agree to rent a home or purchase heating oil for delivery over the course of the winter.[29] Experience goods and relational contracts routinely involve asymmetric information, and this may require government regulations to help restrain conflicts of interest and abusive practices.

James Galbraith argues that when people purchase a good they are actually purchasing both the item and some assurance that the product is safe and effective. For a market system to work well, there must be 'a *credible* guarantee of product authenticity and quality. The customer must have reason to believe that the product is what it claims to be, and that it will function as it is supposed to do. This is what a strong system of regulation provides'.[30]

Labour is a type of experience good. It takes time for firms to determine the qualities and work habits of workers. But with labour there is an added twist – workers not only have needs, they also care about how fairly they are treated – a typical aspect in relational contracts. We emphasized these points in Chapter 3 when explaining why minimum wage legislation may not cause unemployment because it may elicit more work effort from minimum wage workers, or may prevent a low-level equilibrium if multiple equilibria are possible.

Asymmetric information, inevitable in the cases of experience goods and relational contracts, results in a variety of problems. First, some people can benefit at the expense of others, compared to a situation where everyone was well-informed. Sellers can convince people to pay high prices for shoddy products. Workers may be exposed to unsafe working conditions without their knowledge. Employers may have difficulty monitoring the work effort of their employees. This last example is an instance of the 'principal-agent' problem, mentioned in Chapter 4, in which a principal attempts to get his or her agent to serve the principal's interests, while the agent would otherwise be inclined to do something else.

Second, it contributes to 'moral hazard', where incentives are changed by certain kinds of contracts. For example, individuals may have less incentive to prevent fires after buying fire insurance, and asymmetric information means that insurers can't easily monitor this.

Third, it results in 'adverse selection' if contracts disproportionately attract undesirable customers. This problem afflicts privately provided medical insurance.

A common solution is for government to provide universal healthcare paid for from general tax revenues. Similar issues arise with unemployment insurance and insurance against destitution.

Perfectly competitive markets require perfect information, so imperfect and asymmetric information are associated with noncompetitive markets. Such markets can't work well if these problems are significant. This opens the door to the possibility that government regulation may improve matters.

Prasch believes the failure to distinguish between inspection goods and experience goods, or between spot markets and relational contracts, explains the 'largely fatuous' dichotomy between government regulation and the "free market" that has become a staple of political discourse in the United States and some other countries. Another regrettable consequence is that 'in the making of economic policy, the legal foundations of market systems are either overlooked or, even worse, taken for granted.'[31]

He contends that failing to acknowledge the legal framework contributes to the erroneous belief that the economic realm lies outside of law and politics. A basic knowledge of the importance of contract and property law would illuminate some of the strengths and weaknesses of markets as economic and social institutions.[32]

If government regulations help to restrain conflicts of interest and abusive practices, why would anyone favour deregulation? Joseph Stiglitz explains that the flip side of regulation is that it restrains profits. In previous chapters we have emphasized that larger corporations and business associations have a strong incentive to try to change the rules of the game in their favour. So deregulation means more profits. Stiglitz argues that, in the case of the United States, those who saw this potential were willing to invest to get it, spending lavishly on campaign contributions and lobbyists. They made the standard argument that deregulation would make markets more competitive, benefiting consumers and society in general. 'But this raised an interesting question: basic laws of economics say that competition is supposed to result in zero profits; if the lobbyists really believed their proposals would result in intense competition, why were they investing so much trying to convince the government to adopt these proposals?'[33]

Question for your professor: Is it true that the legal and regulatory system with in which markets function is important in determining whether markets work well or badly? Do you think we are neglecting this topic?

2.7 Conclusion

This chapter has shown that many of the key predictions of the competitive model do not apply to non-competitive markets. Whenever a firm's demand curve is downward sloping, a price ceiling (as in Figure 6.8) can lead to an increase in quantity supplied without causing a shortage. It is strange, therefore, that textbooks treat the competitive model as a generic model whose predictions apparently apply regardless of market structure. One would suppose that since most markets are non-competitive, the non-competitive predictions would be regarded as generic.

A main theme of our *Anti-Textbook* is to try to explain the overwhelming emphasis placed on competitive markets in principles textbooks. Chapter 3 dismissed claims that such emphasis was justified either by the real-world prevalence of competitive markets, or by the generic applicability of the model's predictions. This chapter dismisses the claims that such emphasis is justified by the usefulness of the competitive model as an ideal market type which can be used to guide government policy.

Finally, in emphasizing the importance of the legal framework, we noted the importance of distinguishing between inspection goods and experience goods, and between spot markets and relational contracts. Experience goods routinely involve asymmetric information. In addition, relational contracts involve issues of needs and fairness. In both cases regulations may be needed to help restrain conflicts of interest and abusive practices. Ideally, regulation should seek to transform experience goods into inspection goods. When it does, it modifies the structure of the market, increasing its size and efficiency.

One way of summarizing this chapter would be to say that even if every good were an inspection good sold on a spot market, competitive markets would still not guarantee an ideal social outcome because of equity considerations, dynamic efficiency considerations, and second-best effects. Once we consider other market structures, then both demand and costs are affected. The major problems with estimating the social cost of monopoly precisely involve these issues. Ironically, the faith-based conclusion that the social costs were 'modest' supported those who had a vested interest in furthering an agenda of deregulation.

SUGGESTIONS FOR FURTHER READING

In his 2019 book, *People, Power, and Profits: Progressive Capitalism for an Age of Discontent*, Joseph Stiglitz makes the case the monopoly power has increased in the United States, with undesirable consequences.

Belgian economist Jan Eekhout describes the growth of market power and its detrimental effects on workers in his 2021 book, *The Profit Paradox: How Thriving Firms Threaten the Future of Work*.

Chapter 7

EXTERNALITIES, COMMON ACCESS RESOURCES AND PUBLIC GOODS: THE UBIQUITY OF MARKET FAILURE

```
Invisible hand;
Mother of inflated hope,
Mistress of despair!
                        – Stephen Ziliak[1]
```

In an address to the American Economic Association in 1972, Joan Robinson asked an inconvenient question: 'In what industry, in what line of business, are the true social costs of the activity registered in its accounts?'[2] The answer is 'none'. Yet the default model of the textbooks assumes that producers of goods and services do pay the full social cost of production. Similarly, when someone buys a good or service, she pays the full cost as well. No one else experiences any costs (or benefits).

If producers or consumers impose such 'external' costs (or confer 'external' benefits) on others and don't take those into account in their decisions, the result would be an inefficient use of resources. The invisible hand drops the ball, yet again.

The most obvious examples where both consumers and producers have been failing to pay the full social costs are the activities that contribute to climate change. The standard texts typically mention this issue in their chapter on externalities. Because of its critical importance, a Postscript chapter is devoted to this, examining the content of the texts and providing an anti-text critique. Unfortunately, as we will see, there is no shortage of other pervasive and serious externalities to consider.

Included in this chapter are two other kinds of goods. External costs play a central role in the analysis of 'common access resources' such as water or wild fish, where people using the resource impose costs on others. The concepts of external benefits and costs also appear when considering 'public goods' (or 'public bads') to which everyone has free access and where no one's use of the good (or bad) reduces others' ability to consume it – for example, a quiet (or an unpleasantly noisy) street.

I THE STANDARD TEXT

1.1 Externalities

Suppose that you're making a decision about how much to drive your car in a week. You weigh the benefits to you of doing various things (going to work, shopping and so on) against the costs you have to pay: fuel, and wear and tear on your car, for example.

The result of this rational choice is illustrated in Figure 7.1. You will drive until the marginal benefit to you of an additional kilometre driven just equals the marginal cost to you of driving that kilometre. Beyond that, the extra costs outweigh the extra benefits. These are termed 'private benefits' and 'private costs' because they are what you, the decision-maker, experiences. If the private costs or benefits change, you would respond accordingly. For example, if public transport became cheaper or quicker, the benefits of driving would fall and you would drive less.

Your choices won't lead to the best social outcome, however, because your driving decisions have effects on others which you haven't taken into account.

In his original analysis of such situations, the English economist Arthur Pigou pointed out that driving leads to wear and tear on the road, a cost that others would have to bear either by repairing the road or by having to drive over a poorer surface.[3] There are other costs too: the emission of toxic pollutants, of greenhouse gases into the atmosphere, increased congestion of the roads, which slows the progress of other drivers and increases their chances of having an accident, which, in turn, increases their insurance costs. In high-traffic density regions these added insurance costs are significant. An extra driver in California adds between $2,000 and $3,000 a year to total statewide insurance costs, costs borne by other drivers.[4]

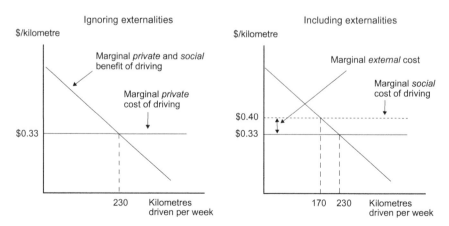

Figure 7.1 Markets are inefficient in the presence of externalities

The person driving the car doesn't bear these costs – they are 'external' to her and are borne by others in the society. The marginal social cost is the marginal private cost to the driver herself plus the marginal external costs she imposes on others. Thus, the marginal social cost of driving another kilometre is greater than the marginal private cost.

In an analogous way, an activity could benefit others. If you plant tulips around your house, others can enjoy the flowers in the spring, but the rational-choice model presumes that you plant the tulips only for your own pleasure, ignoring others' external benefits. (The tulips might even impose external costs on the neighbours if they compare their own properties with yours. A wasteful tulip 'arms race' could take place in which gardens become ever more elaborate and expensive!)

In the case of the driving example, suppose there are no external benefits, so the marginal social benefit is the same as the marginal private benefit to the driver. Suppose the external cost of driving is 7 cents a kilometre. In Figure 7.1, the dashed line shows the marginal social costs of driving a kilometre as 7 cents greater than the marginal private cost. The socially optimal amount of driving is where the marginal social cost equals the marginal social benefit of driving. Clearly, individual decisions result in 'too much' driving from a social point of view, a 'market failure' because resources are not being efficiently used.

There are two solutions to the externality problem. If persons or producers aren't bearing the full costs of their activities, their costs can be raised through appropriate taxes, called Pigouvian taxes, named after Pigou. In Figure 7.1, a tax of 7 cents per kilometre driven would increase the driver's marginal costs by the amount of the externality. This 'internalizes' the externality; the driver now considers the marginal social cost of driving when deciding how much to drive, reducing kilometres driven to the socially optimal amount.

Many governments levy special taxes on motor fuels. These can be justified by the externalities of traffic congestion, damage to roads, and air pollution. (The Postscript examines the case of carbon taxes to deal with greenhouse gas emissions.)

Some cities, notably Stockholm, Milan, Singapore and London have 'congestion charges', special fees that drivers have to pay to enter the city centre at certain times of the day. Research has found that London's congestion fee, currently £15, was successful in reducing accidents, encouraging the use of public transport and bicycles, increasing speed of travel and reducing air pollution.[5]

There is a second, less obvious, way to address some externalities. Externalities arise because there are no markets for some things and hence no price is paid for them. In some cases, markets can be created to do this.

The burning of coal to produce electricity leads to emissions of sulphur dioxide and nitrous oxides which cause 'acid rain'. In the United States, this was successfully controlled by the creation in 1990 of a market for tradable emissions permits. Polluters are required to have a permit, setting a cap on the total amount of pollution. Now using the air for such emissions is no longer free; property rights having been established, they now have a price. The emissions cap was gradually reduced over time, successfully dealing with the problem.

1.2 Common access resources

As seen in the previous example, problems can arise in the absence of property rights in the use of common access resources, such as the air. Sometimes also called common property resources, further examples include water in an aquifer, wild fish and other wild animals, and the classic parable of a field (called the commons) in which everyone may graze their animals. In each case, there is an incentive for overuse.

For example, if a farmer grazes his cows on the village commons, considering only his own animals' benefit, he is imposing an external cost on others by leaving less grass for their animals. The result is overgrazing and a gradual deterioration of the resource, which makes everyone worse off in the long term. This is often called the 'tragedy of the commons'.

An obvious solution is to establish property rights by subdividing the commons among the villagers and a closing the land with fences. The externality disappears and each farmer has an incentive to care properly for his own grazing land.

In the case of a fishery, each fisher, by taking a fish, leaves fewer for others both now and in the future, increasing their costs in finding and catching fish. This external cost can be addressed in various ways including a Pigouvian tax equal to the marginal external cost, or by establishing property rights. The government could issue or sell tradable licences that permit long-term, but limited, access to the common resource. Creating such a market within a country's territorial waters gives everyone in the industry a long-term stake in its future. Credible enforcement is necessary in both cases.

But this cannot address overfishing in international waters, where countries have no jurisdiction. There, the result has been extensive overfishing, threatening many fish stocks with collapse and some species with extinction.

1.3 Public goods

A *pure public good* (also called a collective good) has the characteristic that the benefits any one person gets from it do not reduce the benefits others can get. Because people are not rivals in consuming it, such goods are described as '*non-rival*'. Nor can anyone be excluded from enjoying the benefits, even if they have not contributed toward its cost, a situation termed '*non-excludability*'.

National defence is the classic example. Others are basic research, public health measures, streetlights, TV or radio broadcasts, newspaper and magazine content available on the Internet, fireworks displays, and clean air in a city.

If you drive a noisy motorcycle down the street, you are instead contributing to a '*public bad*', imposing external costs on others from both the noise and the air pollution. Public bads are also non-rival and non-excludable.

Some public goods, such as a city street, are subject to congestion. Because there can be some rivalry in their use, these are called *impure public goods*. Beyond a certain point, as more people consume it, others experience some reduction in their benefits – another example of a negative externality.

Anyone voluntarily producing or contributing to the cost of a public good provides others with an external benefit. If people think only of their own benefits and costs, from a social point of view too few public goods will be provided, if they are provided at all. Self-interested behaviour and 'free riding' by individuals results in too few voluntary contributions to public goods, while resulting in over-contribution to public bads, such as smoggy air.

Collective action is sometimes needed to provide public goods and to restrict public bads. The efficient quantity of a public good is not easy for governments to determine. Ideally, if governments knew the marginal benefit that each person receives from a public good, they could add them up to get the social marginal benefit. The efficient quantity would be that where the social marginal benefit equals the social marginal cost of providing the public good. It would then be paid for through taxation.

But in the same way that no one has an incentive to contribute voluntarily to the public good, no one would have an incentive to accurately state their marginal benefit from the public good if they felt that that would be tied to their tax contribution. Ultimately the amount of publicly provided public goods must be determined by politicians responding to the preferences expressed by citizens in the political process.

The examples of TV and radio broadcasts and free media Internet content shows that (despite the potentially confusing terminology) public goods need not be produced just by the public sector. In those cases, revenues can be raised by selling advertising. Here again, there is no reason to think that the socially optimal amount will be provided.

In general, goods fall into one of four categories, as depicted in Table 7.1. Some goods have the non-rival characteristic of a public good, but, unlike the public good, it's possible to exclude those who don't pay for it. The computer programs used to write this book are a good example. Excludability means that these goods are artificially scarce; otherwise they would be freely available to anyone. Some computer programs are freely available and are pure public goods.

Table 7.1 Classification of types of goods

	Excludable	Non-excludable
Rival	Private goods, e.g. an apple, fish in a fish farm	Common access resources, e.g. air, water, fish in the ocean
Non-rival	Artificially scarce goods, e.g. a computer program	Pure public goods, e.g. a radio programme; open source software

2 THE ANTI-TEXT

The late Joan Robinson of Cambridge University was a sharp critic of textbook economics. She commented on 'the notorious problem of pollution': 'The distinction that Pigou made between private costs and social costs was presented by him as an exception to the benevolent rule of laissez-faire. A moment's thought shows that the exception is the rule and the rule is the exception'.[6]

Unfortunately, current textbook economics downplays the importance of externalities by the 'note but ignore' rhetorical device we have seen before. The texts note the existence of externalities and then largely forget about them. This contributes to the overall message that the market economy is generally efficient.

Mainstream textbook treatment of externalities is remarkably uniform. The topic is always mentioned briefly in an early chapter and is then set aside while the bulk of the book adopts 'no externalities' as its default assumption. Serious consideration of externalities usually reappears only in a chapter towards the end.[7]

If students get this far, they have spent the bulk of the course admiring the works of the invisible hand. It would be easy to get the impression that externalities are of peripheral, not central, importance. This would be the case if external effects were not significant or if governments address them adequately.

In reality, externalities are pervasive and are of great practical importance. Every year, they cost millions of people their lives. They threaten to make the planet uninhabitable for many species, perhaps eventually including our own. They are involved in everyone's consumption decisions every day. They even contribute to the instability of the financial system. The no-externalities default model of the textbooks invites us to forget these simple facts.

Many of the biggest externalities are also remarkably hard to deal with through collective action. It would be easy to get the impression from the textbooks that well-informed economists determine what government policy should be to counteract externalities, and that politicians then implement it. Is this what happens in practice? The textbooks don't say because, for the most part, they don't deal adequately with how government policy is actually determined. (We return to this topic in Chapter 9.)

As we've argued in Chapter 5, business power combined with a poorly informed public often plays a central role in shaping public policy, and that sensitive topic is off limits. As a result, the textbooks give the misleading impression that externalities and related market failures involving public goods and common access resources are minor blots on the landscape.

2.1 Externalities in reality

Let's briefly consider some actual externalities to support our contention that they deserve a central place in the analysis of the modern economy. At the same time, we consider whether these externalities are likely to be adequately addressed in light of the realities of power and information in the societies involved.

Meta-externalities

The classic textbook externality takes place entirely within the economic system: for example, a manufacturing plant puts waste into a river which harms a downstream fishery. Instead, *meta-externalities* are, as Neva Goodwin puts it, the side effects 'of the economic system, as a whole, on the social and ecological environment in which it is embedded — and on whose health the continuing health and vitality of the economy depends'.[8] The term meta-externality does not appear in any standard textbook, despite their importance.

The economic activities contributing to climate change have created the most serious negative meta-externality. As noted earlier, because of its critical importance, we devote the Postscript to a text/anti-text case study of climate change. Here, let's consider some other examples, generally unmentioned by the textbooks.

One reason that meta-externalities are ignored in the standard text is because economic life is typically portrayed in isolation from its social and environmental context. As a result, the connections between these are often overlooked.

For example, the outcomes of the economic system can affect (positively or negatively) the viability of democracy and the quality of communities. The long-term increase in literacy rates and levels of education required for the modern economy have had beneficial effects. The growth of economic inequality in many countries in recent decades has had a negative effect, eroding democracy and strengthening plutocratic power. While unacknowledged in the textbooks, this linkage is recognized in political debates about the taxation of income and wealth in many countries. Another example is the interest that the business sector has in shaping the tastes and preferences of the population, encouraging a culture of consumerism instead of 'promoting the responsibility, frugality, and other values that will be needed in the difficult times of the twenty-first century', as Neva Goodwin observes. Another example she gives are 'the toxins and nonbiodegradable wastes building up in huge quantities throughout the Earth's ecosystems. No single corporation has major responsibility for these; they come from the whole system'.[9]

Plastic pollution 'Geologists are now considering a plastic horizon in the world's soils and sediments as one of the key indicators marking the current geological epoch, the Anthropocene', write Canadian marine biologist Boris Worm and his co-authors, whose focus is on the ocean. Between 5 and 13 million metric tonnes of plastics (1.5 to 4 percent of world production) enter the ocean annually. Once there, it 'cannot be easily removed, accumulates in organisms and sediments, and persists much longer than on land. New evidence indicates a complex toxicology of plastic micro- and nanoparticles on marine life, and transfer up the food chain, including to people.'[10]

Most of the materials used to make plastics, including synthetic fibers, come from fossil hydrocarbons and are not biodegradable. A comprehensive study of all plastics produced since mass production began in the early 1950s concluded that, 'as of 2015, approximately 6300 Mt [million metric tonnes] of plastic waste had been generated, around 9% of which had been recycled, 12% was incinerated, and 79% was accumulated in landfills or the natural environment.' As a result, 'near-permanent contamination of the natural environment with plastic waste is a growing concern.' The authors concluded that 'without a well-designed and tailor-made management strategy for end-of-life plastics, humans are conducting a singular uncontrolled experiment on a global scale, in which billions of metric tons of material will accumulate across all major terrestrial and aquatic ecosystems on the planet' with effects that are only now being investigated.[11]

Micro plastics and even smaller pieces called nano plastics, the result of the breakdown of plastic waste into ever smaller pieces, are now everywhere, 'in the air, soil, rivers and the deepest oceans around the world.'[12] They are in our tap water, in things we eat and in the air we breathe. How many tens or hundreds of thousands of particles the average person ingests each year is unknown as are the long-term consequences.

An important feature of this kind of pollution is that its costs remain unknown and were not properly anticipated. The standard story of the Pigouvian tax assumes that regulators know the costs and so set appropriate taxes. Instead, with the costs unclear but potentially large, we face a problem of dealing with risk. As with the risks from climate change, business as usual, with ever increasing plastic production, should not be an option.

The visible plastic pollution has finally got public attention. Photographs of dead animals, from whales to albatross chicks with plastic in their stomachs, make for unpleasant viewing; many have learned of the existence of the Great North Pacific Garbage Patch, one of five such collections of large and small pieces of plastic and other garbage in the oceans.[13]

In many countries, this is producing a reaction against plastic bags, straws and bottles. By 2020, about 500 billion plastic bottles were being produced annually. Less than half were collected for recycling. Requiring buyers to pay a small deposit, redeemable when the bottle is recycled effectively encourages recycling, but in the United States, only 10 of the 50 states require such deposits. Beverage companies have successfully opposed such legislation for decades.[14]

Of recycled bottles, only a tiny fraction was used to make new bottles.[15] In general, the plastics currently in use have a low value for recycling due to the presence of various additives as well as the loss of important characteristics with each re-use. However, publicly funded research is developing some new plastics which can overcome these problems, allowing them to be recycled and recombined indefinitely, greatly reducing their environmental impact.[16]

Air pollution 10 years. This is the reduction in life expectancy of the average resident in Delhi, India, because of excessive air pollution from fine particulate matter as estimated in 2018 by the Air Quality of Life Index. Living in Beijing costs the average resident eight years of life expectancy; Los Angeles costs almost a year, London 0.4 years. Across the world, if World Health Organization air quality guidelines were met, average life expectancy would rise by almost 2 years. 'This life expectancy loss makes particulate pollution more devastating than communicable diseases like tuberculosis and HIV/AIDS, behavioral killers like cigarette smoking, and even war', as two researchers explain.[17]

Fine particulate matter ($PM_{2.5}$) are small particles less than 2.5 μm (i.e. microns or micrometres) in diameter, less than 1/30 the thickness of a human hair. They are produced by the burning of fossil fuels, which also creates a variety of other pollutants such as carbon monoxide, sulphur dioxide, and nitrogen oxides.[18] Breathing these invisible pollutants and other pollutants that form from them (such as ozone) damage the lungs and directly influence respiratory and cardiovascular illnesses and lung cancers. But the effects of $PM_{2.5}$ are even more pervasive, affecting virtually every organ in the body.[19] As a review of the evidence explains, 'tissue damage may result directly from pollutant toxicity because fine and ultrafine particles can gain access to organs, or indirectly through systemic inflammatory processes.... Harmful effects occur on a continuum of dosage and even at levels below air quality standards previously considered to be safe.' Children are particularly at risk, including through prenatal exposure.[20]

While the thick smog in big Indian and Chinese cities rightly gets a lot of attention, even the much lower levels of particulates (achieved through public pressure) in the world's wealthiest countries are still killing substantial numbers of people and causing health problems, such as asthma, for many more. Worldwide, the WHO estimates that 90 percent of people live where $PM_{2.5}$ pollution exceeds its guidelines, but even these are not a 'safe' level of exposure.[21]

Estimates of the deaths and morbidity from air pollution have increased sharply as both better techniques and better data become available. Worldwide, about 8.9 million people die prematurely given the air pollution levels of 2015 according to two studies.[22] The additional deaths are primarily due to heart disease, strokes, chronic obstructive pulmonary disease, lung cancer, and lower respiratory tract infections.

Even in Europe, an estimated 790,000 people die prematurely annually from its effects, leading to a reduction in average life expectancy of 2.2 years.[23] This is more than twice as high as earlier estimates.

But wait – after all, the textbooks like to emphasize that the optimal level of pollution is not zero. It's a matter of comparing marginal costs and marginal benefits. How do we know that the pollution we're observing is excessive from a social point of view?

However, a cost-benefit analysis can't be done without knowing its health costs and ongoing research is showing that it causes much more damage than had previously been understood. We also can't forget the political realities of regulatory policy. Where democracy is weak or nonexistent, pollution levels can't be said to reflect collective choice, although even nondemocratic governments must pay some attention to public opinion. Even where democracy appears stronger, governments are still susceptible to corporate power. For example, the cheating on emissions tests by Volkswagen and other European diesel-powered car manufacturers seems to have been quietly overlooked by government regulators to protect their own industries.[24]

In the United States it took the emergence of a nascent environmental movement backed by growing public concern about the effects of pollution on human health to greatly strengthen the Clean Air Act in 1970. The reduction in pollution, largely due to this Act, added an estimated 1.5 years to the life of an average American.[25]

The US national standard is an annual average $PM_{2.5}$ of 12 µg/m³, 2 units more than the WHO guideline, but half that of the European Union's 25, and far lower than India's 40. Having standards doesn't mean that they are achieved, only that regulations are supposed to be trying to attain them. In 2015, the average Indian was exposed to 74 µg/m³, almost twice the standard. Compared with a safe level of particulate matter, one study concludes this would result in about 2.2 million premature deaths annually, exceeded only by China's 2.5 million.[26]

The good news in this gloomy picture is that if countries reduce fossil fuel use to deal with climate change, the burden of disease and death from air pollution will fall significantly. For example, eliminating fossil fuel emissions in Europe could reduce premature deaths by more than 400,000 per year, adding 1.2 years to average life expectancy.[27] Many European cities are already acting. Amsterdam, for example, is phasing in measures that will ultimately ban all gasoline and diesel vehicles from the city by 2030.[28]

Chemical pollutants Compared with air pollution, our understanding of the effects of chemical pollutants is still in its infancy. The *Lancet* Commission on Pollution and Health summarized our state of ignorance:

> More than 140,000 new chemicals and pesticides have been synthesised since 1950. Of these materials, the 5000 that are produced in greatest volume have become widely dispersed in the environment and are responsible for nearly universal human exposure. Fewer than half of these high-production volume chemicals have undergone any testing for safety or toxicity, and rigorous pre-market evaluation of new chemicals has become mandatory in only the past decade and in only a few high-income countries.[29]

They worry that the damage from the untested materials of the past, such as lead, asbestos, DDT, PCBs, and ozone-destroying chlorofluorocarbons, will be repeated in the future with newer synthetic chemicals. These include 'developmental neurotoxicants, endocrine disruptors, chemical herbicides, novel insecticides, pharmaceutical wastes, and nanomaterials.' Their concern is 'heightened by the increasing movement of chemical production to low-income and middle-income countries where public health and environmental protections are often scant.'[30]

But firms in all countries, including high income ones, may be asking themselves 'When is it profit maximizing to put a dangerous chemical into the environment, either to dump it as waste or to sell it as/in a product?' If Homo economicus is asking this question, ethical considerations play no role; if firm profits can increase by doing things that will leave people injured, sick or dead, it will do so. It should also consider reputational costs, fines imposed by regulators, and, if those harmed bring successful legal action against it, out of court settlements or court awarded damages. Ideally, such costs should deter a firm from taking socially harmful actions, but often in practice they don't.

Consider persistent organic pollutants, sometimes dubbed "forever chemicals" because they do not biodegrade. One such chemical, PFOA (also called C8), was used to make non-stick cookware and to coat fabrics and carpets among other uses. It is now found in the blood of people worldwide. It is associated with birth defects, among other things.[31]

Economists Roy Shapira and Luigi Zingales examined the behaviour of DuPont, a prominent American chemical company and its illegal dumping of PFOA.[32] DuPont, knowing perfectly well what it was doing, made the rational choice to dump PFOA rather than dispose of it properly. Shapira and Zingales concluded that this decision reflected a more general problem: the deterrents are just too weak. In general, 'chemical companies can use their informational advantage to delay liability, fend off regulators, and cast doubts in ways that limit a reputational sanctioning process.'[33]

On its current path, the global chemical industry will double in size between 2017 and 2030. As the head of the UN Environmental Programme writes: 'Large quantities of hazardous chemicals and pollutants continue to leak into the environment, contaminating food chains and accumulating in our bodies, where they do serious damage. Estimates by the European Environment Agency suggest that 62 per cent of the volume of chemicals consumed in Europe in 2016 were hazardous to health.'[34]

The WHO estimated that in 2016 there were 1.6 million preventable deaths from chemical pollution, with harm to tens of millions more. These are underestimates because they are limited to substances where we have reliable global data.[35] With such disproportionate corporate power and incomplete scientific knowledge, we cannot be observing socially optimal pollution levels.

Antimicrobial resistance Microbes such as bacteria, viruses, and parasites such as malaria, have been major killers throughout human history. In the 20th century, researchers developed drugs such as antibiotics and antivirals, saving countless lives. The use of these drugs involves two kinds of externalities. One is a positive externality: microbes are killed and prevented from spreading to other people, who experience a benefit. The second is a negative externality. The use of the drug, and particularly its misuse, can result in the evolution of microbes resistant to the treatment. Such antimicrobial resistance has been steadily growing and threatens both current and future generations. Diseases that were once treatable, will become untreatable; routine operations that require antibiotics to prevent postoperative infections will become increasingly risky.

In 2019, England's chief medical officer, Sally Davies, said that antimicrobial resistance is a threat as great as climate change, although there is much less awareness about it. At the same time, Haileyesus Getahun, the director of the UN's Interagency Coordination Group on Antimicrobial Resistance (IACG), gave a similar warning: 'We don't see the effects of it yet, but what is coming will be a catastrophe.'[36]

The IACG 2019 report stated that 700,000 people annually are being killed by drug-resistant diseases, a third of these from tuberculosis.[37] If no action is taken, they expect 10 million deaths annually by midcentury. Among their many recommendations is the phasing out of the use of antibiotics in promoting growth in farmed animals.[38] This is already banned in the EU and the US but is common in many countries. For example, an investigation in 2018 found that hundreds of tonnes of colistin, a powerful antibiotic, were being imported into India and used to increase the growth rate of industrially produced chickens. This will hasten the development of resistance to a drug which is 'one of the last lines of defence against serious diseases, including pneumonia, which cannot be treated by other medicines.'[39]

A study of major rivers in 2019 found antibiotics critically important for the treatment of serious infections present in 65 percent of the 711 test sites in 72 countries. 16 percent had antibiotic concentrations exceeding levels at which bacterial resistance is likely to develop. The drugs come from untreated or improperly treated human and animal waste and even leaks from drug manufacturing facilities. Such environmental pollution is an important source of growing antibacterial resistance. Pollution is greatest in poorer countries, but the consequences will be worldwide.[40]

Pharmaceutical companies have shown little interest in developing new antibiotics which would be kept in reserve for only the most hard-to-treat cases. Development costs would be high and sales would be low. As a result, the UN's IACG report, mentioned earlier, called for more investment from public, private, and philanthropic sources. British economist Jim O'Neill, who headed an important British government review of antimicrobial resistance, has suggested offering billion-dollar rewards to companies developing such drugs as a way of overcoming the problem.[41]

```
Question for your professor: Isn't market inefficiency
the norm rather than the exception? If externalities
are pervasive and important, why doesn't the textbook
integrate them throughout the book, rather than
leaving them to a chapter towards the end?
```

Positional externalities in consumption

```
'A house may be large or small; as long as the
surrounding houses are equally small it satisfies all
social demands for a dwelling. But if a palace rises
beside the little house, the little house shrinks
into a hut.' Karl Marx[42]
```

People's assessment of their own material situation depends in part on what other people have. If few people have their own vehicle, for example, then you won't feel the lack of one nearly as much as if everyone else has one and you don't. The same thing holds for other visible consumption goods: houses, cars, clothing, jewellery, furnishings and appliances, and so on.

What others in society have sets your 'frame of reference', as Robert Frank terms it.[43] Everyone is affected by their knowledge of what others have. In subtle but real ways, each person's consumption decisions affect the comparisons everyone makes in assessing their relative position and thus their satisfaction with their own material well-being.

For example, suppose that you notice a beautiful pair of $500 Italian shoes in a store window. Carried away, you buy them. Everyone who notices your shoes will now judge their own consumption standards by a slightly altered frame of reference. If their shoes suddenly look second rate beside yours, your purchase devalued them. Your extravagance created a negative externality by lowering their consumption levels relative to yours.

Frank calls these 'positional externalities'; their cumulative effect adds up in the same way that millions of people driving a few more kilometres adds up in terms of air pollution. This results in people systematically engaging in futile 'expenditure arms races' on those 'positional goods' that most enhance their relative consumption position. The other side of the coin is that too few resources are devoted to 'non-positional' goods whose consumption isn't easily observed by others. These include things we produce and consume individually (going for a walk, taking more holidays, socializing with friends) or consume collectively (public libraries, roads, parks). Thus positional externalities distort the entire pattern of consumption, lowering everyone's well-being. The result resembles outcome of the Prisoners' Dilemma that we saw in the previous chapter. Everyone chooses what's best for them given what others have chosen, but the result is that everyone has too many 'positional goods'.

© Andy Singer

This unhappy result is ruled out by the standard textbook assumption that individual well-being depends only on absolute, not relative, consumption.[44] The problem with this default model is that (as Frank puts it) it 'is inconsistent with our best theoretical understanding of the origins and functions of human motivations; and it is flatly at odds with extensive direct and indirect empirical evidence regarding the nature of utility'.[45]

For example, in a unique study, University of Zürich economist Rainer Winkelmann examined the relationship between the registration of new Ferraris and Porsches in Swiss municipalities and cantons and survey data on people's satisfaction with their incomes. Information about new luxury cars is a rough indicator of the extent of conspicuous consumption in the area. He found that if the rate of registration of such cars were to double, from 0.2 to 0.4 per 1000 population, it 'would have an adverse effect on predicted income satisfaction equal to that of a 5% reduction in income.'[46]

Conspicuous consumption can be reined in only by collective action. Frank has argued that progressive taxes on annual consumption spending are the most effective tool to correct this externality. Under such a scheme, people would be able to deduct from taxable income all savings placed in registered accounts.[47] Because income equals consumption plus saving, the tax base is annual consumption spending. The extra tax paid per dollar of spending would rise with an individual's total annual consumption spending; Frank suggests top marginal tax rates of 70 per cent or so , but (unlike with an income tax) rates of over 100 percent are feasible. This would make the tax 'progressive' in the sense that total tax paid as a share of a person's income would be higher for higher-income persons.[48] He writes:

> If a progressive consumption tax is to curb the waste that springs from excessive spending on conspicuous consumption, its rates at the highest levels must be sufficiently steep to provide meaningful incentives for people atop the consumption pyramid. For unless their spending changes, the spending of those just below them is unlikely to change either, and so on all the way down.[49]

Because the tax would collect more from higher-income households and less from lower-income households than the current US tax system, it would reduce total spending on conspicuous consumption goods. Some spending on $20,000 Hermès Kelly alligator handbags would be replaced by increased spending by lower-income families on necessities. It would also encourage people to engage in untaxed consumption: working less to spend more leisure time with friends and family, going for a walk or reading a library book. All of these activities have been reduced by the wasteful consumption arms race.

Frank thinks opposition to such a tax is based on the widespread, and false, belief that imposing higher tax rates on the rich will cripple the economy. He's not optimistic about such a policy actually being adopted when political programmes apparently have to be explained in ten-second sound bites.

Other forms of collective action can also help to address these consumption externalities. If spending to keep up with the Joneses leads people to work excessively long hours, increases in legislated minimum holidays could help. Business owners, however, have an interest in promoting the cycle of work-and-spend. As the American abolitionist Frederick Douglass famously put it: 'Power concedes nothing without demand. It never did and it never will.' In the European Union, where social democratic parties have a long history in many countries and unions organize a large part of the labour force, people are entitled to a minimum of four weeks of paid vacation per year, although some countries legislate five or six weeks. Australia and New Zealand also have a minimum of four weeks, while Canada and Japan have two. In the United States, where unions are weak and the power of business is exceptionally strong, there is no federal legislation requiring paid vacations. Most high income countries have legislated at least six paid holidays per year; in the United States: none. Without national rules, almost a quarter of American workers have no paid vacation or paid holidays.[50]

Questions for your professor: Do consumption externalities exist? If so, why doesn't the text book mention them?

2.2 Another look at common access resources

Every textbook mentions the problems with common access resources – often at the back of the book and rather briefly. As described in the Standard Text part of this chapter, solutions focus on government regulation or creation of tradable property rights.

Ignored is the fact that communities around the world have typically devised their own ways to successfully manage their local common access resources such as grazing lands, forests, wildlife, inshore fisheries and irrigation systems. American political scientist Elinor Ostrom (and 2009 recipient of the Nobel Memorial Prize in Economics) pointed out that 'When local users feel a sense of ownership and dependence on a local resource, many of them invest intensively in designing and implementing ingenious local institutions – some of which are sustained for centuries.'

How is this possible? Simple – most people are not like the Homo economicus assumed by simple economic theory. The evidence shows that if others offer to cooperate, most people are willing to reciprocate. They are also willing to punish non-cooperators, even at a cost to themselves. This can result in the evolution of lasting cooperation. Ostrom explained that: 'So long as they can identify one another, trustworthy fair reciprocators actually achieve higher material rewards over time than rational egoists!'[51]

She was sharply critical of textbook policies, based as they are on the assumptions that 'only short-term selfish actions are expected from "the common people"' and that 'citizens do not have the knowledge or skills needed to design appropriate institutions to overcome collective-action problems', but must instead rely on professional planners. She considered these 'devastating messages in regard to the long-term development and sustenance of a democratic society.'[52] The result would also be inefficient and ineffective policy.

Furthermore, the assumption that short-term selfish actions are the norm 'basically says that it is okay to be narrowly self interested and to wait for externally imposed inducements for sanctions before voluntarily contributing to collective action', a message that 'undermines the normative foundations of a free society.'[53] Yet this is precisely the view that economics students are invited to accept.

When dealing with larger scale problems with common resources, Ostrom maintained that 'a variety of overlapping policies at city, subnational, national, and international levels is more likely to succeed than are single, overarching binding [international] agreements.' This *polycentric* approach permits rapid evolution and adaption as people learn from each other's experience about what works and what doesn't.[54]

A few texts do contain good factual accounts of the current state of common access resources, focused on fisheries, but most say little or nothing.[55] Let's have a brief look at two issues.

The slow-motion collapse of the world's fisheries Even in the late nineteenth century, biologists declared the world's fisheries 'inexhaustible' and regulation a waste of time.[56] These optimistic assessments were completely wrong. Advances in fishing technology combined with population growth and increased demand has put ever growing pressure on fish stocks. A study of fisheries worldwide found the median fishery to be 'in poor health (overfished, with further overfishing occurring), although 32% of fisheries are in good biological, although not necessarily economic, condition.' Its 'business-as-usual scenario projects further divergence and continued collapse for many of the world's fisheries.'[57] By 2050, 88 percent of stocks would be overfished.

If effective local management, as described by Ostrom, is not an option, the textbook recommendation of 'individual transferable quotas', limiting the total catch, may work within a country's territorial waters. But the country would need strong institutions (to resist industry demands for excessive quotas) and enforcement capabilities.[58] But this may simply shift more fishing fleets into international waters, where no one has jurisdiction, or to the coastal waters of developing countries, many of which lack enforcement capabilities.[59]

Let's try to end on an optimistic note. Fisheries scientist Boris Worm points out that advances in satellite monitoring of fishing vessels offer hope that enforcement can improve, while the United Nations is 'working toward a new implementation Agreement to better protect biodiversity, vital food resources, and natural capital on the high seas.' As if following Ostrom's polycentric prescription, a wide variety of marine protected areas are being established by authorities ranging from local, subnational, and national governments as well as at the international level. Such protected areas currently comprise just over 4 percent of the world's ocean area but have been expanding rapidly. Still, this has fallen short of the international target for 2020 of 10 percent.[60]

Biodiversity and species extinction The problems facing fisheries worldwide from overfishing, pollution, and climate change are just one part of the impact human activity is having on the natural world. A recent study examined the prospects for the world's largest vertebrates among fresh and saltwater fish, birds, amphibians, reptiles and mammals. It asked: 'Are we eating the world's megafauna to extinction?' The answer: for most of them, 'yes'. 70 percent have declining populations; 59 percent are threatened with extinction. The primary cause? Killing for human use.[61]

The authors report that about one fifth of the world's vertebrate species are threatened with extinction. The major causes are overexploitation and habitat loss as the human population has grown. Because of human actions more broadly, including climate change, there is 'mounting evidence that humans are poised to cause a sixth mass extinction event.'[62]

Unfortunately, the major international group studying this, the Intergovernmental Science-Policy Platform on Biodiversity and Ecosystem Services (IPBES), agrees. In a 2019 report it concluded that biodiversity and ecosystems are deteriorating worldwide, pointing to land-use changes, pollution, and climate change as the major drivers.

> Human actions threaten more species with global extinction now than ever before. An average of around 25 per cent of species in assessed animal and plant groups are threatened... suggesting that around 1 million species [of a total of 8 million, 75 percent of which are insects] already face extinction, many within decades, unless action is taken ... Without such action, there will be a further acceleration in the global rate of species extinction, which is already at least tens to hundreds of times higher than it has averaged over the past 10 million years.[63]

The IPBES says that what's required are 'transformative changes', which means a 'fundamental, system-wide reorganization across technological, economic and social factors, including paradigms, goals and values.'[64] If that sounds like the same daunting set of things that are needed to tackle climate change adequately, it's no coincidence. Both the pressures on the biosphere and climate change are the product of meta-externalities with both societal and ecological impacts.

2.3 Public goods – a second look

We will focus on two main problems with the textbook treatment of public goods. First, the importance of public goods is understated, in part because certain public goods are ignored even though they are central features of human society. Second, the assumption that people are self-interested and will free ride results in predictions that are wrong in important cases. There is no excuse for this because other, more plausible, assumptions about people's motivations are readily available that better explain the facts.

Underemphasized and overlooked public goods As American economist Louis Putterman writes, 'The concept of public goods is well established in economics. But it's not too difficult to come away with the impression that they constitute a small subset of society's requirements and can be dealt with as just "a few special cases".'[65] In fact, as he points out, the physical and social infrastructure provided by public goods are essential in the production of private goods.

The laws, regulations and public policy that underpin social and economic life are public goods. In principle, they apply to everyone within a government's jurisdiction. It follows that actions to change these are also public goods. In Chapter 9, we'll consider aspects of this public good: civic participation – paying some attention to public affairs, voting, and other political activity. Without enough of it, democratic states could never have developed and could not sustain themselves. If civic participation declines, civil society could become too weak to sustain democracy. The result could be a new equilibrium with dysfunctional institutions from which it would be hard to escape.

We saw in Chapter 4 that average levels of trust in private and public institutions and the extent of social connections and supports among people were important in explaining differences in subjective well-being between countries. Social connectedness and trust in others are components of *social capital* and are public goods. Everyone in a society would benefit from high levels of trust, the absence of corruption, and extensive social connections among people.

American political scientist Robert Putnam describes social capital as 'connections among individuals – social networks and the norms of reciprocity and trustworthiness that arise from them.' Forming interpersonal connections is done for private benefit, but they have important external benefits, giving social capital both a private and the public good dimension.[66] As in Elinor Ostrom's account of the development and maintenance of cooperation in managing common access resources, social norms – 'shared understandings about actions that are obligatory, permitted, or forbidden' – play a central role.[67] The social norms of reciprocity and trustworthiness are public goods which are self-reinforcing and critical in facilitating economic, social and civic life more broadly.

Given the fundamental importance of these public goods, it is remarkable that they go virtually unmentioned in the texts. There are other public goods which are largely ignored.

Earlier in this chapter, we saw Robert Frank's point that each person's consumption decisions about positional goods affect the frame of reference that others use to judge their own consumption standards. Everyone's decisions, in turn, influence the frame of reference, which evolves over time. This frame of reference satisfies all the definitions of a public good: it is non-rival and nonexcludable. Its importance is clear: it can result in a wasteful positional goods 'arms race' leaving everyone worse off.

Everyone is also affected by the distribution of income – a public good to be examined in Chapter 9. As we'll see, it matters a lot whether you and your fellow citizens live in an egalitarian society with low income inequality or, at the other extreme, a highly unequal one.

Voluntary contributions to public goods Getting voluntary payments for a public good resembles the prisoner's dilemma that we saw in the previous chapter. There, both firms would be better off if they each charged the monopoly price, but faced difficulties coordinating their actions, because each is tempted to charge a lower price. With a public good, everyone would be best off if each contributed, but each is tempted to free ride. With many people involved, the coordination problem is more difficult. If people are self-interested, there will be no contributions. If some have a social conscience, they will quickly be discouraged by the presence of free riders. Hence the need for public provision paid for by taxation. This reasoning works well enough for things like the standard examples of financing national defence and basic research. But let's go beyond that.

One exception is any situation where the private benefits of a contribution exceed the private costs, although the texts assume this to be rare or trivial (e.g planting flowers that others also enjoy). An important everyday example is the case when individuals form connections that result in the social networks described by Robert Putnam. Another, discussed further below, are individual actions that adhere to social norms.

The fundamental problem with the general prediction of no contribution to a public good, as Elinor Ostrom observed, is that it

> contradicts observations of everyday life. After all, many people vote, do not cheat on their taxes, and contribute effort to voluntary associations. Extensive fieldwork has by now established that individuals in all walks of life and all parts of the world voluntarily organize themselves so as to gain the benefits of trade, to provide mutual protection against risk, and to create and enforce rules that protect natural resources.[68]

Other striking examples can be found in the newspapers every day. Here is one selected virtually at random.

In the fall of 2020, Chileans voted overwhelmingly to establish a new constitution to replace the one imposed by the 1973–1990 Pinochet military dictatorship, which had been written with the assistance of economists such as James Buchanan (whom we will encounter again in Chapter 9).[69] The referendum followed a year of mass protests carried out by millions of people in the face of police violence. At least three dozen were killed, thousands injured, hundreds with eye damage or loss of vision because of munitions fired by the police.[70]

Such an attempt to change the constitution and thus what public policy could be is a public good (or a public bad, depending on your political viewpoint). The textbook model would predict that everyone would be sitting at home, hoping that others would take to the streets to face the police.

Ostrom wrote that while cooperative behaviour is widespread, it is not inevitable. What's needed is a better understanding of how it can evolve and be sustained.

Experimental economists have tackled this question by creating many different public goods games. These explore how people behave when offered an opportunity to gain through collective action by contributing resources to a public good.

For example, imagine 10 people in a laboratory setting in which they can't communicate with each other. Each person receives 10 tokens for each round of play, each token worth a certain amount of money. Everyone chooses how much to contribute to a public good which provides benefits for everyone. For instance, if a person contributes all 10 tokens to the public good, every participant would receive 5 tokens. If every person contributed all of their tokens, 100 in total, each person would receive 50 tokens. Collectively, this is obviously the best outcome, but if an uncooperative *Homo economicus* is participating, he will free ride, letting the others contribute 90, giving everyone a payoff of 45. By keeping his 10 tokens, he ends up with 55 tokens. Obviously if everyone thinks this way, no one will contribute anything – the prediction of standard theory.[71]

The experimental evidence overwhelmingly rejects this prediction. Whether played once or repeatedly a fixed number of times, the average contribution in the first round of the game is about half of the tokens, not zero. In general, these experiments provide evidence that many people are willing to cooperate with others if they hope or expect that a sufficient number will reciprocate. In games in which players can punish others at a cost to themselves (e.g. losing one token while the other player loses four tokens), some will do this to inflict costs on low contributors, possibly leading them to contribute more in future rounds of the game. Face-to-face communication before the game also enhances cooperation.[72]

All in all, the results suggest that people fall into different broad categories. Ostrom calls them 'conditional cooperators', 'willing punishers', and 'rational egoists'. Despite the presence of the rational egoists, who would like to free ride if it were profitable, even they can be induced to cooperate if credibly threatened with punishment for noncooperation. Experiments where punishment is possible have shown that it takes only a small fraction of 'willing punishers' to bring about this kind of self-reinforcing and sustained cooperation.[73] It's not hard to see how this has real world parallels.

This does not surprise evolutionary psychologists. Over most of the last several million years of human evolution, people have lived in small bands of hunter gatherers. While individuals had to look out for their own interests, cooperation and risk sharing were necessary for the group to prosper. The result was the evolution of a preference to cooperate, at least on the part of most people, as well as of skills in recognizing who can and can't be trusted.[74]

Another product of evolution is people's ability to learn and to internalize the social norms of their society. Those who do are likely to be recognized by others as 'trustworthy reciprocators', to their benefit. They voluntarily contribute to this public good by reinforcing it through their own behaviour. It pays them to do so because violating social norms would cause feelings of guilt as well as potential shame if others found out. Clearly, not everyone in the same society is socialized in the same way and personalities differ. The need remains to watch out for norm violators.

Despite their artificial nature, the laboratory experiments described earlier provide insights into actual societies which have many collective action problems to solve – persuading people to go to the trouble of recycling, to pay their taxes, not to shirk at work or steal from their employers, and on and on. The behaviour of people in the experiments have their real-world counterparts: people who are willing to do their part if others do as well; people who, perhaps motivated by indignation, are willing to pay some price to impose a cost on norm violators. By providing this public good they help to reduced norm violation and to enhance cooperation.

As well, based on experiments conducted in different parts of the world, Louis Putterman notes 'a link between norms of social cooperation and the quality of institutions across societies, one that may even contribute to explaining why some of the societies are more economically developed than others.' They also give insights into how institutions could evolve to enhance cooperation, learning from past experience and from the experience of others. Putterman writes that 'diffusion from organization to organization, company to company, city to city, country to country, and so forth doubtless accounts for some real improvements in economic and social practices over both short and long spans of time.'[75]

Finally, with their analysis of public goods the textbooks are doing students no favour by telling them that it is 'rational' to free ride. Unfortunately, there is some evidence from experimental economics that this message has an effect. Public goods experiments have been conducted with economics students and people with other backgrounds. Not surprisingly, they consistently find that economics students are much more likely to free ride than others. After reviewing the studies, Norbert Häring and Niall Douglas remark: 'Thus do economic theories influence social norms of accepted behavior and become self-fulfilling.'[76]

2.4 Summing up: externalities, common access resources, public goods and the market economy

The idealized perfectly competitive market economy that allocates scarce resources efficiently is also one that presumes that there are no market failures. But the conclusion that such a fictitious 'free market' economy is efficient (although, admittedly, not equitable) is no justification for a presumption of laissez-faire. At best, it's an intellectual toy that could be used to stress just how different the actual economy is from this imaginary world.

But instead of stressing the differences, the texts stress the similarities. For example, at the beginning of their text, Paul Krugman and Robin Wells offer a list of fundamental principles. The eighth reads: 'Markets Usually Lead to Efficiency, But When They Don't, Government Intervention Can Improve Society's Welfare'. Efficiency is portrayed as the norm 'because in most cases the invisible hand does the job' as people go about exploiting the gains from trade with each other.[77]

The modern market economy has indeed produced a high material standard of living for many people in the developed world and a growing number in the developing world. But this is not the same thing as 'efficiency'. As we've tried to show, it's compatible with very serious problems of pollution (of which we've given only a few examples), misuse of resources, and even with long-term catastrophe.

In fact, this may not contradict what is in some of the texts themselves if they are read carefully and completely by those willing to draw their own conclusions and to follow it up with their own research. Earlier in the chapter where Krugman and Wells set out the principle quoted above, they write 'But the invisible hand isn't always our friend. It's also important to understand when and why the individual pursuit of self-interest can lead to counterproductive behavior.' They mention traffic congestion, air and water pollution, and the overexploitation of natural resources. 'The environmental costs of self-interested behavior can sometimes be huge. And as the world becomes more crowded and the environmental footprint of human activity continues to grow, issues like climate change and ocean acidification will become increasingly important.'[78]

True enough, but by then setting out the principle that markets usually lead to efficiency, the student is invited to set these facts aside. This is reinforced by the assurance that economics can identify market failures and often 'can also be used to devise solutions.' Presumably once these have been devised and implemented, the market failures will have been dealt with and something approximating efficiency restored.

In reality, because of the pervasive nature of important negative externalities that are not adequately addressed by policy, the costs of current production and consumption are seriously understated. The profit motive, particularly when we include the profitability of corporate investments in shaping public policy, leads to the systematic misallocation of resources. In short, in the existing political economy, markets lead to inefficiency.

Despite the success in managing many local common access resources, as described by Elinor Ostrom, very serious problems remain at the global level. The extent and rate of species extinction due to human activities surely rates more than a passing mention in few of the textbooks.

The standard portrayal of public goods both marginalizes their importance and is excessively narrow. By neglecting social capital, and particularly social norms and trust, it omits their central importance to the fabric of human society and its ability to produce private goods. Clinging to the assumption of narrow self-interest leads to predictions of universal free riding that are falsified by the evidence of everyday life, while teaching students that uncooperative, antisocial behaviour is 'rational'. Including an account of what experimental economists and others have concluded, sketched out in the previous section, would surely be more interesting.

SUGGESTIONS FOR FURTHER READING

Robert Frank's 1999 book, *Luxury Fever: Why money fails to satisfy in an era of excess*, is a thought-provoking exploration of the effects of consumption externalities.

Among the many good accounts of the behaviour of industrial polluters and the makers of dangerous products are David Michaels's *The Triumph of Doubt: Dark Money and the Science of Deception*, and Carey Gillam's book on the herbicide glyphosate, also known by its brand name Roundup, *Whitewash: The Story of a Weed Killer, Cancer, and the Corruption of Science*.

The 2018 documentary film *The Devil We Know: The Chemistry of the Cover-Up* examines how a Dupont factory contaminated a town in West Virginia with PFOA, a pollutant now found worldwide. See thedevilweknow. com for details on where it may be viewed.

The film "Albatross" vividly documents the plastic pollution on and near the island of Midway in the Pacific and its effects on the albatross populations who breed on the island. It's available at albatrossthefilm. com/watch-albatross.

The Sixth Extinction: An Unnatural History by Elizabeth Kolbert is a first-class reporter's account of the slowly unfolding sixth mass extinction event, put in the context of the previous five.

Chapter 8

THE MARGINAL PRODUCTIVITY THEORY OF INCOME DISTRIBUTION – OR YOU'RE WORTH WHAT YOU CAN GET

'In theory there is no difference between theory and practice. In practice there is.' – Anonymous[1]

We've emphasized in previous chapters how standard textbooks downplay one of the main economic goals – equity – in favour of the other – efficiency. This emphasis shows up again in the placement of chapters explaining the factor distribution of income – the determination of factor prices in other words. They are invariably towards the end of the book, and, because of time constraints, the typical introductory economics course may not cover them. The implicit message is that the subject isn't that important.

The textbooks teach the neo-classical model where the prices of factors of production are determined primarily by technology, tastes, and factor supplies. Mere lip-service is given to conventions or norms, government decisions over public spending, bargaining power, notions of fairness, discrimination, or the legal framework.

In its pure form, the neoclassical model assumes perfect competition (including perfect information) and predicts that *all factors earn the value of what they contribute to output.* Though proponents of this view are prepared to admit that almost no markets are perfectly competitive, and there is almost never perfect information, they hypothesize that that competitive forces are prevalent enough, and information good enough, to justify using the theory as an approximation.

I THE STANDARD TEXT

1.1 Introduction

Goods and services are produced by factors of production whose rewards are determined in factor markets. Factors are often broadly classified as land, labour and capital. Land encompasses the contribution of nature and natural resources to production. Some of those natural resources are exhaustible, meaning they are limited in supply, so they might be classified separately. Similarly, labour includes all the ways in which people's activities contribute to production. Economists often identify 'entrepreneurship' as a separate factor of production; entrepreneurs try to take advantage of profit opportunities by creating new firms, products and technologies. Capital includes all things produced in the past that have been invested and are available to produce goods and services in the present. A special category of capital is 'human capital', the result of past investments in education and skill acquisition.

What do these factors of production earn? The usual terminology has land earning rent, labour earning wages, capital earning interest, and entrepreneurship (or stockholders) receiving profits. In the long run in a competitive market, this will be normal profit; in the short run, some economic profit or loss may occur.

1.2 Demand for Factors of Production

The demand for any factor of production depends on its productivity, and the revenue generated from selling additional output. Applying the usual marginal reasoning, the profit-maximizing firm will hire an additional unit of a factor as long as it adds more to revenues than to costs.

On the revenue side, an additional unit of a factor produces its marginal product, *MP*. Further, each extra unit of output generates some marginal revenue, *MR*. (For a perfectly competitive firm, marginal revenue is simply the market output price, *P*.) Hence, the additional revenue from hiring one more unit of a factor is the product of the two, *MR x MP*, referred to as the marginal revenue product, *MRP*.

Additional revenue from one more unit of a factor is MRP = MR x MP

If the firm is a price taker in the factor market, then the cost of one more unit of the factor is simply the factor price, P_F. We'll assume that this price includes all fringe benefits: payroll taxes, paid vacation, paid sick leave, and pension contributions.

Additional cost of one more unit of a factor is its market price, P_F

Therefore, the firm should hire each factor up to the point where it price equals its marginal revenue product, $P_F = MRP$. In other words, the marginal revenue product (MRP) is the firm's factor demand schedule. This is downward sloping for two reasons: *the law of diminishing returns* (explained in Chapter 5) guarantees that *MP* eventually falls as more units of the factor are employed; and second, for imperfectly competitive firms, downward sloping demand curves guarantee that *MR* falls as more output is sold.

Applying the decision rule $P_F = MRP$ in the short run (when the only variable factor of production is labour), the firm maximizes its profits by hiring labour up to the point where the wage, W, equals the marginal revenue product of labour, $MR \times MP_L$.

The firm's decision about how much labour to hire also determines how much output it produces. However, in Chapter 5 we saw that to maximize profit, the firm produces up the point where marginal revenue equals marginal cost. Is the new decision rule consistent with the earlier one?

It is easily shown that the two rules are equivalent. The new rule says hire labour until $MR \times MP_L = W$. Divide both sides by MP_L, to get: $MR = W/MP_L$. A moment's reflection confirms that the wage divided by the marginal product of labour *is* the marginal cost. It costs the firm W (say $16) to hire one more unit of labour, but the labour produces MP_L units of output (say 8 units). Therefore, the cost of producing one of those extra units of output, which is marginal cost, is W divided by MP_L (or $2 per unit).

In the long-run, when all factors of production are variable, they are all hired up to the point where their marginal revenue product equals their factor price, $P_X = MR \times MP_X$. Rearranging this expression gives the optimal combination of factors: $MR = P_X/MP_X = P_Y/MP_Y$, for factors of production X and Y. This is known as the 'least cost rule': the firm will hire every factor up to the point where the productivity of a dollar's worth of every factor is equal.

The least cost rule means that a change in one factor's price will have ripple effects on the demand for all other factors of production. For example, suppose capital goods become cheaper. This generates two effects: first, firms respond by using more capital and less labour – a substitution effect; second, since costs have fallen, competitive supply curves shift right, leading to increased output – an output effect. The net effect on the position of the labour demand function depends on which effect dominates.

1.3 Determination of Wages in a Perfectly Competitive Labour Market

To obtain the market demand for a particular type of worker, say welders, we must horizontally sum the *MRP* curves of all the firms across all the industries that employ welders, as shown in Figure 8.1. The supply of a particular type of worker is normally depicted as upward sloping, reflecting the assumption that a higher wage is required to induce a greater supply of work time or to induce more people to offer to work as welders. The overall supply and demand for a particular skill (welding) determines the market wage. The firm then decides how many workers to hire by equating the wage to its MRP.

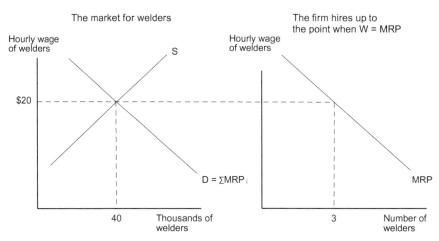

Figure 8.1 Competitive determination of the wage of welders

1.4 Wage Differentials in Competitive Labour Markets

Why do top professional athletes earn more than surgeons? Why do surgeons earn more than fast food workers? To answer questions such as these, we must consider the forces operating on the demand and supply of different types of labour in competitive labour markets. We'll begin with the principle of equal net benefit.

The principle of equal net benefit: If there were no intrinsic (or innate) differences between workers, and no barriers to entering an occupation, then in equilibrium the *present value of net benefits should be the same* in all jobs. Otherwise people would move from a lower benefit job to a higher benefit one.

The principle of compensating differences: Because 'net benefits' include non-monetary benefits, dirty, dangerous or dull jobs would receive higher pay than clean, safe and interesting jobs. This could help to explain why construction workers earn more than sales clerks, since construction involves dirtier and more hazardous conditions, and more irregular employment, than clerical work.

Differences in acquired abilities: the principle of equal net benefit implies that wage differentials must be enough to compensate individuals for their investments in acquiring necessary skills. Accountants must earn more than waiters because of the many years of training required. They have acquired human capital, which earns a market return.

On its own, human capital can't explain big wage differentials. If it takes four years and $100,000 to become an accountant rather than a waiter, then (assuming an interest rate of 8% amortized over a 25-year career)

accountancy should pay around $9,000 more a year than being a waiter.[2] So, differences in acquired abilities must be supplemented with differences in inherent abilities or barriers to occupational entry (perhaps caused by unions) to come close to explaining real world wage differentials.[3]

Differences in inherent abilities: Large wage differentials require non-competing groups. For example, how many of us have the ability (or aptitude) to become a concert violinist, a surgeon, or a top athlete? Since the answer is 'very few', and since millions of people are willing to pay billions of dollars on sports entertainment, top professional athletes have very high marginal revenue products.

Union-Caused Wage Differentials: Unions and professional associations, by restricting the availability of labour, force up wages. In the left-hand diagram of Figure 8.2, 'craft unions' seek to restrict supply of qualified workers by enforcing long apprenticeships, high initiation fees, and limits on the number of new members admitted. Examples are occupational licensing of barbers, physicians, plumbers, and cosmetologists. Many progressive social initiatives have a similar effect: for example, laws prohibiting child labour, compulsory retirement, or a fixed length of the working week.

In the right-hand diagram of Figure 8.2, the 'industrial' (or economy-wide) union tries to organize all available workers to force wages above equilibrium. Like the craft union, this increases wages at the expense of employment.

To try to offset employment reductions, unions could try to increase demand for union workers, for example through efforts to increase productivity or by encouraging consumers to buy goods made by unionized workers. Union workers would benefit at the expense of others as demand switches away from the products made by other workers. Another strategy

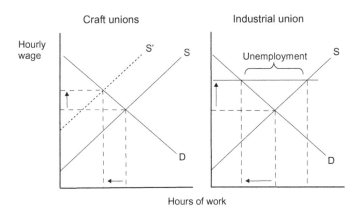

Figure 8.2 Two types of unions in otherwise competitive markets

is to support increases in the minimum wage since this makes non-union workers more costly. In short, unions benefit some workers at the expense of other workers.

Efficiency wages: Even without unions, firms may choose to pay more than the equilibrium wage as an incentive for better performance, especially when monitoring work effort is difficult. This makes workers less likely to shirk; being caught and fired now implies a lower wage in an alternative job. If all firms pay wages that are above the market equilibrium, the result will be a pool of workers who want higher-paying jobs but can't find them. The penalty for being caught shirking is now a longer period unemployed.

The theory of efficiency wages is a theory of market failure, which arises because of a lack of information about worker effort. Those who retain their jobs still earn their marginal revenue product since the higher-than-equilibrium wage elicits greater effort. But the market failure manifests itself as unemployment.

Winner-take-all markets: American labour economists Edward Lazear and Sherwin Rosen point out: 'On the day that a given individual is promoted from vice-president to president, his salary may triple. It is difficult to argue that his skills have tripled in that one-day period, presenting difficulties for standard theory.'[4] They go on to say: 'It is not a puzzle, however, when interpreted in the context of a prize.' In winner-take-all markets, CEO pay is like the prizes professional golfers and tennis players receive for winning tournaments. Those prizes increase the productivity of everyone who competes for them. In this view, CEO pay is still based on high productivity, but now it is the productivity of the whole team of executives striving for the top job – not just the CEO alone.

Discrimination: Economic discrimination against different groups of people, such as women or racial or religious minorities, can take many forms: differing access to education and occupations, different treatment in hiring, training, promotion, wages and working conditions. The extent of discrimination is often estimated by comparing the wages paid to individuals in different groups. But we cannot simply compare the average wages of men and women, for example, without considering differences in human capital, compensating differentials, occupational choice and so on. Once we control for these differences, some of the unexplained differences that remain may be due to discrimination.

There are several sources of potential discrimination. For example, suppose black and white workers are otherwise identical in terms of skills, work ethic and so on, but that some employers dislike hiring black workers. Compared to the situation without racial prejudice, black workers' wages will be lower. Employers who are not prejudiced will hire more black workers, who are now available at a lower wage, and will be able to produce at lower cost than employers who are prejudiced. Their market share will expand at the expense of discriminating firms. This increases the demand for black workers and increases their wages. In the long run, the high-cost discriminating firms don't survive, and the discriminatory wage gap disappears.

However, discriminatory wage gaps persist, so what other kinds of discrimination could account for that? What if the source of prejudice is customers, not employers? For example, suppose customers are willing to pay more to be served by white workers. Now the demand for black workers falls and so do their wages as firms act to maximize profits. Competition does not eliminate the black-white wage gap, which persists if customers' prejudice persists.

1.5 Monopsonistic Labour Markets

Monopsony means 'single buyer'. This is the relatively rare case of a single employer of a particular type of labour, which is relatively immobile – either geographically or in terms of skill. An example is the 'company town' where there is just one large employer.

Since the monopsonistic employer faces an upward-sloping labour supply curve, to hire an extra worker it must increase the wage for all workers hired. As a result, the marginal cost of an additional worker is not just the wage paid to that worker, but also the additional cost of all the other workers it previously employed at a lower wage.

For example, the first two columns in Table 8.1 describe an upward sloping labour supply curve – a higher hourly wage inducing the supply of more workers. The third column shows total daily labour cost, and is the product of the first two columns multiplied by the length of the working day (8 hours). The last column shows marginal hourly labour cost, and is the change in total labour cost as we move from one row to the next in column (3) divided by 8 – the change in hours worked as an additional worker is hired. Note that (except for the first worker) marginal hourly labour cost exceeds the wage.

Figure 8.3 illustrates the situation. To maximize profits, the monopsonist hires labour until its marginal cost equals its marginal revenue product at point A where the profit maximizing number of workers is four. The wage at which they will work is given by the labour supply schedule at point B. According

Table 8.1 Marginal cost of labour for a monopsonist

Number of workers (1)	Hourly wage (2)	Total daily labour cost (3)	Marginal hourly labour cost (4)
1	$6	$48	$6
2	$7	$112	$8
3	$8	$192	$10
4	$9	$288	$12
5	$10	$400	$14

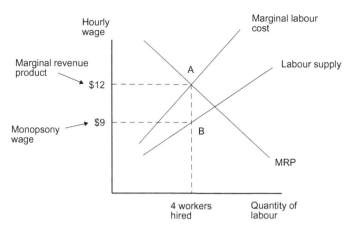

Figure 8.3 Monopsony in the labour market

to Figure 8.3, they will be willing to work for $9 an hour even though their marginal revenue product is $12 an hour.

Monopsony and the minimum wage: What happens if the government sets a minimum wage that is higher than the wage the monopsonist is paying? Since the minimum wage is a legally binding constraint, the marginal cost of labour is just the minimum wage, at least up to the point where the labour supply curve shows that a higher wage is needed to induce a greater supply of labour. Figure 8.4 shows the simple case where the minimum wage is set equal to what the wage would be in a competitive labour market, which we suppose is $10 an hour. The effect is to *increase* employment. In contrast to the competitive model, a binding minimum wage offsets the monopsonist's market power. In this case, it eliminates the inefficiency caused by the gap between the value

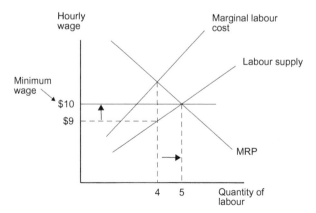

Figure 8.4 Monopsony with minimum wage

of what an extra worker could produce (the MRP) at what a worker would be willing to accept to produce it (shown by the supply curve).

Note that a union could also offset the market power of the monopsonist. Figure 8.3 shows that the monopsonist could pay up to $12 an hour, the fourth worker's marginal revenue product. Bargaining in a *bilateral monopoly* situation leads to a wage somewhere between $12 and $9 an hour with no adverse effect on employment.

1.6 Markets for other factors of production

The markets for other factors such as capital equipment and land can be dealt with briefly because they rely upon the same principles that we described in section 1.2 above. If these markets are perfectly competitive, the firm is a price taker and compares the marginal revenue product that it would get from employing additional amounts of a factor with that factor's price. Diminishing marginal returns are assumed for each factor.

Suppose the firm needs to use machines to produce its product. For simplicity, let's assume that firms rent the services of this capital equipment. The cost of using an hour of machine time is the rental rate of that kind of capital. The firm will hire hours of capital services until capital's marginal revenue product is just equal to the rental rate. As with the market wage, the rental rate of this kind of capital is determined by all firms' demand for it and its total supply.

The rental rate of land would be determined in the same way. Each firm would choose to rent an amount of land such that its marginal revenue product was just equal to the rental rate.

Entrepreneurial talent is sometimes considered to be a separate factor of production. If so, the marginal productivity theory does not apply to it. Entrepreneurs receive a residual: whatever is left over after other factors have been paid. This residual, which can be thought of as economic profits, could be positive or negative.

2 THE ANTI-TEXT

The marginal productivity story has many problems that the textbooks gloss over or fail to mention. We start with the problematic nature of the marginal productivity concept itself. We then have a critical look at compensating differentials – an important explanation of wage differentials since Adam Smith first wrote about them – before turning to the empirical evidence for or against the model of competitive labour markets. As we'll see, economists have developed alternative models to better explain empirical regularities in labour markets. These approaches all acknowledge employers' ability to set wages, a fact of life that the competitive model resolutely denies.

And what about the idea that factor prices, and in particular the wages that emerge from competitive markets, are 'fair'? They have been viewed by some as fair since they reflect the marginal value of each factor's contribution to total output. While this fairness argument was debunked long ago, the explanations offered for the very high incomes received by some come very close to being arguments that those very high incomes are justified and have been earned by their recipients. On that theme, the chapter closes with a brief case study of the compensation received by the senior managers of large corporations.

2.1 Theoretical problems with the standard textbook story

It would be unfair to criticize the textbook model for its simplicity because models are supposed to convey concepts in the simplest possible way. But we do have to ask whether its concepts are clearly set out and have identifiable counterparts in reality. If not, the model's usefulness is surely limited.

Measuring and valuing marginal product Can marginal products be measured? Where output consists of many products produced in a complex organization, one person's contribution to overall output is impossible to determine. As well, the theory has nothing directly to say about people who produce output that is not sold in a market. John Komlos inconveniently asks: 'What is the value of the marginal product of a professor? Of a policeman? Of a nurse?'[5] He points out that a significant fraction of the labour force falls into this category. But it is hardly an explanation to say that the value of their marginal product is whatever they happen to be getting paid.

Even in the simple but not uncommon situation where inputs are used in fixed proportions, the theory has nothing to say because the marginal product of any one of the inputs is zero. Consider the example of a bus and a bus driver; an extra bus without a driver would produce nothing, as would an extra driver without a bus. So, 'neoclassical theory cannot say anything about how much of the jointly produced revenue is contributed by the bus drivers (labor) and how much by the buses (capital)' as Norbert Häring and Niall Douglas observe, pointing out that this problem with the theory was identified by Italian economist Vilfredo Pareto long ago.[6] The same objection could be made in the case of our welders in the Standard Text, who can only weld if they have the appropriate equipment to work with.

If marginal productivity cannot be measured, how do employers make decisions about how much pay to offer? And if it can't be measured, how can the theory be tested?

Questions for your professor: If people work in a team
or a large organization, how do employers identify
the marginal products of any particular individual?
How do we value those marginal products if the
output is not sold, as in the case of government
workers or members of the military?

What does the marginal product theory of distribution specifically say? Setting
the unobservability of marginal products aside, let's examine the theory on
its own terms. When the American economist Lester Thurow began writing
a critique of the textbook marginal productivity analysis, he wrote, 'it is so
amorphous that I have been unable to say what it is.'[7]

For example, does the theory say that the workers are paid their actual
marginal products every hour or every day? Or will they be paid their average
marginal product over some longer period, such as their working life?
Thurow points out that 'seniority wage schedules are not evidence contrary
to the lifetime marginal-productivity hypothesis, but they are evidence
contrary to the instantaneous marginal-productivity hypothesis'.[8]

What about a group of workers of the same seniority all getting the same
pay, while some have higher marginal products than others? If pay in such
cases reflects the average marginal product of the group, is this consistent
with marginal productivity theory? And, given the team nature of much
production, what defines the group?

As we discussed in Chapter 2, a theory can be defended with a protective
belt of auxiliary assumptions that prevent the core proposition from being
refuted. In this case, Thurow points out that 'subsidiary distribution theories
are necessary in every variant except the strict interpretation in which every
individual factor is paid his marginal product at every instant of time'. He
warns that the theory is in danger of becoming a tautology – something that
is true by definition: 'factors in general must be paid in accordance with the
productivity of factors in general'.[9]

Questions for your professor: Does the marginal
productivity theory predict that workers receive the
value of their actual marginal product every hour (for
example), or their average marginal product over a
longer period? Given such things as seniority pay, how
long might that period be? If individuals' marginal
products can't be observed, are they paid the average
marginal product of the group to which they belong?
If so, how can the group be identified?

The adding up problem A theory of factor prices may try to explain the prices of all factors. If so, then the incomes of factor owners must add up to the value of total production. Otherwise there would be something left over or there would be not enough to go around. This is the so-called 'adding-up problem' that preoccupied some economists in the 1890s as the marginal productivity theory was being developed. (Note that the problem can be avoided if the theory includes a factor, such as entrepreneurial talent, that gets whatever is left over. But this leaves the theory unable to explain the returns to that factor.)[10]

While the technical details need not concern us here, it turns out that the incomes of factors do indeed add up to the value of the goods produced if the economy has perfectly competitive factor and product markets. Production must be carried out with constant returns to scale, because perfectly competitive firms are incompatible with increasing returns to scale. In his classic book, *Economic Theory in Retrospect*, Mark Blaug writes:

> The implications of ... economies of scale are disturbing to the marginal productivity theory of factor pricing. If factors are awarded their marginal products, the product is more-than-exhausted under increasing returns to scale: thus, competition cannot survive and there is no mechanism that forces monopolists to pay the factors they hire their marginal products. If economies of scale characterise much of modern manufacturing, marginal productivity theory is simply irrelevant.[11]

```
Questions  for  your  professor  (if  the  marginal
productivity theory in your text claims to explain
payments to all factors): Does this theory of factor
pricing guarantee that the incomes of factors of
production will add up to the value of total output?
Are the assumptions required for that realistic?
```

2.2 Compensating differentials in practice

As we saw in the Standard Text, a clear prediction of the model is that compensating differentials adjust wages appropriately so that the marginal worker is indifferent between jobs with different characteristics. A more unpleasant or dangerous job, all else equal, receives sufficient extra pay. But how does it really work in practice?

The case of workplace health and safety The world's workforce, about 3,500 million in 2018, experiences about 2.8 million deaths per year related to occupation, about 5 percent of global deaths. Of these work-related deaths, 400,000 are fatal accidents while 2.4 million are due to occupationally related diseases. These consist chiefly of circulatory disease, cancers, and respiratory diseases. Respiratory diseases in particular have been growing, the result of exposure to vapours, gases, dust and fumes – for example, coal dust, asbestos, diesel fumes, cement dust and organic solvents, among other things.[12] An additional 374 million workers annually suffer nonfatal injuries on the job.[13]

Textbook economics rules out by assumption any concerns about worker illness, injury and death due to hazardous workplaces. For example, according to *The Guardian*, 'amputations, fractured fingers, second-degree burns and head trauma are just some of the serious injuries suffered by US meat plant workers every week', but no worries.[14] With perfect information, workers demand and get higher wages in exchange for voluntary exposure to added risk. These compensating wage differentials raise firms' costs so that, on average, firms and the buyers of their products pay the true cost of production, including all the costs borne by the workers.

If this proves too costly, firms may find workers in lower-wage countries to accept the risks more cheaply. As Lawrence Summers, then Chief Economist at the World Bank wrote in an internal memo, 'the measurement of the costs of health-impairing pollution depends on the foregone earnings from increased morbidity and mortality'. He concluded (sardonically, as he later explained) that it would be efficient to dump toxic waste in the lowest wage country, or, in this case, to put the dirtiest and most dangerous jobs there.[15]

If workers get appropriate compensating differentials, there is no role for workplace health and safety regulations. They would either be redundant or would reduce efficiency by preventing workers from taking on risks that they would be willing to accept.

The text by Robert Frank and co-authors is unique by offering one refutation of this argument. They contend that individual workers pursue riskier higher wage jobs to try to raise their income relative to others. In their example, workers want to spend more on positional goods like a house in a more desirable neighbourhood. If the supply of such positional goods is fixed, this just increases their prices, leaving these workers having accepted additional risk for no gain. Workplace health and safety regulations could make everyone better off.[16]

In real workplaces, information is imperfect, and the balance of power is tilted towards employers. Workers don't know the extent of the hazards they face; employers, however, often know just what they're doing. Friedrich Engels, writing in 1845 on *The Condition of the Working Class in England*, termed such behaviour 'social murder'. He wrote that society 'placed the workers under such conditions in which they can neither retain health nor live long ... and so hurries them to the grave before their time.'[17]

Choosing false beliefs Even if workers know there may be risks to their work, will they evaluate them properly? The textbook model assumes that they will, resulting in appropriate compensation for the extra risk. But this won't happen if workers experience what psychologists call 'cognitive dissonance'.

People can choose their beliefs about the world, using information selectively to reinforce a belief they would prefer to have.[18] In this case, workers have to reconcile their view of themselves as smart people who make the right choices with the actual job they have. As a result, they can believe their work is safer than it actually is. In this situation, there is no reason to think that wages will adequately compensate workers for the risks they face, and thus internalize these costs in the firms' decision-making.[19] Another idea, leading to the same result, is that workers have differing and incomplete information about job risks. Those who most underestimate the risks take the most dangerous jobs.

Question for your professor: Is there any reason to worry that compensating differentials in wages are not enough to compensate workers for health and safety risks they face?

What about the empirical evidence for these compensating differentials? After all, Sherwin Rosen described the theory decades ago as '*the* fundamental (long-run) market equilibrium construct in labor economics'. Yet even now 'considerable doubt remains about the size, and sometimes even the existence, of differentials for even the most salient of disamenities, including death', as a recent paper put it.[20] Aside from data limitations, its authors point out that 'the standard rationale for the emergence of compensating differentials presumes vigorous and well- informed job search in a world where labor market frictions and incomplete information are absent.' Given that actual labour markets are not at all like that, the resulting complications have left the empirical evidence in the condition they described.

Speaking of empirical evidence, let's now turn to the evidence for the centrepiece of the standard text: the competitive labour market model.

2.3 Empirical evidence and the competitive model

Even when marginal products cannot be directly measured there are indirect ways of testing the textbook competitive labour market model. Let's consider some of the model's predictions that could be compared with the evidence.

The competitive model predicts a single market wage for workers of given characteristics, no matter where they work. They can move costlessly between jobs for which they are qualified and so competition must ensure that they receive the same wage. But there is plenty of evidence showing that workers with the same characteristics receive significantly different wages in different industries and occupations, even taking union status and observable job characteristics into account. This is consistent with the existence of efficiency wages, briefly described in the Standard Text, although omitted in many actual texts.[21] Clearly, efficiency wage models are fundamentally incompatible with the assumption of perfectly competitive labour markets: firms are exercising market power in deciding what wage to set.

George Akerlof and Janet Yellen have developed an efficiency wage model which is based on fairness considerations. They propose that workers' efforts on the job depend on their perception of the fairness of their wage compared with others working in the same firm. Such considerations don't appear in the textbook model, where social context is absent. There, Homo economicus workers only get utility from the goods and services they can purchase with their wages and don't care about what anyone else is getting paid. But humans do care, so fairness considerations will lead firms to prefer wage differentials that are smaller than productivity differentials, a situation termed *wage compression*. The result is better labour relations and higher output per worker although, like the standard efficiency wage model, it also results in a market failure: there is some involuntary unemployment, in this case concentrated among lower skilled workers.[22] Unlike in the competitive model, efficiency wage models predict that wages will not decline despite the excess supply of labour.[23]

Akerlof and Yellen's model helps to explain other important features of labour markets that are inconsistent with the competitive model: industries that have high wages for one occupation (for standard efficiency wage reasons) also have high wages for other occupations for fairness reasons.[24] As well, wages are strongly positively related to industry profits, in contrast to the predictions of the competitive model.

While workers are still getting paid the value of their marginal product in these efficiency wage models, wages would be systematically different from those in a competitive labour market. The resulting equilibria with involuntary unemployment are inefficient.[25]

Robert Frank explained wage compression in some situations in a different way. His article, entitled 'Are workers paid their marginal products?', concluded that they are not. Because of the difficulties of observing individuals' marginal products, discussed earlier, he examined a variety of relatively rare situations in which a worker's marginal product could be directly measured, such as the productivity of real estate and automobile salespeople. He found strong evidence that their earnings varied substantially less than individual productivity. His explanation: the standard model is missing the importance people attach to their relative status in the firm's hierarchy.[26]

Status is like a nonmonetary benefit. If the best workers were paid the value of their marginal products, they would receive their high status for free. But they are willing to work for less and to receive higher status instead. Think of it as a negative compensating differential. Similarly, if the lowest productivity workers were paid the value of their marginal products, they would suffer low status without any compensating payment. Therefore, they are paid more as a compensating differential for their low status. In this case, it seems that the average wage of the group will be the average of their marginal products.

Question for your professor: How important are workers' perceptions of 'fairness' and 'status' in determining a firm's wage structure?

Despite such evidence (and the evidence of pervasive employer power that we discuss below), the default model of the textbooks remains perfect competition. Deviations from this are portrayed as the exception rather than the rule. For example, Krugman and Wells write: 'Although there are some important exceptions, most factor markets in the modern American economy are perfectly competitive, meaning that buyers and sellers of a given factor are price-takers.'[27]

Questions for your professor: Is the competitive labour market model in the text consistent with the evidence about wages? For example, more profitable industries also pay higher wages for a given kind of work. Is that predicted by the competitive model? Do efficiency wage models explain features of the labour market that the competitive labour market model doesn't?

Even if labour markets were perfectly competitive, there is no guarantee that this would result in an efficient outcome because labour supply is influenced by considerations of relative position. It is easy to see how people can get caught in a rat race as they try to improve their income and consumption possibilities relative to others. They may accept riskier or less pleasant jobs, as we saw when considering compensating differentials. They may invest in more or better education, only to find their credentials have been devalued as everyone else pursues the same strategy. They may work longer hours hoping to improve their chances of promotion, but when all do it the result is a futile arms race that may simply benefit their employer if they are salaried workers. Or they may simply be caught up in the cycle of work and spend, trying to keep up with the Joneses, that we looked at in Chapter 4. As Robert Frank and Philip Cook have written, 'if we worked less than we currently do, we would have less income, but then if everyone worked less, we would need less income, because the amount of income we *need* is in part determined by the amount that others have ... private incentives favor excessive work'.[28]

The externalities involved, discussed in the previous chapter, help to explain the attraction of collective measures to reduce the number of hours people work. Examples include legislation requiring a certain number of weeks of paid holidays or requiring overtime premiums for national holidays and all hours worked in excess of a standard work week. From the point of view of the standard textbook model of the labour market, such regulation is simply unwarranted interference with freedom of contract.

2.4 Labour markets are not like the market for bananas

When Tim Bray resigned as a Vice President of Amazon over the firing of employees who had protested workplace safety during the pandemic, he wrote the following on his blog: 'At the end of the day, the big problem isn't the specifics of Covid-19 response. It's that Amazon treats the humans in the warehouses as fungible units of pick-and-pack potential. Only that's not just Amazon, that's how 21st-century capitalism is done.'[29]

The treatment of workers that Mr. Bray describes is the very same treatment they receive in the standard text's model of the labour market. It makes a critical assumption that it hides in plain sight: 'it assumes that labour can be purchased in a manner similar to the way bananas change hands in some fruit market', as Yanis Varoufakis describes it.[30] He adds that once it's assumed that labour can be quantified like this, it is also assumed that these quantities of labour can be combined with other factors of production to produce specific amounts of output. This is the assumption that was made in the Standard Text part of Chapter 5 when we consider the firm's production and costs.

The ideas that we looked at in the previous section suggest that labour is a special commodity. The workers who are renting out their time care about fair treatment and are sensitive to their social status in the workplace, among other things. People also care about what they do, unlike in the standard model where hours of work are hired by whoever pays the most.[31]

The version of efficiency wages that appears in some texts (and in our Standard Text) acknowledges that the amount of work effort that the employer receives from hiring an hour of work is not constant, but it does not pursue its implications. Workers will increase their work effort the greater the opportunity cost of losing their jobs as reflected by time spent unemployed. The texts fail to note the link between the general level of unemployment and employers' power to extract more work effort. If employers could costlessly monitor workers, that link would be even stronger. Technological developments now allow almost costless monitoring for some jobs, such as the pick-and-pack jobs in Amazon warehouses.

Because contracts between employers and workers are necessarily incomplete and can't specify the level of work effort, employers can try to dictate the pace of work using 'the threat of dismissal and other psychological methods. It is these important determinants of the profit/ wage link that the textbook theory does not account for', as Yanis Varoufakis explains.[32] By portraying labour as just another commodity, it serves to obscure, whether intentionally or not, the incentive and ability of employers to exercise some degree of power over employees, who may resist that in various ways.

If there is no firm link between hours of work and work effort, the diagrams illustrating inputs and outputs (the production function) and outputs and costs (the total and marginal cost functions) technically don't exist. They are fuzzy things where the actual relationships depend on 'the social relations between bosses and workers, between workers themselves or about the social environment in which firms operate. It would be like admitting that history, sociology, politics, etc. should have a say in the theory of the firm', as Varoufakis writes.[33]

> Questions for your professor: If a business hires a certain number of hours of work, doesn't that involve a kind of 'power struggle' over how much work effort the employer will get from the employees? Do you think that is an important feature of actual workplaces that our textbook is ignoring?

Clearly a model that treats labour as if it were no different than bananas is missing crucial features of what determines wages. For example, unlike the price of bananas, people's views about what wages should be affects what wages actually are. For example, it was long considered acceptable to pay women less than men because men were considered to be the primary earners in a family, where women's income was merely supplementary.[34] When that became socially unacceptable, "equal pay for equal work" regulations helped to shrink the gap, something that would be hard to explain if women and men had earlier been paid the value of their marginal products.[35]

The ideas that lie behind the supply and demand framework are not useless, but they need to be put in an appropriate setting that recognizes the special nature of what is being traded. John Komlos gives some examples of what should be considered in explaining wages: 'the history of wages, custom, the degree of unionization, concentration within the industry, the rate of profit of the firm, and the institutional structures in place'.[36] David Colander's text is unusual in agreeing with this need for a broader view, pointing out that the standard model of wage determination has to be augmented to recognize the importance of cultural, political, and social forces.[37]

Let's now consider a better alternative to the standard model of supply and demand. It is a view of the labour market that recognizes the reality of employers' wage setting power and its consequences.

2.5 How about dynamic monopsony?

Many economists now believe that the competitive labour market model is not an appropriate default model. Like Alan Manning of the London School of Economics, they think that a version of the monopsony model should be central to the study of labour markets, even where there are many small firms.[38]

A central problem with the textbook competitive model is that it omits critical features of the labour market, including employers' market power. Did you notice in Figure 8.1 that if a competitive firm reduces its wages by one cent below the equilibrium wage, its entire workforce would quit and instantly get a job somewhere else at the equilibrium wage? From the firm's point of view, if workers leave (to take care of children, to retire, etc.), the firm can instantly and costlessly replace them. The employer–employee relationship is symmetric, with neither being more powerful than the other. Each has the equivalent power to terminate the relationship and instantly find another job or another worker. Such a depiction is completely implausible as a description of the actual labour market.

In general, if a firm reduced its wages, it would not immediately lose all its workers. As Manning says, a firm 'may find that workers quit at a faster rate than before or that recruitment is more difficult, but the extreme predictions of the competitive model do not hold'.[39] Why don't all the workers quit immediately? It's because of what are called 'frictions' in the market. For example, when information

> Questions for your professor: The competitive labour market model predicts that if a firm reduces its wage by one cent below the equilibrium wage, its entire workforce will quit. Because that prediction is wrong, can we conclude that the typical employer does have a choice about what wage to offer?

is not free it takes time and resources to find a new job and taking such a job might entail moving home or increased costs of commuting. Other frictions include personal preferences (such as strongly preferring a certain type of work or attachment to one's coworkers), and the firm-specific training and skills that a worker may have. As Manning explains: 'The existence of frictions gives employers potential market power over their workers. The assumption that firms set wages means that they actually exercise this power.'[40]

A dynamic reinterpretation of monopsony The original monopsony model, due to Joan Robinson, is the one presented in the textbooks.[41] It illustrates the case of a single employer, or perhaps a few large employers, in a labour market. The textbooks say that such cases are exceptional; this helps to justify their reliance on the perfectly competitive model.

However, modern models of 'dynamic monopsony' base their explanation of the firm's upward sloping labour supply curve on the effects of the ubiquitous frictions in the labour market described earlier. These models can also explain well-known features of the labour market that the competitive model cannot. This is why frictionless perfect competition is better seen as a special case rather than the norm. That supply and demand is a special case is underscored by the fact that the demand for labour curve only exists if the labour market is perfectly competitive for analogous reasons that a supply curve for a good only exists in perfectly competitive markets.[42]

How do labour market frictions affect the firm's labour supply? Here is one simple story.

If the firm offers a lower wage, it experiences a higher quit rate as workers more frequently learn about better opportunities elsewhere. The resulting job vacancies (unfilled job openings) are a common feature of labour markets but are missing in perfectly competitive labour markets, where each firm can costlessly hire at the going market wage. Job turnover entails costs of recruiting and training. In their discussion of the low-wage labour market, Card and Krueger depict low-wage employers as fighting a constant 'war of attrition' to maintain their workforces.[43] It is this dynamic setting that gives the modern monopsony model its name.

We illustrate the firm's problem in Figure 8.5. In the left-hand panel, the upward sloping line h(W) shows that a firm's ability to hire new workers

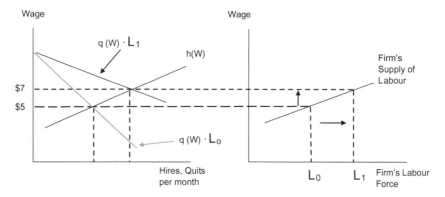

Figure 8.5 Derivation of a firm's upward-sloping supply of labour schedule

each month increases as its offered wage, W, increases.[44] On the other hand, the monthly quit rate, q(W), decreases as the wage increases. As a result, the absolute number of quits, which is the product of the quit rate and the size of the workforce, L, also decreases as the wage increases. This is shown as the downward-sloping line.

To maintain a workforce of L_0 employees, the firm must set the wage at $5 an hour, so that the number of new hires just balances the number of quits: h(w) = q(w)·L_0. If the firm wants to increase the size of its workforce, it must increase its rate of hiring by offering a higher wage. With a larger labour force, the schedule showing the absolute number of quits rotates outwards. At a wage of $7 an hour, quits and hires are in balance, allowing the firm to maintain a larger workforce. As a result, the firm faces an upward-sloping supply of labour schedule, as shown in the right-hand panel of Figure 8.5. From that, we can derive a marginal cost of labour schedule, as shown earlier in Table 8.1, leaving a gap between the marginal revenue product and the wage as in the standard monopsony model (shown in Figures 8.3 and 8.4).

The most direct prediction from Figure 8.5 is that larger firms pay higher wages on average. This is strongly supported by the evidence.[45] A more general version of the model can explain the fact that some firms choose a 'low-wage/high-turnover' policy, and others a 'high-wage/low-turnover' policy, a strategy choice well-known in the human resources literature.[46] In this setting, the wage offered by other firms is determined within the model itself, with the prediction that wages will differ systematically across firms in equilibrium.[47]

Monopsony can be an important cause of the gender pay gap. If employers can identify a group of workers who are less responsive to a wage reduction (i.e. their labour supply is less elastic), it will be profitable to pay them less than other workers doing comparable work, because fewer will quit.[48] Why would this be true for women? There is evidence that women place a higher value than men on the non-wage aspects of a job, such as hours of work and distance from home.[49] These preferences, perhaps reflecting family obligations in the case of married women, also limit their ability to find another suitable job. As a result of this greater attachment to their jobs and the greater difficulty of finding another one, employers have greater market power and can pay them less.[50]

> Questions for your professor: If it is costly for workers to move between jobs, could even small firms have some degree of monopsony power? If so, why isn't the monopsony model the standard model of the labour market, rather than supply and demand?

The dynamic monopsony model is also consistent with efficiency wage models such as those based on considerations of fairness or shirking, mentioned earlier.[51] As we have seen, it is also consistent with much of the evidence concerning the effects of changes in minimum wages.

What empirical evidence is there for an upward sloping labour supply curve for the typical firm? One example is a study by Douglas Webber, who estimated the elasticity of labour supply for a sample of 670,000 American firms. If labour markets were competitive, these elasticities would be infinite: the labour supply curve would be a horizontal line.[52] Instead, Webber found that the average elasticity was about 1.1, meaning that a 1 percent increase in wages would increase labour supply by just over 1 percent. He found large variation around this average, with a small but 'nontrivial fraction of firms who do appear to be operating in an approximately competitive labor market.' Nevertheless, he concluded that most firms have significant power in setting wages. If their elasticity of labour supply increases by one unit, reducing their monopsony power, he estimated that worker earnings increase by 5 to 16 percent. However, 'there is evidence that firms only utilize a fraction of their market power'.[53] That means that workers are left with some share of the mutual gains from the employment relationship.

These mutual gains from an ongoing employment relationship are termed 'rents'. These reflect the fact that a worker experiences a loss if she loses her job, while an employer also experiences a loss. The worker's loss includes the time and effort spent to find another job, possibly the loss of firm-specific human capital (knowledge and skills which were only useful when working with the previous employer) that could result in a lower wage in the next job. The employer had benefited by getting her marginal revenue product while paying her less than that (the difference contributing to profits). If she quits her job, the employer loses that, while facing the expense of hiring a replacement. Manning writes that these rents might be 'in the region of 15 to 30 percent of the wage, with the best guess being that most of them go to the worker'.[54] In contrast, the frictionless perfectly competitive labour market model says nothing about rents because it has assumed them away.

Australian economist John Quiggin comments that after Card and Krueger's work in the 1990s, 'the view that many, perhaps most, labor markets are monopsonistic has gained ground, at least among those economists open to empirical evidence.'[55] The texts' account of labour markets should be open to empirical evidence as well. Most of them already refer to the monopsony model. It would be easy to describe the frictions in the labour market that motivate the modern dynamic monopsony model, which will already be familiar to students from their everyday experience.

Recognizing widespread monopsony power in labour markets gives a different perspective on labour market policies. These include not only the minimum wage, but also legislation regarding such things as hours of work and holidays, trade unions and "equal pay for equal work".[56] Instead, by claiming that most labour markets are perfectly competitive, textbook economics reinforces the message that market outcomes are, for the most part, efficient and that regulating them will create inefficiencies.

2.6 Does the marginal productivity theory help to legitimize actual factor prices?

Many critics of neoclassical economics accuse the marginal productivity theory of doing precisely that: legitimizing existing payments to the owners of factors of production.[57] If these factor payments can somehow be rationalized as legitimate or fair, it would be an important step towards justifying the fairness of the distribution of households' market incomes.

A theory might legitimize an outcome, like a market price, in three ways. It might make the outcome seem: (1) fair; (2) unavoidable; or (3) socially beneficial, or some combination of the three.

The modern marginal productivity theory originated in the late nineteenth century in the work of the American economist John Bates Clark. Clark explicitly argued that having rewards determined by marginal contribution to output was fair because 'what a social class gets is, under natural law, what it contributes to the general output of industry'.[58] It was unavoidable because competition ensures that if an employer tried to pay a worker less than her marginal product, other employers would offer more, bidding her wages up. It also seems (at least at first glance) to be socially beneficial. Given the assumption of competitive markets and no market failures, it allocates society's scarce resources in the most efficient way. Competition also ensures that no market power is exerted by either party in the transaction. Clark's claim came at a politically convenient time because socialists, inspired by the writings of Karl Marx and other critics of capitalism, were arguing that workers were being systematically exploited.

It's worth noting that Clark's theory only applies to the long run of perfectly competitive markets with perfect foresight and perfect mobility of factors. So, as factor markets are continually being disturbed by shifts in demand and supply, at best actual prices would be moving towards that equilibrium. Given this, Mark Blaug comments on Clark's claim, writing: 'It would be less misleading to say the very opposite: marginal productivity theory shows us that market results are by no means "fair" or "equitable".'[59]

In Clark's theory, reproduced in today's textbooks, if more labour is employed with a given amount of capital, its marginal productivity is lower because capital per worker is less. Similarly, if there is less labour, its marginal productivity is higher. Blaug remarks that 'the greater productivity of fewer workers may just as well be attributed to capital.... *There is no such thing as a specific marginal product of a factor considered in isolation: the factors of production are essentially complements and the marginal product of one factor is a consequence of the marginal product of the other factors*' (our emphasis). This 'destroys the idea that a wage in accordance with the marginal productivity of labour is a "just wage".'[60]

In any case, whether wages would be fair in the long-run equilibrium of perfectly competitive markets is an academic question of little interest in a world of dynamically monopsonistic labour markets. There, workers are always paid less than the value of their marginal product. If you believed that a 'just wage' is the value of labour's marginal product, then you would have to conclude that, workers are being 'exploited' in actual labour markets.[61]

What do the texts themselves say about fairness? At best, a brief paragraph is included after a lengthy exposition of the theory. According to the American text by Campbell McConnell and his co-authors, Clark's view is 'controversial' in claiming that 'that fairness and economic justice are one of the outcomes of a competitive capitalist economy.' They write: 'if you are willing to accept the proposition "To each according to the value of what he or she creates," income payments based on marginal revenue product provide a fair and equitable distribution of society's income.' But they warn that there are 'serious criticisms.' They point to discrimination and note that 'not all labor markets are highly competitive', giving the example of collective bargaining where both employers and workers try to exert power. Even if factor prices were somehow fair, the resulting distribution of household income need not be, because it depends on who gets to own what factors.[62]

Krugman and Wells write: 'many people wrongly believe that the marginal productivity theory of income distribution gives a *moral* justification for the [factor] distribution of income, implying that the existing distribution is fair and appropriate.'[63] William Baumol and his co-authors declare that 'no economist today claims that marginal productivity analysis shows that distribution under capitalism is either just or unjust.'[64] However, some texts say nothing one way or the other, contenting themselves with presenting the positive theory and leaving it up to the student to figure out whether it has any normative implications.[65]

While no text explicitly supports the idea that marginal productivity theory justifies existing factor prices, this has not prevented that impression from persisting. After all, the central model presents factor prices as both the inevitable and efficient outcome of competitive markets. While efficiency is not an end in itself, that is all too easily forgotten by the student given the repeated emphasis placed on the concept. (In the case of the labour market, recall the typical discussion of the minimum wage where its alleged inefficiency is put in the foreground of the discussion.)

Derek Bok, a former president of Harvard University, puts the argument for a beneficial outcome this way:

> The theory of marginal productivity, together with the insights of Adam Smith, seem[s] to have persuaded the general public, as well as economists, that large differences in compensation are indispensable to progress and prosperity. [They] ... are needed both to attract people to the occupations for which they are best suited and to induce them to acquire the skills and exert their best efforts at work for the ultimate benefit of the entire society.[66]

In this view, factor prices, from CEO compensation packages to the wages of the humblest worker, give the incentives necessary to create an efficient and dynamic economy. This helps to rationalize the ensuing inequality of personal incomes while readying the argument that redistribution will harm (if not kill) the goose that lays the golden eggs.

Let's consider the fairness argument more carefully. Clark's argument about deserving what one contributes to the general output has a some superficial appeal until you realize that the value of one's marginal contribution, reflected in the demand for the factor, only yields a price when combined with the supply of the factor. In turn, national immigration policies are a crucial determinant of factor supplies in individual economies, although this 'elephant in the room' is so taken for granted that it goes virtually unnoticed. As Ha-Joon Chang puts it, 'wages are largely politically determined'.[67]

Chang also points out that individuals' productivity cannot be considered in isolation from the 'historically inherited collective institutions on which they stand'. People in high income countries don't get high incomes compared with their counterparts in low income countries because of some special individual talents and efforts. Instead, 'they live in economies that have better technologies, better organized firms, better institutions and better physical infrastructure – all things that are in large part products of collective actions taken over generations'.[68]

There is no argument to be made that factor prices, including wages, that emerge from market interactions are ethically justified. It follows from this that individual and household incomes which depend, in part, upon these factor prices also have no special ethical justification. Regardless of this, there is no shortage of "free market" advocates who maintain that people are entitled to their "earnings" and that redistribution through taxation is little more than theft. We come back to this issue in the next chapter.

2.7 CEO and Management Compensation

In an article for *Forbes* magazine, Adam Hartung sought to explain why CEOs of large American corporations with publicly traded stock make so much money. He wrote, 'Honestly, if you could set your own pay what would it be? I reckon most folks would take as much as they could get.'[69] CEO pay is actually determined in a more subtle way, as Hartung and others explain, but the end result is not that much different than this. We

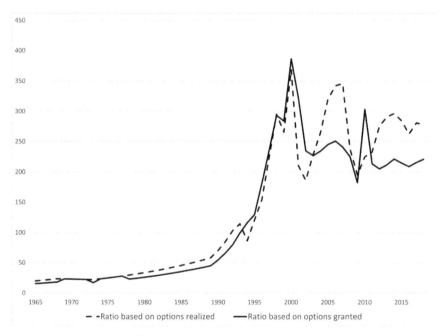

Figure 8.6 CEO pay relative to average earnings, 1965-2018

Source: Mishel and Wolfe (2019: 14, Figure C). Reproduced with permission of the Economic Policy Institute.

conclude this Anti-Text part of the chapter by looking at the compensation of senior corporate executives because it acts as a useful case study of the shortcomings of the marginal productivity theory.

Let's start with a quick look at the facts. Figure 8.6 shows two different measures of CEO compensation for the largest 350 publicly owned US companies, ranked by the value of their sales.[70] These compare annual average payouts to these CEOs with the typical worker's average earnings in the key industry of the firms in the sample. The measures differ in the way they value stock options.

Stock options give the holder the right to buy company stock in the future, generally at prices prevailing when the options are granted. A "fair value" of the option can be estimated and used to value it at that time.[71] An alternative valuation records their "realized' value when the options are exercised and the money received.

The increasing use of stock options arose, in part, from developments in economic theory to address a principal-agent problem (discussed in Chapter 5). In this case, there are two principal-agent relationships: (i) between stockholders as principals and their agents, the Board of Directors, who are to act in stockholders' interests and (ii) between the Board of Directors (now the principals) and their agents, the senior executives of the corporation. In both cases asymmetric information makes it difficult for the principals to monitor their agents.

The 'shareholder value' movement of the 1980s aimed to address the second of these principal agent problems by making management compensation more dependent on company stock price performance, which, in turn, was supposed to reflect expectations of the long-run profitability of the company. As a result, the use of stock options in the United States ballooned.[72]

Unfortunately, this didn't work well in practice. A fundamental problem is that an individual firm's stock price tends to move up and down with the market as a whole. The stock price changes may have little to do with the efforts of management. Another problem is that by more closely tying their pay to stock prices, senior executives have an incentive to focus on actions that influence those prices in the short-term. This has resulted in an emphasis on payouts to shareholders through dividends and stock buybacks instead of long-term investments in physical and human capital.[73]

Most texts in our sample do mention very high levels of CEO pay and offer explanations consistent with the standard marginal productivity theory.[74] They nicely illustrate the very fine line between a positive explanation of their earnings and making a normative case that they have truly earned what they receive. None describe how CEO pay is actually determined. Nor do any link the issue with principal-agent problems and problems with corporate governance, despite the prominence of this theme in the academic literature.

In contrast, this theme dominates the discussion in nonmainstream textbooks.[75] For example, Samuel Bowles and co-authors write:

> In many corporations the chief executive officer (CEO) is also the chair of the board of directors. In addition, ties of friendship or business interests often connect a majority of the directors with the CEO. In such situations the directors might not exercise independent judgment with regard to the practices of the top managers of their companies, and they might have a hard time firing the CEO even if the company is being poorly run.[76]

In their book, *Pay Without Performance*, Lucian Bebchuk and Jesse Fried examine this process in detail. They write: 'Boards of large public companies delegate to compensation committees the task of working out the critical details of executive compensation arrangements. The compensation committee has typically been composed of three or four directors. For some time now, most directors serving on compensation committees have been "independent." '[77]

And how has that worked out? Legendary investor Warren Buffett summed up the lapdog (rather than watchdog) character of such committees at an annual meeting of investors:

> "They don't look for Dobermans on that committee, they look for chihuahuas." He paused amid laughter, then added: "Chihuahuas that have been sedated."[78]

Consider the example of a CEO of Pfizer Corporation who presided over a sharp decline in its stock market value during his five-year tenure. Yet he was paid $65 million and received a $180 million retirement package. The chair of the compensation committee explained that his pay was determined by "market forces".[79]

Instead of looking at institutional details, the standard marginal productivity argument says that, like any other factor of production in a competitive market, top-level management receive the value of their marginal product: in this case, what they are expected to add to the net profits of their company. According to this story, their decisions regarding the strategic directions that the company will take could have a significant impact on profits. The enormous paychecks received by the CEOs of large companies, particularly American ones, then reflect this.

As evidence, some point to the positive relationship between CEO pay and the size of the corporation: the larger the corporation, the greater the impact of the CEOs decisions.[80] However, this cannot explain why CEO pay, adjusted for inflation, was roughly constant from the 1930s through the 1970s, although the companies were growing continually larger. CEO pay started to increase much more rapidly in the 1980s and 1990s.[81] Nor can it explain why American CEOs are apparently much more productive than those leading equally large companies in other countries. In 2018, the CEO-to-average worker compensation ratio was 265 in the United States, compared with 201 in the United Kingdom, 149 in Canada, 136 in Germany, 127 in China, 66 in South Korea, 60 in Sweden, and only 20 in Norway.[82]

The view that CEO pay reflects the value of the marginal product is a position largely based on faith. The value of this marginal product is 'impossible to quantify' and 'it's hard even to describe it clearly' as James Kwak points out, noting that 'business is a team sport'. He adds: 'The idea that good CEOs are entitled to enormous rewards is based on the belief that the success or failure of a company depends on one person—what historian Nancy Koehn calls the business version of the Great Man theory of history.'[83]

The determination of the pay of top executives illustrates several important themes that we have raised in this chapter. First, it is effectively impossible to identify the marginal product of an individual who is part of a team, so claims that CEOs are paid according to their marginal product can never be proven or disproven. Second, social norms play a role in determining how the collective efforts of the team are divided up. Even a few mainstream textbooks acknowledge that how much CEOs can take is limited by how it is perceived by workers and the public. Third, the 'rules of the game' matter in shaping bargaining power. Recent years have seen tinkering with corporate governance to try to rein in the plunder, for example with disclosure requirements about executive pay and by giving shareholders some say over it.

Executive pay also plays a role in the growing inequality of market incomes in some countries. In the United States, of the top 1 percent of the income distribution, more than 30 percent is made up of the incomes of executives of nonfinancial companies.[84] This touches on a central topic in the next chapter: economic inequality and the role of government in dealing with it.

2.8 Concluding Comments

As we've seen, the marginal productivity theory of factor prices has serious limitations. When examined carefully, it seems built on a foundation of sand. The thought experiment described in the texts – marginal increases in a single factor leading to diminishing marginal products – seems superficially plausible. But a little more thought reveals that the marginal product of any particular factor is virtually unmeasurable, inseparable from the contributions of other factors.

Marginal productivity theory is also a story of perfectly competitive, and therefore frictionless, factor markets, when frictions, particularly in labour markets, are of central importance. It fails to explain many well-established facts about wages, which can be explained by models that take those frictions into account. Those alternative approaches all acknowledge employers' power to choose what wage to set. Why shouldn't such a model be at the heart of the textbook story?

The market for labour services is fundamentally different than the market for inanimate objects such as bananas. Labour time is a special commodity; ignoring that misses, among other things, the power struggle between employers and employees about how much work effort will be extracted for an hour's work. A satisfactory model also must acknowledge the importance of custom, social norms, and the institutional framework within which factor rewards are determined.

When the marginal productivity theory was refined in the 1890s by John Bates Clark, he had a normative goal: to show that factor prices are "fair" if they reflect the value of the factor's contribution to output. Some textbooks explicitly reject this, some do not address the question one way or the other, but none support it. In any case, factors are not paid the value of their marginal products, so the issue has no practical relevance.

SUGGESTIONS FOR FURTHER READING

Chapter 7 of Yanis Varoufakis' *Foundations of Economics*, 'Critique: is the textbook's theory of production good economics, good politics, both or neither?', is highly recommended, particularly Chapter 7.2.

More advanced students could explore Mark Blaug's *Economic Theory in Retrospect*, Chapter 11 'Marginal Productivity and Factor Prices'.

About half of Moshe Adler's *Economics for the Rest of Us* is devoted to an insightful examination of theories of wages.

Engels's theme of 'social murder' is taken up by Robert Chernomas and Ian Hudson in their 2007 book *Social Murder and Other Shortcomings of Conservative Economics*, a critique of corporate power and its absence from mainstream economic theory.

On the export of dirty and dangerous jobs, the 2004 documentary film *Shipbreakers*, produced by the National Film Board of Canada, provides a case study. It deals with the work of breaking up ships carried out in Alang, India. Available on YouTube: https://www.youtube.com/watch?v=5jdEG_ACXLw

Chapter 9

GOVERNMENT, TAXATION AND THE (RE)DISTRIBUTION OF INCOME: IS A JUST SOCIETY JUST TOO EXPENSIVE?

```
'The people who own the country ought to govern
it.' - John Jay, first Chief Justice of the US
Supreme Court¹
```

I THE STANDARD TEXT

What should governments do? This is a normative question. It assumes that social goals exist, such as an efficient use of society's resources and an equitable distribution of the goods and services that society produces, and that governments may need to act to further these goals if the market economy fails to achieve them.

Governments have four main roles. First, governments maintain a legal system within which people can make contracts and have them enforced – a precondition for modern economic life. Second, because the market economy sometimes fails to allocate resources efficiently, governments may have a role in trying to fix these market failures. Dealing with externalities and public goods are prominent examples. Governments can also act to constrain monopoly power if it causes inefficiencies or to create it (by granting and enforcing intellectual property rights). Third, they can play an important role in stabilizing the overall level of economic activity and keeping unemployment low. This is the domain of macroeconomic policy, which is beyond the scope of this book. Fourth, because the market economy on its own is unlikely to produce an equitable distribution of income and wealth among individuals, governments can use taxes, transfers of cash and the direct provision of goods and services to improve equity. This chapter examines this last role of government.

We begin by describing the theory of how government policy is determined in the first place. Government activity inevitably involves taxation, whose costs we briefly review. We then describe the measurement of inequality in the distribution of income and wealth, and how and why inequality has changed in recent decades. After a brief discussion of the measurement of poverty, we turn to the trade-offs involved in using taxes and transfers to redistribute income in pursuit of greater equity.

1.1 Public choice and government failure

If markets fail to allocate resources efficiently, government policy could potentially correct it. Our major examples were (i) a Pigouvian tax (or subsidy) to offset an external cost (or benefit); (ii) competition policy, regulation or public ownership to deal with monopoly power; and (iii) providing public goods if the private sector failed to do so adequately. Because the social costs of some market failures are smaller than the costs of government action, sometimes it's better for government to do nothing.

Up to this point, we have implicitly assumed that governments will appropriately address such economic inefficiencies. But why couldn't we also have *government failures* as well as market failures? These could occur if government policymakers fail to recognize the problem, if they don't have the information to address it adequately, or if they choose inappropriate policies, perhaps creating greater inefficiencies. We need theories of the *political marketplace*, where policies are determined, to assess the likelihood of government success or failure.

In the same way that we assume that self-interested consumers maximize utility and firms maximize profits, we could assume that actors in the political marketplace also act in their own self-interest. *Public choice theory* uses this approach. It originated in the United States in the late 1950s and the 1960s with the work of economists including James Buchanan, winner of the 1986 Nobel Memorial Prize in Economics.

In this view, politicians, motivated by the desire for money, prestige and power, seek to gain and to keep public office by attracting the votes that are needed to do that. Bureaucrats are assumed to want to maximize the size of their bureaus and budgets, as this provides them with greater pay and status. People, in their role as voters, support those policies which most closely conform to their own economic interests. They can also further those interests by lobbying politicians, donating to political parties and so on.

What determines which policies will be chosen? Among other things, that depends on the nature of the political institutions and the way that people can express their preferences about policy choices.

The median voter model Let's consider a simple example of this influential model that's relevant to the subject of this chapter.

The policy in question is how much income to redistribute to reduce income inequality. This could involve setting income tax rates and providing certain cash transfers to households. Different people will have different preferences, depending upon their interests. Those with low incomes would prefer a significant reduction in income inequality (e.g. through progressive taxes and cash transfers of income to themselves), while at the other extreme those with high incomes would prefer that no inequality-reducing redistribution take place. Imagine voters lined up from left to right, those on the left preferring the largest reduction in inequality, those on the right preferring the least reduction.

If there are two political parties each offering voters choices about how much redistribution will take place, the option that wins is the one that gets majority support. People will vote for the proposal closest to their preferred outcome. The decisive vote that creates the majority will be cast by the person in the middle, who has an equal number of people to her left as to her right. This is the *median voter* and the model predicts that the two political parties will adjust their policy offerings to closely resemble her preferences. A vote maximizing political party would have no interest in proposing an extreme choice, because it would have no chance of winning a majority. This model helps to explain why in two-party political systems the policies offered by the parties are often quite similar: both are trying to appeal to the crucial median voter.

This simple model provides some useful insights, even if people don't vote directly about particular policies except in referenda. Instead they usually elect representatives from political parties to make decisions on their behalf about many different policies. Those policies could potentially still be packaged to fit on something like the left-right spectrum described earlier, but that is not guaranteed.

The median voter model presumes that people know their own interests. But many people without a large stake in a particular policy may find that being well informed takes time and effort that isn't worth the cost. Their 'rational ignorance' leaves room for those that do have a strong interest to organize to influence the policy making process.

Rent seeking Special interest groups lobby politicians for policies that are in their collective interest. A typical country could have hundreds or thousands of them actively trying to influence policy from the local to the national level. Examples of such groups are farmers, pensioners, environmentalists, human rights advocates, unions, bankers, lawyers, doctors, teachers, and corporations seeking tariffs or tax breaks. They invest resources to persuade governments to change the 'rules of the game' for their own benefit and at the expense of the majority. This is termed 'rent seeking'.

Rent seeking is socially unproductive, because it uses resources that could have produced additional goods and services, rather than merely transferring income from one group to another. Even more resources can be wasted if special interest groups lobby for and against a particular policy, offsetting each other's efforts. The result could be policies whose social costs exceed its social benefits (if any) – an example of government failure. Public choice economists believe that much of the resulting taxes and government expenditures bring little social benefit but leave government excessively large. This is compounded by bureaucrats' incentives to expand their budgets, providing their monopoly services at excessive cost.

Implications for income distribution and redistribution Public policies, determined by the interaction of politicians, voters and interest groups, influence both the market distribution of income and its redistribution. For example, in the labour market, certain professions may successfully lobby to restrict entry, raising their incomes above what they would otherwise be. Labour unions can lobby for increases in the minimum wage, indirectly increasing demand for higher-wage unionized workers (whose hiring becomes less unattractive), and so on.

Taxes and transfers to households and businesses will be determined in a similar process of contending forces. The result depends very much on the country's specific institutions and individuals' ability to advance their interests, particularly through interest group formation.

1.2 The costs of taxation

Taxation is costly not only because it is costly for government to collect the revenues and for individuals and business to comply with the tax law, but because it influences economic decisions. These include decisions by households about what and how much to buy and how much to save, and decisions by firms about what to produce and how and where to produce those things.

If the decisions of consumers and firms in the absence of taxes would lead to an efficient allocation of resources, then taxes must cause inefficiency if they change those decisions. We saw this in the analysis of an excise tax using the supply and demand framework in Chapter 3. In that case, the result was a loss to society of producing less of the taxed good. This loss occurs because some mutually beneficial exchanges no longer take place. A similar analysis can be done for any kind of tax. As long as taxes influence choices that would otherwise be optimal, they create 'efficiency losses'.

1.3 Taxes: an international comparison

A simple way to compare taxes across countries is to express total tax revenues collected by all levels of government as a percentage of the country's total production, or gross domestic product (GDP), as shown in Table 9.1 for some of the member countries of the Organisation for Economic Co-operation and Development (OECD). Clearly, countries differ considerably in their overall levels of taxation. The other side of the coin is that they differ in terms of the goods and services provided by the state. The extent of social insurance – public pensions, public healthcare and education, unemployment insurance and other forms of income supports – is a major cause of these differences between countries. Incidentally, adding all taxes together like this obscures the significant differences in the way countries raise tax revenues. They can choose different mixes of direct taxes on individuals, social insurance contributions, taxes on business income, on property values, and on consumption spending. These choices affect how people respond to taxes and therefore the extent of the efficiency losses due to taxation.[2]

Table 9.1 Tax Revenues as Percent of GDP, Selected OECD Countries, 2018

France	46.1	Spain	34.4
Denmark	44.9	United Kingdom	33.5
Belgium	44.8	Canada	33.0
Sweden	43.9	New Zealand	32.7
Finland	42.7	Japan	31.4*
Austria	42.2	Australia	28.5*
Italy	42.1	South Korea	28.4
Norway	39.0	Switzerland	27.9
Netherlands	38.8	Turkey	24.4
Greece	38.7	United States	24.3
Germany	38.2	Ireland	22.3
Hungary	36.6	Chile	21.1
Czech Republic	35.3	Mexico	16.1
Poland	35.0	*OECD average*	34.3

Source: Organisation for Economic Co-operation and Development (2019: Table 1.1)

Note: 2018 data is a provisional estimate. *denotes 2017 value. The OECD average is unweighted.

1.4 The distribution of income and wealth

Countries are usually compared using per-person average income. Because of inequality, however, we need to know about the distribution of income and of wealth to judge how a society is doing in terms of equity. Inequality has been increasing in many countries in recent decades, leading to debate about why this has happened. It has also led to questions about what, if anything, to do about it.

The distribution of income The distribution of income can be measured in two ways. One is the functional distribution of income, breaking income down into its sources like wages and salaries, rent, and profits as we did in Chapter 8. The Classical economists from Adam Smith to Karl Marx used this approach to think about the incomes of workers, landowners and capitalists. This distinction is now no longer as relevant, so economists now focus on the distribution of household incomes.

Incomes can be measured in different ways. 'Market income' includes wages and salaries and income from savings (dividends, interest, capital gains). Alternatively, 'disposable income' is market income plus cash transfers from government minus income taxes and other direct taxes on wages and salaries (e.g. premiums to national pension plans or for unemployment insurance). Comparing the two allows us to see some of the effects of government on the distribution of income.

Suppose, as in Figure 9.1, households are lined up on the horizontal axis from the lowest income on the left to the highest income on the right. The vertical axis shows the percentage shares of total household income that various groupings of households have. In this example, the poorest 50 per cent of households have 20 per cent of total market income. If household incomes were equally distributed, those households would have 50 per cent of total

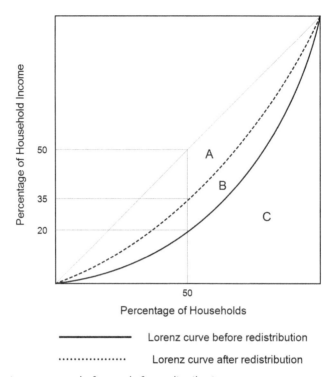

Figure 9.1 Lorenz curves before and after redistribution

income, the amount shown on the 45-degree line. The gap between the points showing actual household incomes (called the Lorenz curve) and this reference line indicates the nature and extent of market income inequality.

Income inequality can be summarized in a single number to aid in comparing inequality over time and across countries. The most widely used measure that summarizes the entire income distribution is the Gini coefficient. This is the ratio of the area between the Lorenz curve and the 45-degree line and the entire area under the 45-degree line. In Figure 9.1, the Gini coefficient for market incomes is (A+B)/(A+B+C). Its value ranges between zero and one. It's zero if income is equally distributed; it's 1 if one household has everything. This method is commonly used to measure both inequality in a country over time and to compare inequality in different countries.

The Gini coefficient can also show how taxation and government transfers of money to households change the distribution of income among households. If governments act to reduce inequality, the Lorenz curve shifts as shown in Figure 9.1. In the example, the half of households with the lowest incomes now have 35 percent of total disposable income compared with 20 percent before taxes and transfers. The Gini coefficient now falls to A/(A+B+C). The extent of redistribution can be measured by the difference in the two Gini coefficients.

Table 9.2 Extent of Redistribution Through Taxes and Transfers

Country	Year	Gini Coefficient		Reduction in Gini coefficient due to redistribution
		Market Income	Disposable Income	
Australia	2018	0.454	0.325	0.129
Belgium	2017	0.486	0.264	0.222
Canada	2017	0.438	0.310	0.128
Chile	2017	0.495	0.460	0.035
Costa Rica	2019	0.532	0.478	0.054
Czech Republic	2017	0.436	0.249	0.187
Denmark	2016	0.447	0.261	0.186
Finland	2018	0.509	0.269	0.240
France	2017	0.519	0.292	0.227
Germany	2017	0.500	0.289	0.211
India	2011	0.508	0.495	0.013
Italy	2017	0.516	0.334	0.182
Japan	2015	0.504	0.339	0.165
Netherlands	2016	0.445	0.285	0.160
New Zealand	2014	0.462	0.349	0.113
Norway	2018	0.429	0.262	0.167
Russia	2016	0.446	0.331	0.115
Sweden	2018	0.428	0.275	0.153
Turkey	2015	0.429	0.404	0.025
United Kingdom	2018	0.513	0.366	0.147
United States	2017	0.505	0.390	0.115

Source: OECD Income Distribution Database (IDD) available at oecd.org/social/income-distribution-database.htm

Table 9.2 shows the Gini coefficients of market incomes and of disposable incomes and the differences between them for a selection of countries. Inequality of market incomes varies considerably as does the extent of redistribution. In some countries such as Chile, redistribution is minimal; in others, such as Finland, inequality of market incomes is as high as in the United States, but redistribution results in a relatively egalitarian outcome.

Inequality in disposable incomes has been rising in many countries since the mid-1980s as seen in Table 9.3. This shows the net result of changing inequality in market incomes and the extent to which redistribution has offset any increases in market income inequality.

Causes of increasing income inequality Economists are debating why inequality in market incomes has increased in many countries One contributing factor is *technological change* favouring those with higher levels of education. This has increased demand for jobs with high levels of skill and talent relative to other jobs. If changes in supply have not kept pace, the gap between high wage and low-wage jobs would grow.

Table 9.3 Changing inequality of disposable incomes

Country	Year	Gini Coefficient	Year	Gini Coefficient
Australia	1995	0.309	2018	0.325
Belgium	1983	0.257	2017	0.263
Canada	1985	0.293	2017	0.310
Czech Republic	1992	0.232	2017	0.249
Denmark	1985	0.221	2016	0.261
Finland	1987	0.209	2017	0.266
France	1984	0.300	2017	0.292
Germany	1985	0.251	2017	0.289
Greece	1985	0.352	2017	0.319
Israel	1985	0.326	2018	0.348
Italy	1985	0.291	2017	0.334
Japan	1985	0.304	2015	0.339
Mexico	1984	0.452	2016	0.458
Netherlands	1985	0.272	2016	0.285
New Zealand	1985	0.271	2014	0.349
Norway	1986	0.222	2017	0.262
Sweden	1983	0.198	2017	0.282
Turkey	1987	0.434	2015	0.404
United Kingdom	1985	0.309	2017	0.357
United States	1985	0.340	2017	0.390
Some Non-OECD Countries				
Brazil	--	--	2013	0.47
China, PR of	--	--	2011	0.51
South Africa	--	--	2015	0.62

Sources: Earlier year data: OECD (2015, Figure 1.3). Recent data: OECD Income Distribution Database (IDD) available at oecd.org/social/income-distribution-database.htm
Note: Gini coefficient estimates are for household disposable income after taxes and transfers.

Globalization – changes in international trade and investment – has changed the pattern of industrial production, shifting significant amounts of manufacturing to rapidly developing countries such as China. This has decreased demand for less educated workers in some countries.

For some countries, the decline in the percentage of private sector workers represented by *trade unions* has been important. As we saw in the previous chapter, unions raise wages above what they would otherwise be. Immigration can also affect wages depending on immigrants' skill levels.

Among well-educated workers, there has also been an increase in earnings inequality. In some countries, particularly in the United States, there have been large increases in the earnings of those at the top of the income distribution – the so-called "1 percent". These include increases in the pay of senior corporate executives, top athletes and entertainers.

As we will see in the next section, wealth is quite unevenly distributed. Income from wealth – interest, dividends and capital gains (i.e. increases in the value of the assets the people own) will be unevenly distributed as well. As emphasized by French economist Thomas Piketty, if wealth inequality grows, this will contribute to increases in income inequality, particularly if those assets are getting high rates of return compared with the growth of wages.

Remember that the changes in inequality shown in Table 9.3 reflect income inequality after taxes and transfers. These typically reduce inequalities created by changes in market incomes, but these policies can also change and could contribute to increasing inequality.

The distribution of wealth Wealth is important because it offers economic security, status and power (including borrowing power), things not adequately captured by measures of income alone. A household's wealth includes the value of physical and financial assets net of debts, but cannot include the value of human capital, an omission that must be kept in mind when thinking about wealth inequality measures.

Wealth is distributed more unequally than income, as Table 9.4 shows. As with income inequality, differences in wealth inequality between countries are large. The share of wealth held by the top 1 percent in the United States is almost four times larger than that in some other countries and has almost doubled since the late 1970s.[3] Russia, India and China, the non-OECD countries included here, also have high wealth inequality. Incidentally, the negative shares

Table 9.4 Distribution of household net wealth

Country	Share of total wealth held by			Ratio of Average to Median Net Wealth
	Top 1%	Top 10%	Bottom 60% *(50%)	
Australia (2014)	15.0	46.5	16.5	1.7
Canada (2016)	16.7	51.1	12.4	2.2 (2012)
*China (2015)	29.6	67.4	6.4	n/a
Denmark (2015)	23.6	64.0	-4	4.7
France (2014)	18.7	50.6	12.1	2.2
Germany (2014)	23.7	59.8	6.5	3.5
*India (2012)	30.7	62.3	6.4	n/a
Italy (2014)	11.7	42.8	17.3	1.6
Japan (2014)	10.8	41.0	17.8	1.6
Netherlands (2015)	27.8	68.4	-4	8.1
Poland (2014)	11.7	41.8	18.3	1.7
*Russia (2015)	42.6	71.3	3.5	n/a
United Kingdom (2015)	19.9	52.0	11.8	2.4
United States (2016)	42.5	78.2	2.4	8.2

Sources: OECD Income Distribution Database, stats.oecd.org/Index.aspx?DataSetCode=IDD; *indicates source is World Inequality Database, wid.world/data/.n/a denotes 'not available'.

Table 9.5 Percentage of children in households with less than 50 percent of median disposable income

Country	Year	Poverty Rate (%)
Australia	2018	13.3
Canada	2017	11.6
Chile	2017	21.5
Denmark	2016	2.7
Finland	2017	3.6
France	2017	11.2
Germany	2017	11.3
Greece	2017	15.9
Israel	2018	22.2
Italy	2017	18.7
Japan	2015	13.9
Mexico	2016	19.8
Netherlands	2016	10.9
Norway	2017	8.0
Spain	2017	19.6
Sweden	2017	9.3
Turkey	2015	25.3
United Kingdom	2017	12.9
United States	2017	21.2
Non-OECD Countries		
Brazil	2013	30.1
China, PR of	2011	33.1
India	2011	23.6
Russia	2016	19.6
South Africa	2015	32.0

Source: OECD Family Database, oecd.org/els/family/database.htm.

of wealth held by the bottom 60 percent of the population in Denmark and the Netherlands are not typographical errors! Collectively, these households have debts which exceed their assets.[4]

The right-hand column of Table 9.4 shows the ratio of average wealth to median wealth. Median wealth is the wealth of the household in the middle of the wealth distribution, so its value best reflects that of the typical household. Because wealth is very unequally distributed, the presence of large fortunes pulls the average above the median. The ratio of the two is a good indicator of wealth inequality.[5] Within this group of OECD countries, the United States and the Netherlands have by far the most unequal wealth distributions.

1.5 Poverty

Households with incomes below a certain level can be defined as living in poverty. That income level, or 'poverty line', can be defined in two ways. An *absolute poverty* line is the income a household would need to permit some minimal standard of living. For example, in the United States, the official poverty line is based on 1964 estimates of a minimally adequate diet, adjusted for family size and then multiplied by three (the purchase of other necessities presumably taking up two-thirds of the budget). It has since been adjusted only for changes in the cost of living.[6] If everyone's incomes rise with economic growth, poverty defined in this way will steadily decline (because a smaller share of income will be needed to meet the minimal food requirements). This hasn't happened in the United States because while average inflation-adjusted incomes have continued to grow, since the mid-1970s the incomes of the poorest households have not, and inequality has increased.[7]

A *relative poverty* line is one that is set relative to the incomes of other households. Half of the median household's income after adjusting for family size is commonly used. This approach views 'necessities' as culturally determined. As community standards increase with the growth of average incomes, those who are too far away from the median will feel relative deprivation, or poverty, even if their absolute standard of living were increasing. The growing gap between themselves and others causes them to experience 'social exclusion' as opposed to 'social inclusion'.

The two approaches are not mutually exclusive. An absolute poverty line could be defined as the cost of buying the goods and services a household would need to attain a modest, basic standard of living. The goods and services included could gradually change as living standards rose.[8]

Poverty among families with children is sometimes viewed with particular concern because it further worsens inequalities of opportunity. Table 9.4 shows the enormous range of variation across the high-income countries; the child poverty rate is eight times higher in the United States than in Denmark.

There are useful absolute measures of poverty and deprivation, however, which have become more widely used as a result of arguments such as those of Indian economist Amartya Sen, which stress the importance of also measuring people's capabilities to lead a decent life.[9] Fundamental to this are things like children's abilities to avoid premature death and to receive adequate nutrition.

This approach is reflected in the World Development Indicators published by the World Bank.[10] These include the prevalence of malnutrition of children under age five and the under-five mortality rate. It has also influenced the Global Multidimensional Poverty Index for developing countries. This combines 10 indicators of health, education, and living standards into a single number to measure poverty along these different dimensions. By this measure, there were about 1.3 billion people in poverty around 2016, about half of them children.[11]

Some of the United Nations' Sustainable Development Goals, (SDGs) established in 2016, deal with poverty.[12] The first SDG is to reduce extreme poverty worldwide from 10 percent in 2015 to less than 3 percent of the world's population by 2030. Here, extreme poverty is defined in absolute terms: persons living on less than US$1.90 per day.[13] It also includes the goal of reducing national

> Question for your professor: If poverty is defined with
> respect to the income that others have, this indicates
> that well-being is determined by relative income, not
> just a person's own income in isolation. Shouldn't
> this idea and its implications [e.g. as explored in
> the anti-text sections of Chapters 4 and 7 of this
> book] be mentioned elsewhere in the text?

poverty rates everywhere by 50 percent.[14] The second SDG is to end hunger by 2030, as measured by undernourishment and measures of food insecurity.

1.6 Income redistribution

How much redistribution of income should take place is a normative question about which economists have no more ethical expertise than other citizens. What they hope to contribute is a framework for thinking clearly about the question. The benefits of income redistribution are greater 'equity', or social justice, although views differ greatly about how much redistribution is appropriate. The costs are less efficiency. This trade-off is illustrated by Arthur Okun's famous 'leaky bucket' metaphor which we referred to in Chapter 1: redistributing income is like carrying water from the rich to the poor using a leaky bucket – the result may improve equity, but comes at a cost of water spilled on the ground.

The result is an application of the familiar logic of comparing marginal benefits and marginal costs. The general idea of the trade-off is sketched out in Figure 9.2. So that we have something measurable on the horizontal axis, let greater 'equity' mean less income inequality. Thus to get more equity, we would have to accept less efficiency. Lower average incomes are the price of reducing income inequality.

As drawn, the line shows diminishing returns: when equity is low (and inequality is high), as at A, equity improvements have relatively little cost in terms of economic efficiency. The leaks in Okun's 'leaky bucket' are small. Further reductions in inequality require sacrificing increasing amounts of efficiency, and hence income. The bucket gets leakier and leakier.

The leaks are chiefly the adverse effects on incentives as redistribution takes place. Redistribution is not just cutting up the 'economic pie' in different slices; it affects the size of the pie itself. For example, it may affect the work effort of those who pay taxes and those who get transfers. A certain amount of inequality is necessary to maintain individual incentives to produce income.

The job of the economist is not to say where on this trade-off society should be. Rather the job of the economist is just to do positive economics: to inform public debate, and if possible to think of ways of improving the trade-off. As described in the earlier discussion of public choice, where a society ends up depends on individual preferences and how society's political institutions

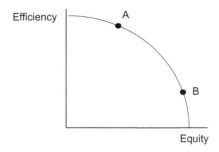

Figure 9.2 The equity–efficiency trade-off

translate these into a collective choice about taxes and transfers and other measures affecting the distribution of income.

2 THE ANTI-TEXT

Our goal for the remainder of the chapter will be to make a case for the following claims:

1 Those textbooks that describe public choice theory in any detail, while providing no critique, invite students to give up on the possibility of government action to improve social outcomes. All that can be expected is 'government failure', with the recipe that the less government does, the better. While examples of government failure are real enough, the theory's assumptions are clearly false as are many of its predictions.

2 The texts contain subtle biases against government action to alter market outcomes by carrying out significant redistribution. This begins with a paucity of treatment compared with the focus on efficient resource use as well as by burying the topic towards the end of the text. They fail to link some of the important causes of changes in the inequality of market incomes to public policy choices.

3 The empirical evidence says that the textbook claim of a significant equity-efficiency trade-off is wrong. If policies are well designed, poverty and inequality in many countries can be greatly reduced without any cost in terms of economic growth.

4 The texts mention equity as an abstract social objective, but spend little or no time discussing the real effects of social and economic inequalities that would be reduced in a more equitable society. They ignore a mountain of evidence that shows that these socioeconomic inequalities are responsible for large inequalities in health and life expectancies that cost millions of people many years of life.

2.1 Public Choice and the unsubtle bias against taxation, government spending and income redistribution

Unlike the basic description of the roles of government set out at the beginning of the Standard Text, the treatment of public choice varies across the texts. In our sample, a couple barely mention it, while most set out some of its central concepts in varying detail. Our Standard Text collects these to give a complete sketch.[15]

Public choice as an ideological project The unflattering picture of the public sector that emerges from public choice theory is no accident. British economist Charles Rowley, a prominent supporter of the approach, described the result of one of the first books on the subject, co-authored by James Buchanan: 'The scene was set for a program of scientific endeavour that exposed government failure *coupled to a program of moral philosophy* that supported constitutional reform designed to limit government, *even to the role of the nightwatchman state*' (our emphasis).[16] A nightwatchman state is the libertarian capitalist ideal: a minimal state that does nothing more than operate a military for defence, police to deal with theft and violence, and a judicial system to enforce contracts and prevent fraud.[17] The 'constitutional reform' Rowley refers to would strip governments of the ability to provide social insurance (healthcare, public education, unemployment insurance, pensions, childcare, assistance to the destitute and so on), to redistribute income in other ways, to regulate business and to address market failures. The result would be 'democracy in chains' – the title of American historian Nancy MacLean's book about James Buchanan, with the subtitle 'the radical right's stealth plan for America'. Big business, owned or controlled largely by the wealthy, would be left the dominant force in society.

This extremist agenda has a powerful cult following, notably among right-wing billionaires, libertarian capitalist 'think tanks' and like-minded academics, but almost no popular support, hence the need for stealth in advancing their cause. Rowley was effectively saying that public choice theory was designed from the beginning to undermine support for collective action through government. In considering Buchanan's economics, American economist Gary Mongiovi concluded that his work 'is a modern manifestation of what [Karl] Marx called "vulgar economy", that is, ruling-class ideology posing as science.'[18] Ironically, Buchanan himself was not shy about publicly accusing other economists of being 'advocates for ideological interests' – in this case, David Card and Alan Krueger, whose empirical findings about the minimum wage had no place in his ideology.[19]

Compare the textbook picture of the cost-efficient profit maximizing firm with the public choice story of cost-inefficient monopolistic government bureaucracies presided over by self-interested politicians with no interest in the public good. Compare the story of efficient markets, where market failures are the exception rather than the rule, with the story of inevitable government failure as policies are determined either by ignorant voters or by the power struggles of special interest groups. Even if there are real problems with market outcomes, the government cure is portrayed as worse than the disease. If a student accepts public choice theory uncritically – and no text that describes public choice ideas in some detail offers any critique – then reducing the size of the state by cutting taxes and spending, privatizing public services and so on starts to look attractive.

False assumptions and falsified predictions Public choice theory begins with a set of assumptions to deduce predictions about the political marketplace. Neither the assumptions nor many of the predictions are in accord with the empirical evidence, but as a rhetorical device, it can be effective. As John Quiggin comments, 'in most areas of politics the facts are not so obvious. Thus, it is possible for quite inaccurate propositions to go unrefuted because they have the seeming surety of deductive logic.'[20]

Public choice begins by extending the assumption of purely self-interested behaviour from the marketplace to the political realm. Otherwise, in James Buchanan's view, one would have to show that there is something in political life that 'suppresses these motives and brings out more "noble" ones'. But political scientist Steven Kelman says that is exactly what happens: self-interest remains, but what he calls 'public spirit' has 'an important role in the political process'. He adds: 'That political decisions involve the community as a whole – and often future generations as well – encourages people to think about others when taking a stand. This is in contrast to personal decisions involving mainly oneself, which encourage people to think mainly of themselves when making them.'[21]

Let's start with the assumptions: the simplistic picture of purely self-interested politicians, bureaucrats and voters. Like any caricature, it has a grain of truth. Everyone can imagine some who might behave like that – a politician whose positions change with the direction of the political winds or a voter who would support policies that benefit himself at the expense of others – but as a generalization it is clearly false.

Politicians are typically members of political parties, which consist of people who broadly share a common view of what constitutes the public good and the kind of policies required to promote it. Some like-minded citizens join such parties, volunteering time and financial support. There is no place for such organizations in public choice theory, where no one has any interest in 'the public good'.[22] Yet, much political debate centres around which policies are in the public interest. That debate is directed at the voters, whom it's presumed also care to some extent about the public good, again violating the assumption of pure self-interest on their part.

> Questions for your professor: (IF APPLICABLE) Our
> text describes a theory of politics called "public
> choice". Were the founders of the public choice
> school libertarians? [Right answer: for the most
> part, yes.] What would be the role of government in
> a libertarian state?

The portrayal of voters as ignorant and greedy harkens back to arguments used long ago to oppose the vote for the working class on the grounds that they were an 'irrational, easily manipulated mob', as Quiggin insightfully observes, highlighting the fundamentally antidemocratic nature of the project.[23] But rather than being rationally ignorant, many voters watch the news on television, read newspapers, and discuss politics with friends and family. They are not well-informed on every issue, but many clearly try to judge how well government is performing given their values as well as their material interests. People may pay attention to public affairs for variety of reasons: a sense of civic duty, a desire not to appear ignorant, or simply because they find it intrinsically interesting.

As for 'bureaucrats' (not civil or public servants, terms with positive connotations), the public choice story underestimates politicians' incentives and ability to control costs. More importantly, the narrow self-interest assumption is as inappropriate here as it is in thinking about people's behaviour in business firms. Large organizations, whether public or private, simply could not function if everyone behaved that way. As Ha-Joon Chang points out, 'successful companies are run on trust and loyalty, rather than suspicion and self-seeking.' Good management, in both the public and the private sector, is about cultivating such qualities in people. He adds that people have 'many other motives – honesty, self-respect, altruism, love, sympathy, faith, sense of duty, solidarity, loyalty, public-spiritedness, patriotism, and so on – that are sometimes even more important than self-seeking as the driver of our behaviours.'[24] In part, these are the product of the social norms and moral codes of our societies, which people internalize as they grow up.

Louis Putterman takes this one step further. He argues that '[a]ccountable, democratic government is impossible assuming that the self-interested, rational individuals of traditional economic theory are the only available citizens and officials.' Why? Because the development of such states from the autocratic ones that preceded them required 'the aid of the actual human impulses that underlie attraction to norms of fairness, capacities to cooperate, desire for social approval, and anger at norm violators.'[25] Such behaviour is also required to maintain these states and to improve their performance. This is what we saw in Chapter 7 when examining how people have dealt with public goods problems. Creating and monitoring an accountable, democratic government is a public good and requires widespread voluntary contributions.

As we saw in Chapter 2, it wouldn't matter if a model's assumptions were empirically false if their violation had a negligible effect on the predictions of the theory. But that's not the case here.

One of the first predictions that came out of public choice theory was that rational self-interested people will not bother to vote.[26] Voting involves time and effort, while the expected benefits are essentially zero: the probability that any one person's vote is going to be decisive is extremely small. Even if it did decide the election in voting for a representative, how likely is it that that would determine who forms a government? Only then would the voter have affected her personal circumstances, which is all she supposedly cares about.

Yet people do vote in significant numbers. The result is a 'paradox' that public choice theorists have struggled unconvincingly to resolve. If they admit that people vote out of a sense of civic duty which it gives them pleasure to fulfill or because they want to punish a government that is done a poor job, their entire theory would begin to unravel.

There is also good evidence that people don't cast their votes based solely on their own economic self-interest. Instead, many appear to judge the performance of politicians based on the general economic situation, not on how they themselves are doing.[27]

```
Questions for your professor: (IF APPLICABLE) Our
text describes a theory of politics called "public
choice" that assumes pure self-interest on the part
of politicians, bureaucrats, and voters. (a) If
that were true, would people even bother to vote?
[Answer: likely 'no'.] (b) If the theory makes a
wrong prediction about something so fundamental,
shouldn't the theory be modified? If so, how? [Possible
answer: Throw the pure self-interest assumption
aside and recognize people's complex motivations.]
```

Corporate (and elite) power… and its limitations In Chapter 5, we introduced some public choice ideas to explain corporate power. Firms in concentrated or well-organized industries can often profitably invest resources in changing the rules of the game to their advantage and to the disadvantage of their workers or customers.

The extent of corporate power in any time and place is an empirical question. Who lobbies policymakers and how effectively? The Standard Text's list of lobbying groups (farmers, pensioners, environmentalists, human rights advocates, unions, bankers, lawyers, doctors, teachers, and corporations seeking tariffs or tax breaks) were the actual examples in our sample of texts. None offered any indication of the relative power of these groups should their interests conflict, although some evidence exists in the case of the United States.

Between 2000 and 2016, $53.5 billion was spent on lobbying the US federal government.[28] Spending by corporations and their trade associations dwarfed those of unions and other interest groups. By one estimate, corporate interests had between 21 and 35 times as much lobbying power as that of public interest groups and labour unions.[29]

This has not gone unnoticed by the general public. In a 2020 poll by the Pew Research Center, 82 percent agreed that 'big corporations and the wealthy have too much power and influence in today's economy'.[30] Similar views have been expressed for decades.

'The wealthy' do not fit neatly into the list of lobby groups typically considered in public choice. Yet research by political scientists is revealing the disproportionate influence of the preferences of the wealthy on public policy. In a study that attracted considerable attention, Martin Gilens and Benjamin Page concluded that in the United States the median voter theory explained *nothing* about public policy. They write, 'the preferences of the average American appear to have only a minuscule, near-zero, statistically non-significant impact upon public policy.'[31] Instead, they find that the preferences of the wealthy and of business interest groups dominate. The view of John Jay, quoted in the epigraph to this chapter, is not far off the mark today.

Given its high levels of income and wealth inequality, the weakness of labour unions, and the role that private money plays in the electoral process, this result for the United States may not be surprising. However, ongoing work by other political scientists is uncovering evidence of the disproportionate role of the preferences of the wealthy in a wide variety of democracies. The result is not plutocracy but a bias in the responsiveness of political systems towards the views of the high-income part of the population. For example, in a study of 30 affluent democracies American political scientist Larry Bartels estimates that this has resulted in social spending being 10 to 15 percent lower, on average, than it would be if everyone's views had equal weight.[32]

But let's not forget that economic policy is not determined solely by the kind of self-interested power struggles described by public choice theory. As we've seen, it ignores the fact that politicians and civil servants are motivated, to a greater or lesser extent, by 'public spirit' and their understanding of the public good beyond their own narrow interests. Similarly, people as citizens voluntarily contribute, to a greater or lesser extent, to the monitoring of government, a public good as discussed earlier. Such action is motivated by ideas about what a better, more just, society would look like. As John Maynard Keynes famously wrote, 'I am sure that the power of vested interests is vastly exaggerated compared with the gradual encroachment of ideas.'[33]

The strength of democracy in a country can wax and wane depending on the extent of civic life and participation. But it's a fact that in the affluent democracies, even in the United States, corporations are constrained by laws regarding competition, consumer and environmental protection, health and safety in the workplace, and so on that a century ago would have been unimaginable.

Stronger democracies have been able to evolve welfare states that offer a broad range of social insurance to citizens while also allowing private business to flourish. Table 9.2 shows that considerable redistribution is possible and, as we'll argue shortly, it need not come at any significant cost in terms of economic growth. More radical – and truly libertarian – ideas, such as extending democracy to economic life, remain to be implemented, but are not going to go away.

Discrediting redistribution As we saw in section 2.6 in the previous chapter, there is no moral justification for people's market incomes It is people's incomes after taxes and transfers which is protected by the legal system as their property.

The libertarian philosophy underlying public choice theory, however, believes that people have a right to their *market* incomes, at least as a kind of ideal. But it can't go so far as to claim that taxation is theft because even the nightwatchman state, described earlier, requires some taxation. The goal is to minimize it.[34] Any redistribution would be done voluntarily through charities.

By portraying the political marketplace as an amoral exchange between self-interested interest groups and politicians, any resulting redistribution of income is neatly delegitimized. The strong have simply used the coercive power of the state to acquire resources at the expense of the weak. In the median voter version of the theory, the majority use the power of the state to extract resources for themselves at the expense of the minority.

A destructive self-fulfilling prophecy? The ideas in public choice theory, if widely believed, have the perverse potential to bring about the kind of dysfunction that the theory predicts. Steven Kelman writes that public choice theory is part of an assault on the 'norm of public spiritedness in political action – a view that people should not simply be selfish in their political behavior.'[35] If a society has been able to establish such a norm, its maintenance and strengthening is critically important. But if people come to believe that the assumptions of public choice theory are true, this would weaken the norm. The result would be an erosion of civic engagement, of the respect people get from public service, whether as civil servants or as politicians, reducing the attractiveness of these activities for people with prosocial values.[36]

There are indications that public choice economists and their allies in libertarian capitalist 'think tanks' and in the media are having some success in bringing about this self-fulfilling prophecy, at least in some countries. Writing in England, Jonathan Aldred asserts that '[n]owadays there is a wide consensus that government is bloated, incompetent, inefficient, vulnerable to capture by special interests and that its interference in ordinary life knows no bounds. ... Public choice theory has done more than help shape this consensus view: it has *become* the consensus about government and politics.'[37] As a result, '[i]f each of us assumes politicians, bureaucrats and voters are all selfish, and each of us acts accordingly, then we cannot expect much from politics.'[38]

2.2 The subtle bias against taxation, government spending and income redistribution

In a study of the rhetoric of the textbooks, American economist David George points out that given the order of topics in the texts, government 'tends to be treated as an entity emerging only after the private sector has established itself.'[39] The government then 'interferes' with markets for private goods through taxes and regulation.

With taxes, the texts focus attention on how the 'burden' will be shared and on technical explanations of the efficiency cost of taxes. (Ironically, the goods usually chosen to illustrate the 'efficiency loss' of excise taxes are goods, such as fuel, cigarettes and alcohol, that have negative externalities. Hence, as discussed in Chapter 7, there may be efficiency *gains*, not losses!)[40] The benefits from increased government spending that taxes make possible are made much less clear. In a book already weighted towards the importance of attaining efficiency in the use of scarce resources, what choice is the reader invited to make when it comes to the equity–efficiency trade-off?

The emphasis on the inefficiency of taxes reinforces the examples given in the texts in the supply and demand applications (reviewed in Chapter 3). They are typically ones in which the government appears to mess things up: minimum wages increase unemployment, rent controls create apartment shortages, subsidies create inefficiencies and taxes create efficiency losses. Warnings about 'government failures' (particularly if public choice theory is emphasized) further reinforce this. All this might have been what former US president Ronald Reagan was referring to when he said: 'The nine most terrifying words in the English language are "I'm from the government and I'm here to help" '.[41]

Marginalizing economic inequality For much of the 20th century, the subject of income inequality was marginalized and ignored, according to the English economist Anthony Atkinson who spent much of his professional life studying the subject. Not surprisingly, he 'believed that it should be central to the study of economics', yet (as he wrote) 'a glance at today's best-selling textbooks shows that the structure has remained much the same as in the past, with discussion of inequality kept separate from the central chapters'.[42] (It's in the same relative location as we have placed this chapter given that this book parallels the structure of the typical text.) We suspect that many economics courses never quite manage to get to the topic.

Atkinson justified his claim of the central importance of inequality, pointing out that the 'distribution and redistribution of the current total of income *do* matter to individuals. The extent of differences has a profound effect on the nature of our societies. It does matter that some people can buy tickets for space travel when others are queuing for food banks.'[43] Inequality affects the degree of social cohesion and shared purpose that the society has. He also noted that the distribution of income affects total production, as we'll see in the next section.

We made the case in Chapter 4 that a person's situation relative to others influences well-being. Growing income and wealth inequalities also fuel the wasteful 'conspicuous consumption' arms race that we examined in Chapter 7. We'll see more evidence shortly of the serious damage that inequality causes.

Yet the main part of the microeconomics texts is spent developing an imaginary world of perfect competition in which resources are used efficiently, and then comparing that with other market structures. This must reflect an implicit value judgement that issues of income distribution and redistribution are of secondary importance. This is all the more puzzling because economic inequality has become increasingly prominent in economics research in recent years, perhaps because inequality has been growing significantly in many countries, particularly the United States.

Swedish economist Gunnar Myrdal, an early recipient of the Nobel Memorial Prize in Economics, dismissed any pretence that social scientists might make about their 'objectivity' and pointed out that value judgements must permeate their work. Instead, he advocated making one's value judgements explicit so the reader would be aware of them and could decide whether to accept them.[44] Sadly, his advice has gone largely unheeded and readers must be alert to detect hidden value judgements on their own.

```
Questions for your professor: Why does the text
give so little attention to economic inequality?
Does that reflect a value judgement that it's not
very important?
```

Marginalizing the political choices behind growing economic inequality In countries where market income and/or disposable income inequality are growing, political decisions are inevitably involved. For example, government policy can influence market incomes by making it easier or harder for labour unions to form, or by changing minimum wages or immigration policy. Tax and transfer policy choices determine the inequality of disposable incomes, which is what really matters for people. Different policy choices can result in radically different degrees of redistribution, as seen in Table 9.2. In short, the degree of inequality in a society is ultimately a political choice.

Yet in our sample of texts, explanations for growing income inequality focused solely on factors affecting market incomes and made no mention of policy decisions behind them. It's as if globalization, immigration or a decline of the bargaining power of workers are natural events outside of government influence.[45]

The Pareto principle: when is 'a society' better off? Let's consider an example of a hidden value judgement. Introductory textbooks rarely give a careful and explicit discussion about how we can think about the welfare of society as a whole. 'When professional economists think about economic policies, they generally start with the principle that a change is good if it makes someone better off without making anyone else worse off. That idea … is referred to as the Pareto principle,' explains Harvard professor Martin Feldstein.[46]

When it's not possible to make anyone better off without making someone else worse off, we have a 'Pareto optimal' outcome. If 'better off' and 'worse off' refer to individuals' utilities, determined as they see fit, at first glance this seems innocuous. As David Colander puts it, 'It's hard to object to the notion of Pareto optimal policies because, by definition, they improve life for some people while hurting no one.'[47]

But, as Stephen Marglin notes, 'this appears to offer a way of talking about societal well-being without invoking value judgements', yet 'value judgements continue to be present, hidden in the foundational assumptions that social well-being consists of satisfying the rational, calculating individual's self-interested pursuit of consumption'.[48]

If we accept that value judgement, and if we also accept the claim that individuals' utilities can't be compared directly, how do we implement the Pareto principle to think about whether an economic policy is desirable? As discussed in Chapter 4, the texts assume that utility goes up if income goes up (with prices unchanged) and, despite the evidence, slip in an unstated assumption that no one cares about what others have. Then the Pareto principle becomes: *'If some people's incomes go up and other people's incomes are unchanged, society is better off.'*

It's easy to overlook the assumption that the income distribution doesn't matter, that it's irrelevant whether a policy increases inequality or not. Consider situations A and B in Figure 9.3. The only difference between them is that one person's income has gone up in B compared with A. If people care about how their incomes compare to those of others, the people whose absolute incomes remain the same will judge themselves worse off in B than in A. If so, the Pareto principle can't be used to say that B is better than A because some people's utilities have decreased.

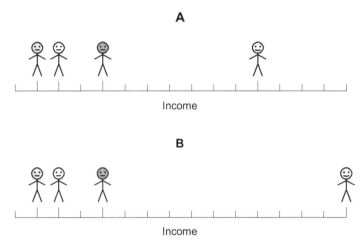

Figure 9.3 Is society better off in B than in A?

Rather than sweeping the question of rising inequality under the rug, Martin Feldstein confronts it in an interesting way. He writes,

> I am interested only in evaluating changes that increase the incomes of high-income individuals without decreasing the incomes of others. Such a change clearly satisfies the common-sense Pareto principle: It is good because it makes some people better off without making anyone else worse off. I think such a change should be regarded as good even though it increases inequality.[49]

Feldstein has neatly substituted the original 'common-sense Pareto principle' that refers to utilities for the version that refers to incomes. He does this while going on to acknowledge that some people 'regard increasing the income of the wealthy as a "bad thing", even if that increased income does not come at anyone else's expense'. How does Feldstein conclude that there has been a Pareto improvement when some people feel worse off? He does it by labelling such malcontents 'spiteful egalitarians' whose views should be ignored. They simply don't count as members of society! Given that concern about one's relative position seems to be a part of human nature and not some moral defect, Feldstein's position is peculiar. It is also a politically expedient position at a time when incomes at the top soared while the incomes for much of the rest of the US population largely stagnated.

When the texts offer the Pareto principle (or words to that effect) and define whether people are 'better off' and 'worse off' in terms of changes in individual incomes, they are agreeing with Feldstein. They just don't state the consequences as openly and candidly as he did.

There is evidence of how people actually think about this Feldstein/ textbook version of the Pareto principle. Yoram Amiel and Frank Cowell investigated this through a series of carefully constructed surveys, asking people to evaluate situations like that illustrated in Figure 9.3. They noted that it 'is perfectly reasonable to suppose that … well-being may be affected by other people's incomes'.[50] They found that in situations like Figure 9.3, the greater the addition to the income of the 'rich' person, the smaller the proportion of respondents who considered that the society as a whole was made better off. Not surprisingly, they reported stark differences between Israeli economics and sociology students who answered these questions. Economics students were almost twice as likely to agree that society was better off in moving from situations like A to B in Figure 9.3.[51]

The 'Pareto optimal' outcomes available to society depend on the initial distribution of wealth and income. With perfectly competitive markets, each possible distribution leads to demands and supplies that result in a particular 'Pareto efficient' allocation of society's resources. A highly unequal society might see a lot of resources devoted to security systems to protect the mansions of the rich; a society where wealth inequality is low might devote resources to universal childcare and healthcare. Both outcomes could be 'Pareto efficient', but not equally desirable.[52]

In any case, given the distribution of income and wealth, the scope for Pareto gains is virtually non-existent. Economic policy typically results in some people being made better off and some worse off. We'll discuss in the next chapter how economists judge society as a whole to be better off or worse off in such situations.

> Questions for your professor: If a policy increases
> the incomes of the rich without decreasing any
> other people's incomes, does the Pareto principle
> say that that policy is desirable? What does the
> text say or imply about such policies?

The rhetoric of reaction Claims of an equity–efficiency trade-off fit neatly into a pattern identified by Albert Hirschman in *The Rhetoric of Reaction*, his study of the arguments used over the last 200 years against the development of civil, political, social and economic rights. What we're interested in here are arguments against the 'welfare state', which

> … in the twentieth century extended the concept of citizenship to the
> *social and economic* sphere by recognizing that minimal conditions of
> education, health, economic well-being, and security are basic to the life
> of a civilized being as well as to the meaningful exercise of the civil and
> political attributes of citizenship.[53]

Welfare state programmes typically include: a guaranteed minimum income of some kind (insurance against destitution); cash transfers to provide greater security in the event of illness, unemployment and old age; and equality of access to certain social services as a right of citizenship, regardless of ability to pay. These include public education, public health services, and possibly housing and personal social services.

Hirschman identifies several claims made in opposition to welfare state programmes. One is that 'the proposed change, though perhaps desirable in itself, involves unacceptable costs or consequences of one sort or another.'[54] Okun's influential book on the equity–efficiency trade-off appeared just after the economic turmoil of the early 1970s. At that time, the argument against the welfare state became 'that it was at odds with economic growth' and 'would jeopardize the conspicuous economic successes of the postwar period.'[55] Okun himself was no reactionary and was optimistic that if his leaky bucket 'is filled in reasonable ways' then 'it can still hold plenty when it reaches the deprived.'[56] This makes the question an empirical one: how leaky is Okun's bucket if 'filled in reasonable ways'?

2.3 The equity–efficiency trade-off, reconsidered

Does it even make sense to talk about an 'equity–efficiency' trade-off? English economist Julian Le Grand points out that 'efficiency' by itself is not a primary social objective like 'equity'; it's just a means to an end, namely attaining primary social objectives, whatever those might be. In his view, efficiency really means that it's not possible to get closer to achieving one social objective without getting farther away from attaining another.

© Andy Singer

In the context of an 'equity–efficiency' trade-off, 'efficiency' is typically used to mean something else, such as maximizing the value of total production or its rate of growth. But Le Grand raises a fundamental point: increasing production or its growth rate is not a primary social objective. It is only useful if it contributes to some primary objective, like a measure of what he calls 'aggregate want-satisfaction'.[57] If there is a trade-off, it is between primary objectives like aggregate well-being and equity. But that is not the trade-off that appears in the texts.

Le Grand is surely right in suggesting that production and its growth have been elevated 'to the status of a primary objective' because it's assumed that 'increases in production lead to increases in individuals' utilities'. We saw the dubious evidence for this assumption in Chapter 4 when considering subjective well-being in wealthy countries. But Le Grand points out another problem: 'the utility *costs* of increased production should also be taken into account. Yet these are frequently neglected'.[58]

He illustrates with an example of a simple policy change that induces a person to work more and so to earn more income, while taking less leisure time.[59] The person ends up with more money income, but less utility. It looks as if 'efficiency' has been increased, but well-being has gone down because of the reduction in leisure. Le Grand argues that it would be better to separate 'the idea of efficiency from that of economic growth and to discuss the issue of any trade-offs between growth and equity explicitly, rather than obscuring the issue by reference to efficiency'.[60]

Let's set aside Le Grand's fundamental objection and consider the textbook story of the equity-efficiency trade-off on its own terms. We'll first consider whether economic theory supports the existence of a trade-off between equity-enhancing redistribution and total income or its rate of growth. Then we'll consider the evidence.

There are two things to keep in mind. First, improving equity is typically equated with reducing economic inequality. Different levels of inequality can affect total income and its growth rate. Second, the costs of redistribution, to move from one level of inequality to another, need to be considered. The equity-efficiency trade-off is the sum of these two effects.

The equity–efficiency trade-off: theory In his book *Inequality*, Anthony Atkinson explained the theoretical basis for the conventional belief that there *must* be a trade-off between equity and efficiency.[61] It is rooted in the model of a competitive economy that has the features we have seen earlier, including perfectly competitive markets for present and future goods and factors of production, no market failures, perfect information, and no explicit role for government. The equilibrium of this imaginary economy produces a certain distribution of individual income, depending on the factors of production each person owns and the prices of those factors. This equilibrium is efficient in the sense that no person can be made better off without at least one other person being made worse off. If income is to be redistributed in such an economy, it will inevitably require 'distortionary' taxation. These taxes 'distort' people's decisions regarding work, saving, spending, and so on, moving the economy away from its previously efficient allocation of resources.[62]

As Atkinson pointed out, the actual economy looks nothing like the one described by this model. The real economy features imperfect competition everywhere, a host of market failures, imperfect and asymmetric information, and government policies that are already influencing market outcomes in many ways. Any taxation and redistribution in this complex situation will change the outcome and economic theory can't say anything about whether the size of the cake (as he puts it) will be bigger or smaller. 'Each proposal has to be evaluated on its merits', as he said. The theory of the perfectly competitive economy is not only irrelevant but using it as the benchmark model makes it more difficult for people to accept the empirical evidence which contradicts it!

Atkinson noted that from the beginning, governments have designed social insurance policies, such as unemployment insurance, to minimize disincentives. For example, unemployment insurance 'increases the attractiveness of working in the market economy, rather than in the informal or domestic economy, and helps bind people into participation.'[63] Theory does not conclude that the cake must be smaller; 'Equity and efficiency may point in the same direction.'

The focus on 'distortionary taxation' also overlooks the possibility that such taxes could help to offset other distortions. Figure 9.3 was a reminder of the importance of relative incomes and how an increase in one person's income worsens other people's relative positions, as seen in panel B. That income increase imposed an external cost on others just like the consumption externalities discussed in Chapter 7. A progressive income tax, reducing inequality, reduces this external cost.

What about the growth of the cake? As Atkinson remarks, the 'standard economic analysis... is typically based on models of economic behaviour that ignore the positive potential contribution of the welfare state to economic performance.'[64]

This raises the distinction between 'static efficiency' and 'dynamic efficiency' mentioned in Chapter 6 in the context of Schumpeterian ideas about the possible dynamic efficiency of oligopolistic markets. The textbook story of the efficiency loss due to taxation is about 'static' inefficiency; reducing distortionary taxes would give a one-time gain in income. An economy that is 'dynamically efficient' is one that optimizes its growth rate. If statically inefficient taxes are used to reduce inequality and that, in turn, increases the rate of economic growth even slightly over time, then the higher growth rates eventually lead to much higher levels of per person income.[65] There would be no trade-off in the long run. What effect that has on subjective well-being is another matter, as discussed in Chapter 4. Let's also set aside, but not forget, that additional growth may come with costs of environmental degradation if not managed sustainably.

Regarding the relationship between inequality and growth, theory provides no decisive answer. The effect depends upon circumstances, such as the level of the country's economic development, or the nature of the inequality. For example, is inequality largely result of a concentration of income at the top of the income distribution? Or does it reflect very low incomes at the bottom of the income distribution? Or is it due to a large spread in incomes between the bottom and the top, with no concentration in any one group?

Surveying the theory, Sarah Voitchovsky writes that 'most of the positive mechanisms can be linked to inequality at the top end of the distribution while many of the detrimental effects can be traced to bottom-end inequality, or to high overall inequality. The ultimate effect of inequality on the economy will therefore depend on the relative strengths of the positive and negative influences'.[66]

Inequality concentrated at the top could describe a dynamic Schumpeterian economy with a class of rich entrepreneurs whose wealth permits savings, investment, and innovation whose benefits might 'trickle down' through increased growth – or not:

> Extreme income or wealth concentration, however, may lead to undesirable distortions and reduced growth when associated with rent-seeking and corruption. While this adverse influence of wealth concentration may be mitigated by strong institutions, high levels of inequality also undermine a country's institutions. High inequality and weak institutions are therefore likely to perpetuate one another, and vice versa for low inequality and strong institutions.[67]

While Voitchovsky comments that developing countries are more likely to have weaker institutions, this feedback between high income and wealth inequality and the weakening of political institutions, leading to further inequality, could happen anywhere.

With high bottom-end or high overall inequality, many people face difficulties acquiring human capital. Taxes to reduce inequality could fund productive private investments in education and productive public investments that could more than offset the effects of distortionary taxes.[68]

The equity–efficiency trade-off: evidence There is now a widespread conclusion about the empirical evidence. It is nicely summarized by a trio of IMF economists who have studied the data extensively. They write: '[E]xcessive levels of inequality are bad not only for social and moral reasons but also for growth and efficiency: although the relation between inequality and growth can be complex, higher levels of inequality are associated, on average, with lower and less durable growth. Hence, even from the perspective of the goal of fostering growth, attention to inequality is necessary.'[69]

As these authors know, and as we discussed in Chapter 2, the conclusions of any particular study depend on the statistical methods employed, the data used, and in this case the way inequality is measured. The relationship between inequality, output, and its growth, will also vary across time and place. The question then becomes: do many different studies, using different methods, point in a similar direction?

The textbooks, while stating the trade-off as fact, fail to summarize, or even acknowledge, the attempts to measure it that have taken place in recent decades. Let's briefly consider some of the empirical evidence about the 'big trade-off', as Arthur Okun originally described it.

The economists who participated in the development of the advanced welfare states of northern Europe in the middle of the twentieth century learned from experience its growth-enhancing effects. Swedish economist Gunnar Myrdal explained that welfare state policies were created despite the belief that they would result in lower growth. But then, as time passed, 'the idea emerged that welfare reforms, instead of being costly for a society, were actually laying the basis for a more steady and rapid economic growth'. Investing in housing, nutrition, health, and education and redistributing income to families with children, especially to underprivileged families, paid off by avoiding future costs and increasing future productivity.[70]

Those countries continue to have high taxes as a share of GDP, comparatively low (although rising) levels of economic inequality yet are among the world's most prosperous countries and their people among the most satisfied with their lives. If there was an unavoidable and significant trade-off between efficiency and equity, how is this possible?

Economists also began statistical examinations of the growth-inequality relationship in large samples of countries once there was enough data to permit it. These try to incorporate the many other factors that economic theory suggests will also influence growth.

For example, in an extensive study, American economist Peter Lindert examined the relationship between economic growth and the social transfers (unemployment insurance, income support, pensions, public healthcare spending, housing subsidies) that are a central part of the welfare state. Looking at the experience of about twenty OECD countries between the early 1960s and the mid-1990s, he found no significant effect of social transfers on economic growth.[71] He sums up by saying: '[T]he social transfers that have always defined the welfare state are indeed a "free lunch" in the sense that they have delivered more equality and longer life expectancy at an essentially zero cost in terms of GDP.'[72]

In 2015, the OECD published a major study, *In It Together: Why Less Inequality Benefits All*. The title gives away the conclusion: inequality inhibits economic growth, while a variety of policies are available that reduce inequality while either promoting growth or not inhibiting it.

In many OECD countries, the bottom 40 percent of the income distribution have suffered a relative decline in disposable incomes as inequality has increased since the 1980s. Setting aside its negative impact on social cohesion, which is hard to quantify, it estimates that rising inequality has reduced overall growth by almost 5 percentage points between 1990 and 2010 across the OECD.

A major cause of this: the 'large amounts of wasted potential and lower social mobility' that result from disadvantaged households being less able to invest in good-quality education and skills development in these high inequality countries.[73] This leads to worse job prospects, less time spent employed, and increased inequality of opportunity for their children. The problem is compounded by increasing wealth disparities, which (unless checked) will reinforce trends in income inequality, reducing growth further.

Notably, its authors write: 'In the public debate, redistribution through taxes and transfers is often claimed to hinder economic growth. The analysis in this report suggests that, if they are well designed, higher taxes and transfers to reduce inequality do not necessarily harm growth.' They recommend that governments consider raising taxes on the wealthy by increasing marginal income tax rates, eliminating or reducing tax deductions that disproportionately benefit them, and 'reassessing the role of taxes on all forms of property and wealth, including the transfer of assets'.[74]

Question for your professor: Our text says that there is a trade-off between reducing income inequality and efficiency. What if taxes were raised on the wealthy, reducing inequality, and used to fund education and training for those who currently can't afford it? Could that raise economic growth?

In their 2019 book *Confronting Inequality: How Societies Can Choose Inclusive Growth*, IMF economists Jonathan Ostry, Prakash Loungani and Andrew Berg describe their studies of the relationship between inequality, redistribution, and economic growth across a wide group of countries. They find that, holding all else constant, greater inequality is associated with significantly lower growth. However, redistribution had 'virtually no effect on output'. (Here, redistribution is measured by the difference between the Gini coefficients of market income and of income after taxes and transfers, as seen in Table 9.2.) So, redistribution, which lowers income inequality, has a positive effect on growth. Only in the cases where redistribution is very high does Okun's leaky bucket kick in – but not to lower growth, simply to offset the positive effect of reducing inequality. In short, their results 'decisively reject' the equity-efficiency trade-off.[75]

The equity–efficiency trade-off lives on despite theory and evidence Why does the equity–efficiency trade-off persist in the textbooks if, in fact, theory is ambiguous and there is no empirical evidence for it, at least within the range of income inequality that we actually observe? Unfortunately, this is an example of a more general phenomenon pointed out by Dani Rodrik, who writes: 'Economists excel at contingent explanations of social life – accounts that are explicit about how markets (and government intervention therein) produce different consequences for efficiency, equity, and economic growth, depending on specific background conditions. Yet economists often come across as pronouncing universal economic laws that hold everywhere, regardless of context.'[76]

In the specific case of the equity-efficiency trade-off, Peter Lindert explains that the source of the declaration of the trade-off as fact 'is ideology and a valid theory that if governments were run badly, they would drag down economic growth'. It is true, Lindert says, that 'if governments did nothing but tax people on the basis of their productivity and give it to other people who were unproductive – encouraging them to be unproductive with those grants – it would make everybody work less, take less risk, and innovate less.'[77] Incidentally, this is exactly the view of government put forward by some public choice theorists; they see society divided between 'makers' and 'takers', with the latter using their voting majority to live parasitically off the 'makers'.[78]

The evidence seems to show that, on average, governments haven't been run badly. More social spending to attain more egalitarian outcomes does not seem to have come at any significant cost in terms of either the level of per-person incomes or their rate of growth. A good deal of evidence suggests that the net effect of such taxes and spending has been positive. It provides a nice counterexample to what is supposed to be a central truth of economics: 'There's no such thing as a free lunch' because there are supposedly always trade-offs. If society collectively wants more of one good (reduced income inequality), it must give up some other good (the size of the cake). But that is not necessarily the case.

The research we've described suggests that the real equity–efficiency trade-off may look something like Figure 9.4. As drawn, this shows no significant relationship between reducing inequality, and efficiency, as reflected by the growth rate, over the range of observed income inequalities. This is the

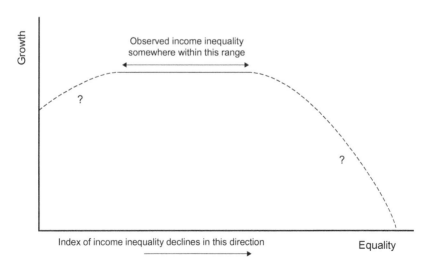

Figure 9.4 The equity–growth trade-off

'free lunch'. This part of the curve could equally well have been drawn with a positive slope, reflecting the results of the OECD and IMF researchers described earlier. As for the rest, the empirical evidence cannot say anything directly about very high or low degrees of inequality that have not been incorporated in past studies. (As drawn, it presumes that reducing very high levels of inequality increases growth, and that at some point a trade-off does emerge if inequality is reduced to very low levels.)

Let's sum up. If you accept Julian Le Grand's view, the textbook equity-efficiency trade-off is asking the wrong question because efficiency is not a final social goal. But if we accept the standard framing of the trade-off, we find that the story has no clear theoretical basis and no empirical support. But by putting the trade-off story in the foreground of the discussion and portraying it as established fact, the textbooks help to tilt the playing field against redistributive measures.

> Questions for your professor: What is the evidence for a significant equity-efficiency trade-off? If there is a significant trade-off, why haven't the high-tax welfare states in Europe experienced low growth and low average living standards compared with lower-tax countries?

2.4 The pervasive costs of inequality

'Social injustice is killing people on a grand scale.' Commission on the Social Determinants of Health, World Health Organization[79]

We've seen earlier, particularly in Chapter 4, evidence of the importance of relative position for individuals' feelings of well-being. But the focus of textbook economics is on the individual removed from social context. As a result, it largely ignores the question of individuals' relative position in society except for admitting its existence briefly if it defines poverty in relative terms. Yet a fundamental feature of human (and many other primate) societies is their social hierarchy and the awareness everyone has of their place in it.

The social gradient of health Within even wealthy countries, life expectancies differ systematically and significantly between different groups of people. People's income, their occupation and the social status attached to it, the degree of economic security and control over work and home life, and their social connectedness (all of which are interrelated) are all important determinants of individual health. Lower levels of these result in increased chances of poor mental and physical health and premature death. This is called the *social gradient of health*: average health and life expectancy decline systematically the lower people are in the social hierarchy, often falling more rapidly at the lowest socioeconomic levels.

The English epidemiologist Michael Marmot, one of the foremost researchers in this area, explains that 'these social inequalities in health ... are not a footnote to the "real" causes of ill-health in countries that are no longer poor; they are the heart of the matter'.[80] The idea of socio-economic inequality as a primary determinant of ill-health may seem surprising. Most public discussion of health policy centres on how well the healthcare system works, and issues of public health regulations (e.g. food and water quality) and individual behaviour, such as smoking, alcohol consumption or exercise. Yet there is ample evidence showing that the effects of socio-economic inequality are deadly.

For example, the gap in life expectancy between those at the top and those at the bottom in affluent countries can be very large, even though it is largely preventable. There are 20 year differences in life expectancy between people at the top and people at the bottom of the income distribution in cities like Glasgow, London, Baltimore, and Washington DC.[81] The health of everyone in between is also affected by their socio-economic position.

Figure 9.5 gives one example, showing life expectancy for men in England according to the characteristics of the neighbourhoods in which they live. An index of multiple deprivation was calculated for each of almost 33,000 neighbourhoods. It combines measures of low income, lack of access to

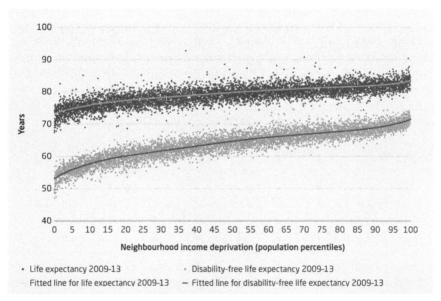

Figure 9.5 Inequalities in male life expectancy and disability-free life expectancy by neighbourhood deprivation, England, 2009–2013

Source: Williams, Buck and Babalola (2020: Figure 1). Reproduced with permission of The King's Fund.

employment, education and skill levels, and crime rates, among other things.[82] The gap in life expectancy between men in the most deprived areas and those in the least deprived is 9.4 years. The key point of the social gradient is that *everyone* is affected, not just those at the very bottom and at the very top. For women, the story is the same although the gap – 7.4 years – is somewhat smaller.

Figure 9.5 also shows estimates of 'disability-free life expectancy' – the amount of time people can expect to remain free of conditions that would restrict their day-to-day activities. For both men and women, the social gradient here is even steeper than that for life expectancy.

In their book for the World Health Organization, *The Social Determinants of Health: The solid facts*, Richard Wilkinson and Michael Marmot explain the psychosocial factors affecting physical health.

> In emergencies, our hormones and nervous system prepare us to deal with an immediate physical threat by triggering the fight or flight response: raising the heart rate, mobilizing stored energy, diverting blood to muscles and increasing alertness ... [T]urning on the stress response diverts energy and resources away from many physiological processes important to long-term health maintenance. Both the cardiovascular and immune systems are affected. For brief periods, this does not matter; but if people feel tense too often or the tension goes on too long, they become vulnerable to a wide range of conditions including infections, diabetes, high blood pressure, heart attack, stroke, depression and aggression.[83]

The effects of socio-economic inequality begin before birth and have lifelong consequences. For example, maternal stress and anxiety reduce blood flow to the uterus, while the fetus experiences the stress hormones directly.[84] Weight at birth is related to the mother's circumstances and shows a remarkably strong correlation with health throughout life. For example, birth weight is negatively associated with the likelihood of heart disease and strokes and with diabetes in middle and old age.[85]

Flattening the social gradient

> 'There will always be inequalities in society but the magnitude of their effects on health is within our control. Why not make things better? It is in all our interests.' Michael Marmot[86]

In an ideal and just society, the social gradient would not exist. In the earlier example of life expectancy in England, everyone would have the same life expectancy as those currently in the least deprived areas. Tens of millions of people would enjoy many more years of life and of disability free life. As Marmot reminds us, the steepness of the social gradient is a matter of choice because it can be influenced by public policy.

A striking example of how social gradients differ between countries and how these differences are also related to the overall level of economic inequality is shown in a 2019 study of the heights of five-year-old children in five countries.[87] (The Gini coefficient for each country is shown beside the country name; recall that a lower Gini coefficient indicates less income inequality.) Children's heights reflect both the socioeconomic conditions they've experienced as well as the general health of the population. They are a good indicator of past and current health and a good predictor of future well-being.

The results for boys and girls are shown in Figure 9.6. Two features stand out.

First, the difference in heights of children at the bottom and children at the top of the income distribution is smaller in the Netherlands and Sweden, countries with lower income inequality. These flatter social

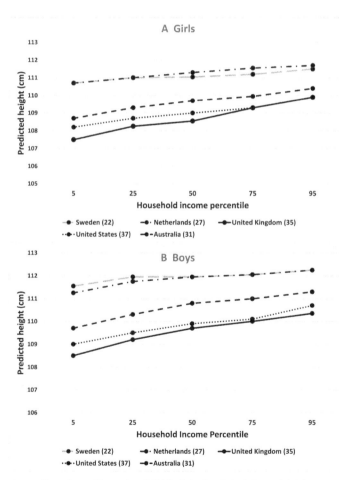

Figure 9.6 Predicted gradients in child height for (A) girls and (B) boys aged exactly 5 years, by equivalised household income percentile
Source: Bird, Pickett, Graham, et al. (2019, Figure 2)

gradients mean that children in the most disadvantaged socioeconomic group suffer a smaller health cost because of their relative position.

How could income inequality affect the social gradient? Family life in more unequal countries can be more stressful for both children and their parents. Sources of stress include the greater likelihood of mental illness and maltreatment of children, and parents having longer working hours. Such societies are likely to have less social cohesion and trust, and to place a greater emphasis on social status, resulting in a greater psychological burden on those with lower social status. The authors add that 'more equal countries also often have more generous welfare systems and more equitable public infrastructure, which may influence both population health and health inequalities.'[88]

This may help to explain a second feature of the data: on average, children in the more equal countries are taller than their counterparts in the less equal countries. The difference is the greatest for the children in the lowest income group. Simply put, societies with greater income inequality have characteristics which seems to be bad for *everyone* in a society.

In their book, *The Spirit Level: Why Equality is Better for Everyone*, Richard Wilkinson and Kate Pickett show the strong relationships between income inequality in different countries and measures of such things as life expectancies, child well-being, mental and physical health, trust and the quality of community life. All tend to be higher in more equal countries.[89]

Questions for your professor: What is the social gradient of health? Would reducing economic inequality and the effects of inequality on people result in a significant improvement in health and life expectancy? Isn't it odd that our textbook does not mention this?

The gradient of health, internationally Typically, textbook discussions of inequality stop at the national border. Redistribution outside the borders is virtually off the agenda. But international inequalities in income are far greater than those within countries. These create what Serbian-American economist Branko Milanovic calls a 'citizenship premium', an accident of birth that gives the typical person born in a high income country advantages and opportunities not available to the typical person born in a low income country, who experience what he calls a 'citizenship penalty'.[90]

Health and life expectancies are reflected in these citizenship premia/penalties. For example, the risk of death in childbirth was (as of 2015) 1 in 16,700 for German women, but 1 in 123 for Nigerian women. In both countries, the risks declined significantly in the previous quarter-century, but the gap remains enormous.[91] The gap in child mortality is also large. As of 2017, one in 10 newborn Nigerian children will not live to the age of five; in Germany, it's one in 270. International differences in child mortality are partly due to diarrheal diseases that account for 10 percent of child deaths worldwide yet are easily preventable and treatable.[92]

If domestic income and health inequalities are unjust, these larger international ones must be even more so. Some philosophers make a strong case for extensive international redistribution.[93] Governments of many high-income countries acknowledge the validity of these arguments with their 'official development assistance', although for most it falls well short of the United Nations target of 0.7 percent of GDP.[94] In many countries international redistribution also has widespread public support through charitable contributions to non-governmental organizations such as Oxfam.[95] Yet the way income distribution, equity and equality of opportunity are discussed in the texts, only people within the national borders count.

Avoidable injustice The World Health Organization's Commission on the Social Determinants of Health set out a detailed plan in 2008 to close the health gap both between people within countries and between countries.[96] The Commission's recommendations included measures to provide affordable housing, improve working conditions, and to enhance economic security through adequate social insurance so that people have assistance in the event of illness, disability, unemployment or lack of adequate income.

The United Nations' Sustainable Development Goals for 2030 contain nine specific targets directly related to health, and others related to poverty, hunger, and inequality.[97] If attained, these will reduce the health gaps identified by the WHO Commission.

Health equity is a matter of life and death for millions of people and the knowledge and resources exist to address it. If economics is concerned with policies to improve people's well-being, why do the textbooks say nothing about the issue?

> Question for your professor: If 'social injustice is killing people on a grand scale', as the World Health Organization's Commission on the Social Determinants of Health claimed, why is this, and policies to address it, not a major theme in an introductory economics course?

2.5 Summing up

What have we seen? While giving lip-service to equity as a social objective, in practice the texts relegate questions of income distribution and redistribution to the back of the book, as if these are of secondary importance to the pursuit of 'efficiency'. For those students whose courses get to this topic in the conventional text, some will encounter the public choice view of politics and policymaking. If they take seriously its stories about rent seeking and pervasive government failure, they will give up hope that much can be done to reduce economic inequalities through government action.

All authors make a faulty theoretical argument for an equity-efficiency trade-off, as we saw that Anthony Atkinson explain. They present no evidence for the trade-off, perhaps because, as we've seen, there is none. They then ignore the evidence about the pervasive effects of economic inequality on health and mortality, documented in detail and beyond dispute, that result in millions of premature deaths every year just in the wealthy countries alone. A simple presentation of the facts would lead inevitably to the question of what to do about this. In those countries with steep social gradients, radical measures would be called for.

But the world-view in the mainstream textbooks is sympathetic to the basic features of the status quo. It appears that textbook authors reflexively shy away from raising questions that would challenge the existing distribution of power and wealth, both within countries and between them. Perhaps they fear that doing so would open them up to accusations of being 'ideological'. But it is equally ideological to avoid raising uncomfortable and inconvenient questions.

SUGGESTIONS FOR FURTHER READING

The story of James Buchanan and the development of public choice theory and the libertarian capitalist ideology behind it is a central part of Nancy MacLean's *Democracy in Chains: The deep history of the radical right's stealth plan for America*.

Hugh Stretton and Lionel Orchard examine and critique public choice theory in their book *Public Goods, Public Enterprise, Public Choice: Theoretical Foundations of the Contemporary Attack on Government*.

In their book *Democracy in America? What has gone wrong and what we can do about it*, Benjamin Page and Martin Gilens describe the extent of corporate and plutocratic dominance in American politics and how citizens can push back against this to strengthen democracy.

American readers should also consult Joseph Stiglitz's *Rewriting the Rules for the American Economy* and *People, Power, and Profits* for an analysis for the causes of growing inequality in the United States and what can be done about it.

Anthony Atkinson's *Inequality: What can be done?* is the culmination of a life's work thinking about economic inequality, offering practical proposals to reduce it.

The World Inequality Database, wid.world, contains data about inequality at the global level and in individual countries. It is maintained by a team at the Paris School of Economics with contributors from around the world. The project periodically produces a *World Inequality Report*, the first appearing in 2018.

Michael Marmot's 2004 book, *The Status Syndrome: How social standing affects our health and longevity*, is a book that may change the way you understand human nature and our social world. His 2015 book, *The Health Gap*, is also written for a general audience.

Chapter 10

TRADE AND GLOBALIZATION WITHOUT THE ROSE-TINTED GLASSES

'There is no branch of economics in which there is a wider gap between orthodox doctrine and actual problems than in the theory of international trade.' Joan Robinson[1]

We saw the idea of comparative advantage and the gains from specialization and trade in the production possibilities frontier model in Chapter 2. We considered there the 'gains from international trade', a theme we examine further here. The case for free trade, presented to students as unassailable wisdom, rests on shallow arguments and the shaky ground of value judgements shared by many economists, but not, it seems, by the general public.

I THE STANDARD TEXT

1.1 The extent and growth of international trade and investment

The importance of trade is typically expressed relative to the size of a country's economy as measured by the total value of all the final goods and services it produces during the year – its gross domestic product (GDP). Trade takes place not only in goods, but also in services such as shipping, tourism and education. Table 10.1 shows the relative size of exports and imports for a variety of countries and how these have changed from 1970 to 2019, almost half a century.

For many countries, the relative importance of trade has increased substantially, particularly for developing countries such was India, China, Mexico and Turkey. Larger economies, such as the United States and Japan, are typically less reliant on trade than smaller countries. The very large values for Belgium and the Netherlands likely reflect the transshipment of goods through their major ports. As well, trade is typically not balanced, with some countries experiencing surpluses (exports exceeding imports) in 2019, such as Germany. Others had deficits, such as the United States. A trade surplus reflects net lending to the rest of the world as the country sells more than it buys from the rest of the world. In effect, it is accumulating IOUs, promises to pay from other countries in the future. Similarly, trade deficits reflect net borrowing from the rest of the world.

Table 10.1 Exports and imports as a percent of GDP, 1970 & 2019

Country	Exports		Imports	
	1970	**2019**	**1970**	**2019**
Australia	12.7	24.1*	12.9	21.6*
Belgium	45.0	81.7	42.8	81.6
Canada	21.6	31.6	19.4	33.3
China, PR of	2.2	19.0*	2.1	18.2*
France	16.0	31.8	15.4	32.6
Germany	15.1	46.9	16.6	41.1
India	4.1	19.0**	4.2	22.0**
Japan	10.4	18.5*	9.2	18.3*
Korea, South	11.1	41.6*	20.4	37.0*
Mexico	6.8	39.3*	9.9	41.2*
Netherlands	43.1	83.3	43.3	72.9
South Africa	21.2	29.9	24.6	29.4
Sweden	22.0	47.2	22.3	43.5
Turkey	3.7	32.7	4.1	29.9
United Kingdom	21.8	31.6	21.0	32.7
United States	5.7	11.7	5.2	14.6

Source: OECD, data.oecd.org/trade/trade-in-goods-and-services.htm.
Notes: n/a denotes "not available". *denotes value for 2018. **denotes value for 2017.

There is nothing inherently good or bad about a trade surplus or deficit; it depends upon the circumstances in which it takes place. For example, a country in which there are good investment opportunities may have a trade deficit as it imports goods and services now to make those investments, enhancing its ability to export in the future.

This increase in trade has occurred for a variety of reasons. Reductions in transportation costs have been significant – consider, for example, the development of containerized shipping. This and improved communications have permitted the development of global supply chains, so that individual products can be produced from components made in many countries. Under a variety of trade agreements, trade barriers have been reduced since the 1970s. The remarkable growth of the Chinese economy since the 1980s and it joining the World Trade Organization (WTO) has been another contributing factor.

In Chapter 2, we explained how trade is determined by comparative advantage, relative costs of production between countries, and how this allows both countries to gain from trade. Restrictions on trade, such as tariffs, can reduce those gains. Let's see how.

1.2 The economics of tariffs and import protection

We'll analyse the effects of a tariff (i.e. tax on imports) on nails. For simplicity, we consider the 'small country' case, where the importing country takes

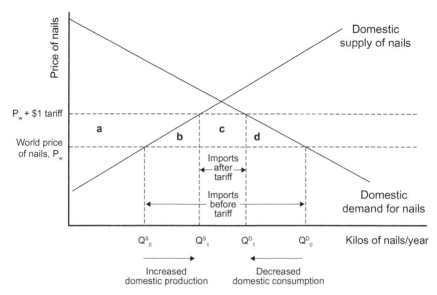

Figure 10.1 The effects of a tariff

the world price of nails (here, $10/kilo of nails) as given: its imports are too small to influence the price in any appreciable way. Figure 10.1 illustrates this situation. At the world price, demand exceeds domestic supply; the difference is imports.

If the government imposes a tariff of $1/kilo on nails, the domestic price rises by the same amount. Foreign suppliers of imported nails must get $11/kilo of nails so that after paying the tariff they still get the world price of $10/kilo. Otherwise, they would sell their nails elsewhere. The rise in price reduces the quantity demanded and increases the quantity produced domestically. As a result, imports decline.

The effect of the tariff is to make consumers of nails worse off and domestic producers of nails better off, while giving the government some revenue from that tariff. What is the net effect?

First, note that the price increase reduces consumers' surplus (the area under the demand curve and above the price) by the areas a + b + c + d in Figure 10.1. Area c is the government's tariff revenue, which involves no loss to society. (Imagine that it is returned to the population as a cash transfer.) The domestic nail producers get areas a + b as they produce more and at a higher price. Part of that (area 'b'), however, represents additional marginal costs of production above the world price, P_w, so really only area 'a' adds to their profits. If those who get these added profits are domestic residents, that results in no loss to society. The net result is that consumers have lost a + b + c + d, producers get 'a', governments get 'c'; thus 'b + d' is the *net loss to society as a whole* from the tariff. The loss comes from two sources: reduced consumption lowers consumer surplus ('d') and the society has accepted higher domestic costs of production of nails than it could have paid to get the nails from abroad ('b').

The analysis of a policy that limits imports to a certain maximum level (called an import quota or a quantitative restriction) is the same with the exception that in that case the government gets no tariff revenue. Either domestic importers or foreign producers get the benefits of the higher price, depending on who gets the valuable rights to import the limited amount of foreign nails.

1.3 The argument for free trade

The net costs of a tariff or a quota are the same as the net gains from removing them. Consumers gain consumer surplus from the lower price and greater consumption; on the production side, society's resources are directed more towards the goods in which it has a comparative advantage. Total income in the country is higher and, as we saw in Chapter 2, every consumer can potentially have more of all goods. Those employed or owning capital in import-competing industries will be made worse off as they have to find employment elsewhere or accept lower incomes, but trade raises the economic well-being of a nation in the sense that the gains of the winners exceed the losses of the losers. Total surplus is increased. Therefore, the winners could compensate the losers and still be better off. In this sense, trade can make everyone better off.

Governments may provide assistance to those hurt by changes in trade policy, but compensation is unlikely to be complete. As a result, changes in trade policy are often controversial. The losers, being smaller in number than those who gain, may be in a better position to organize to obtain tariffs or to block trade liberalization. As a result, nations may fail to fully enjoy the gains from trade.

If all countries pursue free trade, the world would have a more efficient allocation of resources and a higher level of material well-being. Trade has the additional benefit that exposure to foreign competition also keeps domestic producers on their toes, adopting the best technologies to keep costs low and productivity high. The greater interdependence of economies around the world through trade and investment also promotes peace by making war more costly.

1.4 Potentially valid arguments for protecting domestic production against foreign imports

As part of their World Trade Organization obligations, many countries have agreed to increase tariffs only in special circumstances (described below). In international trade negotiations, countries' negotiators label tariff reductions as a 'concession', as if these were costly, rather than beneficial as economic analysis suggests. There are, however, some theoretically defensible arguments for some protection against imports, at least in some circumstances.

National defence Depending on its location and history, a country may view the higher costs of domestic production as a worthwhile price to pay to be able to feed and defend itself in the event of war. How far such a policy should go isn't easy to say, however.

Infant industries and strategic trade policy Comparative advantage is not static; a country's relative costs of production can change over time. If a domestic industry were protected from foreign competition, a sufficiently large domestic market might enable it to expand to take advantage of increasing returns to lower average costs. Average costs could also fall with the experience of producing output ('learning by doing') and with research and product development that, without protection, would not be viable. Eventually, when the fledgling industry grows up, it can survive without protection and could possibly start exporting its product. In the case of an oligopolistic industry where there might be economic profits to be had, this policy secures some of those profits for countries with firms in that industry.

Unfortunately, it may not be clear which industries are good candidates for such treatment, while there will be no shortage of applicants for protection. Other countries could retaliate with tariffs if their exports are affected. Economists also argue that production subsidies would be a more efficient policy. These would support producers without raising consumer prices. (This assumes that taxes needed to pay for the subsidy have low efficiency costs.)

Diversification of production Relying on one or two export industries (usually agricultural commodities or natural resources) exposes the country to risks of large economic fluctuations if world prices are volatile. This is most relevant for developing countries that produce raw materials and for some oil-producing countries. But are tariffs that create a high-cost domestic industry the answer? Perhaps a country could promote other kinds of exports (e.g. tourism, education and other services) through investments in education and infrastructure.

Retaliation against unfair trade practices: subsidies and dumping Under international trade agreements, countries may prevent damage to domestic industries if foreign competitors get subsidies from their governments. Similarly, if foreign firms 'dump' goods in the domestic market at below their cost of production, tariffs can legally be applied to prevent injury to domestic firms. This makes sense if foreign firms are using 'predatory pricing' to destroy domestic firms and establish a monopoly, but not if foreign firms are simply selling in the domestic market at a lower price than they are charging in other markets ('price discrimination'). Yet anti-dumping tariffs may be applied in this way, at the expense of domestic buyers.

Changing the terms of trade The 'terms of trade' reflects the relative value of a country's exports in terms of the imports they can purchase. A country's total consumption can rise if its terms of trade improve: it can export the same amount and get more imported goods. If a country is large enough, it can influence world prices. A tariff on imports, by reducing demand for those products, can drive down their prices in world markets; at the same time, as resources are drawn into the production of import-competing goods, the supply of the country's exports falls, thus raising their price. The country's terms of trade improve. This 'optimal tariff' policy makes the country better off at the expense of people in other countries whose terms of trade worsen. If other countries respond by raising their own tariffs, however, they can cancel out the effects on the terms of trade, leaving everyone worse off.

1.5 Illegitimate arguments for protection

Some arguments for protection are wrong. Here are two examples.

Tariffs increase employment Will the purchase of imports instead of domestic goods cost jobs at home? Not if the country is on its production possibilities frontier, so all resources are employed. Tariff protection can only move workers from the export industry to the import-competing industry, with the losses that we saw earlier in Figure 10.1. If there is unemployment, the claim is true for one country, but it can't be true for all countries. If all countries try this, as in the 1930s, everyone's exports fall and so does employment.

Since we can't compete against low-wage foreign labour, tariffs prevent a 'race to the bottom' High-wage countries sell goods to low-wage countries (and vice versa), so clearly it's possible to 'compete' against low-wage labour. Comparative advantage shows that it is relative, not absolute, costs which matter for the ability to trade. Wage differences reflect productivity differences, as we saw in the Standard Text part of Chapter 8.

1.6 The global trading system

The General Agreement on Tariffs and Trade (GATT) was established in 1948 to provide a system of rules overseeing international trade. This provided predictability and stability for importers and exporters. An international organization of the same name also resolved disputes between member states and provided a forum to negotiate gradual tariff reductions among countries. The World Trade Organization (WTO) replaced the GATT in 1995 but continues to administer the GATT agreement.

Alongside the WTO and allowed within its rules are preferential trade agreements between pairs or groups of countries. These agreements allow trade (and perhaps investment and labour) to move freely between the countries that are members of the preferential agreement, while they maintain separate rules for countries outside it. The European Union is an example of a 'customs union', where all countries within it maintain a common trade policy. The Canada-United States-Mexico Agreement (CUSMA), which replaced the North American Free Trade Agreement (NAFTA) in 2020, is an example of a 'free trade area', in which countries can maintain independent trade policies with countries outside the CUSMA.

2 THE ANTI-TEXT

We will first set out some important points that the textbook analysis slides over. How do the textbooks, and economists more generally, add together the gains and the losses of different people to proclaim that 'the country' as a whole is better off or worse off as a result of some economic policy change? All too often, economists claim to have an answer to this question when they really don't.

What happens if we change the simple assumptions of the Ricardian model? What happens if technologies can change, perhaps moving with foreign investment between countries? What happens if firms face increasing returns instead of constant returns? The simple conclusions of the textbook Ricardian model no longer hold.

Finally, we will see that the problems of externalities, imperfect information and power are just as serious in the international sphere as they are in the domestic sphere. Globalization is a much more complex and double-edged process than the textbooks let on.

2.1 Problems with the textbook model

The analysis of the tariff The analysis of tariff removal compares two equilibrium positions. The implicit assumption is that the economy moves instantly and costlessly from one equilibrium to the other. This is not just a simplification for the convenience of students; it is common in empirical studies of changes in trade policy. These typically simulate what the economy would look like after a change in trade policy, but only consider the new equilibrium when all adjustments have taken place.

Perfectly competitive models of factor markets could be used to describe just such instantaneous and costless reallocations of resources. But in reality, the economy does not hop from one position on the production possibilities frontier to another; it follows a path inside the frontier as factors of production leave the import-competing sectors, and spend time unemployed before perhaps becoming re-employed in other sectors. The income lost during unemployment and the costs of becoming re-employed should be counted. 'Economists have sometimes dismissed such adjustment costs with the comment that the displaced factors become re-employed "in the long run". But this is bad economics, since in discounting streams of costs and benefits ... the near-present counts more heavily than "the long run"', as some well-known international trade economists pointed out long ago.[2] To be fair, many texts go beyond the simple Ricardian model to acknowledge the reality that some workers may lose their jobs and experience unemployment or a permanent reduction in earnings as demand for their skills declines. But as we will see in the next section this does not influence their judgement about the net gains from trade.

As well, the argument is commonly made (as we saw in Figure 10.1) that consumers benefit from lower prices for imported goods, resulting in an expansion of consumer surplus. But did you notice in our earlier 'textbook' exposition that this is only half the story? American economist Robert Driskill writes that in their enthusiasm for free trade, exponents of its benefits sometimes neglect to note that when tariffs are removed, the relative price of exportable goods must rise. People buying those goods will see their consumer surplus shrink. Whether any particular consumer is better off or worse off depends on the balance between the importable and exportable goods they buy.[3]

Questions for your professor: Why do we just compare the equilibrium with the tariff with the equilibrium without it? Are we forgetting the costs of getting from one to the other?

When is 'society' better off? The compensation principle The Pareto principle, which we examined in Chapter 9, does not apply to changes in trade policy. Lowering protection against imports makes some people in society worse off, while others become better off. As in so many practical situations, the Pareto principle offers no guidance.

Recognizing this, British economists John Hicks and Nicholas Kaldor proposed the *compensation principle*.[4] Compare free trade with import protection. If with free trade it is *hypothetically* possible to redistribute income between individuals so that some people have more income and no one has less income than with protection, then free trade is better than protection.[5] Relying on this, Mankiw writes in his text: 'Trade raises the economic well-being of a nation in the sense that the gains of the winners exceed the losses of the losers'.[6]

That is the essence of the texts' argument for free trade. By asserting the Hicks–Kaldor compensation principle (implicitly, if not explicitly), it gives primacy to the supposed social objective of efficiency while downplaying or ignoring questions of equity or income distribution.

We saw in the previous chapter the dubious nature of the Pareto principle as a general criterion for judging whether society is better off or not. The Hicks–Kaldor compensation principle, with its *hypothetical*, not actual, compensation, is far less convincing. Yet despite that, unexplained value judgements abound in the texts. For example: 'Free trade makes the country as a whole better off, even though it may not make every individual in the country better off'.[7]

In a refreshing commentary (aptly entitled 'Why do economists make such dismal arguments about trade?'), Robert Driskill asks: 'Why should people think economists can be, in effect, high priests who tally up benefits and losses to different individuals and pronounce the outcome good or bad for the group as a whole? In fact, people shouldn't.' Judging the outcome is 'a matter of moral philosophy, not number-crunching', and economists are no better moral philosophers than anyone else. 'It's really that simple.' It is hard to overstate the importance of this basic point, which applies to the textbook analysis of economic policy in general.[8]

It's not obvious that everyone would share the value judgement of the textbooks concerning trade policy. What if many people each gain a little bit while a few suffer losses that, as Driskill describes, are 'often large, painful, and traumatic, requiring dramatic life changes'? Is 'society as a whole' necessarily better off if the sum of the gains and losses is positive? A reasonable person could easily say 'no'. Note that the example here also assumes that those whose real income goes up feel better off, but as we've seen in Chapter 4, this is open to question. A relatively small increase in real income experienced by most people could have little effect or no effect on well-being as they quickly adapt to it, while the few who suffer large losses would indeed be worse off as their relative position worsens.

In his book *Straight Talk on Trade*, Dani Rodrik reports that two thirds of Americans support trade restrictions. He then describes meeting a Harvard class who were initially 90 percent in favour of free trade before having studied the subject. He proposed a hypothetical experiment in which $200 would disappear from one student's bank account and $300 would appear in another student's bank account. Only a 'tiny minority' supported this, many were uncertain and even more opposed it. He then asked them why almost all of them had supported free trade which 'entails a similar–in fact, most likely greater–redistribution from losers to winners. They appeared taken aback.'[9]

This description of the nature of the gains and losses from changes in trade policy resembles the conclusions of research on the effects of the North American Free Trade Agreement (NAFTA) on the US economy. There were small decreases in prices for consumers, small net losses in employment, and a small increase in economic welfare as conventionally measured. But while *net* losses in employment may have been small, those losing their jobs because of increased imports from Mexico were unlikely to have the skills or to be in the location to get jobs in industries with improved export opportunities.[10]

In a careful study of local labour markets in the United States, John McLaren and Shushanik Hakobyan identified the industries and localities most vulnerable to increased import competition from Mexico. They found that 'blue-collar workers in vulnerable industries suffered large absolute declines in real wages' and that, in areas with a concentration of such industries, workers in the service sector are substantially worse off too. This happens because workers who lose their jobs because of increased imports must look for jobs elsewhere in the locality, competing down wages for such jobs. McLaren and Hakobyan cite Dani Rodrik's view that changes in trade policy have modest effects on aggregate welfare, but large redistributional effects.[11] The same can be said for significant changes in trade that occur for other reasons; we will have a look at the effects of imports from China on the US labour market shortly.

Such studies deal with job losses and loss of income. But this reflects only a part of the loss in well-being that these workers and those in their communities experience. Research on subjective well-being, measured for example by life satisfaction or happiness, show that for the unemployed well-being declines by much more than the loss of income alone can explain. For most people, work means much more than a paycheck; it's a source of social identity and social contacts. Unemployment also means economic insecurity, not just for the unemployed themselves, but for others in the community.

These spillover effects are significant. In a study of more than 3 million Americans, John Helliwell and Haifang Huang found that for those who remained employed a one percentage point increase in the local unemployment rate had an effect on their subjective well-being 'close to that of a 4 percent fall in household income.'[12] Because there are a lot of such people, this adds up. They summarize the results:

> if the direct monetary loss of the unemployed themselves is 1, the additional SWB [subjective well-being] loss of the unemployed is about 5, while at the population level the indirect or spillover effect is about 16 including the impact of monetary loss to other household members. All together, the total well-being costs of unemployment are about 20 times as large as those directly because of the lower incomes of the unemployed.[13]

Whether or not the workers who have suffered these large redistributive effects deserve help from the government is a matter of ethical judgement. If you care about growing inequality or if you think some social insurance should be available to everyone who suffers significant hardship through no fault of their own, you would probably agree. But if you are a firm believer in the Hicks-Kaldor compensation criterion, then potential compensation is good enough. In the 2018 edition of his text, Gregory Mankiw reprinted a short article by another American economist, Steven Landsburg, who argues that his fellow citizens who were displaced by Mexican imports are owed nothing. In Landsburg's view, they were like bullies, extorting American consumers to pay more for their products by getting the government to protect them from Mexican competition. 'When a free trade agreement allows you to buy from the Mexican after all, rejoice in your liberation', he wrote.[14]

Trade and growing wage inequality While issues of income distribution are important in assessing policy changes, they are also important in judging whether changes in patterns of comparative advantage and trade are making countries as a whole better off or worse off. Trade economists have been debating for years the extent to which globalization and the increasing trade of the industrialized countries with developing countries has put downward pressure on wages of less-skilled workers in the developed countries, contributing to growing income inequality there.[15]

A basic model found in every trade textbook, and sketched out in some introductory texts, explains trade as the result of differences in the relative amounts of factors of production in countries.[16] Some countries have a relative abundance of skilled labour and capital, some have a relative abundance of unskilled labour, for example. The model predicts that countries will specialize in and export goods that use a lot of the relatively abundant factors relative to the less abundant ones.

If a country with an abundance of skilled labour increases imports of goods that use a lot of unskilled labour, the wages of less skilled labour fall. At the same time, an increase in exports of goods that use a lot of capital and highly skilled labour raises the incomes of capital owners and of high-skilled workers. Earnings and income inequality grow. But there are also other explanations for increasing wage inequality. So far, it seems, the debate about the extent to which trade is responsible remains unresolved, if only because of the enormous difficulty in disentangling the causes of changes in wages. (For example, technological change could change wages, but also be a response to import competition.) As we will see shortly, though, there are further reasons for thinking that trade and globalization will be putting downward pressure on wages more generally in the industrialized countries.

The effects of changing trade patterns: the case of China and the United States The remarkable growth of the Chinese economy since 1990 was accompanied by its emergence as a major exporter of manufactured goods. As with NAFTA, economists estimated the effects on local labour markets in the United States of this shift in comparative advantage. Between 1999 and 2011, roughly 2–2.4 million jobs were lost due to increased imports from China, according to one well-known study. This includes not just jobs lost in manufacturing directly but includes its economy wide ramifications. For example, domestic industries supplying those manufacturers would shrink, as would local businesses where plants close.[17]

In the textbook story, there are no frictions in labour markets, so there is always full employment: workers losing their jobs as manufacturing shrinks are immediately reemployed elsewhere. However, to the researchers' surprise, they found no evidence that other sectors expanded. Instead, total spending in the economy declined and lower overall demand prevented employment from growing elsewhere.

In short, both freer trade and rapidly shifting comparative advantage have significant negative consequences for a minority of the workforce, particularly those with the least education. The resulting loss of jobs and income, along with increased inequality and economic insecurity may be contributing to the so-called populist political backlash seen in several countries in recent years.[18]

In contrast here's how Michael Parkin's textbook describes the situation: 'International trade in textiles has cost tens of thousands of U.S. jobs as U.S. textile mills and other factories closed.... And tens of thousands of U.S. workers have better-paying jobs than as textile workers because U.S. export industries have expanded and created new jobs. More jobs have been created than destroyed.'[19] Note how the phrase 'than as textile workers' implies that the displaced textile workers are getting better paying jobs in export industries – ignoring the evidence and turning them into winners instead of losers! As well, the standard model's assumption of full employment of a given labour force has been set aside to have more jobs created than destroyed. Increased imports 'create jobs for retailers that sell imported goods and for firms that service those goods' (as if similar people didn't do the same things for the domestically produced goods that the imports replaced) and the additional imports 'also create jobs by creating income in the rest of the world, some of which is spent on U.S.-made goods and services.' But the evidence, cited above, suggests that the net effect of large increases in imports can be a reduction in total demand in the economy, decreasing employment below what it would otherwise be.

Questions for your professor: When some people gain and some lose following some policy change, how do economists say whether society as a whole is better off or worse off? Is it sufficient to have net gains so that total incomes go up?

2.2 Relaxing the textbook's assumptions

The simple Ricardian model that illustrates comparative advantage and the gains from trade makes some critical assumptions. Technologies can differ permanently between countries; neither the technology nor factors of production can move between them. Only consumption goods can move internationally. It also assumes perfect competition and constant returns in production.

We will briefly consider what happens when each of these assumptions is relaxed. We then get a glimpse of the real world where corporations offshore production, taking their technology with them. Workers lose their jobs, putting downward pressure on wages in rich countries. Increasing returns lead to arbitrary patterns of specialization both within and between countries.

Technological change Paul Samuelson described what happens to countries' national incomes if technology changes as a result of local developments. To adapt his analysis to our simple Ricardian wheat and cloth example from Chapter 2: suppose England experiences a technological improvement in wheat production, the good in which Canada has a comparative advantage. This lowers the world price of wheat and reduces Canada's gains from trade. Canada's national income falls as its terms of trade fall (i.e. it must export more to get a given amount of imports). In the worst case, it eliminates Canada's gains from trade and trade stops.

Samuelson pointed out that this kind of technological catch-up on the part of less developed, lower-wage regions has been common through history, both within countries and between countries. While total incomes rise in the areas 'catching up', income falls in the previously more advanced regions.[20]

Workers, owners, internationally mobile technology and capital The Ricardian model treats everyone like worker-owners, such as farmers who grow wheat and who keep sheep (who provide the wool to make the cloth). They consume some of their own produce and trade the rest. In this simple setting, there are no winners and losers; everyone can gain from trade. Yet, as Stephen Marglin remarks, 'the distinction between worker and owner is basic to capitalism, as is the distinction between producer and consumer', adding: 'it is not just a simplification to ignore these realities but a distortion'.[21]

Marglin offers a more realistic model in a simple numerical example to illustrate what happens when workers and owners are considered separately. In the case he considers, a multinational corporation located in an industrialized country offshores some of its nail production to a developing country.[22] Both technology and the physical capital in which it is embodied move. This is an example of a way in which technological differences between countries can change that is different in an important way from Samuelson's analysis, where the technological change took place abroad, but without a flow of capital.

As a result of their foreign investment, owners of multinational corporations, or MNCs, enjoy larger profits. Nail production falls in the industrialized country as it imports some nails from abroad. Some workers lose their jobs, obtaining instead involuntary 'leisure'. They are worse off, not only from lost income and subjective well-being during unemployment, but also from lower future earnings and, if they have to move, the costly disruption in their lives as they become uprooted from friends, family and community.

In the case Samuelson examined, foreign investment did not bring about the technological change in the foreign country so there was no flow of foreign investment income back to the developed country. This income received by capital owners can offset the income losses of workers who lose their jobs as a result of production cuts, so that national income in both places may rise, unlike in Samuelson's example. But as we have seen, even if the total income in the industrialized country increases, there is no reason to conclude that the nation collectively is better off.

In the developing country, there is greater material prosperity. This benefits people there, particularly if basic needs have not yet been met, and possibly even people in other countries if they care about the international distribution of income. It also involves, however, 'the disruption of community and the substitution of forced-march Westernization for a more gradual evolution' of the indigenous culture, a cost that has no place in textbook thinking.[23] Whether that society is better off or not, or at what pace its transformation should take place, also requires value judgements.

> Question for your professor: The Ricardian model in the text does not allow capital or labour to move internationally. What happens if capital moves to 'offshore' some production? Does this make workers at home worse off?

Increasing returns and globalization Ralph Gomory and William Baumol have examined broadly similar scenarios, but ones in which firms have increasing returns instead of the constant returns of the Ricardian model.[24] In their model, which country ends up specializing in which good is completely arbitrary. The country that first starts producing a particular industrial good has lower average costs than its potential rivals would if they entered the market at initially low levels of output. They will find it more profitable to produce something else instead.

Here, the outcome depends on accidents of history. Except in the unlikely event that average costs are the same in each country, this arbitrary

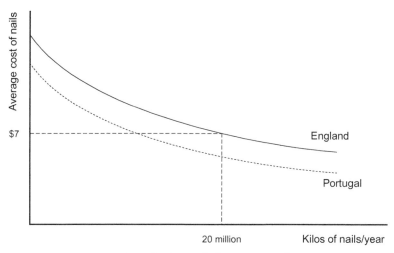

Figure 10.2 Average costs of producing nails in two countries

pattern of production will not maximize total world income. Figure 10.2 gives an example.[25] Portugal could potentially produce nails more cheaply than England, but if England gets a head start, its declining average costs may lock Portugal out of the market.

England produces 20 million kilos of nails at an average cost of $7/kilo. If Portugal tried to enter to take a portion of the world market, its producers would face much higher average costs. When there are increasing returns, 'the invisible hand can blunder' and can lead to inefficient patterns of production.[26]

If increasing returns are an important feature in the production of many goods, the textbook default model of perfect competition is misleading. In that model, free trade produces a globally efficient allocation of resources. In the world of increasing returns, it does not.

As in the Samuelson and Marglin accounts, the transfer of technology from high-income to low-income countries and the 'resulting growth in the effectiveness of competition ... drives wages toward the middle. They end up above the initially low levels in the less-developed economy, but below [their] former level in the wealthier countries'.[27]

None of this means that industrialized countries should sabotage technological progress in developing countries or restrict imports from them. All of these examples serve to stress that comparative advantage evolves and that the distribution of the gains from trade changes with it. The process of 'globalization' produces complex and ever-changing outcomes. No simple conclusions are possible.

Instead of the traditional trade policies – tariffs, quotas and so on – examined in the textbooks in the context of an infant industry, these ideas highlight the importance of broad, economy-wide policies to influence productivity and technological change, and thereby the dynamic pattern of comparative advantage. These could include tax policy and support for research and development, and for education.

> Question for your professor: According to the textbook, specialization with free trade results in the most efficient use of the world's resources. Are other, inefficient, outcomes possible, even with free trade?

2.3 What's missing from the textbooks

Once again, the usual suspects are missing in the textbook account: externalities, asymmetric information and power. In the international context, they raise new problems.

The problem of externalities The textbook analysis of trade assumes the usual default case of no externalities. As we stressed in Chapter 7, externalities are everywhere. When they are not taken into account in decision-making, international trade will be inefficiently large.

The most obvious externalities are global: the greenhouse gas (GHG) emissions that are involved in the transportation of all kinds of traded goods and services, whether it is fresh flowers flown from Kenya to England, container ships travelling from China to Rotterdam, or millions of tourists flying to exotic locations. Neither international aviation nor international shipping were directly included in the 2015 Paris climate agreement. Negotiations and planning to deal with their rapidly growing emissions were left to the UN organizations dealing with these industries.[28] Whether these will be effective remains to be seen.

Indian-British economist Partha Dasgupta gives a nice example of more local externalities.[29] Suppose that the government of a developing country offers timber concessions to private companies which cut down the forest and export the wood. This damages watersheds and the livelihoods of farmers and fishers downstream. They have too little political power to get compensation for the damage they suffer. This effectively subsidizes the country's timber exports and transfers wealth from the poorest people in a poor country to the owners of the forestry companies and to importers in rich countries.

How big are such subsidies and how much is trade influenced by them? Dasgupta writes: 'Unfortunately, I can give you no idea ... because they haven't been estimated. International organizations have the resources to undertake such studies; but, to the best of my knowledge, they haven't done so.' He rightly adds that examples like this do not make a case against free trade, as such, but they do show that the case for free trade must include a consideration of its environmental impacts.[30]

Defenders of globalization, such as economist Martin Wolf of the *Financial Times*, dismiss such concerns about exports being, in effect, subsidized by externalized costs.

> Differences in incomes, preferences and geography could quite reasonably give different localities, or countries, entirely different environmental standards for local environmental spillovers. If polluting industries were then to migrate from high-standard regions or countries to low-standard regions or countries, the world would be unambiguously better off. The high-standard regions or countries would be able to consume the products of polluting activities without having to host them, and the low-standard regions or countries would have more economic activity, in return for pollution to which they are, relatively speaking, indifferent.[31]

That public policy in such countries may not accurately reflect the public's preferences does not seem to occur to him. Setting that aside, there is also the problem of the powerlessness of parts of the population (as Dasgupta noted) and the problem of information. People have to know that the pollution is taking place and to understand fully its consequences.

In recognition of these realities, international conventions are attempting to impose legal restrictions on trade in toxic materials. 187 countries have ratified the Basil Convention on the Control of Transboundary Movements of Hazardous Wastes and their Disposal. 161 countries are parties to the Rotterdam Convention on the Prior Informed Consent Procedure for Certain Hazardous Chemicals and Pesticides in International Trade. Notable among the countries that have failed to ratify these is the United States.

Unfortunately, despite these measures the illegal flow of waste from rich to poor countries continues, taking advantage of lax regulation and enforcement. Electronic equipment that contains lead, mercury, cadmium, chromium and other toxins is causing growing problems, particularly as manufacturers are not required to bear the costs of their proper disposal and thus have no incentive to try to produce them in other ways.

To give just one example, let's consider the gains from trade that occur from the imports that ends up in a large e-waste dump: Agbogbloshie in Accra, Ghana. There, as photojournalist Kevin McElvaney writes:

> Boys and young men smash devices to get to the metals, especially copper. Injuries, such as burns, untreated wounds, eye damage, lung and back problems, go hand in hand with chronic nausea, anorexia, debilitating headaches and respiratory problems. Most workers die from cancer in their 20s.[32]

One 19-year-old worker, Abdoullaye, who makes between £0.5 and £1.3 per day and manages to send £13 each month back to his family in the north of the country, says 'I would like to go back home, but my family needs the money, so I stay.'[33]

Martin Wolf's view, quoted earlier, is economists' (and the textbooks') standard response to this situation: all the exchanges here are voluntary, so everyone must be better off than they would otherwise be. Apparently the young Ghanaians willingly trade their health for cash, given their lack of alternatives. An end to toxic exports from the rich countries would leave them worse off.

If we set aside the fact that the workers still have far from complete information, this could actually be true. What the standard response ignores, because of its narrow focus on efficiency, is the bigger framework of injustice into which all this fits. It is an example of a 'failure of markets' (as opposed to a market failure), David Colander's important distinction, which we explained in Chapter 6. The market may be working efficiently, but it is producing an ethically unacceptable outcome. James Puckett, founder of the non-governmental organization Basel Action Network summed it up perfectly: 'desperate people will do desperate things ... it's a hell of a choice between poverty and poison. We should never make people make that choice.'[34]

Fortunately, in recent years governments in countries are pushing back against the tide of imported waste. In 2018, China banned imports of electronic and plastic waste, which diverted it to countries in Southeast Asia, whose governments also began taking action to halt the trade.[35] The day is slowly but surely approaching when the high-income countries, with their wasteful consumer culture, will have to take responsibility for their own trash.

Questions for your professor: Is trade in toxic waste efficient? Why does it seem to be an unpopular idea?

Information, fair trade and product certification Consumers may care about how the products they buy were produced. Everyone is aware of controversies over child labour and clothing made in 'sweatshops' and other goods produced in poor labour conditions. By not raising these issues, textbook theory seems to suggest that all that matters to the utility-maximizing consumer is the price and information about the physical characteristics of the final good.

Suppose that you are going to buy a $2 cup of coffee. As playwright Wallace Shawn writes, its 'price comes from its history, the history of all the people who were involved in making it and selling it and all the particular relationships they had'. By buying the cup of coffee, you also 'form relationships with all of those people ... The cup of coffee contains the history of the peasants who picked the beans, how some of them fainted in the heat of the sun, some were beaten, some were kicked.'[36] If instead the coffee beans were grown by independent farmers, perhaps buyers with monopsonistic power forced down the price, leaving them in poverty. Perhaps the farming practices were environmentally destructive.

© Andy Singer

If coffee buyers recognize their place in this web of relationships with people and with nature instead of behaving like textbook consumers, they will want to know how the coffee was produced. But how can they find out? Buyers will have no practical way of distinguishing among sellers' claims unless some trusted, independent third party can provide a widely recognized certification.

The development of 'fair trade' certification for coffee and other products is just one example of this. It offers buyers credible assurance that the products were produced by democratically run small farmer cooperatives that are offered above-market prices as a way of reducing poverty and promoting grassroots economic development.[37]

Other examples of certification are those for organic products or certification about how animals were treated in the production of a variety of food products. The development of these certification systems and the rapid growth of sales of 'fair trade' products show that many buyers do indeed care about more than just the price and the physical characteristics of the goods they buy.

When textbook economics ignores these issues, it is only being consistent with its default assumptions, which we have repeatedly highlighted. With perfect information, no externalities, no market power, and the unimportance of economic democracy (in this case, producer cooperatives) because of the absence of power more generally, then the fair trade movement makes no sense.

> Question for your professor: Does the textbook provide
> any explanation about why 'fair trade' products exist?

The problem of power

> 'The strong do as they can, while the weak suffer as
> they must.' Thucydides[38]

Countries differ greatly in terms of population, total production and income per person. In turn, these features influence their bargaining power when dealing with each other. The texts' general neglect of power is particularly apparent when we consider their treatment of the international economy and international economic institutions.

As philosopher Thomas Pogge explains,

> Economic systems, both global and national, are characterized not only by a (generally wholesome) competition under standing rules of the game, but also by a fierce struggle over the design of these rules themselves. The outcomes of this continuous struggle reflect not the well-informed insights of an impartial planner, but the interests, bargaining power and expertise of the various groups of participants.[39]

In the international arena, the 'rules of the game' are formally set out both in international organizations, such as the World Trade Organization (WTO), the World Bank and the International Monetary Fund (IMF), and in an ever-growing number of agreements between countries and groups of countries. In recent decades, the activities of these organizations and the establishment of such agreements have drawn increasing criticism and opposition. Based on the contents of their textbooks, however, economics students would be hard pressed to understand what all the excitement is about.

The World Trade Organization Unless the problem of power is recognized clearly, a good deal of the criticism of the WTO can be baffling. Its decisions are made by consensus; most of its members are at least nominally democratic. What's the problem?

Even sympathetic mainstream economists agree that 'a few rich countries dominate the WTO' negotiations and that 'it is dominated by large corporations', something that is 'probably inevitable, since it is large corporations that do most trade. Corporations have both the incentive and the resources to influence policies, and they do, both within countries and internationally'.[40]

One of the worst examples of the exertion of corporate power has been the creation of the Trade-Related Aspects of Intellectual Property Rights

(TRIPs). It was a top priority of US-based multinationals, particularly pharmaceutical and entertainment companies, and thus of the US government, in the negotiations leading up to the formation of the WTO in 1995. The agreement, to which all WTO members must ultimately adhere, created worldwide protection for 'intellectual property' such as copyrighted materials, including computer programs, protected for fifty years, and patents, protected for twenty years.

It was clear from the beginning that the result would be a substantial increase in transfers, amounting to tens of billions of dollars annually, to the developed-country monopolists who were getting additional protection for their intellectual property. Significant net losers are developing-country residents; patents in those countries are almost entirely controlled by foreign MNCs. The MNCs may enjoy a further benefit of preventing the emergence of potential competitors in developing countries given the increased protection given to patenting processes, as in the production of pharmaceuticals.[41]

Given that intellectual property protection has nothing directly to do with trade, what are these provisions doing in (so-called) trade agreements? Joseph Stiglitz's answer: so that any violations can be punished by trade sanctions, a powerful tool for large countries.[42]

In Chapter 6, we examined the question of dynamic efficiency and Schumpeter's optimistic view that firms' market power would be relatively short-lived in the face of new competition and technological change. Unfortunately, writes Stiglitz, 'the dominant firm has mechanisms to ensure its position becomes entrenched; the resulting equilibrium is inefficient both statically and dynamically. For globalization, this becomes particularly important when a disproportionate share of the entrenched monopolies is in the United States or other advanced countries.' Those countries then 'work to create global rules that, on the one hand, allow the monopoly to remain entrenched, stifling innovation elsewhere and, on the other, to allow the monopoly to avoid paying taxes on the economic activities that occur in the developing countries and emerging markets.'[43]

Bilateral agreements between large and small countries Recent years have seen a growing number of agreements between pairs or small groups of countries. These are sometimes called 'preferential' trade agreements because they give the exports of the members preferential tariff-free treatment. As we will see, calling these 'trade agreements' is misleading. Their scope typically much wider, dealing with such things as the regulation of foreign investment, protection of intellectual property, government purchases of goods and services, competition policy, and regulations to protect people, animals and plants from disease or contaminants.

With multilateral negotiations through the World Trade Organization having apparently come to an end, such arrangements are becoming increasingly common. For example, as of 2019, the United States has such agreements with 20 countries, India with 18.[44] The Comprehensive and Progressive Agreement for Trans-Pacific Partnership (TPP11) involving 11 countries on the Pacific rim is a recent addition to agreements between groups of countries.

As Joseph Stiglitz writes, calling such agreements *free* trade agreements is even more misleading:

> The globalization which emerged at the end of the twentieth century and the beginning of the twenty-first was not based on "free trade," but on managed trade—managed for special corporate interests in the United States and other advanced countries, balancing those interests even as the agreements put little weight on the interests of others—either workers in advanced countries or those elsewhere.[45]

He notes that new laws are often given a name that is the opposite of what they actually do. So "free trade agreements" are not actually about free trade. 'If it were about free trade, it would be short, a few pages— each country gives up its tariffs, its nontariff barriers to trade, and its subsidies.'[46] Instead, the CUSMA is 1800 pages long; the TPP11 has more than 6000 pages.

The focus on portraying these as simple free trade agreements is convenient. Standard trade theory suggests that the gains from an actual free trade agreement goes disproportionately to the small country. The argument is straightforward. We saw from Figure 2.2 in Chapter 2 that a country's consumption possibilities expand more the greater the difference between its prices before trade and its prices after trade begins.

Imagine a simple situation where the world consists of a 'large' and a 'small' country. World supply and demand determine world prices. World prices must be close to those that would prevail in the large country before trade because adding the small country's supply and demand to that of the large country does not change supply or demand very much. As a result, the large country's consumption possibilities do not increase much with trade, while those of the small country increase a lot. The small country gets the lion's share of the total gains from trade, although it also gets the lion's share of the unemployment costs of readjusting its pattern of production – something downplayed by the conventional analysis, as we noted.

Acknowledging the existence of oligopoly and increasing returns reinforces this conclusion. The large country, because of the size of its internal markets, will have already realized the lower average costs associated with increasing returns. In contrast, by obtaining easier and more secure access to the large country's markets, producers in the small country can lower their average costs considerably.

Canadian economists advanced these ideas when considering the consequences of a free trade agreement with the United States in the 1980s.

If the large country signs a preferential trade agreement with a smaller one, the large country is being a good neighbour to the small one. Given that history has no shortage of examples of large countries kicking sand in the faces of small countries, this claim of disinterested benevolence may be too good to be true.

Gerald Helleiner was one Canadian economist who remained skeptical. He suggests that the large country will seek 'side payments' – perhaps unrelated to trade – as a price for preferential access to its markets. He warns that 'it is therefore quite misleading to address the benefits and costs of integration agreements exclusively, or even primarily, on the basis of trade effects', as economists and the textbooks invariably do.[47]

The point is crucial. By focusing attention on the simple arguments from trade theory, economists can make a persuasive-sounding case for freer trade. But by ignoring the actual or potential 'side payments', whose costs may also be hard to quantify, they are ignoring a critical part of the story.

Helleiner suggests that these 'side payments' could include things like: extending monopoly protection of intellectual property (namely patents and copyrights), special protection of foreign investors, privatization of parts of public sector production, 'harmonizing' some laws and regulations to those of the large country, and acceptance by the small country of restrictions on some of its economic policies (e.g. screening of foreign takeovers of domestic firms). The 'side payments' will benefit certain powerful interests in the large country, while at the same time restricting the policy autonomy of the small country in ways that could end up being much more important than just lowering tariffs. Furthermore, as time passes and the economies become more integrated, it could become prohibitively costly to cancel the agreement, effectively locking in these policy constraints.

```
Questions for your professor: 'Free trade' agreements
seem to be about a lot more than tariff reductions.
Doesn't this leave room for corporate power to
influence the rules of the game regarding such things
as intellectual property and rules on protection of
foreign investors?

In bilateral agreements aren't smaller countries
vulnerable to the bargaining power of a larger
country during the negotiation and afterwards?
```

The large country's demands for 'side payments' may well not end once the agreement has been signed. As Canada and Mexico discovered to their cost with NAFTA, the smaller countries remain vulnerable to selective non-compliance or to threats of cancellation or 'renegotiation' of the agreement. This reflects the imbalance in bargaining power that comes from the asymmetry in size between the two countries. It does not just influence the outcome of the initial negotiations, but persists and raises real risks for the smaller country. Helleiner asks an important question: 'will powerful actors actually submit to disagreeable developments, whatever they may previously have said, if they do not suffer greatly in consequence of the failure to do so?'[48]

The large country could stretch or flout the rules and make the small country bear the disproportionate costs of trying to make it comply through whatever time-consuming dispute resolution institutions are set up under their agreement. The US–Canada softwood lumber disputes that began in the early 1980s are an example of such behaviour.

The US government's allegations that Canadian softwood lumber is subsidized and American softwood producers thereby damaged has been defeated at every stage in NAFTA and WTO dispute settlement panels and before American courts. Instead of the dispute settlement process having resolved the problem, however, the end result has not been free trade, but a victory for power politics and managed trade. Time after time, the Canadian government ended up accepting a disadvantageous negotiated settlement.

In the end, it's unclear whether the gains, such as they are, from such agreements are worth the risks for the small country of greater integration with the large country. With greater dependence comes greater vulnerability to lawless behaviour.

In the past, the main alternative was negotiating agreements through the WTO, where small countries could potentially band together and have allies (perhaps even other large countries), rather than facing the large country one on one. However, the last multilateral negotiations which began in Doha in 2001 went nowhere. The weakness of the WTO was emphasized by the US government's refusal during the Trump administration to permit appointments to its Appellate Body, a critical part of process that adjudicates disputes between members. Not coincidentally, this crippling of the WTO's ability to adjudicate disputes happened at the same time that the United States was blatantly violating its GATT obligations, initiating trade wars to press its demands on other countries, even large ones like China.

Foreign direct investment: the problem of power … again The topic of foreign direct investment (i.e. foreign ownership or effective control of firms located in a country) is almost entirely absent from the introductory texts, despite its prominence in many countries. Indeed, multinational corporations (MNCs) receive barely a mention, let alone any serious treatment, despite their central role in the international economy. By leaving MNCs out of the picture, the texts are implicitly taking the position that they are a non-issue. Yet surely the debate about their role deserves serious attention.

Table 10.2 Stock of foreign direct investment as a percent of world GDP, 1980–2020

1980	1990	2000	2010	2020
5	10	23	31	39

Source: Outward FDI data: unctad.org/topic/investment/world-investment-report, Annex Table 04; World GDP: data.worldbank.org/indicator/NY.GDP.MKTP.CD

It's important to note that if the textbooks don't bother to distinguish between whether a firm is domestically owned or foreign owned, they're implying that ownership doesn't matter. All firms in the textbooks maximize profits, so they behave in the same way, regardless of who owns them. But as a general proposition, hardly anyone seems to believe this. Countries routinely prohibit, restrict or review foreign ownership, particularly in sectors associated with cultural and political sovereignty, such as the military industries and the media and publishing industries.

Table 10.3 Developed country shares of world outward and inward foreign direct investment, 1980–2020

	1980	1990	2000	2010	2020
Outward FDI	87	94	90	83	77
Inward FDI	58	77	76	66	69

Source: unctad.org/topic/investment/world-investment-report, Annex Tables 03 & 04.

As shown in Table 10.2, foreign direct investment (FDI) has been growing steadily in importance in this 40 year period. By 2020, FDI was eight times larger than in 1980 relative to the size of the world economy. From the host country's point of view, this results in growing stocks of foreign-owned capital, such as manufacturing plants and equipment or foreign-owned establishments providing services.

Investments owned by residents of developed economies continue their predominant role, as seen in the first row of Table 10.3. Between 1980 and 2000, roughly 90 percent of 'outward' FDI came from developed economies, although that has declined to 77 percent by 2020, in part because of increases in investment originating in China. While the majority of the 'inward' stock of world FDI is located in the developed economies, that share declined significantly from 77 percent in 2000 to 69 percent by 2020. This reflects an expansion of FDI in countries like China.

Notably, the data in these tables omit FDI in Caribbean tax havens, tactfully termed 'financial centres' in official documents. Together, just the Cayman Islands and the British Virgin Islands have more inward FDI than Germany or Canada.[49]

According to French economist Gabriel Zucman, 40 percent of the profits of MNCs (about $600 billion) are moved into tax havens every year. This undermines the corporate income tax base in other countries, forcing ordinary taxpayers, including small businesses, to pay more to make up the shortfall. It has also prompted many countries to start cutting their corporate income tax rates in a self-destructive race to the bottom. The situation undermines the economic and political sustainability of globalization, in Zucman's view. Instead, he suggests that individual countries could, if they wanted, take the simple step of taxing global corporate profits in proportion to where their sales are made. Paper profits can be transferred by creative tax lawyers and accountants to tax havens such as Switzerland, Ireland or the Netherlands, but a corporation's customers cannot be moved to such places.[50]

As this book goes to press in mid-2021, international negotiations have at last begun to address this problem. Whether they will bear fruit, time will tell. That countries failed for so long to take effective action reflects the political influence of these corporations. In keeping with their avoidance of power issues, the textbooks ignore these issues despite their seriousness and growing public awareness of the problem.

Our particular concern here is with the activities in developing countries of MNCs owned in developed countries. This is where disparities in power may be most significant. These activities also draw the most criticism of MNCs' activities. For instance, if the government of a developing country gets into a dispute with an American corporation, the relevant power disparity is that between the United States and the developing country.

State sponsorship and protection of domestic businesses carrying out foreign direct investment have a long, if unattractive, history. In their study of the economics of British imperialism, Lance Davis and Robert Huttenback conclude that British 'imperialism can best be viewed as a mechanism for transferring income from the middle to the upper classes'. The British middle class paid most of the taxes to support the military and administrative structure of the empire, while the upper classes enjoyed higher rates of return on investments abroad than would otherwise have been available to them: 'socialism for the rich, capitalism for the poor'.[51]

American business owners have long enjoyed a similar subsidy. Even before the United States became the dominant world power, it routinely invaded countries in Central America and the Caribbean in support of US business interests. General Smedley Butler of the US Marine Corps candidly described his own exploits this way:

> I spent 33 years ... being a high-class muscle man for Big Business, for Wall Street and the bankers ... I helped purify Nicaragua for the international banking house of Brown Brothers in 1909–1912. I helped make Mexico ... safe for American oil interests in 1914. I brought light to the Dominican Republic for American sugar interests in 1916. I helped make Haiti and

Cuba a decent place for the National City [Bank] boys ... I helped in the rape
of half a dozen Central American republics for the benefit of Wall Street.[52]

After the Second World War, when American power was unrivalled, the
pattern continued but on a larger scale. Particularly notable were the 1953
coup that overthrew the Iranian parliamentary government on behalf of
Anglo-American oil companies (installing the Shah as dictator), the 1954
military coup in Guatemala on behalf of the United Fruit Company, and the
1973 military coup in Chile ousting a democratic government opposed by
the International Telephone and Telegraph Corporation.[53]

Support for multinationals from their home countries' governments
can take more subtle forms. The high-income countries wield considerable
influence over the International Monetary Fund and the World Bank.
Particularly since the 1980s, these institutions have promoted investor-
friendly regulatory environments, particularly in developing countries,
who were pressured to encourage foreign investment. These included
reducing or eliminating environmental protections. If budget cuts were
also forced on governments by these institutions, it weakened their ability
to carry out environmental monitoring. International trade and investment
agreements also constrain host governments from changing laws or
regulations that would reduce the profits of foreign investors, at least not
without significant penalties.[54]

Particularly problematic are the activities of multinational corporations
in extractive industries operating in developing countries, many of
which may already have weak institutions and problems with corruption.
Whether mining for minerals, such as gold and copper, or for fossil fuels,
such MNEs can use their influence to externalize costs through pollution
and displaced communities. The potential costs of future legal liabilities
to their victims is one way to restrain this, but companies may be able to
use their power to limit or evade such payments. An Amnesty International
study found cases in which 'companies had significant input into defining
the legal or regulatory framework governing their operations.' It cites the
example of the Australian mining company Broken Hill which effectively
did this for a mine in Papua New Guinea. It then struck a deal with the
government that allowed it to dump mining waste directly into rivers.[55]
When such environmental damage becomes legal, its victims' access
to justice is effectively eliminated. The law itself has then become an
instrument of illegality.

If rewriting or evading laws and regulations does not suffice, there
is always force, often provided by the host country government, for the
benefit of both foreign and domestic business interests. According to
Global Witness, 212 land and environmental defenders were killed in
2019, the highest number since it began publishing data in 2012. The most
dangerous countries were Columbia, with 64 murders, and the Philippines
(43), Brazil (24), Mexico (18) and Honduras (14). Resisting the damage

caused by mining was the most dangerous activity, costing the lives of 50 with agribusiness second with 34 murders. 'Attacks, murders and massacres were used to clear the path for commodities like palm oil and sugar.'[56]

Global Witness gives an example:

> Vast natural resources and fertile soils have long attracted foreign investment to the Philippines, yet widespread corruption and a culture of impunity for unscrupulous companies has seen the profits disappear into the pockets of a tiny elite. ... Indigenous people who have lived on land for generations are often forced from their homes by large corporations with global connections or investors.
>
> Often, these crimes are aided by the people and institutions meant to prevent them. The Philippines Army, in particular, has been linked to numerous killings of defenders, working in collusion with powerful private interests. Meanwhile, the country's legal system is used to criminalise and intimidate land and environmental defenders, while officials who are complicit in these crimes go unpunished.[57]

Unfortunately, plunder of this kind is not unique to the Philippines.

It's important to acknowledge that, in many places, MNCs have brought real benefits, bringing useful capital investment while assisting in the transfer of technologies and know-how between countries, and offering no threat to local political autonomy. But in other places, destruction and repression follow in their wake. By not offering any serious discussion of the role of MNCs in the international economy, the texts decline to address an issue of worldwide relevance.

> Questions for your professor: Does foreign ownership of firms matter? What does our textbook have to say about this?

2.4 Summing up

We have not attempted to make a case either for free trade or for some form of restricted trade. One of our central points is that things are much less clear cut than the texts let on. In the end, economic theory can prove nothing about whether free trade or some form of restricted trade is best from the point of view of the people living in a particular country. It can provide a variety of models to help to understand the consequences of alternative policies and to identify who is likely to experience gains and losses. Other 'non-economic' considerations may come into play as well, such as national autonomy the kind of occupations available to people, and the quality of community life. Ultimately, value judgements are inescapable.

The second major theme here is that textbook economics slides over a number of important issues concerning globalization. Pervasive externality and informational problems are compounded by inequalities in power, particularly at the national level.

Why do so many economists support free trade and offer advocacy to students rather than an accurate presentation of the benefits and costs? Robert Driskill speculates that in economists' culture, the arguments for free trade are a kind of institution: '200 years of tradition that has short-circuited their critical thinking'.[58] Perhaps, but something deeper may be at work. William Poole (a free trade advocate) stresses that 'the case for free international trade is really part of a more general case for free markets'.[59] If so, what is at stake is much bigger than just whether tariffs are good or bad; it's the ideology of laissez-faire itself.

SUGGESTIONS FOR FURTHER READING

Chapter 8 of James Kwak's *Economism: Bad Economics and the Rise of Inequality* has an excellent critique of the simple stories told about trade in introductory economics.

Robert Driskill's 2012 essay 'Deconstructing the Argument for Free Trade: A Case Study of the Role of Economists in Policy Debates' is a unique critique of the arguments for free trade in the undergraduate international trade textbooks. It's an extended and more academic version of his 2008 essay 'Why economists make such dismal arguments about trade?'.

Dani Rodrik saw the problems with globalization coming long before his peers. Two of his recent books, *The Globalization Paradox: Democracy and The Future of The World Economy* and *Straight Talk on Trade: Ideas for a Sane World Economy*, are excellent.

Globalization and Its Discontents Revisited is Joseph Stiglitz's 2018 update of an earlier book that sets out his ideas about how globalization could be made more equitable.

In *23 Things They Don't Tell You About Capitalism*, Ha-Joon Chang points out that "Free trade policies rarely make poor countries rich" (Thing 7). He also explains that "Capital has a nationality" (Thing 8), something the textbooks implicitly deny by ignoring the distinction between foreign and domestic firms.

Fair Trade, Sustainability, and Social Justice, by Mark Hudson, Ian Hudson and Mara Fridell links fair trade to Marx's concept of commodity fetishism, an idea we sketched out in Section 2.3 using the words of Wallace Shawn, while examining the prospects for the international fair trade movement. Raluca Dragusanu and her co-authors examine

'The Economics of Fair Trade' in a 2014 essay in the *Journal of Economic Perspectives*.

Gabriel Zucman's *The Hidden Wealth of Nations: The Scourge of Tax Havens* is a short clear book explaining the history of tax havens, how multinational companies and the wealthy use them and what can be done about it.

Chapter 11

CONCLUSION

'I wish to urge you to study neoclassical economics carefully and enthusiastically. It is a magnificent edifice, beautifully constructed and full of well-hidden politics and philosophy. By approaching it critically, the student will gain an unmissable glimpse of the highest form of defence of the capitalist society we live in.... [I]t offers a wonderfully spurious apology for an irrational system based on an inadequate model of human nature and on a misleading analysis of the manner in which we produce and reproduce our material existence.' Yanis Varoufakis[1]

In this short chapter, we want to gather together the main points we've raised about what's unsatisfactory with the standard microeconomic textbook – and why it matters.

The distinction between positive and normative economics

The idea that positive and normative economics are clearly distinct is misleading. Implicit value judgements are embedded throughout 'positive' economics. The very definition of economics as the attempt to satisfy *unlimited wants* with limited resources is rooted in judgements about what makes human beings happy. It's an individualistic view that ignores our social links, while shifting our attention towards efficiency (and away from questions of equity).

Indeed, one could argue that the main thrust of textbook economics is not positive. The texts are not describing the world as it is. Instead, the texts explicitly or implicitly make the claim that competitive markets are a reasonable approximation to the real world and that they produce a reasonably efficient outcome. Thus, Krugman and Wells write that 'in most cases the invisible hand does the job' of using resources efficiently. In 'instances of market failure', 'appropriately designed government policy can sometimes move society closer to an efficient outcome'.[2] The reader is invited to think that efficiency is the rule rather than the exception and that, broadly speaking, there should be laissez-faire: a minimum of government 'interference' in market outcomes.

As Stephen Marglin puts it: 'The problem with the idea that economics is purely, or even primarily, a descriptive undertaking is that the apparatus of economics has been shaped by an agenda focused on showing that markets are good for people rather than on discovering how markets actually work. And from this normative agenda has come the constructive agenda.'[3]

What evidence is there for this claim? We've seen in Chapters 3 and 6 how demand and supply were applied to all areas of the economy, regardless of the actual market structure prevailing there. We've seen how demand and supply are applied to explain factor prices and the gains from trade. We've seen how the predictions of the perfectly competitive model – that price ceilings lead to shortages, for example – are presented as universally valid even though a non-competitive market setting results in different conclusions. Finally, we've seen how the textbooks often claim there is a clear body of evidence confirming the inefficiencies resulting from market regulations such as minimum wages and rent control.

In making the argument for markets and (implicitly) for limited government, textbook economics relies on value judgements buried in its fundamental assumptions about self-interested individuals, their full rationality and their unlimited wants, and the nation-state being the only valid measure of community, as Marglin argues.[4] Normative value judgements pervade microeconomics.

The rational individual

Modern research challenges the usefulness of modelling economic life as the choices of rational, fully informed, individuals continuously calculating how best to maximize their own well-being. Bounded willpower, bounded selfishness and bounded rationality are now well established in the behavioural economics literature, although they have made little impact on textbook economics. We know that 'animal spirits' – individuals' impulses to action in the face of fundamental uncertainty – play a dominant role in many important decisions such as investments by entrepreneurs.

Table 11.1 Conventional economics and the blank cells of Akerlof and Shiller

	Rational responses	Irrational responses
Economic motives	Mainstream textbook economics	
Non-economic motives		

We also know that individuals make systematic mistakes that can lead them to regret their choices.

Akerlof and Shiller argue that the current mainstream macroeconomic model focuses on how the economy would behave if people had only the economic motives identified in the textbooks and were fully rational.[5] But the same point can be made about the focus of the microeconomics principles textbooks. In Table 11.1 textbooks and mainstream models inhabit only the upper left-hand cell. These address only the question: How does the economy behave if people have only economic motives and rational responses? It's time that the mainstream textbooks took the blank cells seriously. Non-economic motives include concerns about fairness (which can affect price setting and wages), social status and relative position in the income distribution, considering whether or not to conform to social and moral norms, and making choices based on ethical considerations separate from one's own narrow self-interest.

The goals of equity and efficiency

Textbooks emphasize the importance of efficiency and subtly downplay the importance of equity. For example, with their focus on the maximization of consumer and producer surplus, textbooks implicitly use the compensation principle to justify efficiency-enhancing policies; as long as winners *could* compensate losers and still be better off, society as a whole is supposedly better off, although no one can explain why in any convincing way.

Furthermore, textbooks claim that there is a trade-off between equity and efficiency: transferring income between people is like transferring water in a leaky bucket. They emphasize that taxation causes inefficiencies, while worse, the transfers that make up the social safety net are allegedly costly because they reduce incentives to work and to save. Yet at the same time, the texts ignore the arguments and evidence that reducing inequality can be good for growth. In reality, it seems that, within limits, people in many countries have opportunities to attain both more equity *and* more efficiency.

Recent research has emphasized that lower inequality is associated with greater social cohesion and trust, whereas higher inequality weakens people's sense of reciprocity, and increases the sense of 'us' versus 'them'.[6] By ignoring this subject, textbooks seem to imply that there is no role for virtues like loyalty and trust. Joseph Stiglitz argues that Adam Smith didn't make this mistake: he was aware of the limitations of markets, and knew this was not so. Indeed, modern economics explains why economic systems in which such virtues are prevalent actually work better than those in which they are absent. Stiglitz writes:

> Older theories had simply assumed that it was costless to write and enforce contracts, so that every time anybody did anything for

anybody else, there was a contract that was rigorously adhered to. But in the real world, contracts are ambiguous, contract disputes abound, litigation is extremely expensive, and most economic dealings go on without contracts. In the real world there are often implicit contracts, understandings, norms, which enable society to function well. What makes economic systems work, by and large, is trust.[7]

And, as we have said, trust is enhanced by equity.

The assumption that more is better

When textbooks emphasize the importance of efficiency, they explicitly assume that 'more is better'. At the individual level, well-being and happiness depend only on a person's real income and consumption. This story stumbles into a fallacy of composition by assuming that if one person is better off with more stuff, everyone is better off if everyone has more stuff. This invites readers to adopt a pro-growth consumerist outlook.

The evidence, ignored entirely in the textbooks, shows that in rich countries measures of average happiness have not increased significantly as average incomes have risen substantially. People simply seem to get used to their new circumstances, which quickly become the norm. Good evidence suggests, however, that relative position and status within groups matter a great deal to individuals' happiness.

For example, it's possible for everyone to have more stuff – those at the bottom of the income distribution getting a little bit more, with those further up the income distribution getting increasingly large increases – so that inequality increases. Because of the pervasive effects of inequality, many people could end up with lower well-being. It's even possible that *everyone* could be worse off living in an increasingly dysfunctional society.

Methodological problems

Textbooks teach that we judge the usefulness of a model by the accuracy of its predictions, not by the realism of its assumptions. Textbooks gloss over the difficulty of actually refuting a theory. It is very difficult to reject core hypotheses because they are protected by auxiliary assumptions. If the theory does not seem to fit the facts, this can be blamed on the failure of at least one of these auxiliary assumptions to hold, leaving the core hypothesis untouched. Hence, Deepak Lal's memorable comment: 'ideas – good or bad – never die in economics.'[8]

Deirdre McCloskey maintains that economists are engaged in rhetoric, even if they fail to realize it. In this context 'rhetoric' means 'debate', and in this debate all and every kind of reasoned argument is admissible: analogies (or metaphors), thought experiments, natural experiments, historical precedents and appeals to authority. Even the 'official methodology' – predictive power and hypothesis testing – is used rhetorically according to McCloskey; it's just one more way of trying to persuade.

It is interesting, and perhaps ironic, that the textbooks do not apply the methodology they espouse to the material they present. They do not develop a series of models, generate a variety of predictions, confront these predictions with the facts, and in this way evaluate which model is best. Instead, evidence is presented sporadically and selectively. Evidence is nearly always presented to support the textbook claim that the competitive model is good enough to use as a generic model to answer any question – but contrary evidence is too often ignored.

Ironically, when the textbooks present non-competitive market structures, they choose real-world applications by how closely the market in question conforms to the model's assumptions. They never attempt to apply these models generically to markets that don't conform to the model's assumptions to see how accurate the predictions are. For example, monopsony is said to be of little relevance because the case of a single employer is rarely seen, but a corresponding analysis of the realism of the assumptions of the perfectly competitive labour market is omitted. Adding to the irony is the fact that modern labour economists recognize that monopsony power may derive from imperfect information and imperfect mobility of workers. Since information and mobility are always imperfect, it is entirely reasonable – on a priori grounds – to think that the monopsony model might be a useful generic model of the labour market.

Overemphasis on perfectly competitive markets

Students learn that the realism of a theory's assumptions is irrelevant just before they learn the highly unrealistic perfectly competitive model (in its shorthand 'demand and supply' version). They are then invited to apply it to markets in virtually all sectors of the economy.

Could it be that this model is simpler than others, and this is why it is presented as a generic tool? We don't think so. The perfectly competitive model is rather complex – even if its shorthand version makes it appear simpler than it really is. In any event, one would be hard pressed to show that the competitive model is simpler than (say) the monopoly model. So, why is the competitive model so emphasized?

A main theme of our *Anti-Textbook* is to argue that the overwhelming emphasis placed on the competitive model in principles textbooks reflects – and may produce in readers' minds – a particular ideological outlook. For example, Chapter 3 dismisses claims that the emphasis on competitive markets is justified by either their real-world prevalence, or by the generic applicability of the model's predictions. Chapter 6 dismisses claims that such emphasis is justified by the usefulness of the competitive model as an ideal market type that can be used to guide government policy.

Nor is the competitive model a useful parable – a story that helps us to understand deeper truths about the economy. Certainly, perfect competition contains a germ of truth: the process of entry and exit from industries is driven by a search for profit. But the parable is inadequate in that the process takes place in an environment of constant technological knowledge, with given resources, given tastes and given products. Therefore, it says nothing about some of the most important facts that need explaining – innovation and growth. If there is one thing that capitalism is remarkably good at, for good or ill, it is *innovation*. Monopoly power and the associated profits are its reward. Focusing on a world filled with perfectly competitive markets omits this vitally important feature of the economic landscape.

We believe the overemphasis placed on perfectly competitive markets arises because it is possible to tell a story about their purported ideal characteristics. Textbooks spin a yarn about how competitive markets produce Pareto-efficient outcomes, how they allocate resources to their highest-valued uses and distribute goods to those who value them most. In this market structure, government intervention to change prices or quantities inevitably produces adverse side effects and reduces efficiency. So, the emphasis on competitive markets imparts a market fundamentalist bias to the standard textbook.

Textbooks ignore their own ideological leanings

Textbooks do not acknowledge the possibility that they have adopted a particular ideological position. The authors seem to be unaware that it is impossible for any social science, or any individual researcher, to avoid adopting some world-view. After all, there is necessarily a fine line between explaining why something is the way it is, and justifying the way it is. Since the start of the scientific revolution in the seventeenth century, there have been inevitable interrelationships between science and society.

Social science in particular has largely tended to play a legitimizing role, and economics is no exception. Economics can legitimize aspects of society either through what its dominant theories focus attention on and attempt to explain, or through what they ignore. As the American economist Douglas Dowd wrote: 'it is often alarming to note what mainstream economists do and do *not* examine, what questions they do and do *not* ask, what aspects of the economy (and important connections with the rest of the social process) they do and do *not* take into account.'[9]

As we have seen, textbook economics asks few uncomfortable questions about consumerism. Consumer theory has the notion of 'consumer sovereignty' – that consumers ultimately rule the economy by deciding what to buy and what not to buy. This downplays the role of business in forming consumers' preferences and in determining the products on offer to consumers. All buying decisions are portrayed as the free exercise of individual preferences formed by some unexamined process that apparently falls outside the realm of economics.

Similarly, if corporations pollute the air and water when producing the goods consumers want, this must just reflect voters' rational choices about the trade-offs involved, not a lethal mixture of individual ignorance and corporate influence over the political system. When questions of power are routinely ignored, as they are in the textbooks, this is a subtle way of legitimizing the existing distribution and exercise of power. Similarly, the lack of attention paid to the distribution of income among households and to its equity serves to legitimize existing inequalities. If these issues merit only a single chapter tucked away towards the end of a large textbook, how can they be that important?

The same ideological position is not present in all economic paradigms. Different paradigms contain different world-views. But textbooks don't bother teaching students about how the paradigms reflect world-views, nor do they bother teaching students anything other than one world-view that comes out of its narrow depiction of the dominant neoclassical paradigm.

Indeed, 'economics' has come to be synonymous with the economics of a particular view of capitalism. It wasn't always this way. At one time, economic textbooks routinely contained chapters on alternative economic systems, on the evolution of economic doctrines, and the advantages and disadvantages of the corporate form.[10] In dropping these subjects, perhaps mainstream textbooks have been 'dumbed down'. Certainly, the range of thinking has been narrowed.

The implication that smaller government is better

This follows if – as textbook economics maintains – markets can be generically analysed as if they were perfectly competitive, and if externalities can be analysed as if they are exceptions rather than ubiquitous. Therefore, *in most situations*, government intervention is neither necessary nor beneficial.

Economists in the Public Choice tradition, with their libertarian-capitalist ideology of minimal government, have helped to fuel the popular presumption that governments are inefficient compared to the private sector. But this rests more on ideological belief rather than on evidence. Herbert Simon, who received his Nobel Memorial Prize for important contributions to understanding how organizations behave, put the matter this way:

> Most producers are employees of firms, not owners. Viewed from the vantage point of classical theory, they have no reason to maximize

the profits of firms, except to the extent that they can be controlled by owners. Moreover, profit-making firms, non-profit organizations, and bureaucratic organizations all have exactly the same problem of inducing their employees to work toward the organizational goals. There is no reason, *a priori*, why it should be easier (or harder) to produce this motivation in organizations aimed at maximizing profits than in organizations with different goals. If it is true ... that organizations motivated by profits will be more efficient than other organizations, additional postulates will have to be introduced to account for it.[11]

Downplaying the importance of the legal framework within which markets operate

As noted earlier, trust is important because contracts are necessarily incomplete, potential disputes abound, and litigation is expensive. As Robert Prasch observes: '[A] rudimentary knowledge of the principles of property and contract law opens our minds to their inherent complexity, contingency, and importance. This knowledge, in turn, illuminates some of the strengths and weaknesses of markets as economic and social institutions.'[12]

Imperfect and asymmetric information creates possible conflicts of interest that allow some people to profit at the expense of others. The invisible hand isn't supposed to work like that; it is supposed to transform everyone's selfishness into the greater good.

Prasch explains that the invisible hand only works to produce an efficient allocation of resources if the economy consists of certain special kinds of markets. There must be no externalities, but additionally the quality of the product must be known, and exchanges must be instantaneously completed in 'spot' markets. This describes the proverbial 'widget' of the microeconomic textbooks and occupies the upper left-hand cell in Table 11.2. On the other hand, if quality cannot be determined without owning the product for a while (experience goods as opposed to inspection goods), or if exchanges are ongoing and involve issues of fairness and needs ('relational contracts' as opposed to spot markets), the invisible hand mechanism breaks down and resources will not be efficiently allocated.

Table 11.2 Conventional textbook economics and the blank cells of Robert Prasch

	Spot markets	Relational contracts
Inspection goods	The 'widget'	
Experience goods		

Whenever information about quality is imperfect, markets can break down – as in the market for good used cars (the 'lemons' problem). Even though most consumer durables and capital goods would fit in the lower left cell of Table 11.2, and most labour market contracts and credit market transactions would fit in the lower right-hand cell, textbooks treat all of these as if they were widgets – hence we draw the table with blank cells. Textbooks pretend these cases don't exist. In so doing, they understate the importance of the laws and regulations needed to make these markets function more efficiently. In all the blank cells of Table 11.2, regulations and social norms are needed to help restrain conflicts of interest and abusive practices.

Instead, in the pedagogy of the texts, students' attention is directed to the theory of widget exchange and pricing. This is passed off as the theory of "how markets work".

The omission of power

Textbooks assume all economic relationships are voluntarily entered into. But the choices people make are constrained by the circumstances in which they find themselves. In turn, those circumstances may be shaped by the power of others in the society around them. Should we say that a person 'voluntarily' allows her children to work in a sweatshop or that circumstances forced her into this decision?

The only power that appears in the textbooks is 'market power' – the power of some sellers to influence the prices of their products. Yet in the actual economy, power appears in many forms.

Most people spend much of their lives at work, as employees of companies governed by authoritarian chains of command. Their employers' monopsonistic power influences the pay they receive, which, in turn, rests on the difficulties employees would have in finding another comparable job. As consumers, people's preferences are influenced by a continuous barrage of propaganda crafted by the marketing industry. Perhaps the most glaring example of the omission of power in the standard textbooks is their silence about the influence of the wealthy and of business on government policy, and on the legal and regulatory framework within which markets operate. The acquisition and exercise of this power are economic activities and should not be ignored.

The presumption in favour of free trade

While mainstream texts may appear to take a balanced view on the costs and benefits of free trade, in fact they bias the discussion in favour of it. How is this done? First, the texts downplay adjustment costs and effects on the distribution of income. As. usual, the focus is on efficiency and increasing national income, with the presumption that this, in turn, will increase the wellbeing of society as a whole.

Second, state power is ignored, yet power relations between countries affect the 'rules of the game' that govern trade and international economic relations. 'Free trade agreements' can include rules governing patents and copyright, foreign investment and access to energy resources, for example. Third, the textbooks managed to completely overlook major features of the international economy. Foreign direct investment and the activities of multinational corporations, whose products dominate international trade, are nowhere to be seen. Finally, they ignore the environmental costs of trade – in particular, the production of greenhouse gases in transporting goods and raw materials from one side of the world to the other.

The omission of community

According to the standard account, expanding the realm of the market expands the possibilities for specialization and trade, expands freedom of choice, and necessarily makes people better off. We have noted repeatedly that it doesn't necessarily make *everyone* better off, creating distributional problems that may be compounded when people care about relative position. But there is another issue. Even if everyone were absolutely better off, and even if no one cared about their relative position, there is still a potential problem: markets often undermine community. Stephen Marglin asks what limits should be placed on markets for the sake of community.[13] The greater the role for markets, the more life is commercialized; personal relationships are replaced by anonymous market transactions.

He gives the example of two ways in which a farmer can protect himself against the risk of his barn burning. The old-fashioned way, still practised by the Amish, is to have a commitment to economic reciprocity in the form of community barn-raising. The modern way is to buy insurance. Insurance is much more efficient in terms of time and cost. But it is only more efficient if we focus exclusively on the users of the barn as individuals. If we're interested in the community, then the Amish are on to something by rejecting insurance and sticking to barn-raisings. Economic reciprocity is part of the glue that keeps the community together.

The concept of community doesn't easily fit within the mainstream neoclassical framework, which views society as merely a collection of individuals. Marglin claims that since the benefits of community ties are hard to measure, economists have chosen to ignore them altogether. With wry humour he notes: 'The nineteenth century physicist Lord Kelvin insisted that we know only what we can measure. Economics takes the dictum a step further ... what we can't measure – entities like community – doesn't exist.'[14]

However, the indirect effects of the health of communities on people's well-being can be measured, so economists should take community seriously. Richard Layard writes: 'Happiness requires a sense of belonging – not just to your family or your workplace, but also to your local community more generally.'[15] People living in healthy communities have stronger social connections, higher levels of trust in others, and higher levels of happiness.

When communities weaken, trust declines, and more people become isolated and lonely, with sometimes fatal consequences. In their book *Deaths of Despair and the Future of Capitalism*, American economists Anne Case and Angus Deaton chronicle the increasing rates of death by drug overdoses, alcoholic liver disease, and suicide concentrated among white Americans without university degrees. They trace this back to technological change and particularly to globalization. The resulting unemployment and reductions in income, concentrated in particular parts of the country, has left communities shattered. Needless to say, such costs are not included in economists' calculations of the 'gains from trade'.

Incidentally, the fixation on quantitative measurement has broader implications than the omission of community. It also plays its part in our neglect of the environment. Joseph Stiglitz explains:

> [W]hat we measure affects what we do. If we have poor measures, what we strive to do (say, increase GDP) may actually contribute to a worsening of living standards. We may also be confronted with false choices, seeing trade-offs between output and environmental protection that don't exist. By contrast, a better measure of economic performance might show that steps taken to improve the environment are good for the economy.[16]

Downplaying the ecological crisis facing humanity today

That leads us to the final point in our list: the severe risks that human societies face from climate change. As we describe in the Postscript, the textbooks do an unsatisfactory job of explaining the problem, what policies would be appropriate, and why such policies have not been implemented.

In part, the origins of our environmental problems can be laid at the door of economics itself. As historian J. R. McNeil writes,

> Anglo-American economists (after about 1880) took nature out of economics. The growth fetish, while on balance quite useful in a world of empty land, shoals of undisturbed fish, vast forests, and a robust ozone shield, helped create a more crowded and stressed one ... Economic thought did not adjust to the changed conditions it helped to create; thereby, it continued to legitimate, and indeed indirectly to cause, massive and rapid ecological change.[17]

Economists such as Kenneth Boulding and Herman Daly have written about this distinction between this 'empty-world economics' and the 'full-world economics' that is needed now.[18] But the textbooks are still teaching empty-world economics.

Marglin explains the importance of the distinction:

> But now that we live and work at close quarters to one another, our non-market interactions are much more part of the fabric of our lives, and externalities are of central concern. Pollution, once again, is a case in point. When people lived in small communities with a lot of space between settlements and produced and consumed at relatively modest levels, air and water pollution were relatively minor problems. They become major problems only with the advent of cities and the accompanying growth in population density.[19]

© Andy Singer

The economic system not only produces these increasingly important problems, but some of its features make these problems difficult to address. Firms have an interest in preventing externalized costs from being internalized. They may seek to lessen public pressure for regulation to reduce pollution by 'going green' to improve their image among consumers. But, given asymmetric information, appearance rather than reality counts. Too often the result is 'green-washing' rather than really going green. Alternatively, public ignorance and apathy may allow firms simply to use their political influence to alter or block environmental regulations.

The textbook accounts of externalities ignore these problems and put forward the central story that markets are generally efficient and that market failures, such as pollution, can be remedied. Then the net effect of the market system is, or can be, roughly efficient.

Unfortunately, externalities have not been remedied and should be of central importance to any serious account of how economies actually function. Pretending otherwise is fundamentally misleading.

Critical thinking about economics

Our fundamental aim in writing this *Anti-Textbook* has been to provide economics students with the basic ideas with which they can begin to think critically about what they read in their textbooks. As Noam Chomsky once remarked: 'If the schools were doing their job, which of course they aren't, ... they would be providing people with means of intellectual self-defense' – in this case, the means to defend themselves against the unconscious acceptance of the ideology presented in the textbooks.[20] As a result, students have to think for themselves, not an easy matter to do alone and without some guidance.

Our intention in writing this book has not been to discourage anyone from studying economics. After all, economics deals with matters that are central to individual well-being and to the functioning of human societies. But simply to study a conventional textbook (and to solve the multiple-choice questions that supposedly test understanding of the subject) is not enough. One needs to read with a critical eye, and to note what is omitted and what is unsupported. Such critical thinking will be rewarded with a very different and far more interesting perspective on the world.

SUGGESTIONS FOR FURTHER READING

Yanis Varoufakis' *Foundations of Economics: A Beginner's Companion* is partly a microeconomics anti-textbook and an excellent one, suitable for advanced undergraduate students. The major sections have a chapter on the textbook content, a chapter on the history and evolution of those ideas, and a chapter of critique.

In *Reintroducing Macroeconomics: A Critical Approach*, Steve Cohn provides not only a heterodox critique of textbook macroeconomics, but also of the standard chapters that begin all principles texts, including supply and demand.

Both of Jonathan Aldred's books, *The Skeptical Economist: Revealing the Ethics Inside Economics* and *Licence to be Bad: How Economics Corrupted Us* are highly recommended.

In *Dollars and Change: Economics in Context*, Louis Putterman offers a unique introduction to economic ideas, putting them in a context which is missing in the standard texts by, among other things, incorporating an account of the Industrial Revolution, the development of economic ideas, and issues of economic justice.

James Kwak's *Economism: Bad Economics and the Rise of Inequality* is an insightful critique of the damage caused by the influence of the simplistic model that lies at the heart of the standard microeconomics textbook.

Ha-Joon Chang's *23 Things They Don't Tell You About Capitalism* is a highly readable debunking of the conventional wisdom. Each 'Thing' begins with a short section 'What they tell you', followed by a 'What they don't tell you' critique.

Economists and the Powerful: Convenient Theories, Distorted Facts, Ample Rewards by Norbert Häring and Niall Douglas is an excellent exploration of the neglected theme of power that we have touched on repeatedly throughout this book.

Chapter 12

POSTSCRIPT: A CASE STUDY OF CLIMATE CHANGE AND THE TEXTBOOKS

Climate change research has received surprisingly little space in the leading economics journals.[1] What about the introductory microeconomics textbooks, which constitute most students' exposure to the economics of the subject? Grappling with climate change is surely going to be one of the major preoccupations of politics and public policy debates during the lifetimes of the students who are reading today's texts. That warrants a careful examination of what the texts say and, perhaps even more importantly, what they do *not* say.

GLOBAL WARMING

© Andy Singer

In this postscript, we start with the Standard Text. Unlike the format of earlier chapters, where the Standard Text tries to reflect the content of the typical textbook, the Standard Text here is based on a collection of the best parts found in our sample of texts (supplemented with some additional detail). This was necessary because the texts' treatment of the subject is so variable – from some barely mentioning it to a few with more extensive discussions.

The Anti-Text critique that follows comments on the actual content of the texts and then on the shortcomings that all of them share. It raises many of the issues that we have highlighted throughout the book: the simplistic assumptions about individuals' rationality and motivations; downplaying of the importance of externalities and other market failures (in this case, the greatest market failure of all time); trusting that competitive markets will restore efficiency with a minimum of government action; and ignoring the ability of powerful business interests to influence public opinion and to hinder appropriate policies.

I THE STANDARD TEXT

I.I The greenhouse effect and climate change

It's been known since the 19 century that certain gases in the atmosphere help to prevent the radiation of heat or infrared energy from the earth into space. While carbon dioxide receives the most attention because it is quantitatively the most important and long-lived gas, methane (CH_4) and nitrous oxide (N_2O) are among the other important heat-trapping gases. Together, these gases are called 'greenhouse gases' (GHGs) because their combined effect resembles the effect of the glass roof and walls of a greenhouse.

When the Earth system is in balance, the energy being absorbed from the sun is equal to the energy being radiated away from the earth. The average global temperature then remains roughly constant, in the absence of other natural short-term and long-term events, such as volcanic eruptions and variations in the Earth's orbit.

Increasing CO2 Levels Between about 10,000 years ago, around when agriculture began, and the beginning of the Industrial Revolution in the mid-18th century, atmospheric CO2 averaged about 280 ppm (parts per million) according to the analysis of air bubbles trapped in ice in Greenland and Antarctica. The Industrial Revolution, which began in Britain, was powered by coal. Burning coal and other fossil fuels releases carbon dioxide into the atmosphere, as does the making of cement. (Here we concentrate on CO2 because it is the most important and long-lived greenhouse gas.)

Not all these emissions end up as a net addition to CO2 in the atmosphere; some is absorbed by the oceans, for example. But CO2 emissions are now twice as great as the Earth's absorptive capacity.[2] As a result, atmospheric CO2 is increasing.

Figure 12.1 shows estimates of CO2 concentrations over the last 1000 years. These crept above 280 ppm in the late 1700s and continue to rise. The 2020 average of 414 ppm was 48 percent higher than before industrialization began.

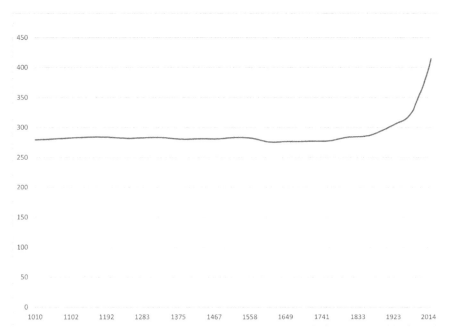

Figure 12.1 Global CO2 levels, 1010–2020

Sources: For 1010-1975, Etheridge et al. (1998), historical CO2 record derived from the Law Dome DSS, DE08, and DE08-2 ice cores. Since 1975, atmospheric measurements at Mauna Loa observatory: Dr. Pieter Tans, NOAA/ GML (www.esrl.noaa.gov/gmd/ccgg/trends/) and Dr. Ralph Keeling, Scripps Institution of Oceanography (scrippsco2.ucsd.edu/).

The net increase in CO2 and other GHGs in the atmosphere has left the Earth system out of equilibrium, absorbing more energy than it radiates. A gradually rising global temperature over the long-term is the result.

Worldwide estimates of average air temperatures over land and sea date only back to 1880. Figure 12.2 shows how average annual temperatures compare with the 20th century average. Clearly, the average temperature is trending upwards.

Modelling climate change Under the auspices of the United Nations, the Intergovernmental Panel on Climate Change (IPCC) is a worldwide collaboration by scientists from many different disciplines who are constructing models of the climate system. Their models simulate possibilities for future average global temperatures, based on different scenarios for future GHG emissions and therefore future stocks of GHGs in the atmosphere.

They also examine other dimensions of climate change. These include how temperatures will be affected in different parts of the world, the likelihood of deadly heat waves, changes in the frequency and strength of typhoons and hurricanes, the rate at which ice sheets will melt, how much sea levels will rise,

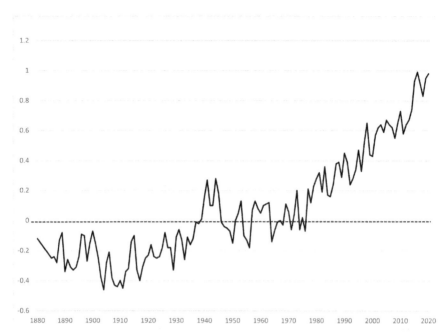

Figure 12.2 Temperature anomaly compared with 20th century average, 1880–2020

Note: Annual average data for land and sea.

Source: NOAA National Centers for Environmental information, Climate at a Glance: Global Time Series, ncdc. noaa.gov/cag/.

and how patterns of rainfall might change (creating droughts or floods). The IPCC issues periodic reports summarizing the current state of knowledge and where more research is required.

1.2 Policies to reduce emissions

Putting a price on emissions: carbon tax or cap and trade? Emissions of greenhouse gases are a case of an externality, which we examined in Chapter 7. There we saw that the externality needs to be 'internalized' so that decision-makers face the marginal social costs of their actions and make their decisions accordingly. Without that, emissions will be inefficiently high.

For a pollutant, such as carbon dioxide, there are two equally efficient ways to price them to reflect an estimate of their marginal external cost. One is a Pigouvian tax, in this case a *'carbon tax'* based on the fuel's carbon content or the emissions involved in some process, such as the production of cement. The idea was illustrated in Figure 7.1, which could be re-labelled as the demand for a fossil fuel, reflecting the marginal benefits of its use, and its supply, reflecting marginal costs of production. An appropriate carbon tax leaves the marginal social benefit equal to the marginal social cost of using the fossil fuel.

A second option is capping emissions at a certain level. The government can issue tradable permits that add up to that amount. These can be distributed to polluters, perhaps based on their past emissions, or sold by auction. If the permits are distributed freely, firms could trade them to establish the permit price. This is the '*cap and trade*' approach. In both cases, the government must be able to monitor emissions.

In principle, the two methods could result in the same price for emissions and reduce them by the same amount. But in practice there is a choice to make between them. With a carbon tax, policy makers must estimate the short run and long-run responses, so how much emissions will decline is uncertain. If instead, emissions are capped, then the decline in emissions is known, but the price for which permits will trade is uncertain and could fluctuate.

Figure 12.3 shows the outcome with the cap and trade policy. Each year the government sets a cap on the maximum amount of emissions, resulting in a new permit price.

The demand curve reflects the benefits that firms get from having a permit: namely, avoiding the costs of reducing emissions. Firms with marginal costs of emissions reduction greater than P* would rather buy a permit instead. Firms with costs less than P* would pay the cost of reducing their emissions rather than pay P* for a permit. In the end, the permit price acts just like an emissions tax set at that rate. If instead a carbon tax had been set at the rate P* per tonne of carbon dioxide, emissions would be the same as under the cap. The carbon tax revenues would be the same as if the government had auctioned off emissions permits, namely P^*Q_s.

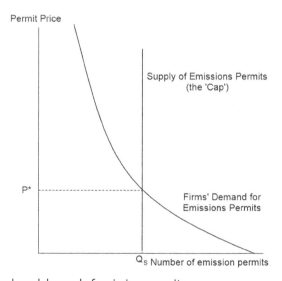

Figure 12.3 Supply and demand of emissions permits

Both the carbon tax and the cap and trade policy reduce emissions in the most efficient way: emissions are reduced by those who face the lowest marginal costs of doing so. Regulations requiring emissions reductions are likely to be costlier because regulators are unlikely to know where emissions can be reduced most cheaply. However, policymakers may use them because their ultimate effect on prices is less clear to the public than a politically unpopular tax.

What price for CO2 emissions? The appropriate price to put on a tonne of CO_2 emissions should reflect its marginal social cost. But that is a matter of considerable debate. It depends on judgements about the uncertain future effects of climate change on output and other less tangible things such as biodiversity. It also depends on how those future costs should be treated today. (Future values are typically discounted, but what should the discount rate be?) Despite the difficulties, estimates have been attempted. For example, in 2018 the OECD estimated the climate change costs of emissions at €30 per tonne of carbon dioxide. At the same time, it surveyed countries' actual policies and noted that most emissions faced no price at all. Where prices existed, they largely fell well short of the levels needed to have a significant effect on climate change.[3]

An effective price on emissions creates incentives to find ways to reduce them. It also increases the attractiveness of technologies which replace the use of fossil fuels – wind and solar power, for example. This encourages innovation in those industries as well.

To meet long-run emissions reductions targets, governments could gradually reduce the number of permits or adjust the level of the carbon tax. The revenues from carbon taxes or the sale of emissions permits could be used in various ways: to reduce other taxes or to fund cash transfers, particularly to low income households, to offset the burden of the tax.

Practical Difficulties with Climate Change Policy Compared with other externalities, climate change poses unique problems. It is global in scope, has very long-term effects and there is considerable uncertainty about the ultimate consequences of various levels of CO_2 in the atmosphere.

The central issue is that emissions reductions are a *global public good*. The cost of reducing emissions are borne now by individual countries and the households within them. But the effects are worldwide, including not just for people alive now but also future generations.

Every country, even large ones, face the temptation to free ride on the efforts of others. This is particularly the case for countries that might consider themselves to be better off with climate change, such as northern countries who could enjoy a longer growing season and make formerly very cold areas more pleasant.[4] This highlights the uneven geographic distribution of the effects of climate change. Some countries will find it in their own self-interest to contribute something; those, such as India and China, facing serious air pollution problems could reduce emissions to deal with that. But this alone will not be enough. The result is like the prisoner's dilemma that we saw in Table 6.1 of Chapter 6; in this case, countries will choose to continue emissions at a higher rate than is in their collective interest.

The ideal would be a uniform worldwide carbon tax, but no international institution exists to enforce it. In its absence, countries that impose carbon taxes may be concerned that their domestic export industries would be at a disadvantage in countries with lower or no carbon taxes. Similarly, import competing industries would face increased competition from the exports of such countries. In principle, imports could be taxed depending on the untaxed carbon emissions involved in their production, as some economists have advocated. However, implementing this could be complex and would also have to be compatible with World Trade Organization rules. The EU is currently planning such a carbon border tax to protect its steel and other energy intensive industries.

Countries' representatives have met numerous times at UN Climate Change Conferences, notably in Paris in 2015. There they reaffirmed the goal of keeping the increase in global temperatures to less than 2°C compared with preindustrial levels and set an aspirational goal of 1.5°C. But the voluntary pledges countries have so far made to reduce emissions would be insufficient to reach their stated goals. A current estimate (as of mid-2021) is that those pledges, if met, could result in an increase in global temperatures of 2.4°C by 2100, with a greater than 66 percent chance of an increase of less than 2.6°C.[5]

2 THE ANTI-TEXT

Even now, more than 30 years after the problem of climate change came to public attention, its treatment in the textbooks has serious shortcomings. In the worst cases, such as Gregory Mankiw's text, the subject is barely mentioned. Yet the importance of the topic is hard to understate. As Nicholas Stern has written:

> The twin defining challenges of our century are overcoming poverty and managing climate change. If we can tackle these issues together, we will create a secure and prosperous world for generations to come. If we don't, the future is at grave risk.[6]

Let's first consider the texts on the science of climate change before turning to questions of policy and then to what is simply missing from the textbooks.

2.1 What do the texts really say about climate change science?

Because of the wide variation in the content of the texts, the preceding Standard Text's description of the science of climate change was more comprehensive than can be found in almost any text. In many, treatment of the science leaves much to be desired.[7] Three of the texts in our sample have virtually nothing explaining the scientific background to the problem or describing its possible consequences.[8] Yet it is the conclusions of the science that motivate policy and explain the urgency of the problem.

Is climate change a real problem caused by human activity? As Krugman and Wells write: 'Science has conclusively shown that emissions of greenhouse gases are changing the earth's climate.'[9] Many other authors echo that view, which reflects an overwhelming consensus among climate scientists.

Yet hints of doubt still linger in some. William Baumol and his co-authors say that 'the subject... *still gives rise to debate*, although the scientific consensus on the dangers and the role of human actions in generating the emissions that are believed to be altering the climate *seems to be strengthening*' (our emphasis here and subsequently). The 'global warming of the past century, and especially in the past decade, *is at least partly* a consequence of human activities' and that '*most* climatologists agree' that burning fossil fuels is 'a primary contributor to this problem'.[10] Another text says that it is 'the most significant and *hotly debated* issue of externalities', although what is hotly debated is left unsaid. It adds: '*Most* scientists predict' that with current policies 'major adverse consequences such as dramatically rising sea levels are likely.'[11]

William McEachern states: 'Though *the science is not yet fully resolved*, fossil fuel used to power the likes of automobiles and electricity generators produces carbon dioxide, which mixes with other greenhouse gases that *could* contribute to climate change'. Worst of all, Gregory Mankiw writes 'Experts disagree about how dangerous this threat is.' According to him, they disagree about whether warming is even happening! At the beginning of his book, as he discusses why economists disagree, he writes: 'recently, climatologists have debated whether the earth is experiencing global warming and, if so, why. Science is an ongoing search to understand the world around us. It is not surprising that as the search continues, scientists sometimes disagree about the direction in which truth lies.'[12]

Question for your professor (IF APPLICABLE): Our text seems to hint at some scepticism about the existence of/extent of human contribution to climate change when it says [quote the applicable passage.] Isn't there overwhelming consensus in the scientific community about that?

2.2 What do the texts not say about climate change science?

Some say little to nothing at all, but even those that do have significant omissions that, taken together, understate the urgency of the problem. The point here is to give a few brief examples that illustrate the complexity of the Earth system's response to GHG emissions, resulting in enormous risks for the future, including for young people alive today.

Ocean acidification Only one text in the sample has a phrase mentioning this.[13] Why is it important?

Oceans currently absorb a quarter of CO_2 emissions. As they do so, carbonic acid is formed. Compared with preindustrial times, the ocean is about 30 percent more acidic.

In 2009, 70 Academies of Sciences issued a statement about ocean acidification. Given the rate of CO_2 emissions, they warned that by mid century the oceans will be more acidic than they had been for tens of millions of years and that this process was 'irreversible for many thousands of years, and the biological consequences could last much longer'.[14]

The increasing acidity makes it more difficult for marine organisms to form skeletons and shells, threatening coral and shellfish. Coral reefs, already affected by warming waters, are home to a quarter of marine species and their demise in the coming century will impact fish populations that are an important food source for hundreds of millions of people. Rapid increases in ocean acidity in the past have been associated with mass extinctions of marine life.[15]

It also turns out that the more CO_2 the ocean absorbs, the slower the rate of absorption becomes, leaving more emissions in the atmosphere. This is an example of a feedback loop, where the more of something that has happened in the past causes either less (or more) of it to occur in the future. Unfortunately, the greenhouse effect involves many feedback loops that can accelerate warming.

Tipping points and feedback loops Not a single text in our sample describes the potential feedback loops involved in climate change, yet they are important and easy to understand.

When sunlight strikes the earth, some of its energy is not absorbed but is reflected by clouds and ice. As the summertime ice in the Arctic Ocean progressively shrinks, more and more energy is absorbed by the dark ocean. Something similar happens in the northern hemisphere as spring snow cover is reduced. Warming also leads to more water vapour in the atmosphere, which also acts as a greenhouse gas. Yet another example is the possible dieback of the Amazon forest and the northern boreal forest, turning them from absorbers of carbon dioxide to emitters, partly through wildfires.

These processes, some of which are already happening, can be triggered or accelerated as the global temperature increases. One reason to keep increases in global temperature below 2°C comes from the risk that warming beyond that (as one study puts it) 'could activate important tipping elements, raising the temperature further to activate other tipping elements in a domino-like cascade that could take the Earth system to even higher temperatures'. The result would be what the authors call a Hothouse Earth which would pose 'severe risks for health, economies, political stability (especially for the most climate vulnerable), and ultimately, the habitability of the planet for humans.' They conclude that 'Humanity is now facing the need for critical decisions and actions that could influence our future for centuries, if not millennia.'[16]

Climate sensitivity and the risk of extreme outcomes The term "climate sensitivity" refers to how much the average global surface temperature would ultimately increase as a result of a doubling of CO_2 concentrations compared with preindustrial levels. Current policies have the world on a path to that during this century.

In its 2021 report, the IPCC set its "likely" range at 2.5°C to 4°C, with 3°C the best estimate. In their terminology, this means that a temperature increase has at least a 66 percent chance of occurring within this range. It went further, stating that it estimated a 90 percent chance of it being between 2°C to 5°C. [17]

In their book, *Climate Shock*, economists Gernot Wagner and Martin Weizmann emphasize two things about such estimates. First, they say nothing about whether the world is going to end up towards the bottom of the range or towards the top, although the consequences of 5°C are vastly different from those of 2°C. Second, estimates like this leave a 10 percent chance of other outcomes. In this case, those outcomes are more likely to be above 5°C then below 2°C. This leaves a significant chance of a global temperature increase of more than 5°C. How much more is unclear, but such outcomes would be 'a near-certain disaster', a 'blind planetary gamble', in Wagner and Weitzman's words. They write that 'risks like on a planetary scale this should not – *must not* – be pushed onto society.'[18]

In short, behind the range of "likely" temperature change estimates presented to the public lie significant risks of much higher temperature increases. Only one text in our sample, that by Robert Frank and co-authors, explicitly cites such a risk – in this case, a 2013 IPCC estimate of a greater than 5 percent chance of more than 4.8°C (8.6°F) by 2100.[19]

> Question for your professor [IF APPLICABLE]: Do you
> think that our text adequately describes the risks
> of possible large temperature increases that would
> have potentially catastrophic results?

2.3 Carbon tax/Cap & trade: Silver bullet or simplistic prescription?

In her book *Economics for Humans*, Julie Nelson was skeptical about the approach of mainstream economics to environmental problems, given its assumptions of 'a mechanical, predictable, controllable world' and its emphasis on marginal thinking. She mused: 'Hmmm ... choosing simple mechanical models designed for examining small changes as the tool for analyzing ethically complicated issues about extremely complex natural and social systems undergoing dramatic upheaval ... what could go possibly wrong?'[20]

Nicholas Stern agrees, writing: 'Risks on this scale take us far outside the familiar policy questions and standard, largely marginal, techniques commonly used by economists.'[21] What does this imply for policy? In Stern's view, 'It is simply not enough to fix the GHG externality through some carbon tax or price, or appropriate regulation and to assert that perfect and complete markets, perfect competition and vibrant entrepreneurship will take care of the rest.'[22] Yet, almost without exception, this is the message of the textbooks who offer the carbon tax or cap and trade as *the* answer to the problem.

The problem itself is boiled down to a single source of market failure: the failure to internalize the external costs of carbon emissions. Pricing carbon is the obvious solution. Apparently, the magic of the market 'will take care of the rest'.

Dealing with climate change requires recognizing and addressing multiple sources of market failure. Stern highlights 'five further and crucial market failures':

> (i) research and development, (ii) imperfections in risk and capital markets, (iii) networks, such as public transport grids, broadband and recycling, (iv) information available to producers and consumers, for example about the efficiency performance of capital equipment and the availability of different options, (v) co-benefits of action on climate, in particular concerning air, water and land pollution. All five involve powerful dynamic elements, as does the fundamental GHG externality [of failing to price emissions appropriately].[23]

From this diagnosis, his policy prescriptions follow: 'by pricing and taxing, by regulating, by R and D investment, by city planning or land management, and so on, we can generate remarkable technical creativity and progress.' He adds that the 'economic response has to be very large, involve dynamic increasing returns, changed economic and urban organisation and design, and the avoidance of potential lock-ins.' It will also involve 'radical change in the way we foster and finance infrastructure.'[24]

To stimulate and to guide a green industrial revolution, the role of government will have to go well beyond the narrow limits described in the textbooks. In *The Entrepreneurial State*, Mariana Mazzucato warns that, if left on their own, markets can get stuck heading in the wrong direction. Past dependence on fossil fuels is self reinforcing. It has created an enormous infrastructure with industries dedicated to maintaining it. That's why governments need to invest in directing technological change in a new direction 'creating and shaping new markets as they regulate existing ones.'[25]

A green industrial revolution is not only about changing sources of energy. It's also about developing recyclable materials, improving waste management, agricultural practices, and energy efficiency.[26]

The first steps for such comprehensive action are already underway in Europe. In January 2020 the European Parliament approved the European Commission's proposed European Green Deal. Among other goals, it aims to achieve zero net emissions of GHGs by 2050.[27]

Questions for your professor: Is just putting a price on carbon emissions going to be enough to reduce emissions to meet the goals set out in Paris in 2015? Aren't there more market failures to consider? Won't a 'green technological revolution' require more government action than that?

Beyond the textbook carbon tax Among the responses to climate change, putting a price on carbon emissions is certainly necessary. Even now, some countries have a *negative* price: in various ways they are actively subsidizing the use of fossil fuels.[28]

Conventional calculations of what a carbon tax should be follow the textbook model. The permit price shown in Figure 12.3 would ideally reflect the marginal external cost of the pollutant, while polluters decide how to reduce emissions based on their marginal cost of doing so.

But GHG emissions create a meta-externality (discussed in Chapter 7), impacting the social and ecological environment in which the economy is embedded. Thus, it entails long-term damages of many different kinds that cannot plausibly be quantified in dollar terms: for example, the consequences of ocean acidification, of species extinction, of the eventual displacement of tens or hundreds of millions of people from areas made uninhabitable by drought, heat, or sea level rise. Another critical and unresolved question: by how much should future costs be the discounted?

As well, the possibility of catastrophic civilization-destroying costs cannot be ruled out, as discussed earlier. How do we deal with an unknown, but non-negligible, chance of what is essentially an infinite loss? Wagner and Weizmann conclude that the problem is one of existential risk management. They recommend a carbon price that ensures, as best we can, that catastrophe will not occur.[29]

A 2017 commission headed by Joseph Stiglitz and Nicholas Stern was asked what 'ranges and paths of carbon prices which, appropriately combined with other policies could deliver on the Paris target' and be compatible with the UN's Sustainable Development Goals.[30] Stern writes that the resulting 'price path is not some estimate of the evolution of social marginal damage, it is a price path that can guide change at the necessary scale and pace. And it has to take into account the need to induce rapid technical innovation as well as investment of the necessary type and scale.'[31]

The Commission recommended a carbon tax of between US$40-US$80 by 2020 and US$50-US$100 by 2030. It added that 'carbon pricing by itself may not be sufficient to induce change at the pace and on the scale' required for the Paris target to be met, so complementary actions are needed. These include 'investing in public transportation infrastructure and urban planning; laying the groundwork for renewable-based power generation; introducing or raising efficiency standards, adapting city design, and land and forest management; investing in relevant R&D initiatives.'[32]

The longer countries take to implement such prices (and few were near this range in 2020), the greater will be the stock of GHGs in the atmosphere. Given other policies, carbon prices would have to be higher than these in the future if the Paris goals are to be met.

> Question for your professor: Is it practical to try to set a carbon tax using estimates of the marginal social cost of emissions when so many of those costs are impossible to quantify?

2.4 Why are we waiting?

So asks Nicholas Stern in the title of his 2015 book on climate change. The IPCC was formed in 1988 and the first international agreement, the Kyoto Protocol dates from 1997. Yet global emissions continue to rise and policies in most countries remain inadequate.

The textbooks spend little time on Stern's question. One claims that 'although there is wide scientific agreement that the earth is slowly warming, there are disagreements over how costly that is. Such disputes make it difficult to agree on concrete policy proposals.'[33] Given that the actual disagreements are over just how bad it will be, this hardly justifies doing so little.

Robert Frank and co-authors conclude that economists' cost-benefit analyses do support action, so 'our failure to enact carbon taxes constitutes a mystery of the highest order. The explanation, perhaps, is that even the soundest policy proposals can sometimes take decades to win legislative approval.'[34] Why decades are required must be yet another 'mystery of the highest order', at least if you forget about corporate power and disinformation as well as the psychological difficulty the public has in grappling with the issues (as discussed below).

The global public goods problem The Standard Text sketched out the global public good/free rider problem as a prisoner's dilemma with a conclusion that self-interested countries will be unable to cooperate in their mutual interest. Nicholas Stern comments: 'The standard, simplistic and pessimistic version of game theory, while not irrelevant, ... appears to be inconsistent with the political reality and real-world experience. Economists may thus need to go beyond the narrow assumptions concerning behavior in that approach.'[35]

As briefly reviewed in Chapter 7, experiments examining people's actual behaviour reveal a complex mix of self-interest, altruism, desires for reciprocity, and an aversion to inequality.[36] A nonstandard text, *The Economy*, written by a team of authors at CORE (Curriculum Open-Access Resources in Economics) gives a simple example where countries act like individuals who are willing to reciprocate if others offer to cooperate and who also dislike inequality. In a simple two country example, they show that two outcomes are possible.[37]

If one country offers to cooperate by restricting emissions, the other country will reciprocate, which also reduces inequality between the two countries. This overcomes the prisoner's dilemma and both attain the best outcome. Instead, if self-interest still dominates one country's decision and it chooses business as usual, the other country will respond in kind, resulting in a bad outcome for both. This illustrates the authors' point that while countries will haggle over their contributions to the mutual gain, 'social preferences and norms such as fairness can facilitate agreement.'[38]

As Stern himself puts it, when it comes major global risks, 'people recognise and are concerned with the consequences of their actions for others. The depth of the understanding and the willingness to act will depend on context, language, communication and the reality of options; and on leadership.'[39]

Given the history of climate change negotiations, there are likely to be evolving agreements and national commitments, which may or may not be fully carried out. In many countries, cities and subnational governments have also undertaken commitments. What may be evolving is a kind of polycentric approach of the kind recommended by Elinor Ostrom that we saw in Chapter 7. She wrote that this 'encourages experimental efforts at multiple levels, as well as the development of methods for assessing the benefits and costs of particular strategies adopted in one type of ecosystem and comparing those with results obtained in other ecosystems'.[40]

Unfortunately, this slow process has left emissions and atmospheric GHGs continuing to rise. But the result has *not* been an equilibrium of 'business as usual'.

By clinging to the self-interest assumption, the texts fail to acknowledge the diversity of motivations both of people and of their governments. The result is an impoverished analysis that is a poor guide to actual events.

> Questions for your professor: The textbook suggests that countries will not reduce emissions beyond what is in their own self-interest (e.g. to reduce local air pollution), free riding on others' contributions. But isn't there evidence, from experimental economics for example, that people will contribute to public goods if they think others are willing to reciprocate? With climate change, don't we see some countries trying to lead by example, setting ambitious targets and hoping to induce others to follow?

The ethics of individual contributions to a global public good Wagner and Weitzman's *Climate Shock* has a chapter entitled 'What You Can Do'. The textbooks don't ask this, perhaps because, in their framework of narrow self-interest, the answer is obvious: voluntary contributions to a public good are irrational. People, including the managers of firms, are assumed to ignore external costs, never reflecting on the ethics of their actions. In this case, you will have already made whatever investments are profitable for yourself, like buying energy efficient appliances. Actions beyond that – flying less to reduce your emissions, for example – are futile sacrifices of utility for no discernible benefit to yourself.

In his book *Climate Matters*, philosopher John Broome says it's obviously your duty as a citizen to try to get your government to fulfill its moral obligation regarding climate change. But individual action is also necessary to fulfill what he calls *duties of justice*.[41] Your emissions are unjust. You emit them intentionally for your own benefit, without making restitution for the harm you cause. Yet you could easily reduce them, at least up to a point.[42]

Marginalist 'thinking like an economist' (e.g. 'Will I go to work today by car or by bicycle?') obscures non-marginal changes. But these are relevant when considering behavioural choices. Broome points out that a typical person in a rich country causes many tonnes of carbon dioxide to be emitted every year and lifetime emissions are significant. Based on World Health Organization estimates of future deaths and disease caused by climate change, Broome writes 'it can be estimated very roughly that your lifetime emissions will wipe out more than six months of healthy human life. Each year, your annual emissions destroy a few days of healthy life in total. These are serious harms.'[43] More recent research suggests even greater harms.[44]

Reframing emissions as causing harm can be (as Nicholas Stern writes) 'more morally motivating... Personal involvement in the causation of harm engages people's emotions in a way that impersonal calculations do not. This phenomenon may partially explain why, historically, many powerful moral campaigns have involved demands to stop causing harm.'[45]

In her original school strike, the flyer that Greta Thunberg handed out to passersby outside the Swedish parliament contained the statement 'I am doing this because you adults are shitting on my future.'[46] This emphasis on the harm that emissions today are doing to the future of today's children became a powerful central theme of the worldwide school strike movement that her action sparked.

Ethical commitments to reduce personal emissions can have a beneficial political side effect. Starting to 'go green' can change your perception of yourself which could further change your behaviour – in this case, encouraging civic engagement and political participation.[47]

How much effort are individuals actually making? A 2019 American survey found that 40 percent reported that friends and family were making 'either "a great deal of effort" (3%), "a lot of effort" (7%), or "a moderate amount of effort" (30%) to reduce global warming.'[48] In a 2019 British survey, 15 percent claimed they were 'very likely' to change their diet in 2020 to reduce their carbon footprint, slightly less than the 17 percent who say they are 'very likely' to 'buy responsibly/ethically-made or secondhand clothes and products'.[49]

Questions for your professor: Do each of us have an ethical obligation to reduce our individual emissions voluntarily? Why doesn't our textbook mention this instead of assuming that people will always ignore the external harms that they cause?

2.5 Corporate power and the strategy of denial and doubt

As we have seen, acknowledgement of business power in the texts is rare indeed. In the case of the attempts to influence climate change policies, this omission is inexcusable, particularly for North American textbooks. After all, the political power of the fossil fuel industry and its allies is hard to overlook in the United States and Canada.[50]

Many books, academic studies and investigative reports have described this decades long campaign to block or to delay effective policy action in the United States, Canada, Australia, and other countries, so only a brief sketch is needed here.[51]

As far back as the 1950s, fossil fuel companies knew that their products would cause long-term climate change that would eventually have to be dealt with. They began internal research. For example, by the early 1980s Exxon's scientists had accurately predicted the CO2 atmospheric concentration and global average temperature increase that would occur by 2020. They also understood its potentially catastrophic long-term consequences.[52]

When climate change finally came to public attention in 1988, the fossil fuel industry acted to protect their future profits by playing a central part in constructing a denial industry, whose objective was to block or to delay policies to address climate change. It consists not only of fossil fuel companies, but also a handful of contrarian scientists, fake experts, public relations firms, industry 'astroturf' front groups, right wing media and commentators, and conservative or libertarian capitalist 'think tanks'.[53]

The denial industry began a well-organized campaign of disinformation targeted both at politicians and at the public. Its primary goal was to convey the impression of disagreement among scientists first about whether climate change was happening and, if it was, whether human activity was primarily responsible for recent changes in the climate. 'Emphasize the uncertainty in scientific conclusions', a 1988 internal Exxon memo stated. Media coverage should then reflect 'balance on climate science'.[54] In *Merchants of Doubt*, Naomi Oreskes and Erik Conway explain that the strategy worked: 'Journalists were constantly pressured to grant the professional deniers equal status – and equal time and newsprint space – and they did.'[55]

If people perceive a consensus among the experts, they will be more likely to accept their conclusions. With the impression of disagreements, politicians would feel less pressure from the public to act.

While there are uncertainties about many aspects of climate change science, there is a strong consensus about the basic facts. Since its fifth report in 2013, the IPCC has attributed virtually *all* global warming since 1950 to human activity.[56] Yet in a 2019 international survey, only 38 percent of Americans agreed that the 'climate is changing and human activity is mainly responsible'. This was slightly more than in Norway(!), Sweden(!) and Saudi Arabia, but well below Thailand and Spain's 69 percent and India's 71 percent.[57] Clearly the public's views differ significantly from the professional consensus – a victory for fossil fuel interests.

Fossil fuel companies also conduct public relations campaigns to improve their corporate image, portraying themselves as socially and environmentally responsible, including taking action to address climate change.[58] At the same time they and their trade associations lobby politicians to stall policy action.

More than $2 billion was spent in the United States between 2000 and 2016 trying to influence federal climate legislation. American sociologist Robert Brulle found that 'environmental organizations and the renewable energy sectors were outspent by the corporate sectors involved in the production or use of fossil fuels by a ratio of approximately 10 to 1.'[59] The result: efforts to put a price on carbon were blocked.

Since the Paris 2015 agreement, the fossil fuel industry has faced increasing pressure. In 2016–2018, the world's five largest publicly-traded oil and gas companies (ExxonMobil, Royal Dutch Shell, Chevron, BP and Total) spent more than $1 billion on a combination of climate-related lobbying and corporate promotion.[60]

By saying virtually nothing about this long and sorry history of corporate misbehaviour in pursuit of profit at all costs, the textbooks have abdicated their responsibility to give a proper analysis of the economics of climate change policy.

> Question for your professor: Why does our textbook say nothing about the profit maximizing efforts of the fossil fuel industry and its allies to influence public opinion and public policy to stop or to delay effective action on climate change?

2.6 Psychology of climate change and evolving social norms

To answer Nicholas Stern's question about why we are waiting, we must also consider individuals' psychological responses to the problem and the social context in which they find themselves. These influence the possibilities people have to escape their state of passive denial and to act to bring political pressure on policymakers.

The psychology of climate change When preparing his book on the psychology of climate change, *Don't Even Think About It*, George Marshall naturally asked the opinion of one of the world's most famous psychologists – Daniel Kahneman. Kahneman's view was bleak: 'I'm extremely skeptical that we can cope with climate change. To mobilize people, this has to become an emotional issue. It has to have the immediacy *and* salience. A distant, abstract, and disputed threat just doesn't have the necessary characteristics for seriously mobilizing public opinion.' And what if people are told about their cognitive biases – would that help? Kahneman's response: 'No amount of psychological awareness will overcome people's reluctance to lower their standard of living. So that's my bottom line: There is not much hope. I'm thoroughly pessimistic. I'm sorry.'[61]

The efforts of the denial industry clearly play a critical role in making it a 'disputed threat'. But the aspects of our nature that Kahneman identifies are critically important.

Norwegian psychologist and economist Per Espen Stoknes points out that as climate science advances and the facts pile up, 'most people either don't believe in or do not act on those facts', what he calls the 'climate paradox'.[62] After you read the facts about the physical science of climate change in the first part of the Standard Text, Stoknes would ask: 'What does your cognitive system get out of all this? An impulse to act? Or fear? An urge to change your life? Or a big yawn?' His guess: likely a big yawn.[63] The information is abstract and, because the changes are slow on a human timescale, the worst effects seem far off. To go from *knowing* to *believing*, and thus acting on that belief, requires an *emotional* reaction.[64] Clearly some people are capable of this, but not enough. At least not yet.

More bad news, as in part 2.2 with its account of feedback loops and the risk of catastrophe, doesn't help either. It increases a sense of helplessness and a desire to avoid thinking about it. This is made easier if others are not talking about it. Surveys of Americans in 2019 found that a majority 'rarely' or 'never' discuss climate change with family and friends. Only 10 to 12 percent say they discuss it 'often'.[65] For most people, the result is a state of active denial ("It's a hoax!"), or more likely, just putting it out of their minds, which amounts to passive denial. To do otherwise would mean having to act, a step with potentially wide-ranging ramifications for one's life.

Yet many cultural and societal shifts have happened in the past, overcoming the inertia of the status quo. How can this one come about?

Framing Words and framing can aid understanding. For example, 'climate change' is bland and doesn't resonate with the typical person. Stoknes and others prefer '*climate disruption*', which more accurately describes the scope of the changes underway and the break with the past that it entails.[66]

Kahneman's work has found that people put much greater weight on losses than on comparable gains. So, policies that emphasize raising costs, like carbon taxes, or demand 'sacrifices' (giving up meat or flying) to avoid future damages are unappealing frames. Effective framing emphasizes gains and opportunities.

Nicholas Stern understands this well, writing:

> the transitions to a low-carbon economy, are likely to be full of discovery, innovation, investment, and growth, much as we have seen in other waves of technological change over the last 250 years. Further, the alternative ways of producing, consuming, and living will likely be cleaner, quieter, safer, more energy-secure, more community-based, and more biodiverse

in the short and medium term as well as involving far lower climate risks in the medium and long term.[67]

When asked how we can afford the cost of such a large-scale transition, he responded with a reframing: 'I don't think of those as costs; I think of those as investments with very strong returns... in terms of reduced costs of production; reduced pollution, and in terms of climate change.'[68]

Evolving social and moral norms History offers many examples of radical, and sometimes rapid, shifts in social and moral norms. Attitudes towards slavery, torture, domestic violence, drunk driving, and (in many countries) racism and smoking are now much different than they used to be. The money poured into 'greenwashing' by fossil fuel companies, portraying themselves as environmentally responsible, is an indication that attitudes are shifting. So are the growing movements for fossil fuel divestment and in opposition to expansion of these companies' activities. For individuals, driving a Rolls-Royce Phantom Coupe (which burns about 17 litres of fuel per 100 km) may someday damage the driver's social status, but we're not quite there yet.

As social animals, our choices are influenced by others' choices, creating the possibility of multiple equilibria. If most people are inactive, that encourages others to do so and the situation can persist; if many are talking about the issue and being active, that encourages people to join them. This 'behavioural contagion', as Robert Frank calls it, is yet another example of an externality.[69]

Each person's choices affect the overall social environment. Someone who buys an electric vehicle or who installs solar panels on her roof will not be thinking about this externality, but each person who does so increases the likelihood that others will follow. This creates the possibility of a virtuous cycle that can gradually bring about widespread change, especially if given a push by public policy initiated by scientific and political leadership.[70]

Questions for your professor: Climate disruption seems likely to lead to serious problems in the lifetimes of today's young people. Yet most people avoid even thinking about it or talking about it with others. Can we expect the appropriate economic policies to be implemented if this is the case? Can we escape this trap?

2.7 Summing up

> 'Our situation is desperate and at the same time hopeful.' Per Espen Stoknes[71]

Dealing with ongoing and future climate disruption – acting to lessen it and adapting to what will happen – surely deserves better treatment than it gets in the standard textbooks. Even those with an adequate description of the basics of the science generally fail to explain the immense risks humanity faces, even in the lifetimes of today's students. An increase in average global temperatures of 2°C, the top end of the target range agreed to in 2015 in Paris, would leave the world very different from today's.[72]

The textbooks' sole policy prescription – a carbon tax or any equivalent cap and trade system – is not enough. A 'green industrial revolution', requiring rapid structural transformation, needs government action on many fronts.

Remarkably, the standard texts largely leave it a mystery as to why governments haven't appropriately priced emissions. The model of self-interested free riders doesn't capture the complexity of actual motivations, while ignoring the ethics of individual action. Inexcusably, they ignore the successful actions of the denial industry. And finally, they don't acknowledge the psychological barriers that people have in feeling the danger of climate disruption and acting on it. Acting, or remaining passive, has an external effect on others via behavioural contagion and in influencing social and ethical norms.

Finally, they fail to convey the urgency of the problem and the importance of the decisions that must be taken in the near future as the world's population and economy grow, cities expand, and critical investment decisions are made that will shape the trajectory of future emissions. As Nicholas Stern said in 2016, 'People have not sufficiently understood the importance of the next 20 years. They are going to be the most decisive two decades in human history.'[73]

Today's economics students are beginning their adult lives during that time. They have a choice to make about how to respond to climate disruption: passive denial or action. If they choose action, they have the unique opportunity to experience what Robert Frank describes as 'the deep satisfaction that would stem from being part of a collaboration to preserve our planet's viability' for humanity.[74] Their economics textbooks have a responsibility to help them make the right choice.

SUGGESTIONS FOR FURTHER READING

An accessible primer on the science of climate change is Michael Mann and Lee Kump's *Dire Predictions: Understanding Climate Change*. A bit more technical is Joseph Romm's *Climate Change: What Everyone Needs to Know*.

Gernot Wagner and Martin Weitzman's 2015 book *Climate Shock: The Economic Consequences of a Hotter Planet* is a very accessible introduction to the economics with an emphasis on risk management.

Nicholas Stern's *Why are we waiting? The logic, urgency, and promise of tackling climate change*, also published in 2015, is an important book for a general audience by the world's leading economist working on climate change. More advanced students can also read his 2014 essays in the journal *Economics and Philosophy* and his 2018 paper in the *Journal of Public Economics*.

Mariane Mazucato details in Chapter 6 of *The Entrepreneurial State* how the state can push (not nudge) a green industrial revolution. She takes up this theme again in her 2021 book *Mission Economy: A Moonshot Guide to Changing Capitalism*.

Robert Pollin's *Greening the Global Economy* and his more recent book with Noam Chomsky, *Climate Crisis and the Global Green New Deal*, describe how global net zero emissions could be attained by 2050 while expanding employment opportunities, economic growth and reducing poverty in developing countries.

In Chapter 10 of *Dark Money: The Hidden History of the Billionaires Behind the Rise of the Radical Right*, Jane Mayer describes the success of Koch Industries' political network in stopping legislation that would have put a price on carbon emissions in the United States.

On the psychology of climate change, George Marshall's *Don't even think about it: why our brains are wired to ignore climate change* details the psychological barriers. He is more optimistic than the title suggests, arguing that we are also 'wired to take action' under the right circumstances. Also recommended is Per Espen Stoknes' *What We Think About When We Try Not To Think About Global Warming: Towards a New Psychology of Climate Action*.

An introduction to economics that deals with climate change themes throughout is Jack Reardon, Maria Alejandra Madi and Molly Scott Cato's *Introducing a New Economics: Pluralist, Sustainable and Progressive*.

NOTES

Introduction: our goals, audience and principal themes

1   Varoufakis (1998: 279). Copyright 1998 from *Foundations of Economics* by Yanis Varoufakis. Reproduced by permission of Taylor and FrancisGroup, LLC, a division of Informa plc.

2   Marglin (2008: 5) Copyright © 2008 by Stephen A. Marglin, reproduced by permission of Harvard University Press.

3   See Arnsperger and Varoufakis (2006) who try to identify the fundamental features of neoclassical economics.

4   Stiglitz sees his work as changing the neoclassical paradigm. For example, the title of his Nobel lecture (Stiglitz 2002) was 'Information and *the change in the paradigm* in economics' (emphasis added).

5   Colander (2003: 1), who describes how the process works and how it affected his text.

6   Zuidhof (2014: 159).

7   Kwak (2017: Kindle loc.333).

8   Arnott (1995: 117).

9   In a 1938 letter to Roy Harrod, cited by King (2020: 33).

10   Basu (2011: 193).

11   Quoted by medialens.org/2018/ empire-journalism-venezuela-the-us-and-john-mccain.

12   Rodrik (2015: 198).

13   Market fundamentalism is essentially a laissez-faire view. Its core belief: markets are efficient and governmental attempts to 'interfere' with markets necessarily create inefficiencies. The term was popularized by George Soros (1998), but has been used by many others.

14   Prasch (2008: 3).

15   Ibid.: 5.

16   See isipe.net/open-letter.

17   The 'Nobel Memorial Prize in Economics' is a commonly used term for 'The Sveriges Riksbank Prize in Economic Sciences in Memory of Alfred Nobel'. Established in 1968 by the Bank of Sweden, it is not one of the original prizes established by Alfred Nobel.

18   Akerlof and Shiller (2009: 173)

19   Zuidhof (2014: 161-6).

20   Ibid.:169.

21   Ibid.

22   Baumol et al. (2020: 4-5).

23   Zuidhof (2014: 170).

Chapter 1

1 Northrop (2000: 57).
2 Smith (1979), Book I, Ch. II and Book IV, Ch. II.
3 Okun (1975).
4 Lavoie (2006: 10).
5 Northrop (2000: 55-56).
6 Keynes (1963 [1931]: 365).
7 Nelson (2016: 196).
8 Raworth (2017, Ch.1).
9 Marglin (2008).
10 Marglin (2008: 10).
11 John K. Galbraith (2004).
12 Ibid.: 25.
13 John K. Galbraith (1973: 5).
14 See Davis (1998) and Schlosser (1998).
15 See Stanley (2004) and Zuboff (2019).
16 Gehl and Porter (2017).
17 John K. Galbraith (1973: 11).
18 Knack and Keefer (1997).
19 Helliwell (2003) and Helliwell et al. (2018).
20 Raworth (2017), Chapter 3, location 1449, Kindle edition.
21 Robinson (1979: 43).
22 Frank et al. (1993).
23 Frey and Meier (2003).
24 Cipriani et al. (2009); Bauman and Rose (2011).
25 This is the preferred term of Aldred (2019: 10 et seq.).
26 Gigerenzer (2008: 81).
27 Thaler (2018: 1281), who then asks 'what are their true preferences?'
28 Badger et al. (2007).
29 Kahneman (2002).
30 Darley and Latane (1968).
31 Redelmeier et al. (1993).
32 An older behavioural economics, pioneered by Herbert Simon, also challenged the rationality assumption. It focused mainly on the behaviour of business firms.
33 Thaler and Bernartzi (2004).
34 Titmus (2004).
35 Dawnay and Shah (2005: 6).
36 Gneezy and Rustichini (2000).
37 Lunn and Harford (2008: 2).
38 Thaler (2018: 1267).
39 Kahneman (2013: 413).
40 Gigerenzer (2008: 86).
41 In our sample of 10 texts, notable exceptions were Colander (2020), with extensive coverage across several chapters, and Frank et al. (2019) and McConnell et al. (2021), both with a full chapter.
42 Marglin (2008: 5).

43 Nelson (2016: 196).
44 FAO et al. (2018: 9-10). The technical term is 'severe food insecurity'.
45 Nelson (2018a: 216).
46 Marglin (2008: 1).
47 We noted earlier that mainstream economics does not restrict preferences, so that altruism is allowed. Still, the typical model assumes pure self-interest.

Chapter 2

1   Salam (1990: 99).
2   In a 1938 letter to Roy Harrod, cited by King (2002: 33).
3   Fuller and Geide-Stevenson (2014).
4   This is a theme in Aldred (2019).
5   Mankiw (2021: 31).
6   Card (1992a, 1992b), Katz and Krueger (1992), Card et al. (1994), Card and Krueger (1994, 1995, 2000). Neumark and Wascher (2004) point out that conflicting empirical evidence can be found for nearly every country in the world.
7   Valentine (1996) on Card and Krueger (1994).
8   Card and Krueger (1995: 186).
9   Doucouliagos and Stanley (2009).
10 Ioannidis et al. (2017).
11 Levine (2001: 161).
12 The minimum wage debate continues. A substantial minimum wage increase in Seattle, Washington, beginning in 2015 led to two studies using different methods and reaching conflicting conclusions. See Jardim et al. (2017) and Reich et al. (2017).
13 Dewald et al. (1986: 600). On the other hand, the errors did not significantly affect the conclusions in the majority of cases.
14 For example, McCullough et al. (2006) and Chang and Li (2021).
15 Hahn (1987: 110).
16 Lakatos (1978).
17 Varoufakis (1998: 344).
18 Rodrik (2015: 65).
19 Leamer (2012: 26).
20 Musgrave (1991) and Mäki (2000) are detailed, but technical, examinations of negligibility and domain assumptions.
21 For example, see Krugman et al. (2018: Ch. 7).
22 Leamer (2012: 27).
23 Ibid.: 19.
24 Ibid.: xx.
25 McCloskey (1998: xii, quoting Booth (1974)).
26 Ibid.: xii).
27 Leamer (2012: 19).
28 Leontief (1983: viii).
29 Friedman (1953: 21).
30 Colander (2020: 20).

31 Bowles et al. (2017: 58).
32 The example is taken from Goodwin et al. (2019: 22).
33 Colander (2020: 18-20), a text that is unique in discussing the idea.
34 Colander (1992: 196).
35 Rodrik (2015: 211).
36 Colander (1992. 196-197).
37 Kuhn (1962).
38 Keynes (1936: viii).
39 Cohn (2007: 41).
40 David Colander's (2020) text is exceptional, ending every chapter with a set of 'Questions from Alternative Perspectives': e.g. Austrian, Institutionalist, Religious, Post-Keynesian, Radical, Feminist.
41 Cohn (2007: 41).
42 George (1996: 28).

Chapter 3

1 Mankiw (2021) and Parkin (2019).
2 Colander (2020: 112).
3 Krugman and Wells (2021: 356).
4 Baumol et al. (2020), Case et al. (2020), and Colander (2020).
5 Krugman and Wells (2021), Mankiw (2021) and McConnell et al. (2021) say nothing about information.
6 Stiglitz (2002: 461).
7 Ibid.: 477.
8 Depending on the market, other consequences could be an equilibrium where the quantity demanded differs from the quantity supplied, or even multiple equilibria.
9 Stiglitz (1985: 34).
10 Stiglitz (2002: 469).
11 Baumol et al. (2020: 196).
12 Krugman and Wells (2021: 439).
13 Mankiw (2021: 63).
14 Goodhue and Russo (2012: 79).
15 Lawrence 2014; Schlosser 2001.
16 Blinder et al. (1998: 12).
17 Ibid.: 298.
18 Krugman and Wells (2021: 438).
19 Dolar (2013).
20 These were McConnell et al. (2021), Parkin (2019) and Ragan (2020).
21 Mankiw (2021: 117).
22 Krueger (2001: 247).
23 Arnott (1995: 112).
24 Ibid.: 117.
25 Ibid.: 99.
26 Parkin (2019: 138).
27 Colander (2020: 95)

28 Baumol et al. (2020: 363).
29 Arrow (1959: 41, 43).
30 Ibid.: 41.
31 Dixon (1990: 361–2).
32 There are no inventories in model. In the real world, inventories are needed because demand is uncertain. In the perfectly competitive market, trade only takes place at the 'market clearing' price; the amount supplied to the market is always the same as the amount sold, so holding inventories would be pointless.
33 Case et al. (2020: 62).
34 Ibid.: 61.
35 Prasch (2008: 88).
36 Ibid.
37 Ibid.: 93.
38 Stiglitz (2002: 471).
39 Textbooks try to make the model seem more applicable to real world markets by telling an ill-defined story of dynamics where both consumers and producers tried to acquire inventories to carryover to the future time periods; this has no place in a comparative static model.
40 Mullainathan and Thaler (2004); Russell and Thaler (1985).
41 For example, Singleton (2014).
42 This is mere anecdotal evidence collected by Myatt (2004) while living in Paris from 2001 to 2002. He claims that the plural of 'anecdote' is 'data'.
43 Chang (2010: 1). The term 'free market' appears with varying frequency in our sample of texts; Baumol et al. (2020) and Ragan (2020) use it the most.
44 Ibid.: 10.
45 Stiglitz (2002: 488).
46 Häring and Douglas (2012: 141-2).
47 Ackerman (2002: 121).
48 Hildenbrand and Kirman (1988: 49).
49 Ibid.: 49, 105.
50 Ackerman (2002: 122).

Chapter 4

1 Varoufakis (2017: 65).
2 There are technical issues with this measure of consumers' surplus (e.g. the requirement that the marginal utility of income be constant and that consumers' utilities can be added up) that advanced students should be aware of. See Slesnick (2008).
3 Friedman (1976: 13).
4 Douglas (1987).
5 Bowles et al. (2018: ch. 2) has an excellent discussion.
6 Leacock (1924: 123). Leacock, a Canadian economist, was best known for his humorous stories.
7 Schmalensee (2008).
8 John K. Galbraith (1958: 122).

9 Schor (2004: 86).

10 Peppers (2014) is an actual example.

11 McPherson (1987: 403).

12 Cohn (2007: 22).

13 From George Carlin's 'Advertising lullaby', available on YouTube.

14 Schor (2004: 86).

15 Nader (2004: 100).

16 Economist Intelligence Unit (2017: 5, 13).

17 Ibid.: 13.

18 Boseley et al. 2018. See takeapart.org/tiny-targets/ for detailed country reports.

19 Victoria et al. (2016).

20 UNICEF and WHO (2018). This is the percentage of infants aged 0-5 months exclusively breastfed the day before the survey (Victoria et al. 2016: 476).

21 Ibid.: 2.

22 Rollins et al. (2016: 495).

23 Ellis-Petersen (2018).

24 The United States was the only UN member to vote against the Code (*Time*, 1 June 1981, p. 26).

25 Beasley and Amir (2007).

26 Boseley (2008).

27 Healy (2006). See also healyprozac.com.

28 E.g. Angell (2004); Moynihan and Cassels (2005); Goldacre (2013).

29 Centers for Disease Control and Prevention, 'Prescription Opioid Data', available at cdc.gov/drugoverdose/data/prescribing.html. Accessed 25 June 2021.

30 Meier (2018: xii). See also Alpert et al. (2019). Other pharmaceutical companies, notably Johnson & Johnson, have faced lawsuits regarding the opioid epidemic.

31 Moynihan and Cassels (2005: Ch.7).

32 Angell (2004: 124-125).

33 Ibid.: xxvi.

34 Singer and Wilson (2009).

35 Angell (2004: 126–55); Moynihan and Cassels (2005); Goldacre (2013).

36 Schlosser (2001: 4); Lawrence (2008 & 2014).

37 Pawlick (2006: 15–16, 26–7).

38 Singer and Mason (2006: 3–6).

39 Nader (2000) is a great collection of essays detailing problems facing consumers.

40 Schor (1998: 69). See also Frank (1999) and Marmot (2004).

41 The textbook assumption is correct only for one person's demand, taking the incomes and consumption of everyone else as given (Pollak 1978).

42 John K. Galbraith (1958: 119).

43 Ibid.: 120–21.

44 Layard with Ward (2020: Kindle loc. 444).

45 The average is calculated using '5' for 'very satisfied', decreasing in increments of one so that '1' is 'very dissatisfied' (Sharpe et al. 2010: 12).

46 Layard with Ward (2020: loc. 96).

47 Kahneman and Deaton (2010: 16492).

48 Jebb et al. (2018).

49 Easterlin (1995).
50 See data.worldbank.org.
51 Easterlin et al. (2017).
52 Stevenson and Wolfers (2008:46-56).
53 Krueger (2008), Easterlin et al. (2010) and Easterlin (2017).
54 Layard with Ward (2020: loc. 1124).
55 Easterlin (2001).
56 Easterlin (1995: 35–6). Solnick and Hemenway (1998) report survey evidence supportive of this.
57 Only three of the texts in our sample give a brief account of Easterlin's ideas: Colander (2020:487), Frank et al. (2019: 283), and McConnell et al. (2021: 161).
58 Linder (1970: 7-8).
59 Ibid.: 143–4).
60 Layard with Ward (2020: p.33).
61 Ibid.: Figure 2.2.
62 Helliwell et al. (2020: Table 2.1).
63 This and following paragraphs draw on the results reported in Helliwell et al. (2020) and Layard with Ward (2020: loc. 829-53).
64 GDP is measured in constant 2011 $US. Ireland's GDP per capita reflects its status as a notorious corporate tax haven. Luxembourg ($93,965 GDP per capita) was omitted for this reason.
65 Deaton (2008: 69).
66 Sen (1999). In our sample of texts, only Colander (2020: 404) briefly mentions these ideas.

Chapter 5

1 Robinson (1972: 4). [Copyright American Economic Association; reproduced with permission of the American Economic Review].
2 Firms often produce more than one product. Here, 'the size of the firm' refers only to how much of the relevant product the firm produces because the concern is about its share of this market.
3 Smith, *Wealth of Nations*, Book V, Chapter 1, Part III.
4 Northrop (2013: 115).
5 For example, Taibbi (2011).
6 Bebchuk and Fried (2004: 2).
7 Stiglitz (2002: 480–81).
8 Stanfield and Stanfield (2004: 81–2).
9 Chandler (1977: 10).
10 Lavoie (2014: 73). Keynes (1936, Chapter 12) famously described such uncertainty and its macroeconomic consequences.
11 Lavoie (2014: 128-147).
12 Ibid.: 170-171. Equivalently, the firm's elasticity of demand is one or less than one. Note that in the standard monopoly model the firm does not produce in the inelastic range of the demand curve, thus avoiding negative marginal revenue.

13 Blinder et al. (1998: 60). The firms were representative of the economy as a whole outside of government, non-profit firms, agriculture and firms with regulated prices.

14 Ibid.: 40–44.

15 Northrop (2013: 114).

16 Friedman (1970).

17 Colander (2020: 257).

18 See bcorporation.net.

19 Northrop (2013: 119-120).

20 Baumol et al. (2020: 333; Parkin (2019: 228).

21 Ragan (2020: 152).

22 Rubinstein (2006: C1).

23 A variant of the survey described profits using an equation and was given to students in economics, MBA, law and mathematics. By dehumanizing workers, who appear as the variable x in the equation, all students became much more (and equally) likely to choose the profit maximizing number of layoffs.

24 Helliwell and Huang (2011).

25 The following sections draw heavily on Cohen (1983, 1996).

26 Miller (2000: 119) explains that the stock-flow distinction is not necessary in the case of land, used in David Ricardo's initial formulation of diminishing marginal returns. Once 'plowed, fertilized, and planted, the land provides services continuously', unlike capital which can be left idle.

27 Mankiw (2021: 247-9).

28 Bowles et al. (2017: 300).

29 Miller (2000, 2001).

30 Miller (2000: 125).

31 Lavoie (2014: 150); Bumas (1999:380); Dorman (2014: 257-259).

32 Miller (2000: 127).

33 Miller (2001: 196).

34 Mansfield (1994: 242).

35 Blinder et al. (1998: 103).

36 Ibid.: 105.

37 Lavoie (2014: 151). See Baumol et al. (2020: 131).

38 Sraffa (1926: 543).

39 Mansfield (1994: 242, our emphasis).

40 Case et al. (2020: 195) is exceptional, discussing the empirical evidence and acknowledging the possibility of an L-shaped long-run average cost curve. However, they fail to say that perfect competition may the no longer occur.

41 Parkin (2019: 266).

42 Cohen (1983: 217). Natural resource industries are an exception; diseconomies arise because the natural resource input is limited and cannot be replicated like a manufacturing plant can (Dorman 2014: 270).

43 Dorman (2014: 156-157). Kroszner and Putterman (2009: 13-16) survey theoretical ideas that dispute this.

44 Simon and Bartel (1986: 23).

45 Cohen (1983: 218).

46 Stiglitz (2002: 460).

47 Cohen (1983: 218).

48 Cohen (1996: 86).
49 Rothschild (1971: 7).
50 Veblen (1965 [1904]: 286).
51 Center for Responsive Politics at opensecrets.org/lobby/. Data for 2019.
52 Jacobs 2019; Greenhalgh 2019.
53 Lavoie (2014).
54 Olson (1971: 1).
55 Ibid.: 29, his emphasis.
56 Ibid.: 43.
57 See statista.com/markets/415/topic/472/tobacco/.
58 Glenza (2017).
59 Boseley (2017).
60 Kalra et al. (2017).
61 For examples, see the Front Groups pages at sourcewatch.org.
62 See centerjd.org/content/fact-sheet-citizens-against-lawsuit-abuse-groups.
63 Nader (2000: 275–309) and (2004: 37–48).
64 Herman and Chomsky (1988: 298, 1).
65 Frank (1989) is particularly insightful.
66 Quoted in Chomsky (2006: 206).
67 James K. Galbraith (2008: 15-24).
68 Bowles et al. (2017: 322).
69 Ibid.
70 Ibid.: 63. who examine the issue carefully.
71 Mill (1965: 775); for other editions, see Book IV, ch. vii, §6.
72 Kalmi (2007).
73 Bowles et al. (2017: 103).
74 Whyte and Whyte (1991).
75 Mondragón (2020).
76 Bowles et al. (2017: 322-323).
77 Lavoie (2014: 150; 166).
78 Kahneman et al. (1986).
79 Thaler (2015:128).
80 Kahneman et al (1986: 738).
81 Lavoie (2014, Chapter 3.6) refers to many empirical studies of price setting.
82 Ibid.: 167.
83 Leonhardt (2005).

Chapter 6

1 Blaug (2002: 38). Reproduced with permission of the Licensor through PLSclear.
2 Chamberlin (1933) and Robinson (1933).
3 High income persons will, on average, have a lower marginal utility of income than a low-income person. The marginal dollar is worth less to them so they'll be willing to pay more for an extra loaf of bread, for example.
4 Colander (2003: 85). His own text is a notable exception.
5 Marx and Engels (2012[1848]: 78).
6 Schumpeter (1950: 84).

7 Ibid.: 77.
8 Frank et al. (2019), Krugman and Wells (2021), Mankiw (2021) and Parkin (2019).
9 A most notable exception was Baumol et al. (2020: 413-419).
10 Stiglitz (2017: 385).
11 Stiglitz and Greenwald (2015: 20).
12 Ibid.: 17.
13 Lipsey and Lancaster (1956/57). In our sample of texts, only Case et al. (2020: 402) and Colander (2020: 166) acknowledge the issue.
14 The nonmainstream text by Dorman (2014: 497-500) gives a clear explanation of second-best issues. The oil price example is based on his.
15 McConnell et al. (2021: 197) and Colander (2020: 166).
16 Blaug (2002: 38).
17 Leibenstein (1966).
18 Schumpeter (1954: 977).
19 The elasticity is the percentage change in quantity divided by the percentage change in the price. This and the change in price allow estimation of the change in quantity (the base of the triangle).
20 Littlechild (1981).
21 Hay and Morris (1991: 586).
22 Scherer and Ross (1990: 666-667).
23 This change in treatment between the earlier edition to the third edition is explained in a footnote on p. 678.
24 Ibid.: 678.
25 Prasch (2008: 3).
26 Colander (2003: 85).
27 Ibid.: 84.
28 Prasch (2008: 8, 13).
29 Ibid.: 56.
30 Galbraith, cited in ibid.: 147.
31 Ibid.: 14.
32 Ibid.: 8-9.
33 Stiglitz (2003: 89–90).

Chapter 7

1 Ziliak (2002: 111), ©Association for Economic and Social Analysis, reprinted by permission of Informa UK Limited, trading as Taylor & Francis Group, www.tandfonline.com on behalf of Association for Economic and Social Analysis.
2 Robinson (1972: 7).
3 Pigou (1932: 193).
4 Edlin and Karaca-Mandic (2006: 936).
5 Green et al. (2016: 21).
6 Robinson (1972: 7).
7 Of the 10 texts surveyed, only three have a chapter on externalities in the first half of the book: McConnell et al. (2021); Colander (2020), and Mankiw (2021).
8 Goodwin (2010: 29). See Cohn (2015: 17) who gives many examples throughout his book.

9   Ibid.: 29-30.
10 Worm et al. (2017: 1).
11 Geyer et al. (2017: 1, 3).
12 Carrington (2019b).
13 The plastic moves with ocean currents called gyres. See www.5gyres.org.
14 Corkery (2019), who notes that public pressure may be weakening their opposition.
15 Laville and Taylor (2017).
16 Christiansen et al. (2019).
17 Greenstone and Fan (2018: 3). See the interactive world map at aqli.epic.uchicago.edu/the-index/. The calculations are for 2016 and assume pollution levels at that time persist.
18 The WHO guideline is an annual average of 10 μg (micrograms) of fine particulate matter per cubic metre of air. Sandstorms are an important source in some parts of the world.
19 Carrington (2019a) summarizes with illustrations the studies by Schraufnagel et al. (2019a and 2019b) both of which are non-technical and publicly available.
20 See Schraufnagel et al. (2019a: 409; 412-4).
21 An annual average of 2-3 $\mu g/m^3$ is safe (Lelieveld et al., 2019: 1595).
22 Burnett et al. (2018) and Lelieveld et al. (2019). The standard of comparison in the former is 2.4 $\mu g/m^3$, the lowest exposure available in the data.
23 Lelieveld et al. (2019: 1590).
24 Vidal (2015). Netflix's *Dirty Money* documentary series has an episode on this: *Hard NO$_x$*.
25 Greenstone and Fan (2018: 3).
26 Burnett et al. (2018: 9595).
27 Lelieveld et al. (2019: 1595).
28 Boffey (2019).
29 Landrigan et al. (2018: 462).
30 Ibid.: 463.
31 Persistent organic pollutants (POPs) do not break down over time and accumulate in the body. An international agreement, the Stockholm Convention, added PFOA to its list of banned substances in 2019. See pops.int.
32 Shapira and Zingales (2017); also Dizik (2018).
33 Shapira and Zingales (2017: 31).
34 United Nations Environmental Programme (2019: v).
35 Ibid.: 150.
36 Harvey (2019).
37 The problem is double-edged; because of global inequality in access, more people are still dying from a lack of antimicrobial drugs than are dying from drug-resistant infections (National Academies of Sciences, Engineering and Medicine 2017: 9).
38 Interagency Coordination Group on Antimicrobial Resistance (2019: 2-3).
39 Harvey (2019 and 2018).
40 Gilbert (2019).
41 O'Neill (2016: 6).
42 Cited by Easterlin (1995: 36).
43 Frank (1997).

44　Of the texts surveyed, only Frank et al. (2019: 282) discusses positional externalities.

45　Frank (2005: 141).

46　Winkelmann (2012: 189).

47　Frank (1999: 211-26). Some countries, such as the US and Canada, have such schemes, but limit annual contributions.

48　This contrasts with existing 'regressive' sales and value-added taxes where higher-income persons tend to pay a lower percentage of their income in tax than lower-income persons.

49　Frank (1999.: 216).

50　Maye (2019: 3).

51　Ostrom (2005: 258; 265).

52　Ibid.: 270.

53　Ibid.

54　Ostrom (2012).

55　Notably Ragan (2020: 388), Krugman and Wells (2021: 503-5), and McConnell et al. (2021: 378-83).

56　Gordon (1954: 126).

57　Costello et al. (2016: 5125).

58　This usually extends up to 200 nautical miles from baselines drawn between the tips of irregular coastlines.

59　Worm (2016: 4896).

60　Worm (2017).

61　Ripple W, C. Wolf, T. Newsome, et al. (2019: 3).

62　Ibid.: 1-2.

63　Díaz, S., J. Settele,, E.Brondízio, et al. (2019: 4, 14).

64　Ibid.: 22.

65　Putterman (2012: 191).

66　Putnam (2020: 19).

67　Ostrom (2000: 143-4).

68　Ibid.: 137-8.

69　MacLean (2017: ch 10).

70　Vergara (2020) and 2019 and 2020 annual reports on Chile at amnesty.org.

71　This is the experiment described by Ostrom (2000: 139).

72　Putterman (2012: ch6) summarizes the experiments and their results.

73　Fehr and Schmidt (2006: 640).

74　Ostrom (2000: 131).

75　Putterman (2012: 137; 141).

76　Häring and Douglas (2012: 38).

77　Krugman and Wells (2021: 16).

78　Ibid.: 3.

Chapter 8

1　Origin unknown, often misattributed to American baseball player Yogi Berra. (See en.wikiquote.org/wiki/Yogi_Berra).

2　It's like a simple mortgage calculation. Find a mortgage calculator online. Set the amortization period to 25 years and choose the interest rate and principal amount.

3 If estimated returns to schooling are much greater than that required from a mortgage amortization point of view, it suggests that there are barriers to entering occupations – including differences in inherited ability – which raises the return above levels implied by the principle of equal net benefits. McConnell et al. (2021: 334) write of the United States: 'Rates of return are estimated at 10 to 13 percent for investments in secondary education and 8 to 12 percent for investments in college education. Overall, *each year* of schooling raises a worker's wage by about 8 percent' [emphasis added].

4 Lazear and Rosen (1981: 847).

5 Komlos (2015: 107).

6 Häring and Douglas (2012: 157).

7 Thurow (1975: viii).

8 Ibid.: 211–112.

9 Ibid.: 215.

10 Steedman (1987).

11 Blaug (1996: Ch.11, Kindle loc.11810).

12 Hämäläinen et al. (2017: 4, 17).

13 ILO (2019: 1).

14 Wasley et al. (2018).

15 Summers (1992). See Swaney (1994) for a critique.

16 Frank et al. (2019: 283). Their analysis does not explain how compensating differentials change in response to the increased supply of those willing to accept less safe work.

17 Engels (1987 [1845]: 128).

18 Akerlof and Dickens (1982).

19 Purse (2003).

20 Carpenter et al. (2017: 50), who quote Rosen.

21 Half of the texts in our sample made at least a brief mention of efficiency wages. At best, this is another example of the 'note but ignore' strategy.

22 Akerlof and Yellen (1988: 45).

23 Akerlof and Yellen (1988 and 1990).

24 The standard efficiency wage model is based on the costs of supervising particular kinds of work. It can't explain why other workers doing easy-to-supervise tasks in the same firm should also be paid more.

25 Another possibility is a dual labour market: workers with the same characteristics are divided between those with high wages in the 'primary labour market' (where jobs are rationed and there is effectively excess supply) and those with lower wages in the 'secondary labour market'.

26 Frank (1984, 1985). This emphasis on status and relative position is consistent with the evidence seen in Chapter 4 on relative position and subjective well-being.

27 Krugman and Wells (2021: 536).

28 Frank and Cook (1995: 144).

29 See tbray.org/ongoing/When/202x/2020/04/29/Leaving-Amazon#p-3

30 Varoufakis (1998: 170).

31 Frank (2003, ch5) gives striking examples of the compensating differentials that exist between jobs based on perceptions of the social responsibility (or irresponsibility) involved in carrying them out.

32 Varoufakis (1998.: 172).

33 Ibid.: 175.
34 Barth (2015).
35 Brown (1987).
36 Komlos (2015: 115).
37 Colander (2020: 378).
38 Manning (2003).
39 Ibid.: 4.
40 Ibid.
41 Robinson (1933).
42 Bumas (1999: 373) gives a detailed example. Different labour supply curves can lead the firm to be willing to pay different wages for the same amount of labour. There is no unique relationship between the wage and labour demanded.
43 Card and Krueger (1995: 373).
44 In this simple case, the firm can only increase hires by increasing the wage. Its hiring costs are assumed fixed, but firms could choose to spend more or less on recruitment efforts, shifting the hiring relationship in the figure. See Manning (2011: 1004).
45 Green et al. (1996); Oi and Idson (1999).
46 For example, Newman et al. (2016).
47 Card and Krueger (1995: 379); Barth (2015) summarizes the model clearly.
48 This parallels discrimination among customers according to their price elasticity of demand. The least price-sensitive customers will be charged a higher price.
49 Manning (2003: Ch. 7.4).
50 Barth (2015).
51 Manning (2003.: 256-63).
52 Labour supply is 'perfectly elastic'.
53 Webber (2015: 132-33). The median elasticity was 0.74.
54 Manning (2011: 1031).
55 Quiggin (2019: 186).
56 Manning (2003: Chs.8, 13).
57 For example Adler (2010: 192).
58 Clark (1891: 319).
59 Blaug (1996: Kindle loc.11115).
60 Ibid.: loc.11129.
61 Ibid.: loc.11142.
62 McConnell et al. (2021: 315-6).
63 Krugman and Wells (2021: 556). Case et al. (2020: 369) stress the inequality of opportunity in acquiring human capital, leading to unjust differences in wages.
64 Baumol et al. (2020: 390).
65 That theory includes analyses of discrimination. The resulting wages may still be both inevitable and, depending on the nature of the discrimination, efficient.
66 Bok (1993: 15).
67 Chang (2010: 23).
68 Ibid.: 29.
69 Hartung (2015).

70 Both series also include salary, bonus, restricted stock awards, and long-term incentive payouts for CEOs.

71 See Mishel and Wolfe (2019: 21, note 1). This estimates the value of the option as if it were tradable in an options market.

72 In 1992 firms in the 'Standard & Poor's 500' index granted employees options worth $11 billion at the time of grant; by 2000, these had increased to $119 billion (Hall and Murphy 2003: 49).

73 Stiglitz et al. (2015: 54-55), who mentions a study showing that stock prices "have difficulty incorporating information more than five years out", not surprising in the face of fundamental uncertainty. But this further reinforces a short-term focus.

74 McEachern (2017: 275-276) has the most comprehensive treatment.

75 For example, Bowles et al. (2018: 166, 219), Dorman (2013: 155), Goodwin et al. (2019: 318).

76 Bowles et al. (2018: 219).

77 Bebchuk and Fried (2004: 24).

78 Zweig (2004).

79 Adler (2010: 143-4).

80 For example, McEachern (2017: 276).

81 Chang (2010: 151-152); on the 1930s-1970s, Stiglitz et al. (2015: 53).

82 Duarte (2019).

83 Kwak (2016: loc. 1376).

84 Stiglitz et al. (2015: 53).

Chapter 9

1 Quoted in Chomsky (1987: 3).

2 The source for Table 9.1 contains these details.

3 See wid.world/country/usa/.

4 This is largely due to mortgage debt exceeding the value of households' property (Balestra and Tonkin, 2018: 15).

5 The Gini coefficient is not very useful because so many households have negative net wealth.

6 See census.gov/topics/income-poverty.html.

7 Mankiw (2021: 401).

8 This is the approach of the Market Basket Measure used in Canada.

9 For example, Sen (1999).

10 See wdi.worldbank.org/tables.

11 For details see ophi.org.uk/ and United Nations Development Programme (UNDP) and Oxford Poverty and Human Development Initiative (2019: 1). See also the most recent UNDP *Human Development Report*.

12 See sustainabledevelopment.un.org/. There are annual updates for each SDG.

13 This is measured using purchasing power parity exchange rates.

14 The poverty line in this case is that defined by each country.

15 Colander (2020), Mankiw (2021), McConnell et al. (2021), and Parkin (2019) have the most. Our sample omits two American texts with emphasis on public choice: Cowen and Tabarrok (2021) and Gwartney et al. (2018).

16 Quoted by Orchard and Stretton (1997: 418).

17 We use the term 'libertarian capitalism' to distinguish this from other versions of libertarianism, such as libertarian socialism or anarchism, which entail economic democracy.
18 Mongiovi (2019: 177).
19 Quoted by Weeks (2014: 35), citing the *Wall Street Journal*, 25 April 1996, p.A20.
20 Quiggin (1987:15).
21 Kelman (1987: 85; 93).
22 Quiggin (1987: 12).
23 Ibid.: 15.
24 Chang (2010: 46, 50).
25 Putterman (2018: 251).
26 Downs (1957: 265-7).
27 Kelman (1987: 89-90).
28 Brulle (2018: 297).
29 Ibid.: 292, quoting Drutman (2015: 36).
30 Igielnik (2020).
31 Gilens and Page (2014: 575).
32 Bartels (2017).
33 Keynes (1936: 340).
34 Aldred (2009: 79-87) examines the issue in detail.
35 Kelman (1987: 81).
36 Putterman (2018: 253-6).
37 Aldred (2019: 84-5).
38 Ibid.: 96.
39 George (1990: 863).
40 In fairness, the examples are probably chosen for simplicity: an excise tax changes the relative price of a single good.
41 Vitullo-Martin and Moskin (1994: 130). And, yes, really this is 11 words.
42 Atkinson (2015: 14-15).
43 Ibid.: 16.
44 Myrdal (1969).
45 Only Colander (2020: 393-4) mentions less redistributive tax and transfer policy as a cause of growing inequality in the USA, so the Standard Text mentions the idea.
46 Feldstein (1999: 34).
47 Colander (2020: 513).
48 Marglin (2008: 180).
49 Feldstein (1999: 34).
50 Amiel and Cowell (1999: 54). Orchard and Stretton (1997: 420) add a more subtle point: 'If the rich get richer, they bid up the prices of limited resources (land, location, positional goods) against the poor.'
51 Ibid.: 64; 120.
52 Colander (2020: 166) is exceptional in stating this clearly, pointing out that one Pareto optimal position would be for one person to have all the world's income and everyone else nothing.
53 Hirschman (1991: 2).
54 Ibid.: 81.
55 Ibid.: 115.
56 Okun (1975: 101).

57 Le Grand (1991: 30).
58 Ibid.: 31.
59 Ibid.: 35–6. 11 The policy change is a reduction in a guaranteed minimum annual income and a reduction in the tax rate on labour. income.
60 Ibid.: 32.
61 This and the following paragraphs draw on Atkinson (2015: 243-7).
62 The alternative is lump sum or poll taxes, taxes which don't depend on any decisions individuals make and so are non-distortionary. However, they are not feasible politically (Aldred 2009: 93), nor does the government have the information to implement them.
63 Atkinson (2015: 254).
64 Ibid.: 262.
65 Osberg (1995).
66 Voitchovsky (2009: 569).
67 Ibid.: 557.
68 Ibid.: 556.
69 Ostry et al. (2019: 107).
70 Myrdal (1973: 40–41).
71 Lindert (2004b: Vol. 2, Ch. 18).
72 Lindert (2006: 236).
73 OECD (2015: 15).
74 Ibid.: 48.
75 Ostry et al. (2019: 102-6).
76 Rodrik (2015: Kindle loc.56).
77 Lindert (2004a: 7).
78 MacLean (2017: xxx; 211).
79 CSDH (2008: 26), ©WHO, reproduced with permission.
80 Marmot (2004: 2).
81 Marmot (2015: 25).
82 See the link in Williams et al. (2020) for details.
83 Wilkinson and Marmot (2003: 12–3).
84 Experiments with rats have shown maternal stress before birth causes worse subsequent health. Otherwise post-natal conditions could be the cause (Wilkinson 2005).
85 Wilkinson (2005: 81ff.) and Wilkinson and Marmot (2003: 15).
86 Marmot (2004: 266).
87 Bird, Pickett, Graham, et al. (2019).
88 Ibid.: 6.
89 Wilkinson and Pickett (2009) and its 2019 sequel *The Inner Level*.
90 Milanovic (2016: 131).
91 Calculated from ourworldindata.org/maternal-mortality, which takes data from the World Bank's World Development Indicators.
92 Calculated from ourworldindata.org/child-mortality.
93 E.g. Singer (2004 and 2019), Pogge (2008).
94 See the development finance data at oecd.org/dac.
95 For suggestions about the most effective international charities, see thelifeyoucansave.org.
96 CSDH (2008).
97 See un.org/sustainabledevelopment/health.

Chapter 10

1 Robinson (1974: 14). Reproduced with permission of the Licensor through PLSclear.
2 Baldwin et al. (1980: 407).
3 Driskill (2012: 20).
4 Hicks (1939); Kaldor (1939).
5 The original compensation principle was stated in terms of unobservable utilities, but it is typically implemented using incomes, as we saw in the last chapter. Hicks and Kaldor made the simplifying assumption that the redistribution of income would not cost anything: total income would remain unchanged.
6 Mankiw (2021: 172).
7 Ragan (2020: 829). This value judgement appears despite his earlier statement: 'Social and distributional concerns may lead to the rational adoption of protectionist policies. But the cost of such protection is a reduction in the country's average living standards', but the gains in equity may offset this (p. 803).
8 Driskill (2008: 2).
9 Rodrik (2018a: 120-121).
10 Kwak (2017: Chapter 8, Kindle location 2784).
11 McLaren and Hakobyan (2016: 741).
12 Helliwell, and Huang (2014: 1501).
13 Ibid.: 1500.
14 Landsburg (2008).
15 Krugman (2008).
16 This is the Heckscher–Ohlin model. Its unrealistic assumptions were mentioned in Chapter 2: all industries are perfectly competitive and all factors can move freely between industries but are unable to move between countries.
17 Acemoglu et al. (2016: S142-S147).
18 For example, Rodrik (2018b).
19 Parkin (2019: 168).
20 Samuelson (2004: 142-143). This is well-known in trade theory. If England has a technological improvement in the production of cloth, Canada experiences a net benefit.
21 Marglin (2008: 278).
22 Ibid.: 274-81. Production is 'outsourced' if contracted out to another company. If 'offshored', it takes place in another country, whether in the same company or not.
23 Ibid.: 280.
24 Gomery and Baumol (2000, 2004).
25 The figure is adapted from Figure 1 in Palley (2006: 11).
26 Gomory and Baumol (2000: 94).
27 Gomory and Baumol (2004: 438).
28 The International Civil Aviation Organization (ICAO) and the International Maritime Organization (IMO).
29 Dasgupta (2007: 121).
30 Ibid.
31 Wolf (2004: 191). Parkin's text (2019: 169) echoes this.

32 McElvaney (2014).
33 Hirsch (2013). See also Beaumont (2019).
34 Puckett appears in CBS (2009). The Basel Action Network promotes adherence to the Basel Convention.
35 Ellis-Petersen (2019).
36 Shawn (1991: 20–21).
37 Fridell et al. (2008: 11–12).
38 Quoted in Chomsky (2007: 175).
39 Pogge (2007: 139).
40 Deardorff and Stern (2002: 418).
41 Stiglitz (2017: 40-42). See also Scherer (2004).
42 Stiglitz (2017: 41).
43 Ibid.: 383, endnote 6. See p. 452.
44 See trade.gov/fta and indiantradeportal.in.
45 Stiglitz (2017: 20).
46 Ibid.
47 Helleiner (1996: 760).
48 Ibid.: 762.
49 Most of the growth took place since 2000.
50 Zucman (2019).
51 Davis and Huttonbeck (1988: 279).
52 Quoted in Chomsky (1987: 94–5) from Smedley's 1935 book is *War is a Racket*.
53 On Iran, Curtis (2003: 303–15). On Guatemala, Schlesinger and Kinzer (1983). On Chile, Hersh (1983: 258–96). Chomsky (1987) explains the broader principles at stake: independent development benefiting the broader population can't be allowed because it would set a bad example that other countries might follow.
54 Amnesty International (2014: 175-180).
55 Ibid.: 174.
56 Global Witness (2020: 6, 9).
57 Global Witness (2019: 15).
58 Driskill (2008: 2).
59 Poole (2004: 4).

Chapter 11

1 Varoufakis (1998: 375). Copyright 1998 from *Foundations of Economics* by Yanis Varoufakis. Reproduced by permission of Taylor and Francis Group, LLC, a division of Informa plc.
2 Krugman and Wells (2021: 16).
3 Marglin (2008: 3).
4 Ibid.
5 Akerlof and Shiller (2009: 168).
6 Wilkinson and Pickett (2009 and 2018).
7 Stiglitz (2003: 274).
8 Lal (2000: 18).
9 Dowd (2000: 14).

10 The ninth edition of Samuelson's principles text, published in 1973, contains all these topics.
11 Simon (1991: 28).
12 Prasch (2008: 8).
13 Marglin (2008).
14 Ibid.: 9.
15 Layard (2020: 322). See Chapter 10 'Community'.
16 Stiglitz (2002: 2).
17 McNeil (2000: 336).
18 Boulding (1966); Daly and Cobb (1994).
19 Marglin (2008: 284).
20 Chomsky (2004: 478).

Chapter 12

1 Oswald and Stern (2019).
2 Kunzig (2009).
3 OECD (2018).
4 Colander (2020: 181).
5 See climateactiontracker.org/global/temperatures/. Accessed July 6, 2021.
6 Stern (2016: 407).
7 Ragan (2020), a Canadian text, is by far the best.
8 McConnell et al. (2021), Colander (2020), and Mankiw (2021).
9 Krugman and Wells (2021: 479).
10 Baumol et al. (2020: 306; 329-330).
11 Case et al. (2020: 331).
12 McEachern (2017: 377); Mankiw (2021: 196; 29).
13 Krugman and Wells (2021: 3).
14 Interacademy Panel on International Issues (2009).
15 Romm (2018: 123-6).
16 Steffen et al. (2018: 8254, 8256, 8257). Mann and Kump (2015: 104-5) and Romm (2018:29-30) are non-technical descriptions.
17 IPCC (2021: 14).
18 Wagner and Weizmann (2015: 55).
19 Frank et al. (2019: 319). Krugman and Wells (2021: 479) and Parkin (2019: 403) use the phrase 'catastrophic climate change' without further detail.
20 Nelson (2018b: 166).
21 Stern (2014: 397).
22 Stern (2018: 15).
23 Ibid. For example, R&D creates a positive externality – knowledge that can be used by others – and so requires subsidies.
24 Ibid.: 13, 14.
25 Mazzucato (2015: 6).
26 Ibid.: 125.
27 European Commission (2019).
28 In these countries, consumers paid 85 percent of the production cost of the fossil fuels in 2019, according to the International Energy Agency: a *-15 percent* carbon tax. See iea.org/topics/energy-subsidies.

29 Wagner and Weizmann (2015: 78).
30 Stern (2018: 14). On the Sustainable Development Goals, see sustainabledevelopment.un.org.
31 Ibid.
32 World Bank (2017: 3).
33 Baumol et al. (2020: 11).
34 Frank et al. (2019: 320).
35 Stern (2015: 250-1).
36 CORE Team (2017: Ch. 4.13).
37 Ibid.: Figure 4.17.
38 Ibid.: Ch. 4.14.
39 Stern (2018: 15).
40 Ostrom (2014: 124).
41 Broome (2012: Kindle loc.1000).
42 Beyond that, you can pay for actions to reduce emissions – 'offsetting' (Ibid.: loc.1072, 1100).
43 Ibid.: loc.1009-15.
44 The current emissions of 3.5 Americans could lead to one extra heat-related death in the coming century. See Milman (2021). The study he cites is freely available in *Nature Communications*.
45 Stern (2016: 314-5).
46 Crouch (2018).
47 Wagner and Weizmann (2015: 131).
48 Leiserowitz et al. (2019: 19).
49 See 'YouGov/Oxfam – Climate Change 191223', January 6, 2020 at yougov. co.uk/topics/politics/explore/issue/Climate_change.
50 In our sample, only Krugman and Wells (2021: 479) manage a few sentences that refer to 'political interference from companies that lobby to get more generous terms', resulting in ineffective carbon prices.
51 American focused books include Oreskes and Conway (2010, Ch.6), Banerjee et al. (2015), Cook et al (2019), Michaels (2020: ch11), and Mann (2021). On Australia, Hamilton (2007) and on Canada, Gutstein (2018) and Taft (2018).
52 Banerjee et al. (2015).
53 Dunlap and McCright (2011).
54 Cook et al. (2019: 7) quoting a 1998 Exxon memo.
55 Oreskes and Conway (2010: 214).
56 Nuccitelli (2013).
57 The next option was 'climate is changing and human activity is partly responsible, together with other factors'. See 'International poll: most expect to feel impact of climate change, many think it will make us extinct', published September 15, 2019 at yougov.co.uk/topics/politics/explore/issue/ Climate_change.
58 Brulle et al. (2020).
59 Brulle (2018: 295; 298).
60 InfluenceMap (2019: 10).
61 Quoted by Marshall (2014: 56, 58).
62 Stoknes (2015: Kindle loc.327).
63 Ibid.: loc.948.
64 See Marshall (2014: 1) on knowing versus believing.

65 Leiserowitz (2019: 16); Washington Post and KFF poll available at kff.org/
     report-section/the-kaiser-family-foundation-washington-post-climate-change-
     survey-main-findings/
66 Stoknes (2015: loc.1192-7).
67 Stern (2015: 304).
68 Stern and Parker (2019).
69 Frank (2020: 261-2).
70 Otto et al. (2020: 2356); Wagner and Zeckhauser (2012).
71 Stoknes (2015: loc.4358).
72 As described in the IPCC's special 2018 report, available at ipcc.ch/sr15/. For
     an accessible introduction, see Buis (2019), part 2.
73 McKie (2016).
74 Frank (2020: 264).

BIBLIOGRAPHY

Acemoglu, D., D. Autor, D. Dorn, G. Hanson, and B. Price (2016) 'Import competition and the great US employment sag of the 2000s', *Journal of Labor Economics* 34(S1, pt. 2): S141–S198.

Ackerman, F. (2002) 'Still dead after all these years: Interpreting the failure of General Equilibrium Theory', *Journal of Economic Methodology*, 9(2): 119–39.

Adler, M. (2010) *Economics for the Rest of Us: Debunking the Science That Makes Life Dismal*, New York: New Press.

Akerlof, G., and W. Dickens (1982) 'The economic consequences of cognitive dissonance', *American Economic Review*, 72(3): 307–19.

Akerlof, G., and R. Shiller (2009) *Animal Spirits: How Human Psychology Drives the Economy and Why It Matters for Global Capitalism*, Princeton, NJ: Princeton University Press.

Akerlof, G., and J. Yellen (1988) 'Fairness and unemployment', *American Economic Review*, 78(2): 44–9.

Akerlof, G., and J. Yellen (1990) 'The fair wage-effort hypothesis and unemployment', *Quarterly Journal of Economics*, 105: 255–83.

Aldred, J. (2009) *The Skeptical Economist: Revealing the Ethics Inside Economics*, London: Earthscan.

Aldred, J. (2019) *Licence to Be Bad: How Economics Corrupted Us*, London: Penguin.

Alpert, A., W. Evans, E. Lieber and D. Powell (2019) 'Origins of the opioid crisis and its enduring impacts', NBER Working Paper No. w26500, available at ssrn.com/abstract=3496477.

Alston, R., J. Kearl and M. Vaughan (1992) 'Is there a consensus among economists in the 1990s?', *American Economic Review*, 82: 203–9.

Amiel, Y., and F. Cowell (1999) *Thinking about Inequality: Personal Judgement and Income Distributions*, Cambridge: Cambridge University Press.

Amnesty International (2014) *Injustice Incorporated: Corporate Abuses and the Human Right to Remedy*, London: Amnesty International.

Angell, M. (2004) *The Truth about the Drug Companies: How They Deceive Us and What to Do about It*, New York: Random House.

Arnott, R. (1995) 'Time for revisionism on rent control', *Journal of Economic Perspectives*, 9: 99–120.

Arnsperger, C., and Y. Varoufakis (2008) 'Neoclassical economics: Three identifying features', in E. Fullbrook (ed.), *Pluralist Economics*, London: Zed Books, pp. 13–25.

Arrow, K. (1959) 'Towards a theory of price adjustment', in M. Abramovitz (ed.), *The Allocation of Economic Resources*, Stanford: Stanford University Press, pp. 41–51.

Atkinson, A. (2015) *Inequality: What Can Be Done?* Cambridge, MA: Harvard University Press.

Badger, G., W. Bickel, L. Giordano, E. Jacobs, G. Loewenstein and L. Marsch (2007) 'Altered states: The impact of immediate craving on the valuation of current and future opioids', *Journal of Health Economics*, 26: 865–76.

Bakan, J. (2004) *The Corporation: The Pathological Pursuit of Profit and Power*, Toronto: Viking Canada.

Bakan, J. (2020) *The New Corporation: How "Good" Corporations Are Bad for Democracy*, Toronto: Allen Lane.

Baldwin, R., J. Mutti and J. D. Richardson (1980) 'Welfare effects on the United States of a significant multilateral tariff reduction', *Journal of International Economics*, 10(3): 405–23.

Balestra, C., and R. Tonkin (2018) 'Inequalities in household wealth across OECD countries: Evidence from the OECD Wealth Distribution Database', Statistics and Data Directorate Working Paper No. 88, Paris: OECD.

Banerjee, N., J. Cushman, Jr, D. Hasemyer and L. Song (2015) *Exxon: The Road Not Taken*, Brooklyn: InsideClimate News.

Bartels, L. (2017) 'Political inequality in affluent democracies: The social welfare deficit', Working Paper No. 5-2017, Vanderbilt University.

Barth, E. (2015) 'Monopsonistic discrimination and the gender wage gap', in Palgrave Macmillan (eds.), *The New Palgrave Dictionary of Economics*, London: Palgrave Macmillan. doi.org/10.1057/978-1-349-95121-5_3010-1.

Basu, K. (2011) *Beyond the Invisible Hand: Groundwork for a New Economics*. Princeton, NJ: Princeton University Press.

Bauman, Y., and E. Rose (2011) 'Selection or indoctrination: Why do economics students donate less than the rest?', *Journal of Economic Behavior & Organization*, 79: 318–47.

Baumol, W., A. Blinder and J. Solow (2020) *Microeconomics: Principles and Policy*, 14th edn, Boston: Cengage.

Baumol, W., and R. Gomory (2001) *Global Trade and Conflicting National Interests*, Cambridge, MA: MIT Press.

Beasley, A., and L. Amir (2007) 'Editorial: Policy on infant formula industry funding, support or sponsorship of articles submitted for publication', *International Breastfeeding Journal*, 2(5): 1–3.

Beaumont, P. (2019) 'Rotten eggs: E-waste from Europe poisons Ghana's food chain', *The Guardian*, 24 April.

Bebchuk, L., and J. Fried (2004) *Pay without Performance: The Unfulfilled Promise of Executive Compensation*, Cambridge, MA: Harvard University Press.

Bird P., K. Pickett, H. Graham et al. (2019) 'Income inequality and social gradients in children's height: A comparison of cohort studies from five high-income countries', *BMJ Paediatrics Open 2019*, 3: e000568.

Blaug, M. (1996) *Economic Theory in Retrospect*, Cambridge: Cambridge University Press.

Blaug, M. (2002) 'Ugly currents in modern economics', in Uskali Mäki (ed.), *Fact and Fiction in Economics: Models, Realism and Social Construction*, Cambridge: Cambridge University Press, pp. 35–56.

Blinder, A., E. Canetti, D. Lebow and J. Rudd (1998) *Asking about Prices: A New Approach to Understanding Price Stickiness*, New York: Russell Sage Foundation.

Boffey, D. (2019) 'Amsterdam to ban petrol and diesel cars and motorbikes by 2030', *The Guardian*, 3 May.

Bok, D. (1993) *The Cost of Talent*, New York: Free Press.

Booth, W. (1974) *Modern Dogma and the Rhetoric of Assent*, Chicago: University of Chicago Press.

Boseley, S. (2008) 'Prozac, used by 40 m people does not work, say scientists', *The Guardian*, 26 February.

Boseley, S. (2017) 'Threats, bullying, lawsuits: Tobacco industry's dirty war for the African market', *The Guardian*, 12 July.

Boseley, S., D.Collyns, K. Lamb and A. Dhillon (2018) 'How children around the world are exposed to cigarette advertising', *The Guardian*, 9 March.

Boulding, K. (1966) 'The economics of the coming Spaceship Earth', in H. Jarret (ed.), *Environmental Quality in a Growing Economy*, Baltimore, MD: Johns Hopkins Press, pp. 1–3.

Bowles, S., R. Edwards, F. Roosevelt and M. Larudee (2018) *Understanding Capitalism: Competition, Command, and Change*, 4th edn, Oxford: Oxford University Press.

Broome, J. (2012) *Climate Matters: Ethics in a Warming World*, New York: W. W. Norton.

Brown, H. (1987) 'Inequality of pay', in Palgrave Macmillan (eds.), *The New Palgrave Dictionary of Economics*, London: Palgrave Macmillan. doi. org/10.1057/978-1-349-95121-5_1122-1.

Brulle, R. (2018) 'The climate lobby: A sectoral analysis of lobbying spending on climate change in the USA, 2000 to 2016', *Climactic Change*, 149: 289–303.

Brulle, R., M. Aronczyk and J. Carmichael (2020) 'Corporate promotion and climate change: An analysis of key variables affecting advertising spending by major oil corporations, 1986–2015,' *Climactic Change*, 159: 87–101.

Buis, A. (2019) 'A degree of concern: Why global temperatures matter', *Global Climate Change*, 19 June, available at climate.nasa.gov/news/2878/a-degree-of-concern-why-global-temperatures-matter/.

Bumas, L. (1999) *Intermediate Microeconomics: Neoclassical and Factually-Oriented Models*, London: Routledge.

Burnett, R., et al. (2018) 'Global estimates of mortality associated with long-term exposure to outdoor fine particulate matter', *Proceedings of the National Academy of Sciences*, 115, 9592–7.

Card, D. (1992a) 'Using the regional variation in wages to measure the effects of the federal minimum wage', *Industrial and Labor Relations Review*, 46: 22–37.

Card, D. (1992b) 'Do minimum wages reduce employment? A case study of California 1987–89', *Industrial and Labor Relations Review*, 46: 38–54.

Card, D., L. Katz and A. Krueger (1994) 'Comment on David Neumark and William Wascher: Employment effects of minimum wages and subminimum wages', *Industrial and Labor Relations Review*, 47: 487–96.

Card, D., and A. Krueger (1994) 'Minimum wages and employment: a case study of the fast food industry in New Jersey and Pennsylvania', *American Economic Review*, 84(4): 772–93.

Card, D., and A. Krueger (1995) *Myth and Measurement: The New Economics of the Minimum Wage*, Princeton, NJ: Princeton University Press.

Card, D., and A. Krueger (2000) 'Minimum wages and employment: A case study of the fast-food industry in New Jersey and Pennsylvania: a reply', *American Economic Review*, 90: 1396–420.

Carpenter, J., P. Matthews and A. Robbett (2017) 'Compensating differentials in experimental labor markets', *Journal of Behavioral and Experimental Economics*, 60: 50–60.

Carrington, D. (2019a) 'Revealed: Air pollution may be damaging "every organ in the body"', *The Guardian*, 17 May.

Carrington, D. (2019b) 'People eat at least 50,000 plastic particles a year, study finds', *The Guardian*, 5 June.

Case, A., and A. Deaton (2020) *Deaths of Despair and the Future of Capitalism*, Princeton, NJ: Princeton University Press.

Case, K., R. Fair and S. Oster (2020) *Principles of Microeconomics*, 13th edn, Boston: Pearson.

CBS News (2009) 'Following the trail of toxic e-waste', *60 Minutes*, 27 August, available at cbsnews.com/news/following-the-trail-of-toxic-e-waste/.

Chamberlin, E. (1933) *The Theory of Monopolistic Competition: A Re-orientation of the Theory of Value*, Cambridge, MA: Harvard University Press.

Chandler, A. D., Jr (1977) *The Visible Hand: The Managerial Revolution in American Business*, Cambridge, MA: Harvard University Press.

Chang, A. C., and P. Li (2021) 'Is economics research replicable? Sixty published papers from thirteen journals say "often not"', *Critical Finance Review*, 10, available at nowpublishers.com/article/Details/CFR-0053.

Chang, H.-J. (2010) *23 Things They Don't Tell You about Capitalism*, London: Bloomsbury.

Chang, H.-J. (2014) *Economics: The User's Guide*, London: Pelican.

Chernomas, R., and I. Hudson (2007) *Social Murder and Other Shortcomings of Conservative Economics*, Winnipeg: Arbeiter Ring.

Chomsky, N. (1987) *Turning the Tide: The US and Latin America*, 2nd rev. edn, Montreal: Black Rose Books.

Chomsky, N. (2004) *Language and Politics*, expanded 2nd edn (ed. C. P. Otero), Edinburgh: AK Books.

Chomsky, N. (2006) *Failed States: The Abuse of Power and the Assault on Democracy*, New York: Metropolitan Books.

Chomsky, N. (2007) *Interventions*, San Francisco: City Lights Books.

Chomsky, N., and R. Pollin with C. Polychroniou (2020) *Climate Crisis and the Global Green New Deal*, London: Verso Books.

Christiansen, P., A. Scheuermann, K. Loeffler and B. Helms (2019) 'Closed-loop recycling of plastics enabled by dynamic covalent diketoenamine bonds', *Nature Chemistry*, 11: 442–8.

Cipriani, G., D. Lubian and A. Zago (2009) 'Natural born economists?', *Journal of Economic Psychology*, 30: 455–68.

Clark, J. B. (1891) 'Distribution as determined by a law of rent', *Quarterly Journal of Economics*, 5: 289–318.

Cohen, A. (1983) ' "The laws of returns under competitive conditions": Progress in microeconomics since Sraffa (1926)?', *Eastern Economic Journal*, 9(3): 213–20.

Cohen, A. (1996) 'Why haven't introductory textbooks resolved Sraffa's 1926 complaints? The realism of U-shaped cost curves and the dominance of perfect competition', in N. Aslanbengui and M. Naples (eds), *Rethinking Economic Principles: Critical Essays on Introductory Textbooks*, Chicago: Irwin, pp. 81–91.

Cohn, S. (2007) *Reintroducing Macroeconomics: A Critical Approach*, New York: Routledge.

Colander, D. (1992) 'The lost art of economics', *Journal of Economic Perspectives*, 6(3): 191–6.

Colander, D. (2003) 'Caveat lector: Living with the 15% rule', Middlebury College Economics Discussion Paper 03-26.

Colander, D. (2020) *Microeconomics*, 11th edn, Dubuque, IA: McGraw-Hill Education.

Cook, J., G. Supran, S. Lewandowsky, N. Oreskes and E. Maibach (2019) *America Misled: How the Fossil Fuel Industry Deliberately Misled Americans about Climate Change*, Fairfax, VA: George Mason University Center for Climate Change Communication.

CORE Team (2017) *The Economy: Economics for a Changing World*, Oxford: Oxford University Press. Available at core-econ.org/project/core-the-economy/.

Corkery, M. (2019) 'Beverage companies embrace recycling, until it costs them', *New York Times*, 5 July, available at nytimes.com/2019/07/04/business/plastic-recycling-bottle-bills.html.

Costello, C., D. Ovandoa, T. Clavellea et al. (2016) 'Global fishery prospects under contrasting management regimes', *Proceedings of the National Academy of Sciences*, 113(18): 5125–9.

Cowen, T., and A. Tabarrok (2021) *Modern Principles of Economics*, 5th edn, New York: Worth.

Crouch, D. (2018) 'The Swedish 15-year-old who's cutting class to fight the climate crisis', *The Guardian*, September 1.

CSDH (Commission on the Social Determinants of Health) (2008) *Closing the Gap in a Generation: Health Equity through Action on the Social Determinants of Health*, Geneva: World Health Organization.

Curtis, M. (2003) *Web of Deceit: Britain's Real Role in the World*, London: Vintage.

Daly, H., and J. Cobb (1994) *For the Common Good*, Boston: Beacon Press.

Darley, J., and D. Latane (1968) 'Bystander intervention in emergencies: Diffusion of responsibility', *Journal of Personality and Social Psychology*, 8: 377–83.

Dasgupta, P. (2007) *Economics: A Very Short Introduction*, Oxford: Oxford University Press.

Davis, A. (1998) 'Masked racism: Reflections on the prison-industrial complex', *ColorLines*, 10 September, available at www.colorlines.com/articles/masked-racism-reflections-prison-industrial-complex.

Davis, L., and R. Huttenback (1988) *Mammon and the Pursuit of Empire: The Economics of British Imperialism*, abridged edn, Cambridge: Cambridge University Press.

Dawnay, E., and H. Shah (2005) *Behavioural Economics: Seven Principles for Policy Makers*, London: New Economics Foundation.

Deardorff, A., and R. R. Stern (2002) 'What you should know about globalization and the World Trade Organization', *Review of International Economics*, 10(3): 404–23.

Deaton, A. (2008) 'Income, health and well-being around the world: Evidence from the Gallup World Poll', *Journal of Economic Perspectives*, 22(2): 53–72.

Dewald, W., J. Thursby and R. Anderson (1986) 'Replication in empirical economics: The *Journal of Money, Credit and Banking* Project', *American Economic Review*, 76(4): 587–603.

Díaz, S., J. Settele, E. Brondízio et al. (2019) 'Summary for policymakers of the global assessment report on biodiversity and ecosystem

services of the Intergovernmental Science-Policy Platform on
    Biodiversity and Ecosystem Services', available at ipbes.net/
    global-assessment-report-biodiversity-ecosystem-services.

Dixon, H. (1990) 'Equilibrium and explanation', in J. Creedy (ed.), *Foundations of
    Economic Thought*, Oxford: Blackwell, pp. 356–93.

Dizik, A. (2018) 'When it makes sense to pollute and how to
    change the equation', *Chicago Booth Review*, 28 August,
    available at review.chicagobooth.edu/economics/2018/article/
    when-it-makes-sense-pollute-and-how-change-equation.

Dolar, V. (2013) 'The treatment of minimum wage in undergraduate economics
    textbooks revisited', *International Journal of Pluralism and Economics Education*,
    4(2): 157–82.

Dorman, P. (2014) *Microeconomics: A Fresh Start*, Heidelberg: Springer.

Doucouliagos, H., and T. D. Stanley (2009) 'Publication selection bias in
    minimum-wage research? A meta-regression analysis', *British Journal of
    Industrial Relations*, 47(2): 406–28.

Douglas, M. (1987) 'Wants', in Palgrave Macmillan (eds.), *New Palgrave
    Dictionary of Economics*, New York: Palgrave Macmillan. doi.
    org/10.1057/978-1-349-95121-5_1709-1.

Dow, G. (2003) *Governing the Firm: Workers' Control in Theory and Practice*,
    Cambridge: Cambridge University Press.

Dowd, D. (2000) *Capitalism and Its Economics: A Critical History*,
    London: Pluto Press.

Downs, A. (1957) *An Economic Theory of Democracy*, New York: Harper and Row.

Dragusanu, R., D. Giovannucci and N. Nunn (2014) 'The economics of fair trade',
    Journal of Economic Perspectives, 28(3): 217–36.

Driskill, R. (2008) 'Why do economists make such dismal arguments about
    trade?', *Foreign Policy*, 27 May, available at foreignpolicy.com/2008/05/27/
    why-do-economists-make-such-dismal-arguments-about-trade/.

Driskill, R. (2012) 'Deconstructing the argument for free trade: A case study of the
    role of economists in policy debates', *Economics and Philosophy*, 28(1): 1–30.

Drutman, L. (2015) *The Business of America Is Lobbying*. New York: Oxford
    University Press.

Duarte, F. (2019) 'It takes a CEO just days to earn your annual
    wage', *Worklife*, 9 January, available at bbc.com/worklife/
    article/20190108-how-long-it-takes-a-ceo-to-earn-more-than-you-do-in-a-year.

Dunlap, R., and A. McCright (2011) 'Organized climate change denial', in J. Dryzek,
    R. Norgaard and D. Schlosberg (eds), *The Oxford Handbook of Climate Change
    and Society*, Oxford: Oxford University Press, pp. 144–60.

Earle, J., C. Moran and Z. Ward-Perkins (2017) *The Econocracy: The Perils of Leaving
    Economics to the Experts*, Manchester: Manchester University Press.

Easterlin, R. (1995) 'Will raising the incomes of all increase the happiness of all?',
    Journal of Economic Behavior and Organization, 27(1): 35–47.

Easterlin, R. (2001) 'Income and happiness: Towards a unified theory', *Economic
    Journal*, 111(473): 465–84.

Easterlin, R. (2005) 'Diminishing marginal utility of income? Caveat emptor',
    Social Indicators Research, 70 (3): 243–55.

Easterlin, R. (2017) 'Paradox lost?', *Review of Behavioral Economics*, 4(4): 311–39.

Easterlin, R., L. McVey, M. Switek, O. Sawangfa and J. Zweig (2010) 'The happiness–income paradox revisited', *Proceedings of the National Academy of Sciences*, 107(52): 22463–8.

Easterlin, R., F. Wang and S. Wang (2017) 'Growth and happiness in China, 1998–2015', in J. Helliwell, R. Layard and J. Sachs (eds), *World Happiness Report 2017*, New York: Sustainable Development Solutions Network, pp. 48–83.

Economist Intelligence Unit (2017) 'The impacts of banning advertising directed at children in Brazil', August. Available at graphics.eiu.com/upload/pp/EIU-Alana-Report-WEB-FINAL.pdf.

Edlin, A., and P. Karaca-Mandic (2006) 'The accident externality from driving', *Journal of Political Economy*, 114(5): 931–55.

Ellis-Petersen, H. (2018) 'Philippines launches inquiry into formula milk firms targeting poor', *The Guardian*, 28 February.

Ellis-Petersen, H. (2019) 'Treated like trash: South-east Asia vows to return mountains of rubbish from west', *The Guardian*, 28 May.

Eeckhout, J. (2021) *The Profit Paradox: How Thriving Firms Threaten the Future of Work*, Princeton: Princeton University Press.

Engels, F. ([1845] 1987) *The Condition of the Working Class in England*, London: Penguin.

Etheridge, D. M., L. P. Steele, R. L. Langenfelds, R. J. Francey, J. M. Barnola and V. I. Morgan (1998), Historical CO_2 Records from the Law Dome DE08, DE08-2, and DSS Ice Cores (1006 A.D.–1978 A.D). Carbon Dioxide Information Analysis Center, Oak Ridge National Laboratory, Oak Ridge, TN, United States. DOI:10.3334/CDIAC/ATG.011.

European Commission (2019) 'The European Green Deal', COM(2019) 640, Brussels: European Commission. Available at ec.europa.eu/info/publications/communication-european-green-deal_en.

FAO, IFAD, UNICEF, WFP and WHO (2018) *The State of Food Security and Nutrition in the World 2018: Building Climate Resilience for Food Security and Nutrition*, Rome, FAO.

Fehr, E., and K. Schmidt (2006) 'The economics of fairness, reciprocity and altruism – experimental evidence and new theories', in S.-C. Kolm and J. M. Ythier (eds), *Handbook of the Economics of Giving, Altruism and Reciprocity*, vol. 1, Amsterdam: Elsevier, pp. 615–91.

Feldstein, M. (1999) 'Reducing poverty, not inequality', *Public Interest*, 137: 33–41.

Fine, B. (2016) *Microeconomics: A Critical Companion*, London: Pluto Press.

Frank, R. (1984) 'Are workers paid their marginal products?', *American Economic Review*, 74(4): 549–71.

Frank, R. (1985) *Choosing the Right Pond: Human Behavior and the Quest for Status*, Oxford: Oxford University Press.

Frank, R. (1989) *Passions within Reason: The Strategic Role of the Emotions*, New York: W. W. Norton.

Frank, R. (1997) 'The frame of reference as a public good', *Economic Journal*, 107: 1832–47.

Frank, R. (1999) *Luxury Fever: Why Money Fails to Satisfy in an Era of Excess*, New York: Free Press.

Frank, R. (2003) *What Price the Moral High Ground? How to Succeed without Selling Your Soul*, Princeton, NJ: Princeton University Press.

Frank, R. (2005) 'Positional externalities cause large and preventable welfare losses', *American Economic Review*, 95(2): 137–41.

Frank, R. (2020) *Under the Influence: Putting Peer Pressure to Work*, Princeton, NJ: Princeton University Press.

Frank, R., B. Bernanke, K. Antonovics and O. Heffetz (2019) *Principles of Microeconomics*, 7th edn, New York: McGraw-Hill.

Frank, R., and P. J. Cook (1995) *The Winner-Take-All Society*, New York: Penguin.

Frank, R., T. Gilovich and D. Regan (1993) 'Does studying economics inhibit cooperation?', *Journal of Economic Perspectives*, 7(2): 159–71.

Frey, B., and S. Meier (2003) 'Are political economists selfish and indoctrinated? Evidence from a natural experiment', *Economic Inquiry*, 41(3): 448–62.

Fridell, M., I. Hudson and M. Hudson (2008) 'With friends like these: The corporate response to fair trade coffee', *Review of Radical Political Economics*, 40(1): 8–34.

Friedman, M. (1953) *Essays in Positive Economics*, Chicago: University of Chicago Press.

Friedman, M. (1970) 'The social responsibility of business is to increase its profits', *New York Times Magazine*, 13 September.

Friedman, M. (1976) *Price Theory*, Chicago: Aldine.

Fuller, D., and D. Geide-Stevenson (2003) 'Consensus among economists: Revisited', *Journal of Economic Education*, 34(4): 369–87.

Fuller, D., and D. Geide-Stevenson (2014) 'Consensus among economists – an update', *Journal of Economic Education*, 45(2): 131–46.

Galbraith, James K. (2008) *The Predator State: How Conservatives Abandoned the Free Market and Why Liberals Should Too*, New York: Free Press.

Galbraith, John K. (1958) *The Affluent Society*, London: Hamish Hamilton.

Galbraith, John K. (1973) 'Power and the useful economist', *American Economic Review*, 63(1): 1–11.

Galbraith, John K. (2004) *The Economics of Innocent Fraud: Truth for Our Time*, New York: Houghton Mifflin.

Gehl, K., and M. Porter (2017) 'Why competition in the politics industry is failing America', Harvard Business School.

George, D. (1990) 'The rhetoric of economics texts', *Journal of Economic Issues*, 24(3): 861–78.

George, D. (1996) 'The rhetoric of economics texts revisited', in N. Aslanbeigui and M. Naples (eds), *Rethinking Economic Principles: Critical Essays on Introductory Textbooks*, Chicago: Richard D. Irwin, pp. 28–43.

Geyer, R., J. Jambeck and K. Law (2017) 'Production, use, and fate of all plastics ever made', *Science Advances*, 3(7): e1700782.

Gigerenzer, G. (2008) *Rationality for Mortals: How People Cope with Uncertainty*, Oxford: Oxford University Press.

Gilbert, N. (2019) 'World's rivers "awash with dangerous levels of antibiotics"', *Guardian*, 27 May.

Gilens, M., and B. Page (2014) 'Testing theories of American politics: Elites, interest groups, and average citizens', *Perspectives on Politics*, 12(3): 564–80.

Gillam, C. (2017) *Whitewash: The Story of a Weed Killer, Cancer, and the Corruption of Science*, Washington, DC: Island Press.

Glenza, J. (2017) 'Tobacco companies tighten hold on Washington under Trump', *The Guardian*, 13 July.

Global Witness (2019) *Enemies of the State? How Governments and Business Silence Land and Environmental Defenders*, available at globalwitness.org/en/campaigns/environmental-activists/enemies-state/.

Global Witness (2020) *Defending Tomorrow: The Climate Crisis and Threats against Land and Environmental Defenders*, available at globalwitness.org/en/campaigns/environmental-activists/defending-tomorrow/.

Gneezy, U., and A. Rustichini (2000) 'A fine is a price', *Journal of Legal Studies*, 29(1, pt. 1): 1–18.

Goldacre, B. (2013) *Bad Pharma: How Drug Companies Mislead Doctors and Harm Patients*, New York: Random House.

Gomory, R., and W. Baumol (2000) *Global Trade and Conflicting National Interests*, Cambridge, MA: MIT Press.

Gomory, R., and W. Baumol (2004) 'Globalization: prospects, promise and problems', *Journal of Policy Modeling*, 26: 425–38.

Goodhue, R., and C. Russo (2012) 'Modeling processor market power and the incidence of agricultural policy: A nonparametric approach', in G. Zivin, S. Joshua and J. Perloff (eds), *The Intended and Unintended Effects of US Agricultural and Biotechnology Policies*, Chicago: University of Chicago Press, pp. 51–81.

Goodwin, N. (2010) 'Good business', *Our Planet*, February, 28–31.

Goodwin, N., J. Harris, J. Nelson, B. Roach and M. Torras (2019) *Microeconomics in Context*, 4th edn, New York: Routledge.

Gordon, H. S. (1954) 'The economic theory of a common-property resource: The fishery', *Journal of Political Economy*, 62(2): 124–42.

Green, C., J. Heywood and M. Navarro (2016) 'Traffic accidents and the London congestion charge', *Journal of Public Economics*, 133: 11–22.

Green, F., S. Matchin and A. Manning (1996) 'The employer size-wage effect: Can dynamic monopsony provide an explanation?', *Oxford Economic Papers*, 38: 433–55.

Greenhalgh, S. (2019) 'Making China safe for Coke: How Coca-Cola shaped obesity science and policy in China', *British Medical Journal*, 9 January.

Greenstone, M., and C. Fan (2018) *Introducing the Air Quality Life Index*, Chicago: Energy Policy Institute at the University of Chicago.

Gutstein, D. (2018) *The Big Stall: How Big Oil and Think Tanks Are Blocking Action on Climate Change in Canada*, Toronto: Lorimer.

Gwartney, J., R. Stroup, R. Sobel and D. Macpherson (2018) *Microeconomics: Private and Public Choice*, 16th edn, Boston: Cengage Learning.

Hahn, F. (1987) 'Review of *The Rhetoric of Economics*', *Journal of Economic Literature*, 25(1): 110–11.

Hall, B., and K. Murphy (2003) 'The trouble with stock options', *Journal of Economic Perspectives*, 17(3): 49–70.

Hämäläinen, P., J. Takala and T. Kiat (2017) *Global Estimates of Occupational Accidents and Work-Related Illnesses 2017*, Singapore: Workplace Safety and Health Institute.

Hamilton, C. (2007) *Scorcher: The Dirty Politics of Climate Change*, Melbourne: Black Inc. Agenda.

Harberger, A. (1954) 'Monopoly and resource allocation', *American Economic Review*, 44: 77–87.

Häring, N., and N. Douglas (2012) *Economists and the Powerful: Convenient Theories, Distorted Facts, Ample Rewards*, London: Anthem Press.

Hartung, A. (2015) 'Why CEOs make so much money', *Forbes*, 22 June, available at forbes.com/sites/adamhartung/2015/06/22/why-ceos-make-so-much-money.

Harvey, F. (2018) 'India's farmed chickens dosed with world's strongest antibiotics, study finds', *The Guardian*, 1 February.

Harvey, F. (2019) 'Antibiotic resistance as big a threat as climate change – chief medic', *The Guardian*, 29 April.

Hay, D., and D. Morris (1991) *Industrial Economics and Organisation: Theory and Evidence*, Oxford: Oxford University Press.

Healy, D. (2006) *Let Them Eat Prozac: The Unhealthy Relationship between the Pharmaceutical Industry and Depression*, New York: New York University Press.

Helleiner, G. (1996) 'Why small countries worry: Neglected issues in current analyses of the benefits and costs for small countries of integrating with large ones', *World Economy*, 19(6): 759–63.

Helliwell, J. (2003) 'How's life? Combining individual and national variables to explain subjective well-being', *Economic Modelling*, 20: 331–60.

Helliwell, J., and H. Huang (2011) 'Well-being and trust in the workplace', *Journal of Happiness Studies*, 12: 747–67.

Helliwell, J., and H. Huang (2014) 'New measures on the costs of unemployment: Evidence from the subjective well-being of 3.3 million Americans', *Economic Inquiry*, 52(4): 1485–502.

Helliwell, J., H. Huang and S. Wang (2018) 'New evidence on trust and well-being', in E. M. Uslaner (ed.), *The Oxford Handbook of Social and Political Trust*. Oxford: Oxford University Press, pp. 409–46.

Helliwell, J., H. Huang, S. Wang and M. Norton (2020) 'Social environments for world happiness', in J. F. Helliwell, R. Layard, J. Sachs and J.-E. De Neve (eds), *World Happiness Report 2020*, New York: Sustainable Development Solutions Network, pp. 13–46.

Herman, E., and N. Chomsky (1988) *Manufacturing Consent: The Political Economy of the Mass Media*, New York: Pantheon.

Hersh, S. (1983) *The Price of Power: Kissinger in the Nixon White House*, New York: Summit Books.

Hicks, J. R. (1939) *Value and Capital*, 1st edn, Oxford: Oxford University Press.

Hildenbrand, W., and A. Kirman (1988) *Equilibrium Analysis: Variations on themes by Edgeworth and Walras*, Amsterdam: North-Holland.

Hirsch, A. (2013) '"This is not a good place to live": Inside Ghana's dump for electronic waste', *The Guardian*, 14 December.

Hirschman, A. (1991) *The Rhetoric of Reaction: Perversity, Futility, Jeopardy*, Cambridge, MA: Belknap Press of Harvard University Press.

Hudson, M., I. Hudson and M. Fridell (2013). *Fair Trade, Sustainability, and Social Justice*, New York: Palgrave Macmillan.

Igielnik, R. (2020) '70% of Americans say U.S. economic system unfairly favors the powerful', *FactTank*, 9 January, available at pewresearch.org/fact-tank/2020/01/09/70-of-americans-say-u-s-economic-system-unfairly-favors-the-powerful.

InfluenceMap (2019) 'Big oil's real agenda on climate change', London: InfluenceMap, available at influencemap.org/report/How-Big-Oil-Continues-to-Oppose-the-Paris-Agreement-38212275958aa21196dae3b76220bddc.

Interacademy Panel on International Issues (2009) *IAP Statement on Ocean Acidification*, available at interacademies.org/statement/iap-statement-ocean-acidification.

Interagency Coordination Group on Antimicrobial Resistance (2019) *No Time to Wait: Securing the Future from Drug-Resistant Infections*. Report to the Secretary-General of the United Nations. Available at who.int/antimicrobial-resistance/interagency-coordination-group/final-report/en/.

International Labour Organization (2019) *Safety and Health at the Heart of the Future of Work*, Geneva: ILO.

Ioannidis, J., T. Stanley and H. Doucouliagos (2017) 'The power of bias in economics research', *Economic Journal*, 127(October): F236–F265.

IPCC (2021) 'Summary for Policymakers', in V. Masson-Delmotte, P. Zhai, A. Pirani, S. L. Connors, C. Péan, S. Berger, N. Caud, Y. Chen, L. Goldfarb, M. I. Gomis, M. Huang, K. Leitzell, E. Lonnoy, J. B. R. Matthews, T. K. Maycock, T. Waterfield, O. Yelekçi, R. Yu and B. Zhou (eds.), *Climate Change 2021: The Physical Science Basis. Contribution of Working Group I to the Sixth Assessment Report of the Intergovernmental Panel on Climate Change*, Cambridge: Cambridge University Press.

Jacobs, A. (2019) 'How chummy are junk food giants and China's health officials? They share offices', *New York Times*, 9 January.

Jardim, E., M. Long, R. Plotnick, E. van Inwegen, J. Vigdor and H. Wething (2017) 'Minimum wage increases, wages, and low-wage employment: Evidence from Seattle', National Bureau of Economic Research Working Paper No. 35532.

Jebb, A., L. Tay, E. Diener and S. Oishi, (2018) 'Happiness, income satiation and turning points around the world', *Nature Human Behaviour*, 2(January): 33–8.

Kahneman, D. (2002) 'Maps of bounded rationality: A perspective on intuitive judgement and choice', Nobel Memorial Prize Lecture, December.

Kahneman, D. (2013) *Thinking, Fast and Slow*, New York: Farrar, Straus and Giroux.

Kahneman, D., and A. Deaton (2010) 'High income improves evaluation of life but not emotional well-being', *Proceedings of the National Academy of Sciences*, 107(38): 16489–93.

Kahneman, D., J. Knetsch and R. Thaler (1986) 'Fairness as a constraint on profit seeking: Entitlements in the market', *American Economic Review*, 76(4): 728–41.

Kaldor, N. (1939) 'Welfare propositions and interpersonal comparisons of utility', *Economic Journal*, 49: 549–52.

Kalmi, P. (2007) 'The disappearance of cooperatives from economics textbooks', *Cambridge Journal of Economics*, 31(4): 625–47.

Kalra, A., P.Bansal, D. Wilson and T. Lasseter (2017) 'Inside Philip Morris' campaign to subvert the global antismoking treaty', *Reuters*, 13 July.

Katz, L., and A. Krueger (1992) 'The effect of the minimum wage in the fast food industry', *Industrial and Labor Relations Review*, 46: 6–21.

Kay, J. (2010) *Obliquity: Why Our Goals Are Best Achieved Indirectly*, New York: Penguin.

Kearl, J., C. Pope, G. Whiting and L. Whimmer (1979) 'A confusion of economists', *American Economic Review*, 69(2): 28–37.

Kelman, S. (1987) '"Public choice" and public spirit', *Public Interest*, 87: 80–94.

Keynes, J. M. (1936) *The General Theory of Employment, Interest and Money*, London: Macmillan.

Keynes, J. M. ([1931] 1963) 'Economic possibilities for our grandchildren', in *Essays in Persuasion*, New York: W. W. Norton, pp. 278–91.

King, J. (2002) *A History of Post-Keynesian Economics Since 1936*, Cheltenham: Edward Elgar.

Knack, S., and P. Keefer (1997) 'Does social capital have an economic payoff? A cross-country investigation', *Quarterly Journal of Economics*, 112: 1251–88.

Kolbert, E. (2014) *The Sixth Extinction: An Unnatural History*, New York: Henry Holt.

Komlos, J. (2015) *What Every Economics Student Needs to Know and Doesn't Get in the Usual Principles Text*, 1st edn, New York: Taylor and Francis.

Kroszner, S., and L. Putterman (2009) 'Reintroducing the economic nature of the firm', in R. S. Kroszner and L. Putterman (eds), *The Economic Nature of the Firm: A Reader*, 3rd edn, Cambridge: Cambridge University Press, pp. 1–32.

Krueger, A. (2001) 'Teaching the minimum wage in Econ 101 in light of the new economics of the minimum wage', *Journal of Economic Education*, 32: 243–58.

Krueger, A. (2008) 'Comment', *Brookings Papers on Economic Activity*, Spring: 95–100.

Krugman, P. (2008) 'Trade and wages, reconsidered', *Brookings Papers on Economic Activity*, 1: 103–37.

Krugman, P., M. Obstfeld and M. Melitz (2018) *International Trade: Theory and Policy*, Boston: Pearson Education.

Krugman, P., and R. Wells (2021) *Microeconomics*, 6th edn, New York: Worth.

Kuhn, T. (1962) *The Structure of Scientific Revolutions*, Chicago: University of Chicago Press.

Kunzig, R. (2009) 'The Carbon Bathtub', *National Geographic*, December, 26–8.

Kwak, J. (2016) *Economism: Bad Economics and the Rise of Inequality*, New York: Knopf Doubleday.

Lakatos, I. (1978) *The Methodology of Scientific Research Programmes: Philosophical Papers*, vol. 1, ed. J. Worrall and G. Currie, Cambridge: Cambridge University Press.

Lal, D. (2000) *The Poverty of 'Development Economics'*, Cambridge, MA: MIT Press.

Landrigan, P., et al. (2018) 'The Lancet Commission on pollution and health', *The Lancet*, 391, 464–512.

Landsburg, S. (2008) 'What to expect when you're free trading', *New York Times*, 16 January.

Laville, S., and M. Taylor (2017) 'A million bottles a minute: World's plastic binge "as dangerous as climate change"', *The Guardian*, 18 June.

Lavoie, M. (2006) *Introduction to Post-Keynesian Economics*, Houndsmills: Palgrave Macmillan.

Lavoie, M. (2014) *Post-Keynesian Economics: New Foundations*, Cheltenham: Edward Elgar.

Lawrence, F. (2008) *Eat Your Heart Out: Why the Food Business Is Bad for the Planet and Your Health*, London: Penguin.

Lawrence, F. (2014) *Not on the Label: What Really Goes into the Food on Your Plate*, 2nd edn, London: Penguin.

Layard, R., with G. Ward (2020) *Can We Be Happier? Evidence and Ethics*, London: Penguin.

Lazear, E., and S. Rosen (1981) 'Rank-order tournaments as optimum labor contracts', *Journal of Political Economy*, 89(5): 841–61.

Le Grand, J. (1991) *Equity and Choice: An Essay in Economics and Applied Philosophy*, London: HarperCollins.

Leacock, S. (1924) *The Garden of Folly*, New York: Dodd, Mead.

Leamer, E. (2012) *The Craft of Economics: Lessons from the Heckscher-Ohlin Framework*, Cambridge, MA: MIT Press.

Leibenstein, H. (1966) 'Allocative efficiency v. X-efficiency', *American Economic Review*, 56: 392–415.

Lelieveld, J., K. Klingmüller, A. Pozzer, U. Pöschl, M. Fnais, A. Daiber and T. Münzel (2019) 'Cardiovascular disease burden from ambient air pollution in Europe reassessed using novel hazard ratio functions', *European Heart Journal*, 40(20), 1590–6.

Leonhardt, D. (2005) 'Why variable pricing fails at the vending machine', *New York Times*, 27 June.

Leiserowitz, A., et al. (2019). *Climate Change in the American Mind: November 2019*. Yale University and George Mason University. New Haven, CT: Yale Program on Climate Change Communication.

Leontief, W. (1983) 'Foreword', in A. Eichner (ed.), *Why Economics Is Not Yet a Science*, New York: M. E. Sharpe, pp. ix–xiv.

Levine, D. (2001) 'Editor's introduction to "The employment effects of minimum wages: Evidence from a prespecified research design" ', *Industrial Relations*, 40: 161–2.

Linder, S. (1970) *The Harried Leisure Class*, New York: Columbia University Press.

Lindert, P. (2004a) 'Social spending and economic growth. Interview with Peter Lindert', *Challenge*, 47(4): 6–16.

Lindert, P. (2004b) *Growing Public: Social Spending and Economic Growth since the Eighteenth Century*, 2 vols, Cambridge: Cambridge University Press.

Lindert, P. (2006) 'The welfare state is the wrong target: A reply to Bergh', *Econ Journal Watch*, 3(2): 236–50.

Lipsey, R., and K. Lancaster (1956/57) 'The general theory of the second best', *Review of Economic Studies*, 24(1): 11–32.

Littlechild, S. (1981) 'Misleading calculations of the social costs of monopoly power', *Economic Journal*, 91: 348–63.

Lunn, P., and T. Harford (2008) 'Behavioural economics: Is it such a big deal?', *Prospect Magazine*, 150(September). prospectmagazine.co.uk/magazine/behaviouraleconomicsisitsuchabigdeal.

Mäki, U. (2000) 'Kinds of assumptions and their truth: shaking an untwisted F-twist', *Kyklos*, 53: 317–36.

Malleson, T. (2014) *After Occupy: Economic Democracy for the 21st Century*, Oxford: Oxford University Press.

Mankiw, N. G. (2021) *Principles of Microeconomics*, 9th edn, Boston: Cengage.

Mann, M. (2021) *The New Climate War: The Fight to Take the Planet*, New York: PublicAffairs.

Mann, M., and L. Kump (2015) *Dire Predictions: Understanding Climate Change*, 2nd edn, New York: DK.

Manning, A. (2003) *Monopsony in Motion: Imperfect Competition in Labor Markets*, Princeton, NJ: Princeton University Press.

Manning, A. (2011) 'Imperfect competition in the labor market', in O. Ashenfelter and D. Card (eds), *Handbook of Labor Economics*, vol. 4b, Amsterdam: North Holland, pp. 973–1041.

Mansfield, E. (1994) *Microeconomics*, 8th edn, New York: W. W. Norton.

Marglin, S. (2008) *The Dismal Science: How Thinking Like an Economist Undermines Community*, Cambridge, MA: Harvard University Press.

Marmot, M. (2004) *The Status Syndrome: How Social Standing Affects Our Health and Longevity*, New York: Times Books.

Marmot, M. (2015) *The Health Gap: The Challenge of an Unequal World*, London: Bloomsbury.

Marshall, G. (2014) *Don't Even Think about It: Why Our Brains Are Wired to Ignore Climate Change*, New York: Bloomsbury.

Marwell, G., and R. Ames (1981) 'Economists free ride, does anyone else? Experiments on the provision of public goods', *Journal of Public Economics*, 15: 295–310.

Marx, K., and F. Engels ([1848] 2012) *The Communist Manifesto*, ed. J. Isaac, New Haven, CT: Yale University Press.

Maye, A. (2019) 'No-vacation nation, revised', Washington, DC: Center for Economic and Policy Research, available at www.cepr.net/report/no-vacation-nation-revised/.

Mayer, J. (2016) *Dark Money: The Hidden History of the Billionaires behind the Rise of the Radical Right*, New York: Doubleday.

Mazzucato, M. (2015) *The Entrepreneurial State: Debunking Public vs. Private Sector Myths*, New York: Public Affairs.

Mazzucato, M. (2021) *Mission Economy: A Moonshot Guide to Changing Capitalism*, New York: Harper Business.

McCloskey, D. (1998) *The Rhetoric of Economics*, 2nd edn, Madison: University of Wisconsin Press.

McConnell, C., S. Brue, and S. Flynn (2021) *Microeconomics: Principles, Problems, and Policies*, 22nd edn, New York: McGraw-Hill.

McCullough, B., K. McGeary and T. Harrison (2006) 'Lessons from the JMCB archive', *Journal of Money, Credit and Banking*, 38(4): 1093–107.

McEachern, W. (2017) *Microeconomics: A Contemporary Introduction*, 11th edn, Boston: Cengage Learning.

McElvaney, K. (2014) 'Agbogbloshie: The world's largest e-waste dump – in pictures', *The Guardian*, 27 February.

McKie, R. (2016) 'Nicholas Stern: Cost of global warming "is worse than I feared"', *The Guardian*, 6 November.

McLaren, J., and S. Hakobyan (2016) 'Looking for local labor-market effects of NAFTA', *Review of Economics and Statistics*, 98(4): 728–41.

McNeil, J. (2000) *Something New under the Sun: An Environmental History of the Twentieth Century*, New York: W. W. Norton.

McPherson, M. (1987) 'Changes in tastes', in Palgrave Macmillan (eds.), *New Palgrave Dictionary of Economics*, New York: Palgrave Macmillan. doi. org/10.1057/978-1-349-95121-5_305-1.

Meier, B. (2018) *Pain Killer: An Empire of Deceit and the Origin of America's Opioid Epidemic*, New York: Random House.

Michaels, D. (2020) *The Triumph of Doubt: Dark Money and the Science of Deception*, Oxford: Oxford University Press.

Milanovic, B. (2016) *Global Inequality: A New Approach for the Age of Globalization*, Cambridge, MA: Harvard University Press.

Mill, J. S. (1965) *Collected Works*, vol. 3: *Principles of Political Economy*, Books III, IV and V, Toronto: University of Toronto Press.

Miller, R. (2000) 'Ten cheaper spades: Production theory and cost curves in the short run', *Journal of Economic Education*, 31(2): 119–30.

Miller, R. (2001) 'Firms' cost functions: A reconstruction', *Review of Industrial Organization*, 18(2): 183–200.

Milman, O. (2021) 'Three Americans create enough carbon emissions to kill one person, study finds', *The Guardian*, July 29.

Mishel, L., and J. Wolfe (2019) *CEO Compensation Has Grown 940% since 1978*, Washington, DC: Economic Policy Institute.

Mondragon (2020). *2019 Annual Report*. Available at mondragon-corporation. com/2019urtekotxostena/?l=en.

Mongiovi, G. (2019) 'Poking a hornets' nest: The debate on *Democracy in Chains*', *Research in the History of Economic Thought and Methodology*, 37B: 177–96.

Moynihan, R., and A. Cassels (2005) *Selling Sickness: How the World's Largest Pharmaceutical Companies Are Turning Us All into Patients*, Vancouver: Greystone Books.

Mullainathan, S., and R. Thaler (2001) 'Behavioural economics', *International Encyclopaedia of the Social and Behavioural Sciences*, Oxford: Pergamon, pp. 1094–100. Available at doi.org/10.1016/B0-08-043076-7/02247-6.

Musgrave, A. (1981) '"Unrealistic assumptions" in economic theory: The F-twist untwisted', *Kyklos*, 34: 377–87.

Myatt, A. (2004) 'Getting the most from a principles discussion of rent control', *Economic Research Network, ERN Educator: Courses, Cases and Teaching*, Abstract no. 485422, 1–17 January.

Myrdal, G. (1969) *Objectivity in Social Research*, New York: Pantheon Books.

Myrdal, G. (1973) *Against the Stream: Critical Essays on Economics*, New York: Pantheon.

Nader, R. (2000) *The Ralph Nader Reader*, New York: Seven Stories Press.

Nader, R. (2004) *The Good Fight: Declare Your Independence and Close the Democracy Gap*, New York: Regan Books.

National Academies of Sciences, Engineering, and Medicine (2017) *Combating Antimicrobial Resistance: A One Health Approach to a Global Threat; Proceedings of a Workshop*. Washington, DC: National Academies Press.

Nelson, J. (2016) 'Poisoning the well, or How economic theory damages moral imagination', in G. DeMartino and D. McCloskey (eds), *The Oxford Handbook of Professional Economic Ethics*, Oxford: Oxford University Press, pp. 184–99.

Nelson, J. (2018a) 'The complicity of economics', *Forum for Social Economics*, 47(2): 214–9.

Nelson, J. (2018b) *Economics for Humans*, 2nd edn, Chicago: University of Chicago Press.

Neumark, D., and W. Wascher (2004) 'Minimum wages, labor market institutions, and youth employment: A crossnational analysis', *Industrial and Labor Relations Review*, 57: 223–48.

Newman, J., B. Gerhart and G. Milkovich (2016) *Compensation*, 12th edn, New York: McGraw-Hill.

Northrop, E. (2000) 'Normative foundations of introductory economics', *American Economist*, 44(1): 53–61.

Northrop, E. (2013) 'The accuracy, market ethic, and individual morality surrounding the profit maximization assumption', *American Economist*, 58(2): 111–23.

Nuccitelli, D. (2013) 'Global warming: Why is IPCC report so certain about the influence of humans?', *The Guardian*, 27 September.

Oi, W., and T. Idson (1999), 'Firm size and wages', in O. Ashenfelter and D. Card (eds), *Handbook of Labor Economics*, vol. 3, Amsterdam: North-Holland, pp. 166–214.

Okun, A. (1975) *Equality and Efficiency: The Big Tradeoff*, Washington, DC: Brookings Institution Press.

Olson, M. (1971) *The Logic of Collective Action: Public Goods and the Theory of Groups*, Cambridge, MA: Harvard University Press.

O'Neill, J. (2016) *Tackling Drug-Resistant Infections Globally: Final Report and Recommendations*. London: Review on Antimicrobial Resistance. Available at amr-review.org/Publications.html.

Orchard, L., and H. Stretton (1997) 'Public Choice', *Cambridge Journal of Economics*, 21: 409–30.

Oreskes, N., and E. Conway (2010). *Merchants of Doubt*, New York: Bloomsbury.

Organization for Economic Cooperation and Development (2015) *In It Together: Why Less Inequality Benefits All*, Paris: OECD.

Organization for Economic Cooperation and Development (2019) *Revenue Statistics 1965–2018*, Paris: OECD.

Osberg, L. (1995) 'The equity–efficiency trade-off in retrospect', *Canadian Business Economics*, 3(3): 5–20.

Ostrom, E. (2000) 'Collective action and the evolution of social norms', *Journal of Economic Perspectives*, 14(3): 137–58.

Ostrom, E. (2005) 'Policies that crowd out reciprocity and collective action', in H. Gintis, S. Bowles, R. Boyd and E. Fehr (eds), *Moral Sentiments and Material Interests: The Foundations of Cooperation in Economic Life*, Cambridge, MA: MIT Press, pp. 253–76.

Ostrom, E. (2012) 'Green from the Grassroots', 12 June, available at project-syndicate.org/commentary/green-from-the-grassroots.

Ostrom, E. (2014) 'A polycentric approach for coping with climate change', *Annals of Economics and Finance*, 15(1): 97–134.

Ostry, J., P. Loungani and A. Berg (2019) *Confronting Inequality: How Societies Can Choose Inclusive Growth*, New York: Columbia University Press.

Oswald, A., and N. Stern (2019) 'Why are economists letting down the world on climate change?', *VoxEU*, 17 September, available at voxeu.org/article/why-are-economists-letting-down-world-climate-change.

Otto, I., J.Donges, R. Cremades et al. (2020) 'Social tipping dynamics for stabilizing Earth's climate by 2050', *Proceedings of the National Academies of Science*, 117(5): 2354–65.

Page, B., and M. Gilens (2020) *Democracy in America?* Chicago: University of Chicago Press.

Palley, T. (2006) *Rethinking Trade and Trade Policy: Gomory, Baumol and Samuelson on Comparative Advantage*, Public Policy Brief 86, Levy Economics Institute of Bard College.

Parkin, M. (2019) *Microeconomics*, 13th edn, Boston: Pearson.

Pawlick, T. (2006) *The End of Food*, Fort Lee, NJ: Barricade Books.

Peppers, M. (2014) 'The iPhone is back! Anna Wintour upgrades her cell after she was spotted with a $15 flip phone', *Daily Mail*, 8 September.

Pigou, A. C. (1932) *The Economics of Welfare*, 4th edn, London: Macmillan.

Piketty, T. (2014) *Capital in the Twenty-First Century*, Cambridge: Belknap Press of Harvard University Press.

Pogge, T. (2007) 'Why inequality matters', in D. Held and A. Kaya (eds), *Global Inequality: Patterns and Explanations*, London: Polity Press, pp. 132–47.

Pogge, T. (2008) *World Poverty and Human Rights*, 2nd edn, London: Polity Press.

Pollak, R. (1978) 'Endogenous tastes in demand and welfare analysis', *American Economic Review*, 68(2): 374–9.

Pollin, R. (2015) *Greening the Global Economy*, Cambridge, MA: MIT Press.

Poole, W. (2004) 'Free trade: Why are economists and noneconomists so far apart?', *Federal Reserve Bank of St Louis Review*, 86(5): 1–6.

Prasch, R. (2008) *How Markets Work: Supply, Demand and the 'Real World'*, Cheltenham: Edward Elgar.

Proctor, J. C., L. Fischer, J. Hasell, D. Uwakwe, Z. Ward-Perkins and C. Watson (eds.) (2018), *Rethinking Economics: An Introduction to Pluralist Economics*, New York: Routledge.

Purse, K. (2003) 'Work-related fatality risk and neo-classical compensating wage differentials', *Cambridge Journal of Economics*, 28(4): 597–617.

Putnam, R. (2020) *Bowling Alone: The Collapse and Revival of American Community, Revised and Updated*, New York: Simon and Schuster.

Putterman, L. (2001) *Dollars and Change: Economics in Context*, New Haven, CT: Yale University Press.

Putterman, L. (2012) *The Good, the Bad, and the Economy: Does Human Nature Rule Out a Better World?* Minneapolis: Langdon Street Press.

Putterman, L. (2018) 'Democratic, accountable states are impossible without "behavioral" humans', *Annals of Public and Cooperative Economics*, 89(1): 251–8.

Quiggin, J. (1987) 'Egoistic rationality and public choice: A critical review of theory and evidence', *Economic Record*, 63: 10–21.

Quiggin, J. (2019) *Economics in Two Lessons: Why Markets Works So Well, and Why They Can Fail So Badly*, Princeton, NJ: Princeton University Press.

Ragan, C. (2020) *Microeconomics*, 16th Canadian edn, Toronto: Pearson.

Raworth, K. (2017) *Doughnut Economics: Seven Ways to Think like a 21st-Century Economist*, White River Junction, VT: Chelsea Green.

Reardon, J., M. Madi and M. S. Cato (2018) *Introducing a New Economics: Pluralist, Sustainable and Progressive*, London: Pluto Press.

Redelmeier, D., P. Rozin and D. Kahneman (1993) 'Understanding patients' decisions: Cognitive and emotional perspectives', *Journal of the American Medical Association*, 72: 73.

Reich, M., S. Allegretto and A. Godoey (2017) 'Seattle's minimum wage experience 2015–16', Center on Wage and Employment Dynamics, University of California Berkeley.

Ripple W., C. Wolf, T. Newsome et al. (2019) 'Are we eating the world's megafauna to extinction?', *Conservation Letters*, 12: e12627.

Robinson, J. (1933) *Economics of Imperfect Competition*, London: Macmillan.

Robinson, J. (1972) 'The second crisis of economic theory', *American Economic Review*, 62(2): 1–10.

Robinson, J. (1973) *Collected Economic Papers*, vol. 4, Oxford: Basil Blackwell.

Robinson, J. (1979) *Collected Economic Papers*, vol. 5, Oxford: Blackwell.

Rodrik, D. (2012) *The Globalization Paradox: Democracy and the Future of the World Economy*, New York: W. W. Norton.

Rodrik, D. (2015) *Economics Rules: The Rights and Wrongs of the Dismal Science*, New York: W. W. Norton.

Rodrik, D. (2018a) *Straight Talk on Trade: Ideas for a Sane World Economy*, Princeton, NJ: Princeton University Press.

Rodrik, D. (2018b) 'Populism and the economics of globalization', *Journal of International Business Policy*, 1: 12–33.

Rollins, N., et al. (2016) 'Why invest, and what it will take to improve breastfeeding practices?', *The Lancet*, 387: 491–504.

Romm, J. (2018) *Climate Change: What Everyone Needs to Know*, 2nd edn, Oxford: Oxford University Press.

Rothschild, K. (1971) 'Introduction', in K. Rothschild (ed.), *Power in Economics: Selected Readings*, London: Penguin, pp. 7–17.

Rubinstein, A. (2006) 'A sceptic's comment on the study of economics', *Economic Journal*, 116(March): C1–C9.

Russell, T., and R. Thaler (1985) 'The relevance of quasi rationality in competitive markets', *American Economic Review*, 75(5): 1071–82.

Salam, A. (1990) *Unification of Fundamental Forces: The First of the 1988 Dirac Memorial Lectures*, Cambridge: Cambridge University Press.

Samuelson, P. (2004) 'Where Ricardo and Mill rebut and confirm arguments of mainstream economists supporting globalization', *Journal of Economic Perspectives*, 18(3): 135–46.

Scherer, F. (2004) 'A note on global welfare in pharmaceutical patenting', *World Economy*, 27: 1127–42.

Scherer, F., and D. Ross (1990) *Industrial Market Structure and Economic Performance*, 3rd edn, Boston: Houghton Mifflin.

Schlesinger, S., and S. Kinzer (1983) *Bitter Fruit: The Untold Story of the American Coup in Guatemala*, Garden City, NY: Anchor Books.

Schlosser, E. (1998) 'The prison-industrial complex', *The Atlantic*, December, available at www.theatlantic.com/magazine/archive/1998/12/the-prison-industrial-complex/304669/.

Schlosser, E. (2001) *Fast Food Nation: The Dark Side of the American Meal*, Boston: Houghton Mifflin.

Schmalensee, R. (2008) 'Advertising', in Palgrave Macmillan (eds), *The New Palgrave Dictionary of Economics*, London: Palgrave Macmillan. doi.org/10.1057/978-1-349-95121-5_354-2.

Schor, J. (1998) *The Overspent American: Upscaling, Downshifting, and the New Consumer*, New York: Harper Perennial.

Schor, J. (2004) *Born to Buy: The Commercialized Child and the New Consumer Culture*, New York: Scribner.

Schor, J. (2011) *True Wealth*, New York: Penguin.

Schraufnagel, D., et al. (2019a) 'A review by the Forum of International Respiratory Societies' Environmental Committee, part 1: The damaging effects of air pollution', *CHEST*, 155(2): 409–16.

Schraufnagel, D., et al. (2019b) 'A review by the Forum of International Respiratory Societies' Environmental Committee, part 2: Air pollution and organ systems', *CHEST*, 155(2): 417–26.

Schumpeter, J. (1950) *Capitalism, Socialism and Democracy*, New York: Harper and Row.

Schumpeter, J. (1954) *History of Economic Analysis*, New York: Oxford University Press.

Sen, A. (1999) *Development as Freedom*, New York: Knopf.

Shapira, R., and L. Zingales (2017) 'Is pollution profit-maximizing? The DuPont case', National Bureau of Economic Research Working Paper No. 23866.

Sharpe, A., A. Ghanghro, E. Johnson and A. Kidwai (2010) 'Does money matter? Determining the happiness of Canadians', CSLS Research Report No. 2010-09, Ottawa: Centre for Study of Living Standards.

Shawn, W. (1991) *The Fever*, New York: Grove Press.

Simon, H. (1991) 'Organizations and markets', *Journal of Economic Perspectives*, 5(2): 25–44.

Simon, H., and R. Bartel (1986) 'The failure of armchair economics', *Challenge*, 29(5): 18–25, 23–4.

Singer, N., and D. Wilson (2009) 'Medical editors push for ghostwriting crackdown', *New York Times*, 17 September.

Singer, P. (2004) *One World: The Ethics of Globalization*. New Haven, CT: Yale University Press.

Singer, P. (2019) *The Life You Can Save: How to Do Your Part to End World Poverty*, 10th anniversary edn, freely available at thelifeyoucansave.org.

Singer, P., and J. Mason (2006) *The Ethics of What We Eat: Why Our Food Choices Matter*, Emmaus, PA: Rodale.

Singleton, K. (2014) 'Investor flows and the 2008 boom/bust in oil prices', *Management Science*, 60(2): 300–18.

Skidelsky, R., and E. Skidelsky (2013) *How Much Is Enough? The Love of Money, and the Case for the Good Life*, London: Penguin.

Slesnick, D. (2008) 'Consumer surplus', in Palgrave Macmillan (eds), *The New Palgrave Dictionary of Economics*, London: Palgrave Macmillan. doi. org/10.1057/978-1-349-95121-5_626-2.

Smith, A. ([1776] 1979) *The Nature and Causes of the Wealth of Nations*, Indianapolis: Liberty Press.

Solnick, S. J., and D. Hemenway (1998) 'Is more always better? A survey on positional concerns', *Journal of Economic Behavior and Organization*, 37: 373–83.

Soros, G. (1998) *The Crisis of Global Capitalism: Open Society Endangered*, New York: Perseus Books.

Sraffa, P. (1926) 'The laws of returns under competitive conditions', *Economic Journal*, 36(4): 535–50.

Stanfield, J. R., and J. B. Stanfield (eds) (2004) *Interviews with John Kenneth Galbraith*, Jackson: University of Mississippi Press.

Stanley, J. (2004) *The Surveillance-Industrial Complex*, New York: American Civil Liberties Union, available at aclu.org/files/FilesPDFs/surveillance_report.pdf.

Steedman, I. (1987) 'Adding-up problem', in Palgrave Macmillan (eds), *The New Palgrave Dictionary of Economics*, London: Palgrave Macmillan. doi. org/10.1057/978-1-349-95121-5_507-1.

Steffen, W., et al. (2018) 'Trajectories of the earth system in the Anthropocene', *Proceedings of the National Academy of Sciences*, 115(33): 8252–9.

Stern, N. (2014a) 'Ethics, equity and the economics of climate change paper 1: Science and philosophy', *Economics and Philosophy*, 30: 397–444.

Stern, N. (2014b) 'Ethics, equity and the economics of climate change paper 2: Economics and politics', *Economics and Philosophy*, 30: 445–501.

Stern, N. (2015) *Why Are We Waiting? The Logic, Urgency, and Promise of Tackling Climate Change*, Cambridge, MA: MIT Press.

Stern, N. (2016) 'Current climate models are grossly misleading', *Nature*, 530(25 February): 407–9.

Stern, N. (2018) 'Public economics as if time matters: Climate change and the dynamics of policy', *Journal of Public Economics*, 162, 4–17.

Stern, N., and C. Parker (2019) 'An economist explains how to go carbon neutral in our lifetime', available at weforum.org/agenda/2019/04/an-economist-explains-how-to-turn-the-whole-economy-carbon-neutral/.

Stevenson, B., and J. Wolfers (2008) 'Economic growth and subjective well-being: Reassessing the Easterlin Paradox', *Brookings Papers on Economic Activity*, Spring: 1–87.

Stiglitz, J. (1985) 'Information and economic analysis: a perspective', *Economic Journal*, 95, Supplement: Conference Papers, pp. 21–41.

Stiglitz, J. (2002) 'Information and the change in the paradigm in economics', *American Economic Review*, 92(3): 460–501.

Stiglitz, J. (2003) *The Roaring Nineties: A New History of the World's Most Prosperous Decade*, New York: W. W. Norton.

Stiglitz, J. (2017) *Globalization and Its Discontents Revisited: Anti-Globalization in the Age of Trump*, New York: W. W. Norton.

Stiglitz, J. (2019) *People, Power, and Profits: Progressive Capitalism for an Age of Discontent*, New York: W. W. Norton.

Stiglitz, J., N. Abernathy, A. Hersh, S. Holmberg and M. Konczal (2015) *Rewriting the Rules for the American Economy: An Agenda for Growth and Shared Prosperity*, New York: WW Norton.

Stiglitz, J., and B. Greenwald (2015) *Creating a Learning Society: A New Approach to Growth, Development, and Social Progress*, New York: Columbia University Press.

Stoknes, P. E. (2015) *What We Think about When We Try Not to Think about Global Warming: Towards a New Psychology of Climate Action*, White River Junction, VT: Chelsea Green.

Stretton, H., and L. Orchard (1994) *Public Goods, Public Enterprise, Public Choice: Theoretical Foundations of the Contemporary Attack on Government*, London: Macmillan.

Summers, L. (1992) 'Let them eat pollution', *The Economist*, 8 February.

Swaney, J. (1994) 'So what's wrong with dumping on Africa?', *Journal of Economic Issues*, 28(2): 367–77.

Taft, K. (2018) *Oil's Deep State: How the Petroleum Industry Undermines Democracy and Stops Action on Global Warming – in Alberta and in Ottawa*, Toronto: Lorimer.

Taibbi, M. (2011) *Griftopia: A Story of Bankers, Politicians, and the Most Audacious Power Grab in American History*. New York: Spiegel and Grau.

Thaler, R. (2015) *Misbehaving: The Making of Behavioral Economics*, New York: W. W. Norton.

Thaler, R. (2018) 'From cashews to nudges: The evolution of behavioral economics', *American Economic Review*, 108(6): 1265–87.

Thaler, R., and S. Bernartzi (2004) 'Save more tomorrow: Using behavioural economics to increase employee savings', *Journal of Political Economy*, 112(1): S164–S187.

Thurow, L. (1975) *Generating Inequality: Mechanisms of distribution in the US economy*, New York: Basic Books.

Titmuss, R. M. (1970) *The Gift Relationship*, London: Allen and Unwin.

UNICEF and WHO (2018) 'Breastfeeding and the international code of marketing of breastmilk substitutes', available at unicef.org/nutrition/files/9_BF_and_the_Code.pdf.

United Nations Development Programme and Oxford Poverty and Human Development Initiative (2019) *Global Multinational Poverty Index 2019: Illuminating Inequalities*, available at ophi.org.uk/global-multidimensional-poverty-index-2019-illuminating-inequalities/.

United Nations Environmental Programme (2019) *Global Chemicals Outlook II. From Legacies to Innovative Solutions: Implementing the 2030 Agenda for Sustainable Development*, unep.org/explore-topics/chemicals-waste/what-we-do/policy-and-governance/global-chemicals-outlook.

Valentine, T. (1996) 'The minimum wage debate: Politically correct economics?', *Economic and Labour Relations Review*, 7: 188–97.

Varoufakis, Y. (1998) *Foundations of Economics: A Beginner's Companion*, London: Routledge.

Varoufakis, Y. (2017) 'Taking the red or blue pill?' *Journal of Australian Political Economy*, 80: 65–73.

Veblen, T. ([1904] 1965) *The Theory of Business Enterprise*, New York: Augustus M. Kelley.

Veenhoven, R. (2020) *Distributional Findings on Happiness in Japan*, World Database of Happiness, Erasmus University Rotterdam, The Netherlands. Viewed on 22 August 2020 at worlddatabaseofhappiness.eur.nl/hap_nat/desc_na_genpublic.php?cntry=6.

Vergara, C. (2020) 'Bloody eye sockets, defaced statues: The visual legacy of Chile's unrest', *The Guardian*, 25 February.

Victoria, C., et al. (2016) 'Breastfeeding in the 21st century: Epidemiology, mechanisms, and lifelong effect', *The Lancet*, 387: 475–90.

Vidal, J. (2015) 'Volkswagen is guilty – but it's not the only offender', *The Guardian*, 24 September.

Vitullo-Martin, J., and J. Moskin (1994) *The Executive's Book of Quotations*, Oxford: Oxford University Press.

Voitchovsky, S. (2009) 'Inequality and economic growth', in W. Salverda, B. Nolan and T. Smeeding (eds.) *The Oxford Handbook of Economic Inequality*, Oxford: Oxford University Press, pp. 549–74.

Wagner, G., and M. Weitzman (2015) *Climate Shock: The Economic Consequences of a Hotter Planet*, Princeton, NJ: Princeton University Press.

Wagner, G., and R. Zeckhauser (2012) 'Climate policy: Hard problem, soft thinking', *Climatic Change*, 110: 507–21.

Wasley, A., C. Cook and N. Jones (2018) 'Two amputations a week: The cost of working in a US meat plant', *The Guardian*, July 5.

Webber, D. (2015) 'Firm market power and the earnings distribution', *Labour Economics*, 38: 123–34.

Weeks, J. (2014) *Economics of the 1%: How Mainstream Economics Serves the Rich, Obscures Reality and Distorts Policy*, London: Anthem Press.

Whyte, W. F., and K. K. Whyte (1991) *Making Mondragón: The Growth and Dynamics of the Worker Cooperative Complex*, 2nd rev. edn, Ithaca, NY: Industrial and Labor Relations Press.

Wilkinson, R. (2005) *The Impact of Inequality: How to Make Sick Societies Healthier*, New York: New Press.

Wilkinson, R., and M. Marmot (eds) (2003) *Social Determinants of Health: The solid facts*, 2nd edn, Geneva: World Health Organization.

Wilkinson, R., and K. Pickett (2009) *The Spirit Level: Why More Equal Societies Almost Always Do Better*, London: Allen Lane.

Wilkinson, R., and K. Pickett (2018) *The Inner Level: How More Equal Societies Reduce Stress, Restore Sanity, and Improve Everyone's Well-Being*, New York: Penguin.

Williams, E., D. Buck and G. Babalola (2020) 'What are health inequalities?', Kings Fund, 18 February, available at kingsfund.org.uk/publications/what-are-health-inequalities.

Winkelmann, R. (2012) 'Conspicuous consumption and satisfaction', *Journal of Economic Psychology*, 33: 183–91.

Wolf, M. (2004) *Why Globalization Works*, New Haven, CT: Yale University Press.

World Bank (2017) *The Report of the High-Level Commission on Carbon Prices*, Washington: World Bank.

Worm, B. (2016) 'Averting a global fisheries disaster', *Proceedings of the National Academy of Sciences*, 113(18): 4895–7.

Worm, B. (2017) 'How to heal an ocean', *Nature*, 543: 630–1.

Ziliak, S. (2002) 'Haiku economics', *Rethinking Marxism*, 14(3): 111–3.

Zingales, L. (2017) 'Towards a political theory of the firm', *Journal of Economic Perspectives*, 31: 113–30.

Zuboff, S. (2018) *The Age of Surveillance Capitalism: The Fight for a Human Future at the New Frontier of Power*, New York: PublicAffairs.

Zucman, G. (2015) *The Hidden Wealth of Nations: The Scourge of Tax Havens*, Chicago: University of Chicago Press.

Zucman, G. (2019) 'Taxing multinational corporations in the 21st century', Economists for Inclusive Prosperity, Policy Brief 10, February. Available at econfip.org/policy-briefs/taxing-multinational-corporations-in-the-21st-century/.

Zuidhof, P.-W. (2014) 'Thinking like an economist: The neoliberal politics of the economics textbook', *Review of Social Economy*, 72(2): 157–85.

Zweig, J. (2004) 'What Warren Buffett wants you to know: How do you learn from a master? Start by listening to what he has to say', *MONEY*, 3 May, available at money.cnn.com/2004/05/03/pf/buffett_qanda/.

GLOSSARY

Arrow's Paradox: if everyone is a price-taker in a perfectly competitive demand and supply model, how do prices change? Who or what adjusts them in response to surpluses or shortages?

Asymmetric information: any situation in which some people know more than others about a good or service being exchanged. Its relevance: one party in a transaction may be able to gain an advantage with that better information.

Behavioural economics: the attempt to study how human beings actually behave instead of focusing on how hyper-rational beings would behave if they existed. Notions of limited selfishness, limited self-control and limited rationality have emerged from this discipline.

Comparative advantage: a lower opportunity cost of production. Used to 'demonstrate' that trade is mutually advantageous. Some texts acknowledge that other theories are needed to explain some aspects of trade, such as trade in similar goods between similar countries.

Competitive market: requires large numbers of buyers and sellers who are all small relative to the market such that no one can individually influence the market price. (See *Arrow's Paradox*.) Also requires free entry and exit, and perfect information.

Deadweight loss of monopoly: the supposed cost of monopoly compared to a competitive market. It includes the loss of net benefit from a smaller quantity produced, the loss from costly efforts to secure and to maintain monopoly profits, and an equity cost of a less equitable distribution of income.

Dynamic efficiency: an optimal rate of technological progress resulting from optimal investments in research and development. Relevant to the debate about whether monopolists and oligopolists are more likely to develop better techniques over time than competitive firms. In contrast, static efficiency assumes given technology and products.

Dynamic monopsony: when a firm has market power to set its wage owing to 'frictions' and imperfect information. Since the conditions are pervasive, so is dynamic monopsony. See *Frictions*.

Easterlin Paradox: empirical evidence showing: (1) a positive relationship of income to subjective well-being (SWB) among people at any point in time, and (2) no relationship between average income and SWB in a society over long periods of time. It is explained by the importance of relative position and gradual adaption or adjustment in people's aspirations over time to higher living standards.

Economism: the erroneous belief that the supply and demand model you have learned and/or are employing is an accurate representation of the real world from which you can draw policy conclusions. See James Kwak's book *Economism*.

Equilibrium: a situation where there is no tendency to change. Plans of all relevant economic decision-makers are consistent with each other. An equilibrium may be stable (the system returns to the equilibrium following a small disturbance) or unstable (a small disturbance drives the system away from equilibrium).

Equity: a synonym for fairness. What is equitable or fair requires an ethical or normative judgement. For example, equity may involve the idea of a 'fair go' where everyone has equal opportunity. It may instead involve judgements about the equitability of outcomes, as in utilitarianism. The ultimatum game (described in Chapter 1) shows that people are prepared to make themselves absolutely worse off in order to punish others who have not treated them 'fairly'.

Externalities: cost or benefits imposed on others that do not influence the decisions by the original actor and which are not reflected in market prices. These are of second order of importance according to their treatment in mainstream texts. In reality they are all-pervasive and many are of first-order importance.

Failure of markets: a situation in which the market may produce an efficient outcome, but it is one which is socially or ethically unacceptable. Term suggested by Colander (2003). Compare with *Market failure*.

Free rider problem: exists whenever an individual can receive a benefit from others' contribution to the cost of a good that benefits them all. Using the principles of rational choice, the individual may decide not to contribute but to 'free ride' on the contributions of others. See *Public good*.

Frictions: often refers to things that prevent either job or geographic mobility of the labour force. For example, changing jobs might necessitate retraining. Includes the time and resources it takes to find information, or switch jobs, or move home.

Fundamental uncertainty: unlike the situations of probability and risk, like betting on flips of a coin, many future situations are fundamentally unknowable, like the profitability 10 years from now of an investment in a gold mine today. There is no information to allow calculations of the probabilities of different outcomes. Keynes (1936, ch 12) is a classic discussion.

General equilibrium: occurs when all markets in the economy are in equilibrium simultaneously.

Heterodox economics: an umbrella term used to cover approaches that are outside of mainstream, orthodox economics. It includes institutional, post-Keynesian, socialist, Marxian, feminist, Austrian, ecological and social economics among others.

Homo economicus: an imaginary species of human that inhabits most economic models. Characteristics include hyper rationality, self-regarding behaviour and a lack of social awareness.

Ideology: a theoretical perspective or worldview; a view of human nature and the possibilities for change; usually embodies value judgements about what is good and bad. Different political ideologies give rise to different schools of thought in the social sciences.

Inefficiency, allocative: exists when there is the potential to use resources more efficiently, to make at least one person better off without making anyone worse off, i.e. to move to a Pareto optimal situation. In practice, eliminating an inefficiency may make some better off and some worse off, but those made better off would be able, in principle, to compensate those made worse off.

Laissez-faire: the doctrine that society is better off if the government refrains from 'intervening' in the market economy. Its shortcoming is that the market economy only exists because of government 'intervention'.

Macroeconomics: the study of the economy as a whole. Topics include the determination of GDP, the growth of GDP, unemployment, inflation, interest rates, and the balance of payments.

Marginal thinking: the attempt to maximize monetary or psychological satisfaction by pursuing any activity up to the point where marginal (or additional) cost equals marginal (or additional) benefit.

Market failure: a situation in which markets fail to allocate resources in a statically efficient way owing to an inherent characteristic of the market, such as monopoly, externalities or imperfect information.

Market fundamentalism: the belief that the model of a perfectly competitive market approximates how actual markets operate in the real world. See Economism and *Laissez-faire*.

Microeconomics: the study of individual markets. Topics include the determination of prices, quantities, and relative efficiency of different market structures.

Monopsony: a firm that has market power to choose the wages it offers. Traditionally it was thought to require a single buyer of labour, and therefore to be extremely rare. But see *Dynamic monopsony*.

Multiple equilibria: an economic model may have more than one equilibrium. For example, neither demand nor supply curves have to be linear and they could intersect more than once, resulting in multiple equilibria. See *Equilibrium*.

Neoclassical economics: often used to describe the orthodox or mainstream approach that dominates the undergraduate textbooks. It emphasizes individual rational choice, marginal analysis, and the efficiency of resource allocation at a point in time (static efficiency). It focuses attention on equilibrium outcomes in individual competitive markets and the general equilibrium of the economy as a whole.

Normative: that which embodies a norm, value or moral precept. Normative statements often (though not always) contain the word *should*. For example: there should be no child poverty in a country as rich as Canada. See its opposite, *Positive*.

Opportunity cost: what must be given up to get something; the value of the next best alternative forgone.

Pareto optimal: has the property that it is not possible to make anyone better off without making at least one person worse off – in other words, there would be no waste anywhere in the economy. See *Inefficiency, allocative*.

Partial equilibrium analysis: the analysis of the equilibrium of a single market in isolation. Other markets may or may not be assumed to be in equilibrium, but they are not analysed explicitly.

Positive: dealing only with facts, descriptions of the world. In principle, positive statements can be shown to be right or wrong, although it may not be easy to do so in practice. See its opposite, *Normative*.

Post-Keynesian: an approach to micro and macroeconomics building on themes in Keynes' *General Theory of Employment, Interest, and Money*, with an emphasis on fundamental uncertainty. (See *Fundamental uncertainty*.)

Public choice: a theory of the political marketplace that assumes purely self-interested actors – politicians, 'bureaucrats' (not 'public servants' because they serve only themselves), special interest groups and voters. Emphasizes wasteful rent seeking and the ubiquity of government failure, and hence the importance of strictly limiting government's role in economic life. (See *Rent seeking*.)

Price ceiling: a government-determined maximum price. It will not be 'binding' unless it is below the equilibrium price. Example: rent controls.

Price floor: a government-determined minimum price. It will not be binding unless it is above the equilibrium price. Example: minimum wages.

Prisoner's dilemma: a situation Robert Frank calls 'smart for one, dumb for all'. People make rational choices to do the best they can for themselves, but collectively the result is worse than other outcomes that are possible. For example the dilemma exists whenever people would be collectively better off if everyone contributed to a public good (or reduced their contributions to a public bad, such as pollution) but rational choice leads them to 'free ride' on others' contributions. It is a pervasive social problem, but people's evolve tendency to cooperate if others reduces the problem in important circumstances.

Private good: a good that provides benefits only to the person who consumes it, also termed a 'rival good'. It's assumed that a system of property rights exists to exclude anyone who has not paid for the good from consuming it ('excludable'). See its opposite, a *Public good*.

Public bad: like a public good, only a public bad reduces utility instead of adding to it. Examples: an unjust distribution of income, incompetent and corrupt government, pollution.

Public good: a good that is non-rival, i.e. any one person's use or benefit from it does not reduce the benefits enjoyed by others. Because the opportunity cost of another person consuming it is zero, its socially optimal price is also zero. It's also non-excludable: no one can be excluded from its benefits, even if they fail to contribute towards its cost or maintenance. See *Free rider problem*. See also *Private good*.

Rational choice theory: this assumes that individuals are rational, self-interested, have a stable set of internally consistent preferences, and wish to maximize their own happiness (or 'utility'), given their constraints.

Rent seeking: the wasteful use of resources to try to influence public policy and obtain a benefit at others' expense. Emphasized by public choice theorists, the most extreme of whom see all public-sector activity as a system of legalized theft driven by rent seeking. Useful publicly-provided goods and services are explained as an accidental byproduct of this. (See *Public choice*.)

Scarcity: the starting point for neoclassical economics. It arises out of the assumption of unlimited wants confronting limited resources.

Static efficiency: (a) using existing resources and technology so that no more of any one could can be produced without reducing the production of some other good (productive efficiency). For a firm: minimizing costs of producing a given output; for an economy: being on the production possibility frontier. (b) producing goods and services so that net benefit (consumer + producer surplus) is maximized (allocative efficiency). See *Pareto optimal* and *Dynamic efficiency*.

Supply: the maximum quantity sellers are willing to sell for any given price. It must be independent of demand. The supply curve exists only for price-taking firms – not for firms that set their price.

Theory-induced blindness: an affliction identified by Daniel Kahneman (2013: 276) characterized by a blindness to the flaws of a theory that has been learned and used. Students of economics become more susceptible to it the more they study the subject. Undergraduate economics majors and graduate students are particularly at risk. See *Economism*.

Utility: a measure of happiness or benefit. The term reflects the influence of the philosophy of utilitarianism on neoclassical economics.

Wage compression: when wage differences between workers are much smaller than their productivity differences. It refutes a prediction of marginal productivity theory, and suggests the importance of fairness and status considerations.

INDEX